© Andrew O'Brien Photography   The Right Reverend W. Martin Fair   BA BD DMin   © Church of Scotland
MODERATOR

The Church of Scotland
YEAR BOOK
2020–2021

135th year of issue

Editor
David A. Stewart

Published on behalf of
THE CHURCH OF SCOTLAND
by SAINT ANDREW PRESS
121 George Street, Edinburgh EH2 4YN

THE OFFICES OF THE CHURCH

121 George Street, Edinburgh, EH2 4YN
0131 225 5722
Fax: 0131 220 3113
www.churchofscotland.org.uk

Office Hours: Monday–Friday 9:00am–5:00pm

CrossReach operates from Charis House, 47 Milton Road East, Edinburgh, EH15 2SR
0131 657 2000
Fax: 0131 657 5000
info@crossreach.org.uk
www.crossreach.org.uk

Scottish Charity Numbers

The Church of Scotland: unincorporated Councils and Committees	SC011353
The Church of Scotland General Trustees	SC014574
The Church of Scotland Investors Trust	SC022884
The Church of Scotland Trust	SC020269

(For the Scottish Charity Numbers of congregations, see Section 7)

Corrections and alterations to the Year Book
Contact the Editor:
yearbookeditor@churchofscotland.org.uk
0131 441 3362

The General Assembly of 2021 will convene on
Saturday 22 May

First published in 2020 by SAINT ANDREW PRESS, 121 George Street, Edinburgh EH2 4YN on behalf of THE CHURCH of SCOTLAND

Copyright © THE CHURCH of SCOTLAND, 2020

ISBN 978 0 00000 000 0 [will be supplied by Stephen Rogers of Hymns Ancient and Modern]

It is the Publisher's policy only to use papers that are natural and recyclable and that have been manufactured from timber grown in renewable, properly managed forests. All of the manufacturing processes of the papers are expected to conform to the environmental regulations of the country of origin.

Acceptance of advertisements for inclusion in *The Church of Scotland Year Book* does not imply endorsement of the goods or services or of any views expressed within the advertisements.

British Library Cataloguing in Publication Data
A catalogue record for this book is available from the British Library.

CONTENTS

FROM THE MODERATOR

Everyone who knows me understands well that I have what might be described as a competitive spirit. Some know it to their cost! But though I love the challenge of going head to head in sporting contests, or even just in a game of Scrabble with Elaine, what I love best of all is being part of a team.

The Year Book is a constant reminder to me that as a Church of Scotland minister, I'm part of a fantastic team. As I flick through its pages I see the names of individuals and of groups and organisations, and I'm encouraged to rejoice that 'these are my team mates!' Many of the names of individuals and of congregations are known to me; many more I've never met nor visited. Yet this volume gives me that overwhelming sense of being surrounded by colleagues who have, and will, support and challenge me in my own ministry and with whom I get to work for the Kingdom.

Having played in football teams in earlier years, my skills were most evident on the left side of the pitch, marauding forward in search of a defence-splitting path or a match-winning goal. But there would have been no victories had I not had ten team mates alongside me.

And so in this business of the Kingdom, I'm thankful daily that I'm not on my own and that in fact I'm alongside colleagues who together have the most wonderful array of gifts and experiences, each complementing the other to complete the picture.

The Year Book is in your hands. Open it and give thanks for the team and that you are part of it.

W. Martin Fair

BHON MHODERÀTOR

Tha fios aig a h-uile duine a tha fìor eòlach orm gu bheil mi caran farpaiseach nam ghnè. Tha daor an ceannach air a bhith aig cuid air sgàth sin! Ach ged is toil leam an dùbhlan a bhith a' dol an ugannan a chèile ann am farpaisean spòrs, no eadhon ann an gèam Scrabble le Elaine, 's e an rud as fhìor fheàrr leam a bhith nam phàirt de sgioba.

Tha an Leabhar Bliadhnail daonnan a'cur nam chuimhne gu bheil mi, mar mhinistear Eaglais na h-Alba, nam phàirt de sgioba mhìorbhailich. Chì mi mar a thionndaidheas mi a dhuilleagan ainmean dhaoine fa leth agus chòmhlan is bhuidhnean, agus tha e na mhisneachd dhomh is na ghàirdeachas gu bheil iad sin na mo chompanaich san sgioba. Tha mi eòlach air mòran de na h-ainmean aig daoine agus coitheanalan; tha mòran a bharrachd nach do choinnich mi is air nach do thadhail mi. Ach tha an leabhar seo a' toirt dhomh faireachdainn làidir de bhith cuairtichte le companaich a thug, agus a bheir, taic is dùbhlan dhomh nam mhinistrealachd fhìn agus leis am faigh mi cothrom obrachadh às leth na Rìoghachd.

Nuair a bhithinn a'cluich ann an sgiobaidhean ball-coise sna bliadhnaichean a dh'fhalbh, b'ann air taobh clì na pàirce a b'fhollaisiche mo chuid sgilean, a' brùchdadh air adhart a' lorg slighe a sgoltadh an luchd-dìon no a chosnadh tadhal buannachaidh. Ach cha bhiodh buaidh sam bith air a bhith ann mura biodh deichnear eile san sgioba còmhla rium.

Agus mar san ceudna ann an cùisean na Rìoghachd, tha mi taingeil gach latha nach eil mi nam aonar agus gu bheil feadhainn eile nam chuideachd aig a bheil eatorra an t-sreath as iongantaiche de ghibhtean is de dh'fhiosrachaidhean, gach aon a'cur ris an fheadhainn eile gus an dealbh iomlan a chruthachadh.

Tha an Leabhar Bliadhnail nur làmhan-sa. Fosgail e agus thoir buidheachas dhan sgioba agus gu bheil thu mar phàirt dhith.

W. Martin Fair
Translation by Professor Boyd Robertson

EDITOR'S PREFACE

I was grateful for the feedback on last year's edition and to those who sent corrections and updates. The key changes this year are:

- Section 1 has been adjusted to reflect the creation of Faith Impact Forum (incorporating the work of the former Church and Society Council and the World Mission Council) and the Faith Nurture Forum (incorporating the work of the former Ministries Council and the Mission and Discipleship Council).

- Given the cancellation of the 2020 General Assembly due to the Coronavirus pandemic, in Section 4 there is instead a summary of the decisions of the Commission of Assembly.

- In the Presbytery listings in Section 5, the Presbyteries of Greenock and Paisley (14) and Dumbarton (18) have been united as the Presbytery of Clyde (14) and the Presbyteries of Aberdeen (31) and Shetland (46) have been united as the Presbytery of Aberdeen and Shetland (31). As more unions of Presbyteries will follow, it is not yet appropriate to renumber all the presbyteries.

- In the second part of the Presbytery listings, In other appointments is labelled B and Demitted is C, and the Index of Ministers has been amended accordingly for ease of reference.

- The list of Representatives on Council Education Committees has been restored to the printed book (List 6-N).

Further to the lists of parishes in Section 5, some parishes have more than one church: those additional churches are included as in previous years in the online Section 8. The Rev. Dr Fiona Tweedie has prepared an online map of parish and presbytery boundaries. This can be found at http://arcg.is/11rSXH. These are visible at different scales – zoom in for the parish boundaries and the labelling.

Many people, despite the constraints on normal activities imposed due to the Coronavirus pandemic, contributed to the compilation, production and distribution of the Year Book. I again thank the Presbytery Clerks and their secretaries, the staff in the Church's offices (in particular my correspondents in Faith Nurture – especially Sheila MacRae – and the Communications Department), and those who compile some of the sections or subsections: Boyd Robertson and Duncan Sneddon (Gaelic), Daran Golby (Forces Chaplains), Sheena Orr (Prison Chaplains), Roy Pinkerton (church grid references, parish and congregational changes, index of parishes and places, and editorial advice), Madeleine Sproule (legal names and Scottish charity numbers) and Fiona Tweedie and Sandy Gemmill (statistics). Finally, thanks to Claire Ruben of FairCopy for careful copy editing and to our contacts at Hymns Ancient and Modern who publish the book via the St Andrew Press.

Corrections, amendments and suggestions are always welcome.

David Stewart
yearbookeditor@churchofscotland.org.uk

SECTION 1

Assembly Trustees, Agencies, Committees and Departments

The symbol > used in website information indicates the headings to be selected as they appear

1. OFFICE OF THE GENERAL ASSEMBLY

The Office supports the General Assembly, Presbyteries and Kirk Sessions, the Moderator and the process of Presbytery reform. In addition, the staff service the following: Assembly Business Committee, Legal Questions Committee, Judicial Commission, Judicial Panel, Appeals Committee of the Commission of Assembly, Ministries Appeal Panel, the Committee to Nominate the Moderator, the Chalmers Lectureship Trust, the Committee on Overtures and Cases, the Delegation of Assembly and the Committee on Classifying Returns to Overtures. The Clerks of Assembly are responsible for consultation on matters of Church Law, Practice and Procedure.

Principal Clerk:	Rev. Dr George J. Whyte
Depute Clerk of the General Assembly:	Ms Christine Paterson LLB DipLP
Presbytery Resource Officer:	Dr Hazel Hastie
Executive Assistant to the Principal Clerk:	Ms Susan Taylor, 0131 240 2240
Senior Administration Officer	Miss Catherine McIntosh MA, 0131 225 5722
(Assembly Arrangements	ext. 2250
and Moderatorial Support):	

Personnel in this department are also listed with the Councils and Committees that they serve.
Contact: pcoffice@churchofscotland.org.uk   0131 240 2240   Fax: 0131 240 2239

2. OFFICE OF THE ASSEMBLY TRUSTEES

The Trustees have responsibility for governance, finance and stewardship, budgeting and general oversight of the agencies of the Church. They assist the General Assembly to determine the strategy and priorities of the Church, and seek to ensure the implementation of the policies, priorities and strategic objectives of the General Assembly through working with the agencies of the Church to achieve a collaborative approach to the nurturing of the people of the Church in their witness, worship and service. They are the Charity Trustees of the Church of Scotland (the Unincorporated Entities) Scottish Charity No. SC011353.

Assembly Trustees:

Convener:	Very Rev. Dr John P. Chalmers
Vice-Convener:	Norma Rolls
Administrative Trustee:	James McNeill
Other Trustees:	Brian Ashcroft
	Alan Campbell
	Jean Couper
	David Harrison
	Dr Linda Irvine
	Jamie Lockhart
	Rev. Donald G.B. McCorkindale

Geoff Miller
Ann Nelson
Rev. Anikó Schütz Bradwell
Raymond Young

Chief Officer:	Dave Kendall
Head of Organisational Programmes:	Catherine Skinner
Head of Estates, Procurement and Health and Safety:	Liam Fennell
Executive Officer:	Catherine Forsyth
Audit and Compliance Officer:	Debra Livingstone
Mission Statistics Co-ordinator:	Rev. Dr Fiona J. Tweedie

Contact: OATadmin@churchofscotland.org.uk
Carron Lunt, Executive PA to the Chief Officer
clunt@churchofscotland.org.uk   0131 240 2229

Further information:
www.churchofscotland.org.uk > About us > Our structure > Assembly Trustees

3. FAITH IMPACT FORUM

The Forum's role is to enable the Church of Scotland – its members, adherents, congregations and presbyteries - to participate effectively in the Mission of God in the world, following the example and priorities of Jesus Christ, and seeking the guidance of the Holy Spirit. It seeks to engage, on behalf of the Church, in national, international, political and social issues through research, theological reflection, resourcing the local church, and by engaging with leaders in civic society, public bodies, professional associations and other networks; and to sustain relationships with the Church's international links. This involves presence (an incarnational approach in which relationships of mutual respect can be built); practical action (following Jesus' example in reaching out to the poor, the captive, the sick, and the oppressed); and proclamation (both the explicit proclamation of the Good News and being a prophetic voice for the voiceless and exercising advocacy in support of the powerless). The Forum is also the principal link with Christian Aid.

Convener:	Very Rev. Susan M. Brown BD DipMin DUniv
Vice-Convener:	Rev. Alan F. Miller BA MA BD
Interim Head:	Rev. Ian W. Alexander
Gender Justice:	Ms Katherine Gilmour
Global:	Mr David Bradwell
Political and Social:	Mr Andrew Tomlinson, Ms Irene Mackinnon
Creation Care:	Mr Adrian Shaw
Society, Religion and Technology:	Dr Murdo Macdonald
Interfaith:	Ms Mirella Yandoli
Regional Links:	Mrs Jennie Chinembiri, Mr Sandy Sneddon, Mr Kenny Roger
Outreach and Communication:	Ms Carol Finlay

Contact: world@churchofscotland.org.uk 0131 225 5722

Further information:
www.churchofscotland.org.uk > About us > Councils, committees and departments > Councils
> Church and Society
www.churchofscotland.org.uk > speak out
www.churchofscotland.org.uk > About us > Councils, committees and departments > Councils
> World Mission
www.churchofscotland.org.uk > Serve > World Mission

4. FAITH NURTURE FORUM

The Forum seeks to support and resource congregations and presbyteries in sharing the good news of the Gospel, growing the church as part of the mission of God, nurturing faith and encouraging discipleship. It seeks to develop individual gifts and talents across all ages, and resource young people in their faith formation and participation in decision-making within the Church, building strong and accessible communities of worship and service, and learning from the successes in congregations. The Forum works on recruiting, training and supporting the recognised ministries of the Church, enabling Presbyteries to plan and resource congregations and mission, as congregations seek to give special priority to those living in poverty and at the margins.

Convener:	Rev. Rosemary Frew MA BD
Vice-Convener:	Rev. Dr Karen K. Campbell
Interim Head:	Rev. Angus R. Mathieson MA BD
Depute:	Mr Craig Renton BSc
Church Without Walls:	Mrs Lesley Hamilton-Messer MA
Congregational Learning:	Mr Ronald H. Clarke BEng MSc PGCE
Education and Training:	Ms Kay Cathcart MA PGCE
Partnerships and Development:	Mr Daran Golby BA CIPD
*Priority Areas:	Ms Shirley Grieve BA PGCE (0141 248 2905)
Recruitment and Support:	Rev. Dr Lezley J. Stewart
Resourcing Worship:	Mr Phill Mellstrom BA

Contact: Faith Nurture@churchofscotland.org.uk 0131 240 2205

*The Priority Area Team operates from 759 Argyle Street, Glasgow G3 8DS; 0141 248 2905

Further information:
www.churchofscotland.org.uk > About us > Councils, committees and departments > Councils
> Ministries Council
www.churchofscotland.org.uk > Serve > Ministries Council > Ministries in the Church
www.churchofscotland.org.uk/ascend
www.churchofscotland.org.uk > About us > Councils, committees and departments > Mission
and Discipleship
www.resourcingmission.org.uk
www.churchofscotland.org.uk > Serve > Go For It
Pulpit Supply Fees: www.churchofscotland.org.uk/yearbook > Section 3F

Church Art and Architecture:
Convener: Rev. William T. Hogg MA BD
Contact: gentrustees@churchofscotland.org.uk

Further information:
www.churchofscotland.org.uk > About us > Councils, committees and departments >
Committees > Church Art and Architecture
www.churchofscotland.org.uk > Resources > Subjects > Art and Architecture resources

---

5. CROSSREACH

Charis House, 47 Milton Road East, Edinburgh EH15 2SR
0131 657 2000   Fax: 0131 657 5000
info@crossreach.org.uk   www.crossreach.org.uk

CrossReach, overseen by the **Social Care Council**, provides social-care services as part of the Christian witness of the Church to the people of Scotland, and engages with other bodies in responding to emerging areas of need. CrossReach operates 70 services across the country.

Convener: Rev. Thomas S. Riddell
Vice-Convener: Sarah Wood
Chief Executive Officer: Viv Dickenson (viv.dickenson@crossreach.org.uk)
Director of Services to Older People: Allan Logan (allan.logan@crossreach.org.uk)
Director of Adult Care Services: Calum Murray (calum.murray@crossreach.org.uk)
Director of Children and Families: Sheila Gordon (sheila.gordon@crossreach.org.uk)
Director of Finance and Resources: Eoin McDunphy (eoin.mcdunphy@crossreach.org.uk)
Director of Human Resources and
  Organisational Development: Mari Rennie (mari.rennie@crossreach.org.uk)

Further information: www.crossreach.org.uk

For sharing local experience and initiatives: www.socialcareforum.scot

---

6. ASSEMBLY BUSINESS COMMITTEE

Convener: Rev. Donald G.B. McCorkindale BD DipMin
Vice-Convener: Mrs Susan J. Pym
Secretary: Principal Clerk
                     cmcintosh@churchofscotland.org.uk   0131 240 2240

Further information:
www.churchofscotland.org.uk > About us > General Assembly
www.churchofscotland.org.uk > About us > Councils, committees and departments >
Committees > Assembly Business

7. AUDIT COMMITTEE

Remit: to oversee the financial and other relevant reporting processes implemented by management; to work with the Assembly Trustees in setting appropriate standards of financial management and in overseeing compliance; and to keep under review the effectiveness of the systems for internal financial control, financial reporting and risk management, including compliance with the legal and regulatory environment.

Convener: Andrew Croxford

Contact: Carron Lunt, Executive PA to the Chief Officer
                                   clunt@churchofscotland.org.uk 0131 240 2229

Further information:
www.churchofscotland.org.uk > About us > Councils, committees and departments > Committees > Audit

---

8. CENTRAL PROPERTIES DEPARTMENT

Remit: to provide property, facilities and health and safety services to the Agencies and Departments of the central administration of the Church.

Property, Health and Safety Manager: Colin Wallace
Property, Health and Safety Officer: Jacqueline Collins
Property Officer: Eunice Hessell
Support Assistant: Joyce Anderson

Contact: cpd@churchofscotland.org.uk   0131 240 2254

Further information:
www.churchofscotland.org.uk > About us > Councils, committees and departments > Departments > Central Properties

---

9. CHURCH OF SCOTLAND TRUST

Chairman: Mr Thomas C. Watson
Vice-Chairman: Mr W.F. Stuart Lynch
Treasurer: Mrs Anne F. Macintosh BA CA
Secretary and Clerk: Mrs Madelaine Sproule LLB MSc DipLP NP
                     msproule@churchofscotland.org.uk   0131 240 2215

Further information:
www.churchofscotland.org.uk > About us > Councils, committees and departments > Departments > Church of Scotland Trust

10. COMMUNICATIONS DEPARTMENT

Head of Communications: Ruth MacLeod 0131 240 2243
Communications Manager: Helen Silvis 0131 240 2268
Senior Communications Officer: Cameron Brooks 0131 240 2204
Communications Officer: Jane Bristow 0131 240 2204
Communications Officer: Laura Crawford 0131 240 2268
Web Editor: Brianne Moore
Web Developer: Alan Murray
Design Team Leader: Chris Flexen
Senior Designer: Steve Walker

Contact the Media Team after hours: 07854 783539
Contact department: 0131 240 2268
Further information:
www.churchofscotland.org.uk > About us > Councils, committees and departments > Departments > Communications

11. ECUMENICAL RELATIONS COMMITTEE

The Committee is composed of Convener, Vice Convener and eight members appointed by the General Assembly, plus representatives of other denominations in Scotland and Church of Scotland members elected to British and international ecumenical bodies. The Church of Scotland trustee of ACTS and the co-chair of the Joint Commission on Doctrine attend as co-opted members. The General Secretary of ACTS attends as a corresponding member.

Convener: Rev. Alexander G. Horsburgh MA BD
Vice-Convener: Rev. Eileen A. Miller BD
Secretary and Ecumenical Officer: Rev. Dr John L. McPake

Contact: ecumenical@churchofscotland.org.uk   0131 240 2208

Further information:
www.churchofscotland.org.uk > About us > Councils, committees and departments > Committees > Ecumenical Relations Committee
www.churchofscotland.org.uk > Connect > Ecumenism
www.churchofscotland.org.uk > Resources > Subjects > Ecumenical Resources
World Council of Churches: www.oikumene.org
Churches Together in Britain and Ireland: www.ctbi.org.uk
Action of Churches Together in Scotland: www.acts-scotland.org
For other international ecumenical bodies see Committee's web pages as above
See also 'Other Churches in the United Kingdom' at Section 2 (2)

12. FACILITIES MANAGEMENT DEPARTMENT

Facilities Manager: Carole Tait
                       ctait@churchofscotland.org.uk   0131 240 2214

Further information:
www.churchofscotland.org.uk > About us > Councils, committees and departments > Committees > Facilities Management

13. FORCES CHAPLAINS COMMITTEE

Convener: Rev. Dr Marjory A. MacLean
Vice-Convener: Rev. John C. Duncan MBE BD MPhil
Secretary: Daran Golby, Faith Nurture
                 DGolby@churchofscotland.org.uk   0131 225 5722

Further information:
www.churchofscotland.org.uk > About us > Councils, committees and departments > Forces Chaplains Committee
A list of Chaplains is found at Section 6 G

14. GENERAL TRUSTEES

Chairman: Mr Raymond K. Young CBE BArch FRIAS
Vice-Chairman: Mr Ian T. Townsend FRICS
Secretary and Clerk: Mr David D. Robertson LLB NP
Depute Secretary and Clerk: Mr Keith S. Mason LLB NP
Assistant Secretaries: Mr Brian Auld ChEHO MREHIS FRSPH GradIOSH
                             (Safe Buildings Consultant)
                             Ms Claire L. Cowell LLB (Glebes)
                             Mrs Morag J. Menneer BSc MRICS (Glebes)
                             Mr Brian D. Waller LLB (Ecclesiastical Buildings)
                             Mr. Neil Page BSc MCIOB
                             (Presbytery Strategy and Innovation)
Health and Safety Officer: Vacant
Fire Safety Officer: Mr Robert Speedie GradIFE
Energy Conservation: Mr Robert Lindores FInstPa
Treasurer: Mrs Anne F. Macintosh BA CA
Finance Manager: Mr Alex Semple FCCA

Buildings insurance,	Church of Scotland Insurance Services Ltd.
all enquiries to	121 George Street, Edinburgh EH2 4YN
	enquiries@cosic.co.uk 0131 220 4119

Contact: gentrustees@churchofscotland.org.uk   0131 225 5722 ext. 2261
Further information:
www.churchofscotland.org.uk > About us > Councils, committees and departments > Departments > General Trustees

15. THE GUILD

The Church of Scotland Guild is a movement within the Church of Scotland whose aim is 'to invite and encourage both women and men to commit their lives to Jesus Christ and to enable them to express their faith in worship, prayer and action'.

Convener:	Mabel Wallace
Vice-Convener:	Helen Banks
	Helen Eckford
	Andrea Houston
	Margaret Muir
General Secretary:	Iain W. Whyte BA DCE DMS

Contact: guild@churchofscotland.org.uk   0131 240 2217

Further information:
www.cos-guild.org.uk
www.churchofscotland.org.uk > Serve > The Guild

16. HOUSING AND LOAN FUND

Chair:	Rev. MaryAnn R. Rennie BD MTh
Deputy Chair:	Rev. Dorothy U. Anderson LLB DipLP BD
Secretary:	Hazel Bett
	HBett@churchofscotland.org.uk 0131 225 5722 ext. 2310
Property Manager:	Hilary J. Hardy
Property Assistant:	John Lunn

Further information:
www.churchofscotland.org.uk > About us > Councils, committees and departments > Departments > Housing and Loan Fund

17. HUMAN RESOURCES DEPARTMENT

Head of Human Resources:	Elaine McCloghry
Human Resources Managers:	Karen Smith
	Angela Ocak
Human Resources Advisers:	Sarah-Jayne McVeigh
	Nicola Bird
	Stephanie Thomson

Contact: hr@churchofscotland.org.uk   0131 240 2270

Further information:
www.churchofscotland.org.uk > About us > Councils, committees and departments > Departments > Human Resources

18. INFORMATION TECHNOLOGY DEPARTMENT

Information Technology Manager: David Malcolm
0131 240 2247

Contact: itdept@churchofscotland.org.uk   0131 240 2245

Further information:
www.churchofscotland.org.uk > About us > Councils, committees and departments > Departments > IT

19. INVESTORS TRUST

Chairman:	Mr Brian J. Duffin
Vice-Chairman:	Mr Robert D. Burgon
Treasurer:	Mrs Anne F. Macintosh BA CA
Secretary:	Mrs Nicola Robertson
	investorstrust@churchofscotland.org.uk

Further information:
www.churchofscotland.org.uk > About us > Councils, committees and departments > Departments > Investors Trust

20. LAW DEPARTMENT

Solicitor of the Church
and of the General Trustees: Miss Mary Macleod LLB DipLP NP
Depute Solicitor: Mrs Elspeth Annan LLB DipLP NP
Solicitors: Miss Susan Killean LLB DipLP NP
                         Mrs Anne Steele LLB DipLP NP
                         Mrs Jennifer Campbell LLB LLM DipLP NP
                         Gregor Buick LLB DipLP WS NP
                         Mrs Madelaine Sproule LLB MSc DipLP NP
                         Gordon Barclay LLB DipLP BSc MSc MPhil PhD
                         David Stihler MA LLB DipLP NP
                         David di Paola LLB DipLP NP

Contact: lawdept@churchofscotland.org.uk   0131 225 5722 ext. 2230; Fax: 0131 240 2246.

Further information:
www.churchofscotland.org.uk > About us > Councils, committees and departments > Departments > Law

21. LEGAL QUESTIONS COMMITTEE

Remit: to advise the General Assembly on questions of Church and Constitutional Law, assist Agencies of the Assembly in preparing and interpreting legislation and arrange for the care of Church Records.

Convener: Rev. Dr S. Grant Barclay
Vice-Convener: Mrs Barbara Finlayson LLB WS
Secretary: Principal Clerk
Depute Clerk: Ms Christine Paterson LLB DipLP

Contact: staylor@churchofscotland.org.uk   0131 240 2240

Further information:
www.churchofscotland.org.uk > About us > Councils, committees and departments > Committees > Legal Questions

22. LIFE AND WORK
the Church of Scotland's monthly magazine

The magazine's purpose is to keep the Church informed about events in church life at home and abroad and to provide a forum for Christian opinion and debate on a variety of topics. It has an independent editorial policy. Contributions which are relevant to any aspect of the Christian faith are welcome. The website, www.lifeandwork.org, includes up-to-date news, extracts from the magazine and additional features. To subscribe to the magazine through your church, speak to your Life and Work co-ordinator. To receive by post, call the number below or visit the website. A digital download, for reading on PC, tablet and smartphone, is also available.

Editor: Lynne McNeil   magazine@lifeandwork.org   0131 225 5722

Further information:
www.lifeandwork.org
www.churchofscotland.org.uk > News and Events > Life and Work

---

23. NOMINATION COMMITTEE

Remit: to bring before the General Assembly names of persons to serve on the Standing Committees of the General Assembly; to work with the Standing Committees to ensure an open, fair and robust process for identifying suitable persons to serve as Conveners.

Convener: Rev. Julie M. Rennick BTh
Vice-Convener: William M. Wishart BD
Secretary: Dave Kendall

Contact: Nominations@churchofscotland.org.uk   0131 240 2229

Further information:
www.churchofscotland.org.uk > About us > Councils, committees and departments > Committees > Nomination Committee

---

24. PENSION TRUSTEES

Chair: Mr Graeme R. Caughey BSc FFIA
Vice-Chair: Miss Lin J. Macmillan MA
Scheme Secretary and
Pensions Manager: Miss Jane McLeod BSc FPMI
Senior Pensions Administrator: Mrs Fiona McCulloch-Stevenson
Pensions Administrators: Ms Birgit Mosemann
                                    Mrs Lesley Elder
                                    Mrs Ruth Farquharson
                                    Mr Connor MacFadyen

Contact: pensions@churchofscotland.org.uk   0131 240 2255

Further information:
www.churchofscotland.org.uk > About us > Councils, committees and departments > Departments > Pension Trustees

25. SAFEGUARDING SERVICE

The service ensures that the Church has robust structures and policies in place for the prevention of harm and abuse of children and adults at risk; and to ensure a timely and appropriate response when harm or abuse is witnessed, suspected or reported.

Convener:	Rev. Adam J. Dillon BD ThM
Vice-Convener:	Mrs Caroline Deerin
Service Manager:	Ms Julie Main BA DipSW

Contact: safeguarding@churchofscotland.org.uk   0131 240 2256

Further information:
www.churchofscotland.org.uk > About us > Councils, committees and departments > Departments > Safeguarding Service

26. SAINT ANDREW PRESS

Saint Andrew Press is managed on behalf of the Church of Scotland by Hymns Ancient and Modern Ltd and publishes a broad range of titles, focussing principally on resources for the mission and ministry of the contemporary church but also including backlist favourites such as William Barclay's much-loved *Daily Study Bible* commentaries. The full list of publications can be viewed on the Saint Andrew Press website (see below).

Contact: Christine Smith, Publishing Director christine@hymnsam.co.uk   0207 776 7546

Further information: www.standrewpress.com

27. SCOTTISH CHURCHES PARLIAMENTARY OFFICE
121 George Street, Edinburgh EH2 4YN

The Office exists to build meaningful relationships between churches and the Scottish and UK Parliaments and Governments, seeking to engage reflectively in the political process, translate their commitment to the welfare of Scotland into parliamentary debate, and contribute their experience and faith-based reflection on it to the decision-making process.

Scottish Churches Parliamentary Officer: Irene Mackinnon MA MLitt
   (Acting)   irene.mackinnon@scpo.scot

Contact: 0131 240 2276

Further information:
www.scpo.scot

---

28. SCOTTISH STORYTELLING CENTRE (THE NETHERBOW)
43–45 High Street, Edinburgh EH1 1SR

The integrated facilities of the **Netherbow Theatre** and the **John Knox House**, together with the outstanding conference and reception areas, form an important cultural venue on the Royal Mile in Edinburgh. The Centre captures both the historical roots of storytelling and the forward-looking mission to preserve it: providing advice and assistance nationally in the use of traditional arts in a diversity of settings. Faith Nurture Forum is pleased to host TRACS (Traditional Arts and Culture Scotland), a grant-funded body who provide an extensive year-round cultural and literary programme.

Contact: reception@scottishstorytellingcentre.com   0131 556 9579

Further information:
www.scottishstorytellingcentre.com

---

29. STEWARDSHIP AND FINANCE DEPARTMENT

General Treasurer: Anne F. Macintosh BA CA
Deputy Treasurer (Congregational
   Finance):   Archie McDowall BA CA
Deputy Treasurer (Unincorporated
   Councils and Committees):   Vacant
National Stewardship Co-ordinator: David J. Lynch BA
Finance Managers: Gillian Coghlan MA CA
                                             Lisa Erskine BA FCCA
                                             Elaine Macadie BA CA
                                             Alex Semple FCCA
                                             Leanne Thompson BSc CA

Contact: sfadmin@churchofscotland.org.uk
Further information and details of consultants:
www.churchofscotland.org.uk > About us > Councils, committees and departments > Stewardship and Finance
www.churchofscotland.org.uk > Resources > Stewardship > The Narrative of Generosity
www.churchofscotland.org.uk > About us > Stewardship Finance and Trusts

30. THEOLOGICAL FORUM

The purpose of the Forum is to continue to develop and bring to expression doctrinal understanding of the Church with reference to Scripture and to the confessional standards of the Church of Scotland, and the implications of this for worship and witness in and beyond contemporary Scotland. It responds to requests to undertake enquiries as they arise, draws the Church's attention to particular matters requiring theological work, and promotes theological reflection throughout the Church.

Convener: Rev. Donald G. MacEwan MA BD PhD
Vice-Convener: Rev. Liam J. Fraser LLB BD MTh PhD
Secretary: Nathalie A. Mareš MA MTh

Contact: NMares@churchofscotland.org.uk
Further information:
www.churchofscotland.org.uk > About us > Councils, committees and departments > Committees > Theological Forum

SECTION 2

General Information

(1) GAELIC DEVELOPMENT IN THE CHURCH OF SCOTLAND
Dr Duncan Sneddon

Leasachadh na Gàidhlig ann an Eaglais na h-Alba
Bhon a thòisich mi san dreuchd seo san Dàmhair 2019, tha mi air a bhith ag obair gus Gàidhlig a leasachadh ann an Eaglais na h-Alba, agus comas na h-eaglaise gus Gàidhlig a chleachdadh na h-obair, fo thrì chinn.

Searmonaichean
Anns a' chiad dol a-mach, tha sinn ag aithneachadh gu bheil fìor ghainnead de mhinistearan agus de shearmonaichean eile a tha comasach air searmonachadh ann an Gàidhlig. Mar sin, tha mi air a bhith ag obair air leabhar-làimhe Gàidhlig a' Bhìobaill agus Gàidhlig na h-Eaglaise, oir tha tòrr dhaoine ann, gu sònraichte am measg na h-òigridh, aig nach eil misneachd anns na raointean-cànain sin. Aig an ìre-sa, tha dà sgoilear Gàidhlig ga dhearbhadh, agus bidh e air fhoillseachadh air-loidhne nuair a tha e deiseil. A bharrachd air sin, tha mi air a bhith ag obair gus sgoil shamhraidh a chur air dòigh aig Sabhal Mòr Ostaig, a' toiseachadh ann an 2021. Bidh sin a' leantainn modal cùrsa a rinn an Eaglais Easbaigeach fad beagan bhliadhnaichean, agus bidh e ag amas air dà bhuidheann: an fheadhainn a tha fileanta ann an Gàidhlig, ach a tha feumach air taic ann an, m.e., mar a sgrìobhas tu searmon; agus an fheadhainn a tha eòlach gu leòr air searmonachadh mar-thà, ach a tha feumach air beagan taic ann a bhith a' cleachdadh na Gàidhlig, agus gu hàraidh "Gàidhlig na Cùbaide". Bidh sin fosgailte do dhaoine ann an eaglaisean eadar-dhealaichte, agus bidh e comasach do mhinistearan ann an Eaglais na h-Alba Urras MhicLeòid a chleachdadh ann a bhith a' pàigheadh cìsean a' chùrsa. Leis mar a tha cùisean a-thaobh èiginn COVID-19, dh'fhaoidte gum bi an cùrsa air a lìbhrigeadh air-loidhne, seach aig a' cholaiste fhèin.

Goireasan
'S e an dara rud as motha air a bheil mi air a bhith ag obair, sgioblachadh an làrach-lìn, ansgeulmor.co.uk, agus a' cur barrachd stuthan ris. Chaidh an làrach-lìn seo a stèidheachadh leis an Urr. Iain D Urchardan, agus gheibhear ann ùrnaighean, laoidhean, goireasan chloinne agus ceanglaichean gu bhideothan agus clàraidhean de sheirbheisean Ghàidhlig, am measg ghoireasan eile. 'S e th' anns An Sgeul Mòr àite far an lorg ministearan, teaghlaichean agus daoine fa-leth goireasan airson adhradh a chumail ann an Gàidhlig, an dara cuid san eaglais no san dachaigh. Le cead bhon Fhòram airson Altraim a' Chreideimh (Faith Nurture Forum), tha mi air cruth didseatach a chur air dà leabhar, *Clann ag Ùrnaigh* (1991) agus *Leabhar Sheirbheisean* (1996), agus tha iad rim faotainn air an làrach-lìn a-nis.

Taic do choitheanalan
Chan eil e air a bhith comasach dhomh tadhal air coitheanalan air a' Ghàidhealtachd bho thòisich an glasadh-sluaigh ri linn COVID-19, ach thadhail mi air coitheanalan anns na h-àiteachan a leanas mus do thòisich e: an t-Òban, an t-Eilean Sgitheanach, Glaschu, Dùn Èideann, Inbhir Pheofharain agus An Gearasdan. Bhruidhinn mi riutha mu dhòighean gus Gàidhlig a leasachadh san eaglais, agus ri daoine aig an robh ùidh san sgoil shamhraidh.
     Chaidh stad a chur air iomadh rud anns na h-eaglaisean ri linn COVID-19, ach tha eaglaisean a' cleachdadh an eadar-lìn airson searmonachadh agus adhradh ann an Gàidhlig ann an caochladh dhòighean. Nam measg: Tha Eaglais an t-Strath is Slèite a' cumail nan seirbheisean Gàidhlig cunbhalach aca air Zoom, agus a' craoladh bhideothan dhen Sgoil Shàbaid Ghàidhlig aca; tha Eaglais Tairbeart na Hearadh a' clàradh agus a' sgaoileadh searmon Gàidhlig air an làrach-lìn aca gach cola-deug; tha an dà choitheanal ann an Dùn Èideann agus Glaschu, Eaglais

nam Manach Liath agus Eaglais Ghàidhlig Chaluim Chille, ag obair còmhla gus seirbheisean a chur air YouTube gach Latha na Sàbaid (fo ainm "Eaglais Ghàidhlig Air-loidhne"), agus bidh iad a' cur barrachd stuthan eile ris an t-sianal sin, ùrnaighean, laoidhean agus m.s.a.a.; tha na h-eglaisean ann an Ùig agus Beàrnaraigh Leòdhais a' foillseachadh rudan ann an Gàidhlig air Facebook; tha seirbheis mhìosail eadar-eaglaiseach Inbhir Pheofharain air a sgaoileadh air YouTube a-nis; tha buidheann-leughaidh a' Bhìobaill anns a' Ghearasdan do luchd-ionnsachaidh, a thòisich dìreach cola-deug ron ghlasadh-sluaigh, a' gluasad air-loidhne a-nis, agus bidh mi gan cuideachadh le sin. A bharrachd air sin, tha an ùrnaigh eadar-eaglaiseach a bhios Eaglais na h-Alba agus caochladh eaglaisean a' foillseachadh gach seachdain a' tighinn a-mach le tionndadh Gàidhlig na chois.

An t-Oll. Donnchadh Sneddon
Oifigear Leasachaidh na Gàidhlig

Gaelic Development in the Church of Scotland
Since taking up this role in October 2019, I have been working to help develop Gaelic in the Church of Scotland, and the capacity of the Church to use Gaelic in its work, in three main priority areas.

Preachers
The first has been to address the serious shortage of ministers and other preachers who are able to preach in Gaelic. In order to tackle this, I have been working to produce a short handbook of Biblical and ecclesiastical Gaelic, as these are registers of the language which many speakers, especially younger speakers, lack confidence in using. This is currently being checked by two Gaelic scholars, and will be published freely online when ready. Additionally, I have been working to establish a weeklong summer school at Sabhal Mòr Ostaig, the Gaelic College on the Isle of Skye, starting in 2021. This will follow the model of a similar course run by the Episcopal Church for several years, and will be aimed at two groups: those who are fluent Gaelic speakers but need training in how to write sermons and lead services, and those who are already experienced preachers, but could use some extra support in their Gaelic, especially their "church Gaelic". This will be open to members of different churches, and ministers in the Church of Scotland will be able to make use of the MacLeod Bequest to help pay their fees. It may be, with the current public health crisis and measures taken to counteract it, that this needs to be delivered online rather than on campus.

Resources
Second, I have been working to reorganise and expand the resources available on the website ansgeulmor.co.uk. This is a website that was established by Rev. John D Urquhart, and hosts prayers, hymns, resources for children and links to videos and recordings of Gaelic services, among other resources. The website is a kind of "one-stop-shop" for worship leaders, families and individuals looking for resources for Gaelic worship in church or in the home. With the permission of the Faith Nurture Forum, the books *Clann ag Ùrnaigh* (1991) and *Leabhar Sheirbheisean* (1996) have been digitised and are now available on the website.

Local congregations
With the lockdown measures adopted to counteract the spread of COVID-19, it has of course become impossible to visit Gaelic-speaking congregations, as had been planned, although I had been able visit congregations and clergy in Oban, Glasgow, Edinburgh, Skye, Dingwall and Fort William before the lockdown. I spoke with them about ideas for developing provision for

Gaelic in the church, and identified individuals who were interested in attending the preachers' summer school.

While the lockdown has, of course, brought great disruption to many church activities, congregations are making use of the internet to continue preaching and worship in Gaelic in different ways. The following are examples: Strath and Sleat Church in Skye is continuing to hold regular Gaelic services on Zoom as well as creating Gaelic Sunday School videos (the Sleat Sunday School group is Gaelic-medium); Tarbert Church in Harris continues to produce online Gaelic services every fortnight; the Gaelic congregations of Greyfriars Kirk in Edinburgh and St Columba Gaelic Church in Glasgow have created a joint YouTube channel (Eaglais Ghàidhlig Air-loidhne) and broadcast a service every week – this will be expanded to also include short videos of prayers and recordings of hymns and sung psalms; Uig and Bernera Church in Lewis is producing some Gaelic content on its social media pages; the monthly ecumenical service in Dingwall has started producing services on YouTube; a Bible reading group for Gaelic learners which started in Fort William before the lockdown is moving online. The weekly ecumenical Gaelic prayer is also published with a Gaelic translation.

Dr Duncan Sneddon
Gaelic Language Development Officer

(2) OTHER CHURCHES IN THE UNITED KINGDOM

THE UNITED FREE CHURCH OF SCOTLAND
Principal Clerks: Rev. Martin C. Keane and Rev. Colin C. Bown, United Free Church Offices, 11 Newton Place, Glasgow G3 7PR (0141 332 3435; office@ufcos.org.uk; www.ufcos. org.uk).

THE FREE CHURCH OF SCOTLAND
Principal Clerk: Rev. Callum Macleod, 15 North Bank Street, The Mound, Edinburgh EH1 2LS (0131 226 5286; offices@freechurch.org; www.freechurch.org).

FREE CHURCH OF SCOTLAND (CONTINUING)
Principal Clerk: Rev. John MacLeod, Free Church Manse, Portmahomack, Tain IV20 1YL (01862 871467; principalclerk@fccontinuing.org; www.freechurchcontinuing.org).

THE FREE PRESBYTERIAN CHURCH OF SCOTLAND
Clerk of Synod: Rev. Keith M. Watkins, Free Presbyterian Manse, Ferry Road, Leverburgh, Isle of Harris HS5 3UA (kmwatkins@fpchurch.org.uk; www.fpchurch.org.uk).

ASSOCIATED PRESBYTERIAN CHURCHES
Clerk of Presbytery: Rev. J.R. Ross Macaskill, Bruach Taibh, 2 Borve, Arnisort, Isle of Skye IV51 9PS (01470 582264; emailjrrm@gmail.com; www.apchurches.org).

THE REFORMED PRESBYTERIAN CHURCH OF SCOTLAND
Clerk of Presbytery: Rev. Peter Loughridge, 7 West Pilton Road, Edinburgh EH4 4GX (07791 369626; peterloughridge@hotmail.com; www.rpcscotland.org).

THE PRESBYTERIAN CHURCH IN IRELAND
Clerk of the General Assembly and General Secretary: Rev. Trevor D. Gribben, Assembly Buildings, 2–10 Fisherwick Place, Belfast BT1 6DW (028 9041 7208; clerk@ presbyterianireland.org; www.presbyterianireland.org).

THE PRESBYTERIAN CHURCH OF WALES
General Secretary: Rev. Meiron Morris, Tabernacle Chapel, 81 Merthyr Road, Whitchurch, Cardiff CF14 1DD (02920 627465; swyddfa.office@ebcpcw.org.uk; www.ebcpcw.cymru).

THE UNITED REFORMED CHURCH
General Secretary: Rev. John Proctor, Church House, 86 Tavistock Place, London WC1H 9RT (020 7916 2020; Fax: 020 7916 2021; john.proctor@urc.org.uk; www.urc.org.uk).

UNITED REFORMED CHURCH SYNOD OF SCOTLAND
Synod Clerk: Mr Bill Robson, United Reformed Church, 3/2 Atlantic Chambers, Glasgow G2 6AE (0141 248 5382; brobson@urcscotland.org.uk; www.urcscotland.org.uk).

BAPTIST UNION OF SCOTLAND
General Director: Rev. Martin Hodson, 48 Speirs Wharf, Glasgow G4 9TH (0141 433 4555; martin@scottishbaptist.org.uk; www.scottishbaptist.com).

CONGREGATIONAL FEDERATION IN SCOTLAND
Chair: Rev. May-Kane Logan, 93 Cartside Road, Busby, Glasgow G76 8QD (0141 237 1349; maycita1@virginmedia.com; www.congregational.org.uk).

RELIGIOUS SOCIETY OF FRIENDS (QUAKERS)
Clerk to the General Meeting for Scotland: Adwoa Bittle (Ms), 4 Burnside Park, Pitcairngreen, Perth PH1 3BF (01738 583108; adwoabittle@hotmail.co.uk; www.quakerscotland.org).

ROMAN CATHOLIC CHURCH
Fr. James A. Grant, General Secretary, Bishops' Conference of Scotland, 64 Aitken Street, Airdrie ML6 6LT (01236 764061; gensec@bcos.org.uk; www.bcos.org.uk).

THE SALVATION ARMY
Lt-Col. Carol Bailey, Secretary for Scotland and Divisional Commander East Scotland Division, Scotland Office, 12A Dryden Road, Loanhead EH20 9LZ (0131 440 9109; carol.bailey@salvationarmy.org.uk; www.salvationarmy.org.uk).

SCOTTISH EPISCOPAL CHURCH
Secretary General: Mr John F. Stuart, 21 Grosvenor Crescent, Edinburgh EH12 5EE (0131 225 6357; secgen@scotland.anglican.org; www.scotland.anglican.org).

THE SYNOD OF THE METHODIST CHURCH IN SCOTLAND
District Administrator: Eileen Cox, Methodist Church Office, Old Churches House, Kirk Street, Dunblane FK15 0AL (Tel/Fax: 01786 820295; DistrictAdmin@methodistchurchinscotland. net; methodistchurchinscotland.net).

GENERAL SYNOD OF THE CHURCH OF ENGLAND
Secretary General: Mr William Nye, Church House, Great Smith Street, London SW1P 3AZ (020 7898 1000; enquiry@churchofengland.org).

---

(3) OVERSEAS CHURCHES

See www.churchofscotland.org.uk > Serve > World Mission > Our partner churches

---

(4) HER MAJESTY'S HOUSEHOLD IN SCOTLAND
ECCLESIASTICAL

Dean of the Order of the Thistle and Dean of the Chapel Royal:	Very Rev. Prof. David A.S. Fergusson OBE MA BD DPhil DD FRSE FBA
Domestic Chaplains:	Rev. Kenneth I. Mackenzie DL BD CPS Rev. Neil N. Gardner MA BD
Chaplains in Ordinary:	Rev. Norman W. Drummond CBE MA BD DUniv FRSE Very Rev. Angus Morrison MA BD PhD DD Very Rev. E. Lorna Hood OBE MA BD DD Rev. Alistair G. Bennett BSc BD

Very Rev. Susan M. Brown BD DipMin DUniv
Very Rev. John P. Chalmers BD CPS DD
Rev. George S. Cowie BSc BD
Rev. Elizabeth M. Henderson OBE MA BD MTh
Rev. George J. Whyte BSc BD DMin

Extra Chaplains:

Rev. John MacLeod MA
Very Rev. James A. Simpson BSc BD STM DD
Very Rev. James Harkness KCVO CB OBE MA DD
Rev. John L. Paterson MA BD STM
Rev. Charles Robertson LVO MA
Very Rev. John B. Cairns KCVO LTh LLB LLD DD
Very Rev. Gilleasbuig I. Macmillan
            KCVO MA BD Drhc DD FRSE HRSA FRCSEd
Very Rev. Finlay A.J. Macdonald MA BD PhD DD
Rev. Alastair H. Symington MA BD
Rev. James M. Gibson TD LTh LRAM
Very Rev. Prof. Iain R. Torrance KCVO Kt DD FRSE

(5) RECENT LORD HIGH COMMISSIONERS
TO THE GENERAL ASSEMBLY

* deceased

1969   Her Majesty the Queen attended in person

1980/81   The Earl of Elgin and Kincardine KT DL JP
1982/83   * Colonel Sir John Edward Gilmour Bt DSO TD
1984/85   * Charles Hector Fitzroy Maclean, Baron Maclean of Duart and Morvern
                  KT GCVO KBE
1986/87   * John Campbell Arbuthnott, Viscount of Arbuthnott KT CBE DSC FRSE FRSA
1988/89   * Sir Iain Mark Tennant KT FRSA
1990/91   The Rt Hon. Donald MacArthur Ross FRSE
1992/93   The Rt Hon. Lord Macfarlane of Bearsden KT FRSE
1994/95   * Lady Marion Fraser KT
1996   Her Royal Highness the Princess Royal LT LG GCVO
1997   The Rt Hon. Lord Macfarlane of Bearsden KT FRSE
1998/99   * The Rt Hon. Lord Hogg of Cumbernauld CBE DL JP
2000   His Royal Highness the Prince Charles, Duke of Rothesay KG KT GCB OM
2001/02   * The Rt Hon. Viscount Younger of Leckie KT KCVO TD PC
              Her Majesty the Queen attended the opening of the General Assembly of 2002
2003/04   The Rt Hon. Lord Steel of Aikwood KT KBE
2005/06   The Rt Hon. Lord Mackay of Clashfern KT
2007   His Royal Highness the Prince Andrew, Duke of York KG KCVO
2008/09   The Rt Hon. George Reid PC MA
2010/11   Lord Wilson of Tillyorn KT GCMG PRSE

2012/13	The Rt Hon. Lord Selkirk of Douglas QC MA LLB
2014	His Royal Highness the Prince Edward, Earl of Wessex KG GCVO
2015/16	The Rt Hon. Lord Hope of Craighead KT PC FRSE
2017	Her Royal Highness the Princess Royal KG KT GCVO QSO
2018/19	The Duke of Buccleuch and Queensberry KT KBE DL FSA FRSE
2020	*General Assembly cancelled: HRH the Prince William had been appointed*

(6) RECENT MODERATORS
OF THE GENERAL ASSEMBLY

* deceased

1992	Hugh R. Wyllie MA DD FCIBS, Hamilton: Old
1993	*James L. Weatherhead CBE MA LLB DD, Principal Clerk of Assembly
1994	James A. Simpson BSc BD STM DD, Dornoch Cathedral
1995	James Harkness KCVO CB OBE MA DD, Chaplain General (Emeritus)
1996	John H. McIndoe MA BD STM DD, London: St Columba's linked with Newcastle: St Andrew's
1997	*Alexander McDonald BA DUniv CMIWSc, General Secretary, Department of Ministry
1998	Alan Main TD MA BD STM PhD DD, University of Aberdeen
1999	John B. Cairns KCVO LTh LLB LLD DD, Dumbarton: Riverside
2000	Andrew R.C. McLellan CBE MA BD STM DD, Edinburgh: St Andrew's and St George's
2001	John D. Miller BA BD DD, Glasgow: Castlemilk East
2002	Finlay A.J. Macdonald MA BD PhD DD, Principal Clerk of Assembly
2003	Iain R. Torrance KCVO Kt DD FRSE, University of Aberdeen
2004	Alison Elliot CBE MA MSc PhD LLD DD FRSE, Associate Director, Centre for Theology and Public Issues, University of Edinburgh
2005	David W. Lacy DL BA BD DLitt, Kilmarnock: Henderson
2006	Alan D. McDonald LLB BD MTh DLitt DD, Cameron linked with St Andrews: St Leonard's
2007	Sheilagh M. Kesting BA BD DD DSG, Secretary of Ecumenical Relations Committee
2008	David W. Lunan MA BD DLitt DD, Clerk to the Presbytery of Glasgow
2009	William C. Hewitt BD DipPS, Greenock: Westburn
2010	John C. Christie BSc BD CBiol MRSB, Interim Minister
2011	A. David K. Arnott MA BD, St Andrews: Hope Park linked with Strathkinness
2012	Albert O. Bogle BD MTh, Bo'ness: St Andrew's
2013	E. Lorna Hood OBE MA BD DD, Renfrew: North
2014	John P. Chalmers BD CPS DD, Principal Clerk of Assembly
2015	Angus Morrison MA BD PhD DD, Orwell and Portmoak
2016	G. Russell Barr BA BD MTh DMin, Edinburgh: Cramond
2017	Derek Browning MA BD DMin, Edinburgh: Morningside
2018	Susan M. Brown BD DipMin DUniv, Dornoch Cathedral

2019   Colin A.M. Sinclair BA BD, Edinburgh: Palmerston Place
2020   W. Martin Fair BA BD DMin, Arbroath: St Andrew's

MATTER OF PRECEDENCE
The Lord High Commissioner to the General Assembly of the Church of Scotland (while the Assembly is sitting) ranks next to the Sovereign and the Duke of Edinburgh and before the rest of the Royal Family.

The Moderator of the General Assembly of the Church of Scotland ranks next to the Lord Chancellor of Great Britain and before the Keeper of the Great Seal of Scotland (the First Minister) and the Dukes.

---

(7) SCOTTISH DIVINITY FACULTIES
* denotes a Minister of the Church of Scotland

ABERDEEN
School of Divinity, History and Philosophy
50–52 College Bounds, Old Aberdeen AB24 3DS
Tel 01224 272366; Fax 01224 273750; divinity@abdn.ac.uk

Master of Christ's College: Rev. Professor John Swinton* BD PhD RNM RNMD
                                   christs-college@abdn.ac.uk
Head of School: Dr Paula Sweeney MA PhD
Head of Divinity: Professor Tom Greggs MA PhD PGCE FRSE FHEA
Co-ordinator,
  Centre for Ministry Studies Rev. Kenneth S. Jeffrey* BA BD PhD DMin
                                   ksjeffrey@abdn.ac.uk

For other teaching staff and further information see www.abdn.ac.uk/sdhp/

ST ANDREWS
University College of St Mary
The School of Divinity, South Street, St Andrews, Fife KY16 9JU
Tel: 01334 462850; Fax: 01334 462852; divinity@st-andrews.ac.uk

Principal and Head of School: Rev. Stephen Holmes BA MA MTh PhD
Professor of World Christianity: Professor Sabine Hyland BA MPhil PhD

For other teaching staff and further information see www.st-andrews.ac.uk/divinity/rt/staff/

EDINBURGH
School of Divinity and New College
New College, Mound Place, Edinburgh EH1 2LX
0131 650 8959; divinity@ed.ac.uk

Head of School:	Professor Helen K. Bond MTheol PhD
Principal of New College:	Rev. Professor Susan Hardman Moore* MA MAR PhD
Assistant Principal of New College:	Rev. Alison M. Jack* MA BD PhD SFHEA
Professor of Divinity:	Very Rev. Professor David A.S. Fergusson* OBE MA BD DPhil DD FRSE FBA
T.F. Torrance Lecturer in Theology and Mission:	Rev. Sandy C. Forsyth* LLB BD DipLP MTh PhD

For other teaching staff and further information see www.ed.ac.uk/schools-departments/divinity/

GLASGOW
School of Critical Studies
Theology and Religious Studies
4 The Square, University of Glasgow, Glasgow G12 8QQ
Tel: 0141 330 6526; Fax: 0141 330 4943

Head of Subject:	Professor Scott Spurlock MTh MSc PhD
Professor of Theology:	Rev. Professor George Pattison MA BD PhD
Principal of Trinity College:	Rev. Doug C. Gay* MA BD PhD

For other teaching staff and further information see www.gla.ac.uk Subjects A-Z. Theology and Religious Studies

HIGHLAND THEOLOGICAL COLLEGE UHI
High Street, Dingwall IV15 9HA
Tel: 01349 780000; Fax: 01349 780001;
htc@uhi.ac.uk

Principal of HTC:	Rev. Hector Morrison* BSc BD MTh
Vice-Principal of HTC:	Jamie Grant PhD MA LLB
Lecturer in Youth Ministry:	Rev. Jonathan Fraser* MA(Div) MTh ThM

For other teaching staff and further information see www.htc.uhi.ac.uk

(8) SOCIETIES AND ASSOCIATIONS

1. INTER-CHURCH ASSOCIATIONS

ACTION OF CHURCHES TOGETHER IN SCOTLAND (ACTS) – Eaglaisean Còmhla an Gnìomh an Alba – was formed in 1990 as Scotland's national ecumenical instrument. It brings together nine denominations in Scotland who share a desire for greater oneness between churches, a growth of understanding and common life between churches, and unified action in proclaiming and responding to the gospel in the whole of life. The Member Churches of ACTS are in the process of transitioning the organisation into the Scottish Christian Forum, which would take forward the charitable purposes of ACTS. Assistant General Secretary: Rev Ian Boa, Jubilee House, Forthside Way, Stirling, FK8 1QZ (07527 433460; ianboa@acts-scotland.org; www.acts-scotland.org).

The FELLOWSHIP OF ST ANDREW: The fellowship promotes dialogue between Churches of the east and the west in Scotland. Further information available from the Secretary, Rev. Dr Robert Pickles, The Manse, Thomas Telford Road, Langholm DG13 0BL (01387 380252; RPickles@churchofscotland.org.uk).

The FELLOWSHIP OF ST THOMAS: An ecumenical association formed to promote informed interest in and to learn from the experience of Churches in South Asia (India, Pakistan, Bangladesh, Nepal, Sri Lanka and Burma (Myanmar)). Secretary: Frances Bicket, 9/2 Connaught Place, Edinburgh EH6 4RQ (0131 552 8781; frances.bicket@gmail.com; www. fost.org.uk).

FRONTIER YOUTH TRUST: A movement of pioneering youth workers, committed to reaching young people on the margins. We host a mission community for youth workers. We are resourcing the church to take pioneering risks in their work with young people. And we are calling others to join the pioneer movement to reach young people on the margins. Contact us for training and coaching, or find practical resources on our website at www.fyt.org.uk. Contact us at info@fyt.org.uk, 0121 771 2328 or find us on social media.

INTERSERVE GREAT BRITIAN AND IRELAND: An international, evangelical and interdenominational organisation with 160 years of Christian service. The purpose of Interserve is 'to make Jesus Christ known through *wholistic* ministry in partnership with the global church, among the neediest peoples of Asia and the Arab world', and our vision is 'Lives and communities transformed through encounter with Jesus Christ'. Interserve supports over 800 people in cross-cultural ministry in a wide range of work including children and youth, the environment, evangelism, Bible training, engineering, agriculture, business development and health. We rely on supporters in Scotland for the work in Scotland and for sending mission partners from Scotland overseas. Scotland Ministry Facilitator: Grace Penney, 21 Park Avenue, Bishopbriggs, Glasgow G64 2SN (07971 858318; GraceP@isgbi.org; www.interserve.org.uk).

IONA COMMUNITY: We are an ecumenical Christian community with a dispersed worldwide membership, and an international network of supporters and volunteers. Inspired by our faith, we pursue justice and peace in and through community. Our Glasgow centre is the base for Wild Goose Publications and the Wild Goose Resource Group. The Iona Community welcomes thousands of visitors each year to its daily worship in Iona Abbey, and to its Welcome Centre and Community shop. It also welcomes guests to share in the common life on Iona and at Camas outdoor centre on Mull, which mainly hosts youth groups. Leader: Rev. Ruth Harvey, 21 Carlton

Court, Glasgow, G5 9JP (0141 429 7281, admin@iona.org.uk; Executive Director: tbc; www. iona.org.uk; Facebook: Iona Community; Twitter: @ionacommunity). Iona Warden: Catriona Robertson, Iona Abbey, Isle of Iona, Argyll, PA76 6SN (01681 700404; enquiries@iona.org.uk).

PLACE FOR HOPE: Our churches and faith communities face change, encounter difference and experience conflict at different stages and for a variety of reasons. In times of change or challenge, we know that practical support can help. Place for Hope, a body with its roots in the Church of Scotland and now an independent charity with over a decade of experience, accompanies and equips people and faith communities where relationships have become strained and helps them move towards living well with difference. Through a skilled and highly trained team of Practitioners, we accompany groups navigating conflict and difficult conversations and resource the church and wider faith communities with peacemakers. Place for Hope can:
– support groups and individuals experiencing conflict
– facilitate sensitive or difficult group conversations, such as preparing for change or transition
– provide individual coaching
– host and enable community dialogues on difficult, potentially divisive issues
– offer training, workshops and resources for understanding and working with conflict and change.
While Coronavirus restrictions are in place, much of our support can be offered online. Please get in touch for information, or a confidential conversation: 07884 580359; info@placeforhope. org.uk; www.placeforhope.org.uk.

The ST COLM'S FELLOWSHIP: An association for all from any denomination who have trained, studied or been resident at St Colm's, either when it was a college or later as International House. There is an annual retreat and a meeting for Commemoration; and some local groups meet on a regular basis. Hon. Secretary: Rev. Margaret Nutter, 'Kilmorich', 14 Balloch Road, Balloch G83 8SR (01389 754505; maenutter@gmail.com).

SCOTTISH CHURCHES HOUSING ACTION: Speaks to churches and for churches on homelessness and its challenges; offers advice and support on establishing befriending services and other voluntary action; and provides consultancy advice on using redundant property for affordable housing. Chief Executive: Richard Howat, 25 Nicolson Square, Edinburgh EH8 9BX (0131 477 4500; info@churches-housing.org; www.churches-housing.org; Facebook @ homelessneighbour; Twitter @churcheshousing).

SCOTTISH CHURCHES ORGANIST TRAINING SCHEME (SCOTS): Established in 1995, SCOTS is a partnership between the Scottish Federation of Organists, the Royal School of Church Music, the Royal College of Organists, and the Scottish Churches. It is a self-propelled scheme by which a pianist who seeks competence on the organ, or organists who wish to develop their skills, can follow a three-stage syllabus, receiving a certificate at each stage. Participants each have an Adviser whom they meet occasionally for help and assessment, and also take part in one of the Local Organ Workshops which are held in different parts of Scotland each year. There is a regular e-letter, *Scots Wha Play*. Costs are kept low. SCOTS is an ecumenical scheme. Information from Andrew Macintosh (01382 521210); andrew.macintosh@rco.org.uk.

SCOTTISH JOINT COMMITTEE ON RELIGIOUS AND MORAL EDUCATION: This is an interfaith body that began as a joint partnership between the Educational Institute of Scotland and the Church of Scotland to provide resources, training and support for the work of religious and moral education in schools. Mr Andrew Tomlinson, 121 George Street, Edinburgh EH2 4YN (0131 225 5722; atomlinson@churchofscotland.org.uk), and Mr Lachlan Bradley, 6 Clairmont Gardens, Glasgow G3 7LW (0141 353 3595).

SCRIPTURE UNION SCOTLAND: Scripture Union Scotland's vision is to see the children and young people of Scotland exploring the Bible and responding to the significance of Jesus. SU Scotland works in schools running SU groups and supporting Curriculum for Excellence. Its three activity centres, Lendrick Muir, Alltnacriche and Gowanbank, accommodate school groups and weekends away during term-time. During the school holidays it runs an extensive programme of events for school-age children – including residential holidays (some focused on disadvantaged children and young people), missions and church-based holiday clubs. In addition, it runs discipleship and training programmes for young people and is committed to promoting prayer for, and by, the young people of Scotland through a range of national prayer events and the *Pray for Schools Scotland* initiative. Scripture Union Scotland, 70 Milton Street, Glasgow G4 0HR (Tel: 0141 332 1162; Fax: 0141 352 7600; info@suscotland.org.uk; www.suscotland.org.uk).

STUDENT CHRISTIAN MOVEMENT: SCM is a student-led movement inspired by Jesus to act for justice and show God's love in the world. As a community we come together to pray, worship and explore faith in an open and non-judgemental environment. The movement is made up of a network of groups and individual members across Britain, as well as link churches and chaplaincies. As a national movement we come together at regional and national events to learn more about our faith and spend time as a community, and we take action on issues of social justice chosen by our members. SCM provides resources and training to student groups, churches and chaplaincies on student outreach and engagement, leadership and social action. Chief Executive; Rev. Naomi Nixon, SCM, Grays Court, 3 Nursery Road, Edgbaston, Birmingham B15 3JX (0121 426 4918; scm@movement.org.uk; www.movement.org.uk).

WORLD DAY OF PRAYER: SCOTTISH COMMITTEE: Convener: Mrs Margaret Broster, Bryn a Glyn, 27b Braehead, Beith KA15 1EF (01505 503300; margaretbroster@hotmail.co.uk). Secretary: Marjorie Paton, Muldoanich, Stirling Street, Blackford, Auchterarder PH4 1QG (01764 682234; marjoriepaton.wdp@btinternet.com; www.wdpscotland.org.uk).

YMCA SCOTLAND: Offers support, training and guidance to churches seeking to reach out to love and serve young people's needs. Chief Executive – National General Secretary: Mrs Kerry Reilly, YMCA Scotland, 1 Chesser Avenue, Edinburgh EH14 1TB (0131 228 1464; kerry@ymca.scot; www.ymca.scot).

YOUTH FOR CHRIST: Youth for Christ is a national Christian charity committed to taking the Good News of Jesus Christ relevantly to every young person in Great Britain. In Scotland there are 5 locally governed, staffed and financed centres, communicating and demonstrating the Christian faith. Local Ministries Director: Lauren Fox (0121 502 9620; lauren.fox@yfc.co.uk; www.yfc.co.uk/local-centres/scotland).

2. CHURCH OF SCOTLAND SOCIETIES

ASSEMBLY AND PRESBYTERY CLERKS FORUM: Secretary: Rev. Bryan Kerr, Greyfriars Parish Church, Bloomgate, Lanark ML11 9ET (01555 663363; clerksforum@ churchofscotland.org.uk).

CHURCH OF SCOTLAND ABSTAINERS' ASSOCIATION: Recognising that alcohol is a major – indeed a growing – problem within Scotland, the aim of the Church of Scotland Abstainers' Association, with its motto 'Abstinence makes sense', is to encourage more people to choose a healthy alcohol-free lifestyle. Further details are available from 'Blochairn', 17A Culduthel Road, Inverness IV24 4AG (jamwall@talktalk.net; www.kirkabstainers.org.uk).

The CHURCH OF SCOTLAND CHAPLAINS' ASSOCIATION: The Association consists of serving and retired chaplains to HM Forces. It holds an annual meeting and lunch on Shrove Tuesday, and organises the annual Service of Remembrance in St Giles' Cathedral on Chaplains' Day of the General Assembly. Hon. Secretary: Rev. Stephen A. Blakey BSc BD, Balduff House, Kilry, Blairgowrie PH11 8HS (01575 560226; SBlakey@churchofscotland.org.uk).

The CHURCH OF SCOTLAND RETIRED MINISTERS' ASSOCIATION: The Association meets in St. Andrew's and St. George's West Church, George St., Edinburgh, normally on the first Monday of the month, from October to April. The group is becoming increasingly ecumenical. Meetings include a talk, which can be on a wide variety of topics, which is followed by afternoon tea. Details of the programme from Hon. Secretary: Rev. Douglas A.O. Nicol, 1/2 North Werber Park, Edinburgh EH4 1SY (07811 437075; Douglas.Nicol@churchofscotland.org.uk).

The CHURCH SERVICE SOCIETY: Founded in 1865 to study the development of Christian worship through the ages and in the Reformed tradition, and to work towards renewal in contemporary worship. It has published since 1928, and continues to publish, a liturgical journal, archived on its website. Secretary: Rev. Dr Martin S. Ritchie (07984 466855; martinsritchie@gmail.com; www.churchservicesociety.org).

COVENANT FELLOWSHIP SCOTLAND (formerly FORWARD TOGETHER): An organisation for evangelicals within the Church of Scotland. Contact the Director, Mr Eric C. Smith (07715 665728; director@covenantfellowshipscotland.com), or the Chairman, Rev. Louis Kinsey (07787 145918; LKinsey@churchofscotland.org.uk; http://covenantfellowshipscotland.com).

The FRIENDS OF TABEETHA SCHOOL, JAFFA: The Friends seek to support the only school run by the Church of Scotland in the world. Based in Jaffa, Israel, it seeks to promote tolerance and understanding amongst pupils and staff alike. President: Irene Anderson. Hon. Secretary: Rev. David J. Smith, 1 Cawdor Drive, Glenrothes KY6 2HN (01592 611963; David.Smith@churchofscotland.org.uk).

The IRISH GATHERING: An informal annual meeting with a guest speaker; all those having a connection with or an interest in the Presbyterian Church in Ireland are very welcome. Secretary: Rev. William McLaren, 23 Shamrock Street, Dundee DD4 7AH (01382 459119; WMcLaren@churchofscotland.org.uk).

SCOTTISH CHURCH SOCIETY: Founded in 1892 to 'defend and advance Catholic doctrine as set forth in the Ancient Creeds and embodied in the Standards of the Church of Scotland', the Society meets for worship and discussion at All Saints' Tide, holds a Lenten Quiet Day, an AGM, and other meetings by arrangement; all are open to non members. The Society is also now working closely with the Church Service Society and is arranging meetings which are of joint interest. Secretary: Rev. W. Gerald Jones MA BD MTh, The Manse, Patna Road, Kirkmichael, Maybole KA19 7PJ (01655 750226; WJones@churchofscotland.org.uk).

SCOTTISH CHURCH THEOLOGY SOCIETY: The Society encourages theological exploration and discussion of the main issues confronting the Church in the twenty-first century. Rev. Alexander Shuttleworth, 62 Toll Road, Kincardine, Alloa FK10 4QZ (01259 731002; AShuttleworth@churchofscotland.org.uk).

SOCIETY OF FRIENDS OF ST ANDREW'S JERUSALEM: In co-operation with the Faith Impact Forum, the Society seeks to provide support for the work of the Congregation of St Andrew's Scots Memorial Church, Jerusalem, and St Andrew's Guesthouse. Hon. Secretary and Membership Secretary: Walter T. Dunlop, c/o Faith Impact Forum, 121 George Street, Edinburgh, EH2 4YN.

3. BIBLE SOCIETIES

The SCOTTISH BIBLE SOCIETY: Chief Executive: Elaine Duncan, 7 Hampton Terrace, Edinburgh EH12 5XU (0131 337 9701; info@scottishbiblesociety.org; https://scottishbiblesociety.org).

WEST OF SCOTLAND BIBLE SOCIETY: Secretary: Rev. Robert Craig (07968 283095; secretary@westofscotlandbiblesociety.com; www.westofscotlandbiblesociety.com).

4. GENERAL

The BOYS' BRIGADE: A volunteer-led Christian youth organisation which was founded in Scotland in 1883 and now operates in many different countries around the world. Our vision is that children and young people experience life to the full (John 10:10). We provide opportunities for young people to learn, grow and discover in a safe, caring and fun environment. John Sharp, Director for Scotland, Scottish Headquarters, Carronvale House, Carronvale Road, Larbert FK5 3LH (01324 562008; scottishhq@boys-brigade.org.uk; www.boys-brigade.org.uk/Scotland). Scottish Chaplain for the Brigade: Rev Derek Gunn (scottishchaplain@boys-brigade.org.uk).

BROKEN RITES: Support group for divorced and separated clergy spouses. (01896 759254; eshirleydouglas@hotmail.co.uk; www.brokenrites.org).

CHRISTIAN AID SCOTLAND: Sally Foster-Fulton, Head of Christian Aid Scotland, Sycamore House, 290 Bath Street, Glasgow G2 4JR (0141 221 7475; glasgow@christian-aid.org; Edinburgh Office: 0131 220 1254; edinburgh@christian-aid.org; www.christianaid.org.uk/get-involved-locally/scotland).

CHRISTIAN ENDEAVOUR IN SCOTLAND: Challenging and encouraging children and young people in the service of Christ and the Church, especially through the CE Award Scheme: 16 Queen Street, Alloa FK10 2AR (01259 215101; admin@cescotland.org; www.cescotland.org).

DAY ONE CHRISTIAN MINISTRIES: Day One has produced Christian literature for over 35 years. A variety of books are published for both adults and young people, as well as cards, bookmarks and stationery items. Ryelands Road, Leominster, Herefordshire HR6 8NZ. Contact Mark Roberts for further information (01568 613740; mark@dayone.co.uk; www.dayone.co.uk).

ECO-CONGREGATION SCOTLAND: Eco-Congregation Scotland is the largest movement of community-based environment groups in Scotland. We offer a programme to help congregations reduce their impact on climate change and live sustainably in a world of limited resources. 121 George Street, Edinburgh EH2 4YN (0131 240 2274; manager@ecocongregationscotland.org; www.ecocongregationscotland.org).

GIRLGUIDING SCOTLAND: 16 Coates Crescent, Edinburgh EH3 7AH (Tel: 0131 226 4511; Fax: 0131 220 4828; administrator@girlguiding-scot.org.uk; www.girlguidingscotland.org.uk).

GIRLS' BRIGADE SCOTLAND: 11A Woodside Crescent, Glasgow G3 7UL (0141 332 1765; caroline.goodfellow@girls-brigade-scotland.org.uk; www.girls-brigade-scotland.org.uk).

The LEPROSY MISSION SCOTLAND: Working in over 30 countries, the Leprosy Mission is a global fellowship united by our Christian faith and commitment to seeing leprosy defeated and lives transformed. The Leprosy Mission Scotland, Suite 2, Earlsgate Lodge, Livilands Lane, Stirling FK8 2BG (01786 449266; contactus@leprosymission.scot; www.leprosymission.scot).

RELATIONSHIPS SCOTLAND: Scotland's largest provider of relationship counselling, family mediation and child contact centre services. Chief Executive: Mr Stuart Valentine, 18 York Place, Edinburgh EH1 3EP (Tel: 0345 119 2020; Fax: 0845 119 6089; enquiries@relationships-scotland.org.uk; www.relationships-scotland.org.uk).

SCOTTISH CHURCH HISTORY SOCIETY: Promoting interest in the history of Christianity in Scotland. Journal: *Scottish Church History*. Secretary: Dr Tristram Clarke (schssec@outlook.com; www.schs.org.uk).

SCOTTISH EVANGELICAL THEOLOGY SOCIETY: Seeks to promote theology which serves the church, is faithful to Scripture, grounded in scholarship, informed by worship, sharpened in debate, catholic in scope, with a care for Scotland and its people. Secretary: Rev. M.G. Smith, 0/2, 2008 Maryhill Road, Glasgow G20 0AB (0141 570 8680; sets.secretary@gmail.com; www.s-e-t-s.org.uk).

The SCOTTISH REFORMATION SOCIETY: Exists to defend and promote the work of the Protestant Reformation in Scotland by organising meetings, publishing literature and running an essay competition. Chairman: Rev. Kenneth Macdonald. Vice-Chairman: Mr Allan McCulloch. Secretary: Rev. Dr Douglas Somerset. Treasurer: Mr Hugh Morrison. The Magdalen Chapel, 41 Cowgate, Edinburgh EH1 1JR (0131 220 1450; info@scottishreformationsociety.org; www.scottishreformationsociety.org).

SCOUTS SCOTLAND: Scottish Headquarters, Fordell Firs, Hillend, Dunfermline KY11 7HQ (01383 419073; hello@scouts.scot; www.scouts.scot).

TEARFUND: Helps communities overcome the worst effects of poverty and disasters, working alongside local churches and other locally-based organisations in over 50 countries. 100 Church Road, Teddington TW11 8QE (0208 977 9144). Acting Director: Graeme McMeekin, Tearfund Scotland, Baltic Chambers, Suite 529, 50 Wellington Street, Glasgow G2 6HJ (0141 332 3621; scotland@tearfund.org; www.tearfund.org/scotland).

The WALDENSIAN MISSIONS AID SOCIETY FOR WORK IN ITALY: Supporting the outreach of the Waldensian Churches, including important work with immigrant communities in the *Mediterranean Hope* project. Scottish Charity No. SC001346. David A. Lamb SSC,

36 Liberton Drive, Edinburgh EH16 6NN (0131 664 3059; david@dlamb.co.uk; www. scottishwaldensian.org.uk).

YOUTH SCOTLAND: Balfour House, 19 Bonnington Grove, Edinburgh EH6 4BL (Tel: 0131 554 2561; Fax: 0131 454 3438; office@youthscotland.org.uk; www.youthscotland.org.uk).

THE YOUNG WOMEN'S MOVEMENT: Our vision is a world where every woman can shape her own life journey and fulfil her potential, where the voices of women are heard, respected and celebrated. We help to bring this about by creating empowering spaces for girls and young women to meet together in groups and clubs, activities and conversations. Director: Patrycja Kupiec, Office 5, 19 Smith's Place, Edinburgh EH6 8NT (0131 652 0248; hello@ywcascotland. org; www.ywcascotland.org).

(9) TRUSTS AND FUNDS

ABERNETHY ADVENTURE CENTRES: Full board residential accommodation and adventure activities available for all Church groups, plus a range of Christian summer camps at our four centres across Scotland. 01479 818005; marketing@abernethy.org.uk; www.abernethy.org.uk).

The BAIRD TRUST: Assists in the building and repair of churches and halls, and generally assists the work of the Church of Scotland. Apply to Iain A.T. Mowat CA, 182 Bath Street, Glasgow G2 4HG (0141 332 0476; info@bairdtrust.org.uk; www.bairdtrust.org.uk).

The Rev. Alexander BARCLAY BEQUEST: Assists a family member of a deceased minister of the Church of Scotland who at the time of his/her death was acting as his/her housekeeper and who is in needy circumstances, and in certain circumstances assists Ministers, Deacons, Ministries Development Staff and their spouses facing financial hardship. Applications can only be submitted to the trustees by the Ministries Council Pastoral Support Team, 121 George Street, Edinburgh EH2 4YN (0131 225 5722; pastoralsupport@churchofscotland.org.uk).

BELLAHOUSTON BEQUEST FUND: Gives grants to Protestant denominations in the City of Glasgow and certain areas within five miles of the city boundary for building and repairing churches and halls and the promotion of religion. Apply to Mr Donald B. Reid, Mitchells Roberton, 36 North Hanover Street, Glasgow G1 2AD (0141 552 3422; info@mitchells-roberton.co.uk).

BEQUEST FUND FOR MINISTERS: Provides financial assistance to ministers in outlying districts towards the cost of manse furnishings, pastoral efficiency aids, and personal and family medical or educational (including university) costs. Apply to A. Linda Parkhill CA, 60 Wellington Street, Glasgow G2 6HJ (0141 226 4994; mail@parkhillmackie.co.uk).

CARNEGIE TRUST FOR THE UNIVERSITIES OF SCOTLAND: The Carnegie Trust invites applications by students who have had at least two years education at a secondary school in Scotland (or can demonstrate evidence of a substantial link to Scotland), for Tuition Fee Grants towards tuition fee costs for a first undergraduate degree at a Scottish university. For more information and a link to the online application form visit the Trust's website (https://www. carnegie-trust.org/award-schemes/undergraduate-tuition-fee-grants/) or contact the Carnegie Trust for the Universities of Scotland, Andrew Carnegie House, Pittencrieff Street, Dunfermline KY12 8AW (01383 724990; admin@carnegie-trust.org; www.carnegie-trust.org).

CHURCH HYMNARY TRUST: The trust is 'formed for the advancement of the Christian Faith through the promotion and development of hymnody in Scotland with particular reference to the Church of Scotland by assisting in the development, promotion, provision and understanding of hymns, psalms and paraphrases suitable for use in public worship, and in the distribution and making available of the same in books, discs, electronically and in other media for use by the Church of Scotland ....' The trust wishes to encourage applications for projects or schemes which are consistent with its purposes. These can include training courses, provision of music and guides to music, but the trust is not limited to those activities. The trust usually meets annually in early February, though applications may be considered out of committee. Applications should be made to the secretary and treasurer Hugh Angus, 56-66 Frederick Street, Edinburgh EH2 1LS, hugh.angus@balfour-manson.co.uk.

CHURCH OF SCOTLAND INSURANCE SERVICES LTD: Insurance intermediary, authorised and regulated by the Financial Conduct Authority, which arranges and manages the facility providing insurance protection for Church of Scotland congregations, including their activities and assets. Cover can also be arranged for other religious groups, charities, and non-profitmaking organisations, with household insurance is available for members. All profits are distributed to the General Trustees of the Church of Scotland through Gift Aid. Contact 121 George Street, Edinburgh EH2 4YN (Tel: 0131 220 4119; Fax: 0131 220 3113; b.clarkson@ cosic.co.uk; www.cosic.co.uk).

CHURCH OF SCOTLAND MINISTRIES BENEVOLENT FUND: Makes grants to the following beneficiaries who are in need:
(a) any retired person who has been ordained or commissioned for the Ministry of the Church of Scotland;
(b) Minsters inducted or introduced to a charge or Ordained National Ministers appointed to posts under approval of Presbytery;
(c) Ministries Development Staff appointed to a Presbytery planned post (including Deacons);
(d) Ordained Local Minsters, Auxiliary Ministers or Deacons serving under the appointment of Presbytery;
(e) Readers set apart by Presbytery to carry out the work of the Church;
(f) any widow, widower and/or orphan of any person categorised in (a) to (e) above;
(g) any spouse or former spouse and/or child (natural or otherwise) of any person categorised by (a) to (e) above.
Apply to Ministries Council Pastoral Support Team, 121 George Street, Edinburgh EH2 4YN (0131 225 5722).

The CINTRA BEQUEST: See 'Tod Endowment Trust ...' entry below.

CLARK BURSARY: Awarded to accepted candidate(s) for the ministry of the Church of Scotland whose studies for the ministry are pursued at the University of Aberdeen. Applications or recommendations for the Bursary to the Clerk to the Presbytery of Aberdeen, Mastrick Church, Greenfern Road, Aberdeen AB16 6TR.

CRAIGCROOK MORTIFICATION: The Trust has power to award grants or pensions (1) to men and women of 60 years of age or over born in Scotland or who have resided in Scotland for not less than 10 years who appear to be in poor circumstances, and (2) to children of deceased persons who met those conditions at the time of death and who appear to require assistance. The Trust has made single payments but normally awards pensions of £1,030 payable biannually. Ministers are invited to notify the Clerk and Factor, Jennifer Law CA, Exchange Place 3, Semple Street, Edinburgh EH3 8BL (0131 473 3500; charity@scott-moncrieff.com) of deserving persons and should be prepared to act as a referee on the application form. Application process currently suspended.

The DRUMMOND TRUST: Makes grants towards the cost of publication of books of 'sound Christian doctrine and outreach'. The Trustees are also willing to receive grant requests towards the cost of audio-visual programme material, but not equipment, software but not hardware. Requests for application forms should be made to the Secretaries, Hill and Robb Limited, 3 Pitt Terrace, Stirling FK8 2EY (01786 450985; fleurmcintosh@hillandrobb.co.uk). Manuscripts should *not* be sent.

The DUNCAN McCLEMENTS TRUST FOR ECUMENICAL TRAINING: Makes grants towards the cost of attendance at ecumenical assemblies and conferences; gatherings of young people; short courses or conferences promoting ecumenical understanding. Also to enable schools to organise one-off events to promote better understanding among differing communities and cultures with different religious backgrounds. The Trust also helps towards the cost of resources and study materials. Enquiries to: Committee on Ecumenical Relations, Church of Scotland, 121 George Street, Edinburgh EH2 4YN (ecumenical@churchofscotland.org.uk).

The David DUNCAN TRUST: Makes grants annually to students for the ministry and students in training to become deacons in the Church of Scotland in the Faculties of Arts and Divinity. Preference is given to those born or educated within the bounds of the former Presbytery of Arbroath. Applications not later than 31 October to Thorntons Law LLP, Brothockbank House, Arbroath DD11 1NE (reference: Glyn Roberts (Trust Manager); 01382 346299; groberts@thorntons-law.co.uk).

ERSKINE CUNNINGHAM HILL TRUST: Donates its annual income to charities and to CrossReach. Individual donations are in the region of £1,000. Priority is given to charities administered by voluntary or honorary officials, in particular charities registered and operating in Scotland and relating to the elderly, young people, ex-service personnel or seafarers. Application forms from the Secretary, Alan Ritchie, 121 George Street, Edinburgh EH2 4YN (0131 240 2260; aritchie@churchofscotland.org.uk).

ESDAILE TRUST: Assists the education and advancement of daughters of ministers, missionaries and widowed deaconesses of the Church of Scotland between 12 and 25 years of age. Applications are to be lodged by 31 May in each year with the Clerk and Treasurer, Jennifer Law CA, Exchange Place 3, Semple Street, Edinburgh EH3 8BL (0131 473 3500; charity@scott-moncrieff.com).

FERGUSON BEQUEST FUND: Assists with the building and repair of churches and halls and, more generally, with the work of the Church of Scotland. Priority is given to the Counties of Ayr, Kirkcudbright, Wigtown, Lanark, Dunbarton and Renfrew, and to Greenock, Glasgow, Falkirk and Ardrossan; applications are, however, accepted from across Scotland. Apply to Iain A.T.

Mowat CA, 182 Bath Street, Glasgow G2 4HG (0141 332 0476; info@fergusonbequestfund. org.uk; www.fergusonbequestfund.org.uk).

James GILLAN'S BURSARY FUND: Bursaries are available for male or female Candidates for the Ministry in the Church of Scotland who are currently resident in, or were born and had their home for not less than three years continually in the Parishes of Dyke, Edinkillie, Forres St Leonard's and Rafford. In certain circumstances the Trustees may be able to make a grant to Church Candidates resident in the old counties of Moray or Nairn, but only while resident. Apply in writing to The Minister, St Leonard's Manse, Nelson Road, Forres IV36 IDR (01309 672380).

The GLASGOW SOCIETY OF THE SONS AND DAUGHTERS OF MINISTERS OF THE CHURCH OF SCOTLAND: The Society's primary purpose is to grant financial assistance to children (no matter what age) of deceased ministers of the Church of Scotland. Applications for first grants can be lodged at any time. Thereafter annual applications must be lodged by 31 December for consideration by Council in February. To the extent that funds are available, grants are also given for the children of ministers or retired ministers, although such grants are normally restricted to university and college students. These latter grants are considered in conjunction with the Edinburgh-based Societies. Limited funds are also available for individual application for special needs or projects. Applications are to be submitted by 31 May in each year. Emergency applications can be dealt with at any time when need arises. More information can be found at www.mansebairnsnetwork.org. Application forms may be obtained from the Secretary and Treasurer, Jennifer Law CA, Exchange Place 3, Semple Street, Edinburgh EH3 8BL (0131 473 3500; charity@scott-moncrieff.com).

HAMILTON BURSARY: Awarded, subject to the intention on graduation to serve overseas under the Church of Scotland World Mission Council or to serve with some other Overseas Mission Agency approved by the Council, to a student at the University of Aberdeen (failing whom to Accepted Candidate(s) for the Ministry of the Church of Scotland whose studies for the Ministry are pursued at Aberdeen University). Applications or recommendations for the Bursary to the Clerk to the Presbytery of Aberdeen, Mastrick Church, Greenfern Road, Aberdeen AB16 6TR.

Martin HARCUS BEQUEST: Makes annual grants to candidates for the ministry resident within the Presbytery of Edinburgh and currently under the jurisdiction of the Presbytery. Applications to the Principal's Secretary, New College, Mound Place, Edinburgh EH1 2LX (NewCollege@ ed.ac.uk) by 15 October.

The HOPE TRUST: In terms of its new constitution, gives support to organisations that (1) advance the cause of temperance through the promotion of temperance work and the combatting of all forms of substance abuse and (2) promote Reformed theology and Reformed church life especially in Scotland and the social mission of charities with historical or contemporary links to the Reformed tradition, and includes a scholarship programme, the appointment of a part-time post-doctoral fellowship and support for students in full time training. Apply to the Secretary, Lyn Sutherland, Glenorchy House, 20 Union Street, Edinburgh, EH1 3LR (Tel: 0131 226 5151; Fax: 0131 556 5354 or Email: hopetrust@drummondmiller.co.uk).

KEAY THOM TRUST: The principal purposes of the Keay Thom Trust are:
1.   To benefit the widows, daughters or other dependent female relatives of deceased ministers, or wives of ministers who are now divorced or separated, all of whom have supported the

minister in the fulfilment of his duties and who, by reason of death, divorce or separation, have been required to leave the manse. The Trust can assist them in the purchase of a house or by providing financial or material assistance whether it be for the provision of accommodation or not.
2.   To assist in the education or training of the above female relatives or any other children of deceased ministers.
Further information and application forms are available from Miller Hendry, Solicitors, 10 Blackfriars Street, Perth PH1 5NS (01738 637311; johnthom@millerhendry.co.uk).

LADIES' GAELIC SCHOOLS AND HIGHLAND BURSARY ASSOCIATION: Distributes money to students, preferably with a Highland/Gaelic background, who are training to be ministers in the Church of Scotland. Apply by 15 October in each year to the Secretary, Mrs Marion McGill, 61 Ladysmith Road, Edinburgh EH9 3EY (0131 667 4243; marionmcgill61@gmail.com).

The LYALL BEQUEST (Scottish Charity Number SC005542): Offers grants to ministers:
1.   Grants to individual ministers, couples and families, for a holiday for a minimum of seven nights. No reapplication within a three-year period; and thereafter a 50 per cent grant to those reapplying.
2.   Grants towards sickness and convalescence costs so far as not covered by the National Health Service. Applications should be made to the Secretary and Clerk, The Church of Scotland Trust, 121 George Street, Edinburgh EH2 4YN (0131 240 2260; msproule@churchofscotland.org.uk).

REV DR MACINNES AND MRS MACINNES TRUST: Provides grants to (1) retired ministers who have spent part of their ministry in the Counties of Nairn, Ross & Cromarty or Argyll and are solely dependent upon their pensions and preaching fees and (2) widows or widowers of such ministers solely dependent on their pensions. Applications should be made to the Secretary and Clerk, The Church of Scotland Trust, 121 George Street, Edinburgh EH2 4YN (0131 240 2260; msproule@churchofscotland.org.uk).

Gillian MACLAINE BURSARY FUND: Open to candidates for the ministry of the Church of Scotland of Scottish or Canadian nationality. Preference is given to Gaelic-speakers. Application forms available from Mr W Stewart Shaw DL BSc, Clerk to the Presbytery of Argyll, 59 Barone Road, Rothesay, Isle of Bute PA20 0DZ (07470 520240; argyll@churchofscotland.org.uk). Closing date for receipt of applications is 31 October.

The E. McLAREN FUND: The persons intended to be benefited are widows and unmarried ladies, preference being given to ladies above 40 years of age in the following order:
(a) Widows and daughters of Officers in the Highland Regiment, and
(b) Widows and daughters of Scotsmen.
Further details from the Secretary, The E. McLaren Fund, Messrs Wright, Johnston & Mackenzie LLP, Solicitors, 302 St Vincent Street, Glasgow G2 5RZ (Tel: 0141 248 3434; Fax: 0141 221 1226; rmd@wjm.co.uk).

THE MEIKLE AND PATON TRUST: Grants are available to Ministers, Missionaries and other Christian Workers, as agreed by the Trustees, for rest and recuperation at the following hotels: Crieff Hydro; Murraypark Hotel, Crieff; Peebles Hydro; Park Hotel, Peebles; Ballachulish Hotel and Isle of Glencoe Hotel. Grants give a subsidy for overnight residence, such subsidy being decreed by the Trustees at any given time. Booking may be made by telephone or on line and applicants will be required to state their page in the Church of Scotland Year Book or their unique number from the CSC list to obtain Meikle Paton benefit. Chairman: Rev. Iain F. Paton (iain.f.paton@btinternet.com).

MORGAN BURSARY FUND: Makes grants to candidates for the Church of Scotland ministry studying at the University of Glasgow. Apply to the Clerk to the Presbytery of Glasgow, 260 Bath Street, Glasgow G2 4JP (0141 332 6606; glasgow@churchofscotland.org.uk). Closing date October 31.

NEW MINISTERS' FURNISHING LOAN FUND: Makes loans (of £1,000) to ministers in their first charge to assist with furnishing the manse. Apply to Elaine Macadie, Finance Manager, Ministries Council, 121 George Street, Edinburgh EH2 4YN.

NOVUM TRUST: Provides small short-term grants – typically between £200 and £2,500 – to initiate projects in Christian action and research which cannot readily be financed from other sources. Trustees welcome applications from projects that are essentially Scottish, are distinctively new, and are focused on the welfare of young people, on the training of lay people or on new ways of communicating the Christian faith. The Trust cannot support large building projects, staff salaries or individuals applying for maintenance during courses or training. Application forms and guidance notes from novumt@cofscotland.org.uk or Mrs Susan Masterton, Blair Cadell WS, The Bond House, 5 Breadalbane Street, Edinburgh EH6 5JH (0131 555 5800; www.novum.org.uk).

PARK MEMORIAL BURSARY FUND: Provides grants for the benefit of candidates for the ministry of the Church of Scotland from the Presbytery of Glasgow under full-time training. Apply to the Clerk to the Presbytery of Glasgow, 260 Bath Street, Glasgow G2 4JP (0141 332 6606; glasgow@churchofscotland.org.uk). Closing date November 15.

PATON TRUST: Assists ministers in ill health to have a recuperative holiday outwith, and free from the cares of, their parishes. Apply to Alan S. Cunningham CA, Alexander Sloan, Accountants and Business Advisers, 180 St Vincent Street, Glasgow G2 5SG (Tel: 0141 204 8989; alan.cunningham@alexandersloan.co.uk).

PRESBYTERY OF ARGYLL BURSARY FUND: Open to students who have been accepted as candidates for the ministry and the readership of the Church of Scotland. Preference is given to applicants who are natives of the bounds of the Presbytery, or are resident within the bounds of the Presbytery, or who have a strong connection with the bounds of the Presbytery. Application forms available from Mr W Stewart Shaw DL BSc, Clerk to the Presbytery of Argyll, 59 Barone Road, Rothesay, Isle of Bute PA20 0DZ (07470 520240; argyll@churchofscotland.org.uk). Closing date for receipt of applications is 31 October.

Margaret and John ROSS TRAVELLING FUND: Offers grants to ministers and their spouses for travelling and other expenses for trips to the Holy Land where the purpose is recuperation or relaxation. Applications should be made to the Secretary and Clerk, The Church of Scotland Trust, 121 George Street, Edinburgh EH2 4YN (0131 240 2260; msproule@churchofscotland. org.uk).

SCOTLAND'S CHURCHES TRUST: Assists, through grants, with the preservation of the fabric of buildings in use for public worship by any denomination. Also supports the playing of church organs by grants for public concerts, and through tuition bursaries for suitably proficient piano or organ players wishing to improve skills or techniques. SCT promotes visitor interest in churches through the trust's Pilgrim Journeys covering Scotland. Criteria and how to apply at www.scotlandschurchestrust.org.uk. Scotland's Churches Trust, 15 North Bank Street, Edinburgh EH1 2LP (info@scotlandschurchestrust.org.uk).

SMIETON FUND: To assist ministers who would benefit from a holiday because of a recent pastoral need. Administered at the discretion of the pastoral staff, who will give priority in cases of need. Applications to the Recruitment and Support Secretary, Ministries Council, 121 George Street, Edinburgh EH2 4YN (pastoralsupport@churchofscotland.org.uk).

Mary Davidson SMITH CLERICAL AND EDUCATIONAL FUND FOR ABERDEENSHIRE: Assists ministers who have been ordained for five years or over and are in full charge of a congregation in Aberdeen, Aberdeenshire and the north, to purchase books, or to travel for educational purposes, and assists their children with scholarships for further education or vocational training. Apply to Alan J. Innes MA LLB, 100 Union Street, Aberdeen AB10 1QR (01224 428000).

The SOCIETY FOR THE BENEFIT OF THE SONS AND DAUGHTERS OF THE CLERGY OF THE CHURCH OF SCOTLAND: Annual grants are made to assist in the education of the children (normally between the ages of 12 and 25 years) of ministers of the Church of Scotland. The Society also gives grants to aged and infirm daughters of ministers and ministers' unmarried daughters and sisters who are in need. Applications are to be lodged by 31 May in each year with the Secretary and Treasurer, Jennifer Law CA, Exchange Place 3, Semple Street, Edinburgh EH3 8BL (0131 473 3500; charity@scott-moncrieff.com).

The SOCIETY IN SCOTLAND FOR PROPAGATING CHRISTIAN KNOWLEDGE: The SSPCK gives grants to: 1. Resourcing mission within Scotland; 2. The training and education of Christians in Commonwealth countries overseas, aimed to equip them for service in the mission and outreach of the Church; 3.The training of British young people volunteering for periods of service in Christian mission and education overseas; 4. The resourcing of new initiatives in worldwide Christian misson. Chairman: Rev. Michael W. Frew; Secretary: Rev. Ian W. Alexander, SSPCK, c/o Faith Impact, 121 George Street, Edinburgh EH2 4YN (0131 225 5722; SSPCK@churchofscotland.org.uk; www.sspck.co.uk).

The Nan STEVENSON CHARITABLE TRUST FOR RETIRED MINISTERS: Provides houses, or loans to purchase houses, on similar terms to the Housing and Loan Fund, for any retired paid church worker with a North Ayrshire connection. Secretary and Treasurer: Mrs Christine Thomas, 18 Brisbane Street, Largs KA30 8QN (01475 338564; 07891 838778; cathomas54@gmail.com).

Miss M.E. SWINTON PATERSON'S CHARITABLE TRUST: The Trust can give modest grants to support smaller congregations in urban or rural areas who require to fund essential maintenance or improvement works at their buildings. Applications for grants should be made via the Trust's online application form available at www.swintonpaterson.org.uk.

SYNOD OF GRAMPIAN CHILDREN OF THE CLERGY FUND: Makes annual grants to children of deceased ministers. Apply to Rev. Iain U. Thomson, Clerk and Treasurer, 4 Keirhill Gardens, Westhill AB32 6AZ (01224 746743; iainuthomson@googlemail.com).

SYNOD OF GRAMPIAN WIDOWS' FUND: Makes annual grants (currently £350 p.a.) to widows or widowers of deceased ministers who have served in a charge in the former Synod. Apply to Rev. Iain U. Thomson, Clerk and Treasurer, 4 Keirhill Gardens, Westhill AB32 6AZ (01224 746743; iainuthomson@googlemail.com).

TOD ENDOWMENT TRUST; CINTRA BEQUEST; TOD ENDOWMENT SCOTLAND HOLIDAY FUND: The Trustees of the Cintra Bequest and of the Tod Endowment Scotland Holiday Fund can consider an application for a grant from the Tod Endowment funds from any ordained or commissioned minister or deacon in Scotland of at least two years' standing before the date of application, to assist with the cost of the beneficiary and his or her spouse or partner and dependants obtaining rest and recuperation in Scotland. The Trustees of the Tod Endowment Scotland Holiday Fund can also consider an application from an ordained or commissioned minister or deacon who has retired. Application forms are available from Madelaine Sproule, Law Department (for the Cintra Bequest), and from Ministries Council Pastoral Support Team (for the Tod Endowment Scotland Holiday Fund). The address in both cases is 121 George Street, Edinburgh EH2 4YN (0131 225 5722). (Attention is drawn to the separate entry above for the Church of Scotland Ministries' Benevolent Fund.)

STEPHEN WILLIAMSON & ALEX BALFOUR FUND: Offers grants to Ministers in Scotland, with first priority being given to Ministers in the Presbyteries of Angus and Dundee, followed by the Presbyteries in Fife, to assist with the cost of educational school/ college/ university trips for sons and daughters of the Manse who are under 25 years and in full time education. Application for trips in any year will be considered by the Trustees in the January of that year, when the income of the previous financial year will be awarded in grants. The applications for trips in that calendar year must be submitted by 31 December of the preceding year. For applications from outwith the 5 priority Presbyteries the total cost of the trip must be in excess of £500, with the maximum grant which can be awarded being £200. The trustees will always give priority to new applicants. If funds still remain for distribution after the allocation of grants in January further applications for that year will be considered. Applications from the Presbyteries of Angus, Dundee, Dunfermline, Kirkcaldy and St Andrews will be considered at any time of year as the Trustees have retained income for these grants. Applications should be made to the Secretary and Clerk, The Church of Scotland Trust, 121 George Street, Edinburgh EH2 4YN (0131 240 2260; msproule@churchofscotland.org.uk).

---

(10) LONG SERVICE CERTIFICATES

Long Service Certificates, signed by the Moderator, are available for presentation to elders and voluntary office bearers in respect of not less than thirty years of service. At the General Assembly of 2015, it was agreed that further certificates could be issued at intervals of ten years thereafter. It should be noted that the period is years of *service*, not (for example) years of ordination in the case of an elder. In the case of those volunteers engaged in children's and youth work, the qualifying period is twenty-one years of service. Certificates are not issued posthumously, nor is it possible to make exceptions to the rules, for example by recognising quality of service in order to reduce the qualifying period, or by reducing the qualifying period on compassionate grounds, such as serious illness. Applications for Long Service Certificates should be made in writing to the Principal Clerk at 121 George Street, Edinburgh EH2 4YN by the parish minister, or by the session clerk on behalf of the Kirk Session. Certificates are not issued from this office to the individual recipients, nor should individuals make application themselves. If a note of the award of the Certificate is to be inserted in *Life and Work* contact should be made with that publication direct.

(11) RECORDS OF THE CHURCH OF SCOTLAND

Church records more than fifty years old, unless still in use, should be sent or delivered to the Principal Clerk for onward transmission to the National Records of Scotland. Where ministers or session clerks are approached by a local repository seeking a transfer of their records, they should inform the Principal Clerk, who will take the matter up with the National Records of Scotland.

SECTION 3

Church Procedure

A. THE MINISTER AND BAPTISM

See www.churchofscotland.org.uk > Resources > Yearbook > Section 3A

B. THE MINISTER AND MARRIAGE

See www.churchofscotland.org.uk > Resources > Yearbook > Section 3B

C. CONDUCT OF MARRIAGE SERVICES (CODE OF GOOD PRACTICE)

See www.churchofscotland.org.uk > Resources > Yearbook > Section 3C

D. MARRIAGE AND CIVIL PARTNERSHIP (SCOTLAND) ACT 2014

See www.churchofscotland.org.uk > Resources > Yearbook > Section 3D

E. CONDUCT OF FUNERAL SERVICES: FEES

See www.churchofscotland.org.uk > Resources > Yearbook > Section 3E

F. PULPIT SUPPLY FEES AND EXPENSES

See www.churchofscotland.org.uk > Resources > Yearbook > Section 3F

G. PROCEDURE IN A VACANCY

A full coverage can be found in two handbooks listed under *Interim Moderators and Nominating Committees* on the Ministries Resources pages on the Church of Scotland website, which also includes information on locum appointments:
www.churchofscotland.org.uk > Resources > Subjects > Ministries resources > Interim Moderators and Nominating Committees

SECTION 4

General Assembly 2020

The General Assembly of 2020 was cancelled due to the coronavirus (COVID-19) pandemic, which led to the cancelling of all public gatherings, including public worship and meetings.

Those appointed to the Commission of Assembly by the General Assembly of 2019 were therefore invited to take certain 'straightforward, time-critical and non-controversial' decisions in relation to papers circulated in April 2020. In summary, the decisions thus agreed were to:

- Elect the Rev. Dr W. Martin Fair of Arbroath: St Andrew's as Moderator of the General Assembly 2020.
- Unite the Presbyteries of Aberdeen and of Shetland as the Presbytery of Aberdeen and Shetland on 1 June 2020.
- Unite the Presbyteries of Greenock and Paisley and of Dumbarton as the Presbytery of Clyde on 1 September 2020.
- Unite the Presbyteries of Dunfermline, of Kirkcaldy and of St Andrews as the Presbytery of Fife on 1 January 2021.
- Reduce the membership of the Social Care Council to 12 on 1 June 2020 and appoint the Rev. Thomas S. Riddell as Convener.
- Appoint the Rev. Donald G.B. McCorkindale as Convener of the Assembly Business Committee.
- Make appointments to the Forums, Committees and Trusts as proposed by the Nomination Committee.
- Agree that the Ecumenical Relations Committee shall act on behalf of the General Assembly in the dissolution of Local Ecumenical Partnerships.
- Amend Regulation I 2013 on the Nomination of the Moderator of the General Assembly and instruct the Nomination Committee to populate the Committee to Nominate the Moderator.
- Pass an Act amending the Income Protection and Ill-Health Act (Act V1 2019).

The installation of the Moderator, Rt. Rev. W. Martin Fair, was held on Saturday, 16 May 2020, following strict social distancing guidelines, and streamed live from the General Assembly Hall in Edinburgh.

THE MODERATOR

The Right Reverend W. Martin Fair BA BD DMin

Lou Reed's song, *A Perfect Day*, reaches out to each of us as something of an invitation – what would that 'perfect day' look like?

For Martin, it would almost certainly involve a ridiculously early start and a day in the high mountains of Scotland. He goes there for the company of trusted friends and for the love of wild places. But through all the years and countless trips, he has found there – in hill and vale and under big skies – that the sense of God's presence is sharpened and that perspective returns and inner healing begins.

Or in other circumstances, you might find him on a Saturday afternoon at Ibrox, watching his beloved Rangers, or nearer to home cheering on the Red Lichties of Arbroath. With football 'in the blood' he travels near and far to cheer on Scotland and along with other members of the Tartan Army has learned the hard way that bitter disappointment is the stuff of life!

Of an evening, Martin enjoys cooking – an interest developed only in later years – and then sitting down to good food and wine and long hours of chat. Or, heading off for a trip to the cinema or settling down at home for the latest Netflix drama.

He loves travelling and through that, seeing other ways of life and meeting new people. He lists the USA (from where he gained his Doctor of Ministry degree) as his favourite place to visit and has on his bucket list to set foot in all fifty states – after completing his other list of climbing all of Scotland's 282 Munros!

Martin is married to Elaine, his childhood sweetheart and best friend. They've shared all of life together, through school days, finding faith to call their own in their mid-teens, and through all of the thrills and spills of marriage and family life. Their three boys, Callum (presently living in Australia), Andrew and Fraser have ensured that life has never been dull and continue to be a source of much joy to their parents.

Martin and Elaine were raised close to each other and on the day of their wedding in July 1987 were able to walk to the church from their respective homes. Even so Elaine insisted on being driven!

Together they attended Thornliebank Primary and Woodfarm Secondary Schools on the south side of Glasgow before going their separate ways, Elaine to train as a primary teacher, Martin to study politics and geography at Strathclyde University. Following his graduation, Martin worked as a street youth worker for the Church of England in Leeds before returning to Glasgow to take up studies in Divinity. Accepted as a candidate for ministry, he was licensed by the Presbytery of Glasgow in July 1989 before heading with Elaine to Bermuda a couple of months later for what served as his probationary period. He has often remarked that it was a tough assignment but that someone had to go!

Returning to home territory in the summer of 1991, he undertook a short placement at Dundee: St. Mary's before accepting the call to Arbroath: St. Andrew's where he was ordained and inducted on the 28th January 1992.

And there he remains to this day, thoroughly committed to ministry in the parish. Together with his congregation, these have been years of exciting discovery as they have sought new ways to offer ministry and mission in a town struggling through serious social and economic malaise and a country largely 'moved on' from meaningful involvement with the Christian Church. Congregational life in Arbroath has revolved around 'growing and going' – growing in faith and in love of the Lord and going, more intentionally, out from the church into the wider community, according to need. Central to that has been the establishment of the widely-recognised Havilah project – a ministry through which an ever-growing number of isolated and broken people have been supported through struggles with addiction towards freedom and fullness of life.

Within Angus Presbytery, Martin has served as Moderator and on various of the groups and committees and, nationally, most fully as Convener of the Parish Development Fund and as Vice-Convener of the Mission and Discipleship Council.

Martin cares passionately about the Church and continues to pray for and reflect deeply about its life and work – not least in the light of the coronavirus crisis through which so many of its tried and tested approaches have been rendered redundant overnight. From being raised in a loving Christian family and within the church at Thornliebank, and the ongoing supportive friendships of many from youth fellowship and summer mission days, he owes much to the Kirk and hopes that through his period of office as Moderator of the General Assembly, he can inspire and support the Church to find new ways for new days.

Catherine Beattie and Gregor McIntyre
Moderator's Chaplains

SECTION 5

Presbytery Lists

In each Presbytery list, the parishes/congregations ('charges') are listed in alphabetical order. In a linked charge, the names appear under the first-named. Under the name of the charge will be found the name of the minister and, where applicable, that of an associate minister, ordained local minister, auxiliary minister and member of the Diaconate. The years indicated after a name in the congregational section of each Presbytery list are the years of ordination (column 1) and the year of current appointment (column 2). Where only one date is given, it is both the year of ordination and the year of appointment. Where no other name is listed, the name of the session clerk(s) or interim moderator is given. (Some parishes have more than one church – see Section 8. For presbytery and parish boundaries, see the online map at http://arcg.is/11rSXH.)

In the second part of each Presbytery list, **B** comprises those ministers and deacons in other appointments (if any), while **C** covers those demitted/retired. The first date is the year of ordination, and the following date is the year of appointment or retirement. If the person concerned is retired, then the appointment last held will be shown in brackets.

F   A charge with a Facebook page.
GD A charge where it is desirable that the minister should have a knowledge of Gaelic.
GE A charge where public worship must be regularly conducted in Gaelic.
H   A hearing aid loop system has been installed.
L   A chair lift or lift has been installed.
T   A charge with a Twitter account.
W   A charge with a website.

PRESBYTERY NUMBERS (following unions, numbers 15, 18, 20, 21 and 46 are no longer used)

1	Edinburgh	17	Hamilton	35	Moray
2	West Lothian	19	Argyll	36	Abernethy
3	Lothian	22	Falkirk	37	Inverness
4	Melrose and Peebles	23	Stirling	38	Lochaber
5	Duns	24	Dunfermline	39	Ross
6	Jedburgh	25	Kirkcaldy	40	Sutherland
7	Annandale and Eskdale	26	St Andrews	41	Caithness
8	Dumfries and Kirkcudbright	27	Dunkeld and Meigle	42	Lochcarron – Skye
9	Wigtown and Stranraer	28	Perth	43	Uist
10	Ayr	29	Dundee	44	Lewis
11	Irvine and Kilmarnock	30	Angus	45	Orkney
12	Ardrossan	31	Aberdeen and Shetland	47	England
13	Lanark	32	Kincardine and Deeside	48	Europe
14	Clyde	33	Gordon	49	Jerusalem
16	Glasgow	34	Buchan		

(1) EDINBURGH (F W)

The Presbytery meets at Palmerston Place Church, Edinburgh, on (2020) 3 November and 1 December, and (2021) in February, June, September and October. It also meets for conference in April or May and November; dates to be intimated.

| Clerk: | REV. MARJORY McPHERSON LLB BD MTh | 10/1 Palmerston Place, Edinburgh EH12 5AA edinburgh@churchofscotland.org.uk | 0131 225 9137 |
| Depute Clerk: | HAZEL HASTIE MA CQSW PhD AIWS | 10/1 Palmerston Place, Edinburgh EH12 5AA HHastie@churchofscotland.org.uk | 07827 314374 |

1 Edinburgh: Albany Deaf Church of Edinburgh (F H)
info@stagw.org.uk — 0131 444 2054
Albany Deaf Church is a Mission Initiative of Edinburgh: St Andrew's and St George's West

2 Edinburgh: Balerno (F H W)
Andre J. Groenewald BA BD MDiv DD   1994   2016
bpc-admin@balernochurch.org.uk — 0131 449 7245
3 Johnsburn Road, Balerno EH14 7DN — 0131 449 3830
AGroenewald@churchofscotland.org.uk

3 Edinburgh: Barclay Viewforth (F W)
David Clarkson BSc BA MTh   2010   2020
admin@barclaychurch.org.uk — 0131 229 6810
113 Meadowspot, Edinburgh EH10 5UY — 0131 478 2376
DClarkson@churchofscotland.org.uk

4 Edinburgh: Blackhall St Columba's (T W)
Fergus M. Cook BD   2020
secretary@blackhallstcolumba.org.uk — 0131 332 4431
5 Blinkbonny Crescent, Edinburgh EH4 3NB — 0131 466 7503
FCook@churchofscotland.org.uk

5 Edinburgh: Bristo Memorial Craigmillar (F W)
Vacant
Interim Moderator: Donald H. Scott
72 Blackchapel Close, Edinburgh EH15 3SL — 0131 657 3266
Donald.Scott@churchofscotland.org.uk — 0131 468 1254

6 Edinburgh: Broughton St Mary's (F H L W)
Vacant
Interim Moderator: Karen K. Campbell
mail@bstmchurch.org.uk — 0131 556 4252
78 March Road, Edinburgh EH4 3SY — 0131 312 7440
KKCampbell@churchofscotland.org.uk — 0131 447 2834

7 Edinburgh: Canongate (F H T W)
Neil N. Gardner MA BD   1991   2006
canongatekirk@btinternet.com — 0131 556 3515
The Manse of Canongate, Edinburgh EH8 8BR — 0131 556 3515
NGardner@churchofscotland.org.uk

No.	Charge / Minister	Ord.	Ind.	Contact	Tel.
8	**Edinburgh: Carrick Knowe (H W)** Fiona M. Mathieson (Mrs) BEd BD PGCommEd MTh	1988	2001	**ckchurch@talktalk.net** 21 Traquair Park West, Edinburgh EH12 7AN FMathieson@churchofscotland.org.uk	**0131 334 1505** 0131 334 9774
9	**Edinburgh: Colinton (F H W)** Rolf H. Billes BD	1996	2009	**church.office@colinton-parish.com** The Manse, Colinton, Edinburgh EH13 0JR RBilles@churchofscotland.org.uk	**0131 441 2232** 0131 466 8384
10	**Edinburgh: Corstorphine Craigsbank (H T W)** Alan Childs BA BD MBA	2000	2019	**admin@craigsbankchurch.org.uk** 17 Craigs Bank, Edinburgh EH12 8HD AChilds@churchofscotland.org.uk	**0131 334 6365** 0131 466 5196
11	**Edinburgh: Corstorphine Old (F H W)** Moira McDonald MA BD	1997	2005	**corold@aol.com** 23 Manse Road, Edinburgh EH12 7SW MMcDonald@churchofscotland.org.uk	**0131 334 7864** 0131 476 5893
12	**Edinburgh: Corstorphine St Anne's (F H L T W)** James J. Griggs BD MTh ALCM PGCE	2011	2013	**office@stannes.corstorphine.org.uk** 1/5 Morham Gait, Edinburgh EH10 5GH JGriggs@churchofscotland.org.uk	**0131 316 4740** 0131 466 3269
13	**Edinburgh: Corstorphine St Ninian's (F H W)** James D. Aitken BD	2002	2017	**office@st-ninians.co.uk** 17 Templeland Road, Edinburgh EH12 8RZ JAitken@churchofscotland.org.uk	**0131 539 6204** 0131 334 2978
14	**Edinburgh: Craiglockhart (F H T W)** Gordon Kennedy BSc BD MTh	1993	2012	**office@craiglockhartchurch.org** 20 Craiglockhart Quadrant, Edinburgh EH14 1HD GKennedy@churchofscotland.org.uk	**0131 455 8229** 0131 444 1615
15	**Edinburgh: Craigmillar Park (H W)** **linked with Edinburgh: Reid Memorial (F H W)** Alexander T. McAspurren BD MTh	2002	2019	**cpkirk@btinternet.com** **reid.memorial@btinternet.com** 14 Hallhead Road, Edinburgh EH16 5QJ AMcAspurren@churchofscotland.org.uk	**0131 667 5862** **0131 662 1203** 0131 667 1623
16	**Edinburgh: Cramond (F H T W)** G. Russell Barr BA BD MTh DMin	1979	1993	**cramond.kirk@blueyonder.co.uk** Manse of Cramond, Edinburgh EH4 6NS GBarr@churchofscotland.org.uk	**0131 336 2036** 0131 336 2036

17 Edinburgh: Currie (F H W)
V. Easter Smart BA MDiv DMin   1996   2015
currie_kirk@btconnect.com
43 Lanark Road West, Currie EH14 5JX
ESmart@churchofscotland.org.uk
0131 451 5141
0131 449 4719

18 Edinburgh: Dalmeny (F W) linked with Edinburgh: Queensferry (F H W)   office@qpcweb.org
David C. Cameron BD CertMin   1993   2009
1 Station Road, South Queensferry EH30 9HY
DavidCCameron@churchofscotland.org.uk
0131 331 1100
0131 331 1100

19 Edinburgh: Davidson's Mains (F H W)
Daniel Robertson BA BD   2009   2016
life@dmainschurch.plus.com
1 Hillpark Terrace, Edinburgh EH4 7SX
Daniel.Robertson@churchofscotland.org.uk
0131 312 6282
0131 336 3078
07909 840654

20 Edinburgh: Drylaw (F W)
Jenny M. Williams BSc CQSW BD MTh   1996   2017
(Transition Minister)
drylawparishchurch@btinternet.com
15 House o' Hill Gardens, Edinburgh EH4 2AR
JWilliams@churchofscotland.org.uk
0131 332 6863
0131 332 0896

21 Edinburgh: Duddingston (F H W)
James A.P. Jack   1989   2001
BSc BArch BD DMin RIBA ARIAS
dodinskirk@aol.com
Manse of Duddingston, Old Church Lane, Edinburgh EH15 3PX
JJack@churchofscotland.org.uk
0131 661 4240
0131 661 4240

22 Edinburgh: Fairmilehead (F H W)
Cheryl S. McKellar-Young (Mrs)   2013   2018
BA BD MSc
office@fhpc.org.uk
14 Margaret Rose Drive, Edinburgh EH10 7ER
CMcKellarYoung@churchofscotland.org.uk
0131 445 2374
07590 230121

23 Edinburgh: Gorgie Dalry Stenhouse (F H T W)
Peter I. Barber MA BD   1984   1995
contactus@gdschurch.org.uk
90 Myreside Road, Edinburgh EH10 5BZ
PBarber@churchofscotland.org.uk
0131 337 7936
0131 337 2284

24 Edinburgh: Gracemount (W) linked with Edinburgh: Liberton (F H T W)   churchsecretary@libertonkirk.net
John N. Young MA BD PhD   1996
7 Kirk Park, Edinburgh EH16 6HZ
JYoung@churchofscotland.org.uk
0131 664 8264
0131 664 3067

25 Edinburgh: Granton (F H T W)
Norman A. Smith MA BD   1997   2005
info@granton.org.uk
8 Wardie Crescent, Edinburgh EH5 1AG
NSmith@churchofscotland.org.uk
0131 552 3033
0131 551 2159

26 Edinburgh: Greenbank (F H W)
Martin S. Ritchie MA BD PhD   2018
greenbankchurch@btconnect.com
112 Greenbank Crescent, Edinburgh EH10 5SZ
MRitchie@churchofscotland.org.uk
0131 447 9969
0131 447 4032

27 Edinburgh: Greenside (H W)
Guardianship of the Presbytery
Interim Moderator: Suzie Stark
office@greenside.org.uk
1B Royal Terrace, Edinburgh EH7 5AB
sstark1962@btinternet.com
0131 557 2124
0131 551 1381

28 Edinburgh: Greyfriars Kirk (F GE H T W)
Richard E. Frazer BA BD DMin — 1986
Kenneth L. Luscombe DipPhysEd TSTC BTh BD ThM (Associate Minister) — 1982
enquiries@greyfriarskirk.com
12 Tantallon Place, Edinburgh EH9 1NZ
RFrazer@churchofscotland.org.uk
Greyfriars Kirk, Greyfriars Place, Edinburgh EH1 2QQ
KLuscombe@churchofscotland.org.uk
0131 225 1900
0131 667 6610
0131 225 1900

29 Edinburgh: High (St Giles') (F T W)
Calum I. MacLeod BA BD — 1996
alison.wylie@stgilescathedral.org.uk
St Giles' Cathedral, High Street, Edinburgh EH1 1RE
Calum.MacLeod@churchofscotland.org.uk
0131 225 4363
0131 225 4363

30 Edinburgh: Holy Trinity (F H W)
Ian A. MacDonald BD MTh — 2005
Rita M. Welsh BA PhD (Ordained Local Minister) — 2017
admin@holytrinitywesterhailes.org.uk
5 Baberton Mains Terrace, Edinburgh EH14 3DG
Ian.Angus.MacDonald@churchofscotland.org.uk
19 Muir Wood Road, Currie EH14 5JW
RWelsh@churchofscotland.org.uk
0131 442 3304
0131 281 6153
0131 451 5943

31 Edinburgh: Inverleith St Serf's (F H W)
Joanne G. Foster (Mrs) — 1996
DipTMus BD AdvDipCouns MBACP(Acc)
78 Pilrig Street, Edinburgh EH6 5AS
JFoster@churchofscotland.org.uk
0131 561 1392

32 Edinburgh: Juniper Green (F H W)
James S. Dewar MA BD — 1983
jigpc@supanet.com
476 Lanark Road, Juniper Green, Edinburgh EH14 5BQ
JDewar@churchofscotland.org.uk
0131 458 5147
0131 453 3494

33 Edinburgh: Kirkliston (W)
Vacant
Interim Moderator: John A. Cowie
43 Main Street, Kirkliston EH29 9AF
JCowie@churchofscotland.org.uk
0131 333 3298
0131 557 6052
07506 104416

34 Edinburgh: Leith North (F H W)
Vacant
Interim Moderator: R. Russell McLarty
nlpc-office@btinternet.com
Russell.McLarty@churchofscotland.org.uk
0131 553 7378
01875 614496
07751 755986

35 Edinburgh: Leith St Andrew's (H W)
A. Robert A. Mackenzie LLB BD   1993   2013
leithstandrews@yahoo.co.uk
30 Lochend Road, Edinburgh EH6 8BS
AMacKenzie@churchofscotlandorg.uk
0131 553 8839
0131 553 2122

36 Edinburgh: Leith South (H W)
John S. (Iain) May BSc MBA BD   2012
slpcoffice@gmail.com
37 Claremont Road, Edinburgh EH6 7NN
JMay@churchofscotland.org.uk
0131 554 2578
0131 555 0392

37 Edinburgh: Liberton See Edinburgh: Gracemount

38 Edinburgh: Liberton Northfield (F H W)
Attie van Wyk BTh LMus MDiv MTh   2005   2020
9 Claverhouse Drive, Edinburgh EH16 6BR
AvanWyk@churchofscotland.org.uk
0131 551 3847
0131 664 5490
07523 906272

39 Edinburgh: Marchmont St Giles' (F H T W)
Karen K. Campbell BD MTh DMin   1997   2002
office@marchmontstgiles.org.uk
2 Trotter Haugh, Edinburgh EH9 2GZ,
KKCampbell@churchofscotland.org.uk
0131 447 4359
0131 447 2834

40 Edinburgh: Mayfield Salisbury (F W)
Vacant
Interim Moderator: Neil N. Gardner
Kay McIntosh (Mrs) DCS   1990   2018
(member of West Lothian Presbytery)
churchmanager@googlemail.com
26 Seton Place, Edinburgh EH9 2JT
NGardner@churchofscotland.org.uk
4 Jacklin Green, Livingston EH54 8PZ,
kay@backedge.co.uk
0131 667 1522
0131 667 1286
0131 556 3515
01506 440543

41 Edinburgh: Meadowbank (F T W)
R. Russell McLarty MA BD   1985   2017
(Transition Minister)
meadowbank@meadowbankchurch.com
9 Sanderson's Wynd, Tranent EH33 1DA
RussellMcLarty@churchofscotland.org.uk
01875 614496
07751 755986

42 Edinburgh: Morningside (F H W)
Derek Browning MA BD DMin   1987   2001
office@morningsideparishchurch.org.uk
20 Braidburn Crescent, Edinburgh EH10 6EN
Derek.Browning@churchofscotland.org.uk
0131 447 6745
0131 447 1617

43 Edinburgh: Morningside United (H W)
Steven Manders LLB BD STB MTh   2008   2015
Morningside United is a Local Ecumenical Partnership with the United Reformed Church
churchoffice.muc@gmail.com
1 Midmar Avenue, Edinburgh EH10 6BS
stevenmanders@hotmail.com
0131 447 3152
0131 447 7943
07808 476733

44 Edinburgh: Murrayfield (F H W)
Keith Edwin Graham MA PGDip BD MTh   2008   2014
mpchurch@btconnect.com
45 Murrayfield Gardens, Edinburgh EH12 6DH
KEGraham@churchofscotland.org.uk
0131 337 1091
0131 337 1364

No.	Charge / Minister			Address / Email	Telephone
45	**Edinburgh: Newhaven (F H W)** Peter B. Bluett BTh	1996	2007	158 Granton Road, Edinburgh EH5 3RF PBluett@churchofscotland.org.uk	0131 476 5212
46	**Edinburgh: Old Kirk and Muirhouse (F H T W)** Vacant Interim Moderator: Douglas A.O. Nicol			35 Silverknowes Road, Edinburgh EH4 5LL Douglas.Nicol@churchofscotland.org.uk	0131 476 2580 07811 437075
47	**Edinburgh: Palmerston Place (F H T W)** Colin A.M. Sinclair BA BD	1981	1996	**admin@palmerstonplacechurch.com** 30B Cluny Gardens, Edinburgh EH10 6BJ CSinclair@churchofscotland.org.uk	**0131 220 1690** 0131 447 9598 Fax 0131 225 3312
48	**Edinburgh: Pilrig St Paul's (F W)** Mark M. Foster BSc BD	1998	2013	**mail@pilrigstpauls.org.uk** 78 Pilrig Street, Edinburgh EH6 5AS MFoster@churchofscotland.org.uk	**0131 553 1876** 0131 332 5736
49	**Edinburgh: Polwarth (F H W)** Jack Holt BSc BD MTh	1985	2011	**office@polwarth.org.uk** 88 Craiglockhart Road, Edinburgh EH14 1EP JHolt@churchofscotland.org.uk	**0131 346 2711** 0131 441 6105
50	**Edinburgh: Portobello and Joppa (F H W)** Stewart G. Weaver BA BD PhD	2003	2014	**office@portyjoppachurch.org** 6 St Mary's Place, Edinburgh EH15 2QF SWeaver@churchofscotland.org.uk	**0131 657 3401** 0131 669 2410
	Lourens de Jager PgDip MDiv BTh (Associate Minister)	2013	2015	1 Brunstane Road North, Edinburgh EH15 2DL LDeJager@churchofscotland.org.uk	07521 426644
51	**Edinburgh: Priestfield (F H W)** Donald H. Scott BA BD	1983	2018	13 Lady Road, Edinburgh EH16 5PA Donald.Scott@churchofscotland.org.uk	**0131 667 5644** 0131 468 1254
52	**Edinburgh: Queensferry** See Edinburgh: Dalmeny				
53	**Edinburgh: Ratho (F W)** Ian J. Wells BD	1999		2 Freelands Road, Ratho, Newbridge EH28 8NP IWells@churchofscotland.org.uk	0131 333 1346
54	**Edinburgh: Reid Memorial** See Edinburgh: Craigmillar Park				

55 Edinburgh: Richmond Craigmillar (F H)
Elizabeth M. Henderson   1985   1997
OBE MA BD MTh
Manse of Duddingston, Old Church Lane, Edinburgh EH15 3PX
EHenderson@churchofscotland.org.uk
0131 661 6561
0131 661 4240

56 Edinburgh: St Andrew's and St George's West (F H L W)
Rosemary E. Magee   2009   2019
BSc MSc MDiv DMin
info@stagw.org.uk
25 Comely Bank, Edinburgh EH4 1AJ
RMagee@churchofscotland.org.uk
0131 225 3847
0131 332 5848

57 Edinburgh: St Andrew's Clermiston (F W)
Alistair H. Keil   BD DipMin   1989
87 Drum Brae South, Edinburgh EH12 8TD
AKeil@churchofscotland.org.uk
0131 339 4149

58 Edinburgh: St Catherine's Argyle (H W)
Stuart D. Irvin   BD   2013   2016
5 Palmerston Road, Edinburgh EH9 1TL
SIrvin@churchofscotland.org.uk
0131 667 7220
0131 667 9344

59 Edinburgh: St Cuthbert's (F H L T W)
Peter R.B. Sutton BA(AKC) BD MTh   2017
PGCertCouns
office@st-cuthberts.net
St Cuthbert's Church, 5 Lothian Road, Edinburgh EH1 2EP
PSutton@churchofscotland.org.uk
0131 229 1142
07718 311319

60 Edinburgh: St David's Broomhouse (F H W)
Michael J. Mair   BD   2014
33 Traquair Park West, Edinburgh EH12 7AN
MMair@churchofscotland.org.uk
0131 443 9851
0131 334 1730

61 Edinburgh: St John's Colinton Mains (F W)
Peter Nelson BSc BD   2015
2 Caiystane Terrace, Edinburgh EH10 6SR
PNelson@churchofscotland.org.uk
07500 057889

62 Edinburgh: St Margaret's (F H W)
John R. Wells   BD PGCE DipMin   1991   2020
stmpc@btconnect.com
43 Moira Terrace, Edinburgh EH7 6TD
JWells@churchofscotland.org.uk
0131 554 7400
0131 322 9272

63 Edinburgh: St Martin's (F W)
William M. Wishart   BD   2017
1 Toll House Gardens, Tranent EH33 2QQ
BWishart@churchofscotland.org.uk
01875 704071

64 Edinburgh: St Michael's (H W)
Andrea E. Price (Mrs)   1997   2018
office@stmichaels-kirk.co.uk
13 Dovecot Park, Edinburgh EH14 2LN
0131 478 9675
0131 443 4355

No.	Name			Address	Phone
65	**Edinburgh: St Nicholas' Sighthill (F W)**	1993	2015	122 Sighthill Loan, Edinburgh EH11 4NT	**07306 100111**
	Thomas M. Kisitu BD MTh PhD			TMKisitu@churchofscotland.org.uk	0131 442 3978
66	**Edinburgh: St Stephen's Comely Bank (F W)**	2000	2015	office@comelybankchurch.com	**0131 315 4616**
	George Vidits BD MTh			8 Blinkbonny Crescent, Edinburgh EH4 3NB	0131 332 3364
				GVidits@churchofscotland.org.uk	
67	**Edinburgh: Slateford Longstone (F W)**	1995	2019	50 Kingsknowe Road South, Edinburgh EH14 2JW	0131 466 5308
	Samuel A.R. Torrens BD			STorrens@churchofscotland.org.uk	
68	**Edinburgh: Stockbridge (F H T W)**	1983	2013	stockbridgechurch@btconnect.com	**0131 332 0122**
	John A. Cowie BSc BD DMin			19 Eildon Street, Edinburgh EH3 5JU	0131 557 6052
				JCowie@churchofscotland.org.uk	07506 104416
69	**Edinburgh: Tron Kirk (Gilmerton and Moredun) (F W)**	1997	2010	467 Gilmerton Road, Edinburgh EH17 7JG	0131 664 7538
	Cameron Mackenzie BD			Cammy.Mackenzie@churchofscotland.org.uk	
	Janet R. McKenzie (Mrs)	2016		80C Colinton Road, Edinburgh EH14 1DD	0131 444 2054
	(Ordained Local Minister)			JMcKenzie@churchofscotland.org.uk	07980 884653
	Liz Crocker DipComEd DCS	1985	2015	77c Craigcrook Road, Edinburgh EH4 3PH	0131 332 0227
				ECrocker@churchofscotland.org.uk	
70	**Edinburgh: Wardie (H T W)**			churchoffice@wardie.org.uk	**0131 551 3847**
	Vacant			35 Lomond Road, Edinburgh EH5 3JN	0131 552 0190
	Interim Moderator: Ann Inglis			revainglis@gmail.com	0131 629 0233
71	**Edinburgh: Willowbrae (F H W)**	1986	2017	office.willowbrae@gmail.com	**0131 661 8259**
	A. Malcolm Ramsay BA LLB DipMin			19 Abercorn Road, Edinburgh EH8 7DP	0131 652 2938
	(Transition Minister)			MRamsay@churchofscotland.org.uk	

B. In other appointments

Name			Appointment	Address	Phone
Alexander, Ian W. BA BD STM	1990	2020	Interim Head of Faith Impact Forum	121 George Street, Edinburgh EH2 4YN	0131 225 5722
				IAlexander@churchofscotland.org.uk	
Ashley-Emery, Stephen BD DPS RN	2006	2019	Royal Naval Chaplain, Portsmouth	Holmhill, East Main Street, Chirnside, Duns TD11 3XR	(Home) 07882 885684
Barclay, Iain C. MBE TD MA BD	1976	2020	Chaplain: The Robin Chapel	The Thistle Foundation, Edinburgh EH16 4EA	(Office) 07393 232736
MTh MPhil PhD FRSA				chaplain@robinchapel.org.uk	

Name	Role			Address / Email	Telephone
Donald, Alistair P. MA PhD BD	Chaplain: Heriot-Watt University	1999	2009	The Chaplaincy, Heriot-Watt University, Edinburgh EH14 4AS a.p.donald@hw.ac.uk	0131 451 4508
Evans, Mark BSc MSc DCS	Head of Spiritual Care NHS Fife	1988	2006	13 Easter Drylaw Drive, Edinburgh EH4 2QA (Home) mark.evans59@nhs.net (Office)	0131 343 3089 01383 674136
Fergusson, David A.S. (Prof.) OBE MA BD DPhil DD FRSE FBA	University of Edinburgh: New College	1984	2000	23 Riselaw Crescent, Edinburgh EH10 6HN	0131 447 4022
Hardman Moore, Susan (Prof.) MA MAR PhD	Principal, New College, University of Edinburgh (Ordained Local Minister)	2013	2018	New College, Mound Place, Edinburgh EH1 2LX SHardman-Moore@churchofscotland.org.uk	0131 650 8908 07811 345699
MacMurchie, F. Lynne LLB BD	Healthcare Chaplain	1998	2003	Royal Edinburgh Hospital. Community Mental Health. Astley Ainslie Hospital lynne.macmurchie@nhslothian.scot.nhs.uk	0131 537 6775
McPheat, Elspeth DCS	Deacon: CrossReach	1985	2001	53 Wood Street, Grangemouth FK3 8LS elspeth176@sky.com	01324 282406
McPherson, Marjory (Mrs) LLB BD MTh	Presbytery Clerk: Edinburgh	1990	2017	10/1 Palmerston Place, Edinburgh EH12 5AA MMcPherson@churchofscotland.org.uk	0131 225 9137
Mathieson, Angus R. MA BD	Interim Head of Faith Nurture Forum	1988	2020	21 Traquair Park West, Edinburgh EH12 7AN AMathieson@churchofscotland.org.uk	0131 334 9774
Orr, Sheena BA MSc MBA BD	Chaplaincy Adviser. Scottish Prison Service	2011	2018	Calton House, 5 Redheughs Rigg, South Gyle, Edinburgh EH12 9HW sheena.orr@sps.pnn.gov.uk	0131 330 3575 07922 649160
Pennykid, Gordon J. BD DCS	Chaplain, HMP Edinburgh	2015	2018	8 Glenfield, Livingston EH54 7BG GPennykid@churchofscotland.org.uk	07747 652652
Ridland, Alistair K. MA BD PGDip MRAcS MInstLM RAFAC	Chaplain: Western General Hospital	1982	2000	13 Stewart Place, Kirkliston EH29 0BQ (Home) alistair.ridland@nhslothian.scot.nhs.uk (Office)	0131 333 2711 0131 537 1400
Robertson, Pauline (Mrs) DCS BA CertTheol	Port Chaplain, Sailors' Society	2003	2016	6 Ashville Terrace, Edinburgh EH6 8DD probertson@sailors-society.org	0131 554 6564 07759 436303
Stark, Suzie BD	Hospice Chaplain	2013	2016	St Columba's Hospice, 15 Boswall Road, Edinburgh EH5 3RW SStark@churchofscotland.org.uk	0131 551 1381
Stewart, Lezley J. BD ThM MTh DMin	Faith Nurture Forum: Recruitment and Support	2000	2017	121 George Street, Edinburgh EH2 4YN LStewart@churchofscotland.org.uk	0131 225 5722
Swan, David BVMS BD	Chaplain, HMP Edinburgh and HMYOI Polmont	2005	2018	159 Redhall Drive, Edinburgh EH13 2LR davidswan97@gmail.com	07944 598988
Tweedie, Fiona J. BSc PhD	Ordained Local Minister: Mission Statistics Co-ordinator	2011	2014	121 George Street, Edinburgh EH2 4YN FTweedie@churchofscotland.org.uk	0131 225 5722
Whyte, George J. BSc BD DMin	Principal Clerk	1981	2017	Church Offices, 121 George Street, Edinburgh EH2 4YN GWhyte@churchofscotland.org.uk	0131 240 2240

C. Demitted

Name	Role			Address / Email	Telephone
Alexander, Helen J.R. BD DipSW CQSW	(Assistant, Edinburgh: High (St Giles'))	1981	2019	7 Polwarth Place, Edinburgh EH11 1LG HAlexander@churchofscotland.org.uk	0131 346 0685
Armitage, William L. BSc BD	(Edinburgh: London Road)	1976	2006	Flat 7, 4 Papermill Wynd, Edinburgh EH7 4GJ bil1@billarm.plus.com	0131 558 8534
Baird, Kenneth S. MSc PhD BD MIMarEST	(Edinburgh: Leith North)	1998	2009	3 Maule Terrace, Gullane EH31 2DB	01620 843447

Name			Charge	Address	Telephone
Bicket, Matthew S. BD	1989	2017	(Carnoustie: Panbride)	9/2 Connaught Place, Edinburgh EH6 4RQ	0131 552 8781
Blakey, Ronald S. MA BD MTh	1962	2000	(Assembly Council)	24 Kimmerghame Place, Edinburgh EH4 2GE kathleen.blakey@gmail.com	0131 343 6352
Booth, Jennifer (Mrs) BD	1996	2004	(Associate: Edinburgh: Leith South)	39 Lilyhill Terrace, Edinburgh EH8 7DR	0131 661 3813
Borthwick, Kenneth S. MA BD	1983	2016	(Edinburgh: Holy Trinity)	34 Rodger Crescent, Armadale EH48 3GR kennysamuel@aol.com	07735 749594
Boyd, Kenneth M. (Prof.) MA BD PhD FRCPE	1970	2004	(University of Edinburgh: Medical Ethics)	1 Doune Terrace, Edinburgh EH3 6DY k.boyd@ed.ac.uk	0131 225 6485
Brady, Ian D. BSc ARCST BD	1967	2001	(Edinburgh: Corstorphine Old)	28 Frankfield Crescent, Dalgety Bay, Dunfermline KY11 9LW bradye500@gmail.com	01383 825104
Brook, Stanley A. BD MTh	1977	2016	(Newport-on-Tay)	4 Scotstoun Green, South Queensferry EH30 9YA stan_brook@btinternet.com	0131 331 4237
Brown, William D. BD CQSW	1987	2013	(Edinburgh: Murrayfield)	79 Carnbee Park, Edinburgh EH16 6GG wdb@talktalk.net	0131 261 7297
Clark, Christine M. (Mrs) BA BD MTh	2006	2019	(Chaplain, Royal Hospital for Sick Children, Edinburgh)	40 Pentland Avenue, Edinburgh EH13 0HY CClark@churchofscotland.org.uk	07444 819237
Clinkenbeard, William W. BSc BD STM	1966	2000	(Edinburgh: Carrick Knowe)	3/17 Western Harbour Breakwater, Edinburgh EH6 6PA bjclinks@compuserve.com	0131 629 0519
Curran, Elizabeth M. (Miss) BD	1995	2008	(Aberlour)	Blackford Grange, 39/2 Blackford Avenue, Edinburgh EH9 3HN curran311@btinternet.com	0131 664 1358
Cuthell, Tom C. MA BD	1965	2007	(Edinburgh: St Cuthbert's)	Flat 10, 2 Kingsburgh Crescent, Waterfront, Edinburgh EH5 1JS	0131 476 3864
Davidson, D. Hugh MA	1965	2009	(Edinburgh: Inverleith)	Flat 1/2, 22 Summerside Place, Edinburgh EH6 4NZ hdavidson35@btinternet.com	0131 554 8420
Dawson, Michael S. BTech BD	1979	2005	(Associate: Edinburgh: Holy Trinity)	9 The Broich, Alva FK12 5NR mixpen.dawson@btinternet.com	01259 769309
Douglas, Alexander B. BD	1979	2014	(Edinburgh: Blackhall St Columba's)	15 Inchview Gardens, Dalgety Bay, Dunfermline KY11 9SA alexandjill@douglas.net	01383 791080
Dunn, W. Iain C. DA LTh	1983	1998	(Edinburgh: Pilrig and Dalmeny Street)	10 Fox Covert Avenue, Edinburgh EH12 6UQ	0131 334 1665
Embleton, Brian M. BD	1976	2015	(Edinburgh: Reid Memorial)	54 Edinburgh Road, Peebles EH45 8EB bmembleton@gmail.com	01721 602157
Embleton, Sara R. (Mrs) BA BD MTh	1988	2010	(Edinburgh: Leith St Serf's)	54 Edinburgh Road, Peebles EH45 8EB srembleton@gmail.com	01721 602157
Farquharson, Gordon MA BD DipEd	1998	2007	(Stonehaven: Dunnottar)	26 Learmonth Court, Edinburgh EH4 1PB gfarqu@talktalk.net	0131 343 1047
Forrester, Margaret R. (Mrs) MA BD DD	1974	2003	(Edinburgh: St Michael's)	25 Kingsburgh Road, Edinburgh EH12 6DZ margaret@rosskeen.org.uk	0131 337 5646
Fraser, Shirley A. (Miss) MA BD	1992	2008	(Scottish Field Director: Friends International)	6/50 Roseburn Drive, Edinburgh EH12 5NS	0131 347 1400
Frew, Michael W. BSc BD	1978	2017	(Edinburgh: Slateford Longstone)	37 Swanston Terrace, Edinburgh EH10 7DN	07712 162375
Gardner, John V.	1997	2003	(Glamis, Inverarity and Kinnettles)	75/1 Lockharton Avenue, Edinburgh EH14 1BD jvgardnet66@googlemail.com	0131 443 7126

Name	Year	Year	Position	Address / Contact	Telephone
Gilmour, Ian Y. BD	1985	2018	(Edinburgh: St Andrew's and St George's West)	29/7 South Trinity Road, Edinburgh EH5 3PN ianyg@gmail.com	07794 149852
Gordon, Margaret (Mrs) DCS	1998	2012	(Deacon)	92 Lanark Road West, Currie EH14 5LA	0131 449 2554
Graham, W. Peter MA BD	1967	2008	(Presbytery Clerk: Edinburgh)	23/6 East Comiston, Edinburgh EH10 6RZ	0131 445 5763
Harkness, James KVCO CB OBE QHC MA DD	1961	1995	(Chaplain General: Army)	13 Saxe Coburg Place, Edinburgh EH3 5BR	0131 343 1297
Hay, Jared W. BA MTh DipMin DMin	1987	2017	(Edinburgh: Priestfield)	39 Netherbank, Edinburgh EH16 6YR jaredhay3110@gmail.com	07906 662515
Inglis, Ann (Mrs) LLB BD	1986	2015	(Langton and Lammermuir Kirk)	34 Echline View, South Queensferry EH30 9XL revainglis@gmail.com	0131 629 0233
Irving, William D. LTh	1985	2005	(Golspie)	122 Swanston Muir, Edinburgh EH10 7HY	0131 441 3384
Lamont, Stewart J. BSc BD	1972	2015	(Arbirlot with Carmyllie)	13/1 Grosvenor Crescent, Edinburgh EH12 5EL lamontsj@gmail.com	07557 532012
Lane, Margaret R. (Mrs) BA BD MTh	2009	2019	(Edinburgh: Kirkliston)	6 Overhaven, Limekilns KY11 3JH MLane@churchofscotland.org.uk	01383 873328 07897 525692
Lawson, Kenneth C. MA BD	1963	1999	(Adviser in Adult Education)	56 Easter Drylaw View, Edinburgh EH4 2QP	0131 539 3311
Logan, Anne T. (Mrs) MA BD MTh DMin PhD	1981	2012	(Edinburgh: Stockbridge)	Sunnyside Cottage, 18 Upper Broomieknowe, Lasswade EH18 1LP annetlogan@sky.com	0131 663 9550
Lough, Adrian J. BD	2012	2020	(Auchtergaven and Moneydie with Redgorton and Stanley)	12 Dundrennan Cottages, Edinburgh EH16 5RG revlough@btinternet.com	
Macdonald, William J. BD	1976	2002	(Board of National Mission: New Charge Development)	1/13 North Werber Park, Edinburgh EH4 1SY	0131 332 0254
Macgregor, Margaret S. (Miss) MA BD DipEd	1985	1994	(Calcutta)	16 Learmonth Court, Edinburgh EH4 1PB	0131 332 1089
McGregor, T. Stewart MBE MA BD	1957	1998	(Chaplain: Edinburgh Royal Infirmary)	19 Lonsdale Terrace, Edinburgh EH3 9HL cetsm@uwclub.net	0131 229 5332
Mackenzie, James G. BA BD	1980	2005	(Jersey: St Columba's)	26 Drylaw Crescent, Edinburgh EH4 2AU jgmackenzie@jerseymail.co.uk	0131 332 3720
Maclean, Ailsa G. (Mrs) BD DipCE	1979	2017	(Chaplain: George Heriot's School)	28 Swan Spring Avenue, Edinburgh EH10 6NJ	
Macmillan, Gilleasbuig I. KCVO MA BD Drhc DD FRSE HRSA FRCSEd	1969	2013	(Edinburgh: High (St Giles'))	207 Dalkeith Road, Edinburgh EH16 5DS gmacmillan1@btinternet.com	0131 667 5732
McPake, John M. LTh	2000	2013	(Edinburgh: Liberton Northfield)	john_mcpake9@yahoo.co.uk	0131 332 2748
Moir, Ian A. MA BD	1962	2000	(Adviser for Urban Priority Areas)	28/6 Comely Bank Avenue, Edinburgh EH4 1EL	0131 336 4706
Morrison, Mary B. (Mrs) MA BD DipEd	1978	2000	(Edinburgh: Stenhouse St Aidan's)	174 Craigcrook Road, Edinburgh EH4 3PP	0131 664 3426
Mulligan, Anne MA DCS	1974	2013	(Deacon: Hospital Chaplain)	27A Craigour Avenue, Edinburgh EH17 1NH mulliganne@aol.com	
Munro, John P.L. MA BD PhD	1977	2008	(Kinross)	5 Marchmont Crescent, Edinburgh EH9 1HN jplmunro@yahoo.co.uk	0131 623 0198
Munro, John R. BD	1976	2018	(Edinburgh: Fairmilehead)	23 Braid Farm Road, Edinburgh EH10 6LE revjohnmunro@hotmail.com	0131 446 9363
Nicol, Douglas A.O. MA BD	1974	2018	(Hobkirk and Southdean with Ruberslaw)	1/2 North Werber Park, Edinburgh EH4 1SY Douglas.Nicol@churchofscotland.org.uk	07811 437075
Paterson, Douglas S. MA BD	1976	2010	(Edinburgh: St Colm's)	4 Ards Place, High Street, Aberlady EH32 0DB	01875 870192
Rennie, Agnes M. (Miss) DCS	1974	2012	(Deacon)	3/1 Craigmillar Court, Edinburgh EH16 4AD	0131 661 8475

Name			Role	Address / email	Phone
Robertson, Charles LVO MA	1965	2005	(Edinburgh: Canongate)	3 Ross Gardens, Edinburgh EH9 3BS canongate1@aol.com	0131 662 9025
Ross, Keith W. MA BD MTh	1984	2015	(Congregational Development Officer)	Easter Bavelaw House, Pentland Hills Regional Park, Balerno EH14 7JS keithwross@outlook.com	07855 163449
Scott, Jayne E. BA MEd MBA	1988	2019	(Secretary, Ministries Council)	52 Ravenscroft Gardens, Edinburgh EH17 8RP jayneescott@gmail.com	0131 431 4195
Scott, Martin C. DipMusEd RSAM BD PhD	1986	2019	(Secretary, Council of Assembly)	52 Ravenscroft Gardens, Edinburgh EH17 8RP martin.scott14@sky.com	0131 431 4195 07856 165820
Smith, Angus MA LTh	1965	2006	(Chaplain to the Oil Industry)	3/7 West Powburn, West Savile Gait, Edinburgh EH9 3EW	0131 667 1761
Stephen, Donald M. TD MA BD ThM	1962	2001	(Edinburgh: Marchmont St Giles')	10 Hawkhead Crescent, Edinburgh EH16 6LR donaldmstephen@gmail.com	0131 658 1216
Stevenson, John MA BD PhD	1963	2001	(Department of Education)	12 Swanston Gardens, Edinburgh EH10 7DL	0131 445 3960
Tait, John M. BSc BD	1985	2012	(Edinburgh: Pilrig St Paul's)	82 Greenend Gardens, Edinburgh EH17 7QH johnmtait@me.com	0131 258 9105
Taylor, William R. MA BD MTh	1983	2018	(Chaplaincy Adviser, Scottish Prison Service)	33 Kingsknowe Drive EH14 2JY wlretl@outlook.com	0131 443 5590 07447 258525
Teague, Yvonne (Mrs) DCS	1965	2002	(Board of Ministry)	46 Craigcrook Avenue, Edinburgh EH4 3PX y.teague.1@blueyonder.co.uk	0131 336 3113
Thomson, Donald M. BD	1975	2013	(Tullibody: St Serf's)	50 Sighthill Road, Edinburgh EH11 4NY donniethomson@tiscali.co.uk	
Torrance, Iain R. (Prof.) KCVO Kt DD FRSE	1982	2012	(President: Princeton Theological Seminary)	25 The Causeway, Duddingston Village, Edinburgh EH15 3QA irt@ptsem.edu	0131 661 3092
Watson, Nigel G. MA	1998	2012	(Associate: East Kilbride: Old/Stewartfield/West)	7 St Catherine's Place, Edinburgh EH9 1NU nigel.g.watson@gmail.com	0131 662 4191
Wynne, Alistair T.E. BA BD	1982	2009	(Nicosia Community Church, Cyprus)	Flat 6, 14 Burnbrae Drive, Edinburgh EH12 8AS awynne2@googlemail.com	0131 339 6462

EDINBURGH ADDRESSES

Church	Address
Albany	at St Andrew's and St George's West
Balerno	Johnsburn Road, Balerno
Barclay Viewforth	Barclay Place
Blackhall St Columba's	Queensferry Road
Bristo Memorial	Peffermill Road, Craigmillar
Broughton St Mary's	Bellevue Crescent
Canongate	Canongate
Carrick Knowe	North Saughton Road
Colinton	Dell Road
Corstorphine	
Craigsbank	Craigs Crescent
Old	Kirk Loan
St Anne's	Kaimes Road
St Ninian's	St John's Road
Craiglockhart	Craiglockhart Avenue
Craigmillar Park	Craigmillar Park
Cramond	Cramond Glebe Road
Currie	Kirkgate, Currie
Dalmeny	Main Street, Dalmeny
Davidson's Mains	Quality Street
Drylaw	Groathill Road North
Duddingston	Old Church Lane, Duddingston
Fairmilehead	Frogston Road West, Fairmilehead
Gorgie Dalry Stenhouse	Gorgie Road
Gracemount	Gracemount Primary School
Granton	Boswall Parkway
Greenbank	Braidburn Terrace
Greenside	Royal Terrace
Greyfriars Kirk	Greyfriars Place
High (St Giles')	High Street
Holy Trinity	Hailesland Place, Wester Hailes
Inverleith St Serf's	Ferry Road
Juniper Green	Lanark Road, Juniper Green
Kirkliston	The Square, Kirkliston
Leith	
North	Madeira Street off Ferry Road
St Andrew's	Easter Road
South	Kirkgate, Leith
Liberton	Kirkgate, Liberton
Northfield	Gilmerton Road, Liberton
Marchmont St Giles'	Kilgraston Road
Mayfield Salisbury	Mayfield Road x West Mayfield
Meadowbank	Dalziel Place x London Road
Morningside	Cluny Gardens
Morningside United	Bruntsfield Place x Chamberlain Rd
Murrayfield	Abinger Gardens
Newhaven	Craighall Road
Old Kirk and Muirhouse	Pennywell Gardens
Palmerston Place	Palmerston Place
Pilrig St Paul's	Pilrig Street
Polwarth	Polwarth Terrace x Harrison Road
Portobello and Joppa	Abercorn Terrace
Priestfield	Dalkeith Road x Marchhall Place
Queensferry	The Loan, South Queensferry
Ratho	Baird Road, Ratho
Reid Memorial	West Savile Terrace
Richmond Craigmillar	Niddrie Mains Road
St Andrew's and	
St George's West	George Street
St Andrew's Clermiston	Clermiston View
St Catherine's Argyle	Grange Road x Chalmers Crescent
St Cuthbert's	Lothian Road
St David's Broomhouse	Broomhouse Crescent
St John's Colinton Mains	Oxgangs Road North
St Margaret's	Restalrig Road South
St Martin's	Magdalene Drive
St Michael's	Slateford Road
St Nicholas' Sighthill	Calder Road
St Stephen's Comely Bank	Comely Bank
Slateford Longstone	Kingsknowe Road North
Stockbridge	Saxe Coburg Street
Tron Kirk	Craigour Gardens and
(Gilmerton and Moredun)	Ravenscroft Street
Wardie	Primrosebank Road
Willowbrae	Willowbrae Road

(2) WEST LOTHIAN (F W)

Meets in the church of the incoming Moderator on the first Tuesday of September and in St John's Church Hall, Bathgate, on the first Tuesday of every other month, except June and December, when the meeting is on the second Tuesday, and January, April, July and August, when there is no meeting.

Clerk:	**REV. THOMAS S. RIDDELL BSc CEng FIChemE**	**4 The Maltings, Linlithgow EH49 6DS** **westlothian@churchofscotland.org.uk**	**01506 843251**
Depute Clerk and Treasurer:	**REV. GORDON D. JAMIESON MA BD**	**41 Goldpark Place, Livingston EH54 6LW** **gordonjamieson182@gmail.com**	**01506 412020**

Abercorn (H W) linked with Pardovan, Kingscavil (H) and Winchburgh (H W)

A. Scott Marshall DipComm BD	1984	The Manse, Winchburgh, Broxburn EH52 6TT SMarshall@churchofscotland.org.uk	01506 890919 07415 028678
Derek R. Henderson MA DipTP DipCS (Ordained Local Minister)	2017	45 Priory Road, Linlithgow EH49 6BP DHenderson@churchofscotland.org.uk	01506 844787 07968 491441

Armadale (H W)

Julia C. Wiley (Ms) MA(CE) MDiv	1998	70 Mount Pleasant, Armadale, Bathgate EH48 3HB JWiley@churchofscotland.org.uk	01501 730358
Margaret Corrie (Miss) DCS	1989	44 Sunnyside Street, Camelon, Falkirk FK1 4BH MCorrie@churchofscotland.org.uk	07955 633969

Avonbridge (H) linked with Torphichen (F H W)

Vacant		Manse Road, Torphichen, Bathgate EH48 4LT innesduncan57@hotmail.com	01506 635957 01506 652169
Session Clerk, Torphichen: Innes Duncan (Dr)			

Bathgate: Boghall (F H W)

Christopher G. Galbraith BA LLB BD	2012	1 Manse Place, Ash Grove, Bathgate EH48 1NJ CGalbraith@churchofscotland.org.uk	01506 652715

Bathgate: High (F H W)

Vacant		**info@bathgatehigh.com**	**01506 650217**
Session Clerk: John Macfarlane		john.macfarlane@gmx.com	01506 632283

Bathgate: St John's (H W)

Vacant		St John's Manse, Mid Street, Bathgate EH48 1QD annenoble1@hotmail.com	01506 653146 07834 365119
Session Clerk: Anne Noble (Mrs)			

Blackburn and Seafield (F H W)
Sandra Boyd (Mrs) BEd BD — 2007   2019 — The Manse, 5 MacDonald Gardens, Blackburn, Bathgate   EH47 7RE — 07919 676242
SBoyd@churchofscotland.org.uk

Blackridge (H) linked with Harthill: St Andrew's (F H)
Vacant
Session Clerk, Blackridge: Jean Mowitt (Mrs) — East Main Street, Harthill, Shotts   ML7 5QW — 01501 751239
jean.mowitt@yahoo.com — 01501 750401
— 07590 901933
Session Clerk, Harthill: Alexander Kennedy — alex.kend@gmail.com — 01501 752594

Breich Valley (F H)
Vacant
Session Clerk: Mary McKenzie (Mrs) — Breich Valley Manse, Stoneyburn, Bathgate   EH47 8AU — 01501 763142
mmckenzie889@hotmail.co.uk — 01506 635818

Broxburn (F H W)
Vacant
Session Clerk: Anne Gunn (Mrs) — 2 Church Street, Broxburn   EH52 5EL — 01506 337560
anne.gunn42@gmail.com — 07833 701274

Fauldhouse: St Andrew's (H)
Scott Raby LTh CertMin — 1991   2018 — 7 Glebe Court, Fauldhouse, Bathgate   EH47 9DX — 01501 771190
SRaby@churchofscotland.org.uk

Harthill: St Andrew's   See Blackridge

Kirknewton (H) and East Calder (F H W)
Alistair J. Cowper BSc BD — 2011   2018 — 8 Manse Court, East Calder, Livingston   EH53 0HF — 01506 357083
ACowper@churchofscotland.org.uk — 07791 524504

Kirk of Calder (F H W)
John M. Povey DL MA BD — 1981 — 19 Maryfield Park, Mid Calder, Livingston   EH53 0SB — 01506 882495
JPovey@churchofscotland.org.uk

Linlithgow: St Michael's (F H W)
Liam J. Fraser LLB BD MTh PhD — 2017   2019 — **info@stmichaels-parish.org.uk** — **01506 842188**
St Michael's Manse, Kirkgate, Linlithgow   EH49 7AL — 01506 842195
LFraser@churchofscotland.org.uk
Thomas S. Riddell BSc CEng FIChemE — 1993   1994 — 4 The Malings, Linlithgow   EH49 6DS — 01506 843251
(Auxiliary Minister) — TRiddell@churchofscotland.org.uk

Linlithgow: St Ninian's Craigmailen (H W)
W. Richard Houston BSc BD MTh — 1998 — 2004 — 29 Philip Avenue, Linlithgow EH49 7BH / WHouston@churchofscotland.org.uk — 01506 202246

Livingston: Old (F H W)
Nelu I. Balaj BD MA ThD — 2010 — 2017 — Manse of Livingston, Charlesfield Lane, Livingston EH54 7AJ / NBalaj@churchofscotland.org.uk — 01506 411888

Livingston United (F W)
Marc B. Kenton BTh MTh — 1997 — 2019 — 2 Eastcroft Court, Livingston EH54 7ET / MKenton@churchofscotland.org.uk — 01506 467426

Livingston United is a Local Ecumenical Partnership with the Scottish Episcopal, Methodist and United Reformed Churches

Pardovan, Kingscavil and Winchburgh See Abercorn

Polbeth Harwood (F W) linked with West Kirk of Calder (F H W)
Jonanda Groenewald BA BD MTh DD — 2000 — 2014 — 3 Johnsburn Road, Balerno EH14 7DN / JGroenewald@churchofscotland.org.uk — 0131 261 7977

Alison Quilter — 2018 — 27 Northfield Meadows, Longridge, Bathgate   EH47 8SA / AQuilter@churchofscotland.org.uk — 07741 985597
(Ordained Local Minister)

Strathbrock (F H T W)
Vacant — 1 Manse Park, Uphall, Broxburn EH52 6NX / lynnemcewen@hotmail.co.uk — 01506 856433 / 01506 852550 / 01506 855513
Session Clerk: Lynne McEwen (Mrs)

Torphichen See Avonbridge

Uphall: South (F H W)
Ian D. Maxwell MA BD PhD — 1977 — 2013 — 8 Fernlea, Uphall, Broxburn EH52 6DF / IMaxwell@churchofscotland.org.uk — 01506 239840

West Kirk of Calder (H) See Polbeth Harwood

Whitburn: Brucefield (F H W)
Vacant — contact@brucefieldchurch.org.uk / 48 Gleneagles Court, Whitburn, Bathgate   EH47 8PG — 01501 748666 / 01501 229354

Whitburn: South (H W)
Vacant
Session Clerk: James A.R. Brown

admin@whitburnsouthparishchurch.org.uk
5 Mansewood Crescent, Whitburn, Bathgate EH47 8HA
jim3059@gmail.com

01501 740333
01506 813914

B. In other appointments

Name	Appointment	From	To	Address	Phone
Dunphy, Rhona B. (Mrs) BD DPTheol DrPhil	Pastoral Support, Faith Nurture Forum	2005	2016	92 The Vennel, Linlithgow EH49 7ET / RDunphy@churchofscotland.org.uk	07791 007158
McIntosh, Kay (Mrs) DCS	Deacon, Edinburgh: Mayfield Salisbury	1990	2018	4 Jacklin Green, Livingston EH54 8PZ / kay@backedge.co.uk	01506 440543
Nelson, Georgina MA BD PhD DipEd	Hospital Chaplain, NHS Lothian	1990	1995	63 Hawthorn Bank, Seafield, Bathgate EH47 7EB / georgina.nelson@nhslothian.scot.nhs.uk	

C. Demitted

Name	Charge	From	To	Address	Phone
Darroch, Richard J.G. BD MTh MA(CMS)	(Whitburn: Brucefield)	1993	2010	23 Barnes Green, Livingston EH54 8PP / richdarr@aol.com	01506 436648
Dunleavy, Suzanne BD DipEd	(Bridge of Weir: St Machar's Ranfurly)	1990	2016	44 Tantallon Gardens, Bellsquarry, Livingston EH54 9AT / suzanne.dunleavy@btinternet.com	
Greig, Ronald G. MA BD	(Livingston United)	1987	2018	47 Mallace Avenue, Armadale EH48 2QD / rgglep@gmail.com	01501 731969 / 07787 887427
Jamieson, Gordon D. MA BD	(Head of Stewardship)	1974	2012	41 Goldpark Place, Livingston EH54 6LW / gordonjamieson182@gmail.com	01506 412020
Kerr, Angus BD CertMin ThM DMin	(Whitburn: South)	1983	2019	27 Pelham Court, Jackton, East Kilbride G74 5PZ	01355 570962
Mackay, Kenneth J. MA BD	(Edinburgh: St Nicholas' Sighthill)	1971	2007	46 Chuckethall Road, Livingston EH54 8FB / kmth_mackay@yahoo.co.uk	01506 410884
McLaren, Glenda M. (Ms) DCS	(Deacon)	1990	2020	17 Heatherwood, Seafield, Bathgate EH47 7BX / gmmclaren1330@gmail.com	01506 651401
Roger, Alexander M. BD PhD	(Whitburn: Brucefield)	1982	2020	30 Meadowpark Crescent, Bathgate EH48 2SX / amroger1951@outlook.com	01506 654563
Shaw, Duncan BD MTh	(Bathgate: St John's)	1975	2020	76 Bankton Park East, Livingston EH54 9BN	01506 442917
Smith, Graham W. BA BD FSAScot	(Livingston: Old)	1995	2016	smithgraham824@gmail.com	
Walker, Ian BD MEd DipMS	(Rutherglen: Wardlawhill)	1973	2007	92 Carseknowe, Linlithgow EH49 7LG / walk102822@aol.com	01506 844412

(3) LOTHIAN (W)

Meets at Musselburgh: St Andrew's High Parish Church at 7pm on the last Thursday in February, April, June and November, and in a different church on the last Thursday in September.

Clerk:	MR JOHN D. McCULLOCH DL	20 Tipperwell Way, Howgate, Penicuik EH26 8QP lothian@churchofscotland.org.uk	01968 676300
Depute Clerk:	REV MICHAEL D. WATSON	47 Crichton Terrace, Pathhead EH37 5QZ MWatson@churchofscotland.org.uk	01875 320043

Aberlady (F H W) linked with Gullane (F H W)
Brian C. Hilsley LLB BD   1990   2015
The Manse, Hummel Road, Gullane EH31 2BG
BHilsley@churchofscotland.org.uk
01875 870777
01620 843192

Athelstaneford (W) linked with Whitekirk and Tyninghame (W)
Vacant
Michael D. Watson   2013   2019
(Ordained Local Minister)
The Manse, Athelstaneford, North Berwick   EH39 5BE
47 Crichton Terrace, Pathhead EH37 5QZ
MWatson@churchofscotland.org.uk
01620 880378
01875 320043

Belhaven (F H T W) linked with Spott (F W)
Neil H. Watson BD   2017
The Manse, Belhaven Road, Dunbar EH42 1NH
NWatson@churchofscotland.org.uk
01368 860672
07974 074549

Bilston linked with Glencorse (H) linked with Roslin (H)
Vacant
June E. Johnston BSc MEd BD   2013   2020
(Ordained Local Minister)
Interim Moderator: Elisabeth G.B. Spence
31A Manse Road, Roslin EH25 9LG
21 Caberston Road, Walkerburn EH43 6AT
June.Johnston@churchofscotland.org.uk
ESpence@churchofscotland.org.uk
0131 440 2012
01896 870754
07754 448889
07432 528205

Bonnyrigg (F H)
Louise I. Purden BD   2020
9 Viewbank View, Bonnyrigg EH19 2HU
LPurden@churchofscotland.org.uk
0131 258 6219

Cockenzie and Port Seton: Chalmers Memorial (F H W)
Robin N. Allison BD DipMin   1994   2018
contact@chalmerschurch.co.uk
2 Links Road, Port Seton, Prestonpans EH32 0HA
RAllison@churchofscotland.org.uk
01875 812225

Cockenzie and Port Seton: Old (F H)
Guardianship of the Presbytery
Session Clerk: Eizabeth W. Malcolm (Miss) — malcolm771@btinternet.com — 01875 813659

Cockpen and Carrington (F H W) linked with Lasswade (H) and Rosewell (H W)
Lorna M. Souter MA BD MSc — 2016 — 11 Pendreich Terrace, Bonnyrigg EH19 2DT — LSouter@churchofscotland.org.uk — 0131 663 6392 / 07889 556418
Elisabeth G.B. Spence BD DipEd — 1995 — 2016 — 18 Castell Maynes Avenue, Bonnyrigg EH19 3RW — ESpence@churchofscotland.org.uk — 07432 528205
(Pioneer Minister, Hopefield Connections)

Dalkeith: St John's and King's Park (F H W)
Keith L. Mack BD MTh DPS — 2002 — sjkpdalkeith@gmail.com / 13 Weir Crescent, Dalkeith EH22 3JN / KMack@churchofscotland.org.uk — 0131 660 5871 / 0131 454 0206

Dalkeith: St Nicholas Buccleuch (F H T W)
Alexander G. Horsburgh MA BD — 1995 — 2004 — 1 Nungate Gardens, Haddington EH41 4EE — AHorsburgh@churchofscotland.org.uk — 01620 824728

Dirleton (F H) linked with North Berwick: Abbey (F H W)
David J. Graham BSc BD PhD — 1982 — 1998 — abbeychurch@btconnect.com / Sydserff, Old Abbey Road, North Berwick EH39 4BP / DGraham@churchofscotland.org.uk — 01620 892800 / 01620 890800

Dunbar (H W)
Gordon Stevenson BSc BD — 2010 — The Manse, 10 Bayswell Road, Dunbar EH42 1AB / GStevenson@churchofscotland.org.uk — 01368 865482

Dunglass (W)
Suzanne G. Fletcher (Mrs) BA MDiv MA — 2001 — 2011 — The Manse, Cockburnspath TD13 5XZ / SFletcher@churchofscotland.org.uk — 01368 830713 / 07973 960544

Garvald and Morham (W) linked with Haddington: West (H W)
John D. Vischer — 1993 — 2011 — hwcofs@hotmail.com / 15 West Road, Haddington EH41 3RD / JVischer@churchofscotland.org.uk — 01620 822213

Gladsmuir linked with Longniddry (F H W)
Robin E. Hill LLB BD PhD — 2004 — The Manse, Elcho Road, Longniddry EH32 0LB / RHill@churchofscotland.org.uk — 01875 853195

Glencorse (H) See Bilston

Gorebridge (F H W)
Mark S. Nicholas MA BD — 1999
office@gorepc.com
100 Hunterfield Road, Gorebridge EH23 4TT
MNicholas@churchofscotland.org.uk
01875 820387
01875 820387
07816 047493

Gullane See Aberlady

Haddington: St Mary's (F H T W)
Alison P. McDonald MA BD — 1991 2019
1 Nungate Gardens, Haddington EH41 4EE
Alison.McDonald@churchofscotland.org.uk
01620 829354
01620 823109

Haddington: West See Garvald and Morham

Humbie (F W) linked with Yester, Bolton and Saltoun (F W)
Anikó Schütz Bradwell MA BD — 2015
The Manse, Tweeddale Avenue, Gifford, Haddington EH41 4QN
ASchuetzBradwell@churchofscotland.org.uk
01620 811193

Lasswade and Rosewell See Cockpen and Carrington

Loanhead (F T W)
Graham L. Duffin BSc BD DipEd — 1989 2001
120 The Loan, Loanhead EH20 9AJ
GDuffin@churchofscotland.org.uk
0131 448 2459

Longniddry See Gladsmuir

Musselburgh: Northesk (F H W)
Vacant
Interim Moderator: John Mitchell
JMitchell@churchofscotland.org.uk
0131 448 2676

Musselburgh: St Andrew's High (H W)
A. Leslie Milton MA BD PhD — 1996 2019
8 Ferguson Drive, Musselburgh EH21 6XA
AMilton@churchofscotland.org.uk
0131 665 7239
0131 665 1124

Musselburgh: St Clement's and St Ninian's
Guardianship of the Presbytery
Session Clerk: Ivor A. Highley
110 Inveresk Road, Musselburgh EH21 7AY
0131 665 5674

Musselburgh: St Michael's Inveresk (F W)
Malcolm M. Lyon BD — 2007 2017
5 Crookston Ct., Crookston Rd., Inveresk, Musselburgh EH21 7TR
MLyon@churchofscotland.org.uk
0131 653 2411

Newbattle (F H W)
Gayle J.A. Taylor MA BD PGDipCouns 1999 2019 Parish Office, Mayfield and Easthouses Church, Bogwood Court, Easthouses EH22 5DG **0131 663 3245**
(Transition Minister) GTaylor@churchofscotland.org.uk
Malcolm T. Muir LTh 2001 2015 Mayfield and Easthouses Church, Bogwood Court, Mayfield, Dalkeith EH22 5DG 0131 663 3245
(Associate Minister) MMuir@churchofscotland.org.uk 0131 663 3245 07920 855467

Newton
Guardianship of the Presbytery
Andrew Don MBA 2006 2013 5 Eskvale Court, Penicuik EH26 8HT 0131 663 3845
(Ordained Local Minister) ADon@churchofscotland.org.uk 01968 675766

North Berwick: Abbey See Dirleton

North Berwick: St Andrew Blackadder (F H W) admin@standrewblackadder.org.uk
Neil J. Dougall BD DipMin DMin 1991 2003 7 Marine Parade, North Berwick EH39 4LD 01620 892132
NDougall@churchofscotland.org.uk

Ormiston (W) linked with Pencaitland (F W)
David J. Torrance BD DipMin 1993 2009 The Manse, Pencaitland, Tranent EH34 5DL 01875 340963
DTorrance@churchofscotland.org.uk

Pencaitland See Ormiston

Penicuik: North (F H W)
Graham D. Astles BD MSc 2007 2019 35 Esk Bridge, Penicuik EH26 8QR 07906 290568
GAstles@churchofscotland.org.uk

Penicuik: St Mungo's (F H W)
John C.C. Urquhart MA MA BD 2010 2017 10 Fletcher Grove, Penicuik EH26 0JT 01968 382116
JCUrquhart@churchofscotland.org.uk 07821 402901

Penicuik: South and Howgate (H W) admin@psah.church
Guardianship of the Presbytery
Session Clerk: Rosemary Townsley (Mrs) rosemarytownsley@icloud.com 01968 679103

Prestonpans; Prestongrange (F W)				
Kenneth W. Donald BA BD	1982	2014	The Manse, East Loan, Prestonpans EH32 9ED KDonald@churchofscotland.org.uk	01875 813643
Roslin See Bilston				
Spott See Belhaven				
Tranent (F W)				
Erica M. Wishart (Mrs) MA BD		2014	1 Toll House Gardens, Tranent EH33 2QQ EWishart@churchofscotland.org.uk	01875 704071 07503 170173
Traprain (W)				
Vacant				
Session Clerk: Thomas W. Middlemass			tom@marklemains.com	01620 861158 07976 661513
Tyne Valley (F H W)				
Dale K. London BTh FSAScot	2011	2018	Cranstoun Cottage, Ford, Pathhead EH37 5RE DLondon@churchofscotland.org.uk	01875 321329
Whitekirk and Tyninghame See Athelstaneford				
Yester, Bolton and Saltoun See Humbie				
B. In other appointments				
Berry, Geoff T. BD BSc	2009	2011	Army Chaplain	3 SCOTS, Fort George, Ardersier, Inverness IV2 7TE revgeoffberry@gmail.com	01368 860508 07703 527240
Cobain, Alan R. BD	2000	2017	Army Chaplain	HQ 20 Armoured Infantry Brigade, Wing Barracks, Bulford SP4 9NA	
Frail, Nicola R. BLE MBA MDiv	2000	2012	Army Chaplain	HQ 1st Strike Brigade, Delhi Barracks, Tidworth SP9 7DX nrfscot@hotmail.com	
Harrison, Frederick		2013	Ordained Local Minister	24 Comrie Avenue, Dunbar EH42 1ZN FHarrison@churchofscotland.org.uk	
Kellock, Chris N. MA BD	1998	2012	Army Chaplain	HQ 12 Armoured Infantry Brigade, Ward Barracks, Bulford, Wiltshire SP4 9NA nicandchris@hotmail.co.uk	
Wood, Peter J. MA BD	1993	2019	Pioneer New Housing Co-ordinator, Presbytery	49 Oxgangs Farm Drive, Edinburgh EH13 9PT PWood@churchofscotland.org.uk	07776 119901

C. Demitted

Name	Years	Charge	Address	Telephone
Allison, Ann BSc PhD BD	2000 2017	(Crail with Kingsbarns)	99 Coalgate Avenue, Tranent EH33 1JW / revann@sky.com	01875 571778 / 07857 525439
Andrews, J. Edward MA BD DipCG FSAScot	1985 2005	(Armadale)	Dunnichen, 1B Cameron Road, Nairn IV12 5NS / edward.andrews@btinternet.com	01667 459466 / 07808 720708
Atkins, Yvonne E.S. (Mrs) BD	1997 2018	(Musselburgh: St Andrew's High)	6 Robert de Quincy Place, Prestonpans EH32 9NS / yveatkins@yahoo.com	01875 819858
Burt, Thomas W. BD	1982 2013	(Carlops with Kirkurd and Newlands with West Linton: St Andrew's)	7 Arkwright Court, North Berwick EH39 4RT / tomburt@westlinton.com	01620 895494
Cairns, John B. KCVO LTh LLB LLD DD	1974 2009	(Aberlady with Gullane)	Bell House, Roxburghe Park, Dunbar EH42 1LR / johncairns@mail.com	01368 862501
Campbell, Thomas R.	1986 1993	(Paisley: St James)	The White House, Nairns Mains, Haddington EH41 4HF / tom@trcampbell.co.uk	07778 183830
Coltart, Ian O. CA BD	1988 2010	(Airbirlot with Carmyllie)	25 Bothwell Gardens, Dunbar EH42 1PZ	01368 860064
Dick, Andrew B. BD DipMin	1986 2015	(Musselburgh: St Michael's Inveresk)	4 Kirkhill Court, Gorebridge EH23 4TW / dixbit@aol.com	07540 099480
Duncan, Maureen M. (Mrs) BD	1996 2018	(Lochend and New Abbey)	2 Chalybeate, Haddington EH41 4NX / revmo43@gmail.com	01620 248559 / 07443 501738
Fraser, John W. MA BD	1974 2011	(Penicuik: North)	66 Camus Avenue, Edinburgh EH10 6QX / jjijj2005@hotmail.co.uk	0131 623 0647
Glover, Robert L. BMus BD MTh ARCO	1971 2010	(Cockenzie and Port Seton: Chalmers Memorial)	12 Seton Wynd, Port Seton, Prestonpans EH32 0TY / rtglover@btinternet.com	01875 818759
Gordon, Thomas J. MA BD	1974 2009	(Chaplain, Marie Curie Hospice, Edinburgh)	22 Gosford Road, Port Seton, Prestonpans EH32 0HF / tom.swallowsnest@gmail.com	01875 812262
Halley, Ruth D. BEd BD PGCM	2012 2019	(Logie)	24 Comrie Avenue, Dunbar EH42 1ZN / RHalley@churchofscotland.org.uk	07530 307413
Jones, Anne M. (Mrs) BD	1998 2002	(Hospital Chaplain)	7 North Elphinstone Farm, Tranent EH33 2ND / revanjones@aol.com	01875 614442
Macaulay, Glendon D. BD	1999 2012	(Falkirk: Erskine)	43 Gavin's Lee, Tranent EH33 2AP / gd.macaulay@btinternet.com	01875 615851
Mitchell, John LTh CertMin	1991 2018	(Bonnyrigg)	28 Shiel Hall Crescent, Rosewell EH24 9DD / JMitchell@churchofscotland.org.uk	0131 448 2676
Pirie, Donald LTh	1975 2006	(Bolton and Saltoun with Humbie with Yester)	46 Caiystane Avenue, Edinburgh EH10 6SH	0131 445 2654
Scott, Ian G. BSc BD STM	1965 2006	(Edinburgh: Greenbank)	50 Forthview Walk, Tranent EH33 1FE / igscott50@btinternet.com	01875 612907
Simpson, Robert R. BA BD	1994 2014	(Callander)	10 Bellsmains, Gorebridge EH23 4QD / robert@pansmanse.co.uk	01875 820843
Steele, Marilynn J. (Mrs) BD DCS	1999 2012	(Deacon)	2 Northfield Gardens, Prestonpans EH32 9LQ / marilynnsteele@aol.com	01875 811497
Stein, Jock MA BD	1973 2008	(Tulliallan and Kincardine)	35 Dunbar Road, Haddington EH41 3PJ / jstein@handselpress.org.uk	01620 824896
Stein, Margaret E. (Mrs) DA BD DipRE	1984 2008	(Tulliallan and Kincardine)	35 Dunbar Road, Haddington EH41 3PJ / margaretestein@hotmail.com	01620 824896
Steven, Gordon R. BD DCS	1997 2012	(Deacon)	51 Nantwich Drive, Edinburgh EH7 6RB / grsteven@btinternet.com	0131 669 2054 / 07904 385256

| Thornthwaite, Anthony P. MTh | 1995 | 2019 | (Dundee: Coldside) | 19 Dovecote Way, Haddington EH41 4HY
tony.thornthwaite@sky.com | 07706 761841 |
| Watson, James B. BSc | 1969 | 2009 | (Coldstream with Eccles) | 20 Randolph Crescent, Dunbar EH42 1GL | 01368 865045
07825 285660 |

(4) MELROSE AND PEEBLES (W)

Meets at Innerleithen on the first Tuesday of February, March, May, October, November and December, and on the fourth Tuesday of June, and in places to be appointed on the first Tuesday of September.

Clerk: REV. VICTORIA LINFORD LLB BD — 20 Wedale View, Stow, Galashiels TD1 2SJ, melrosepeebles@churchofscotland.org.uk — 01578 730237

Assistant Clerk: MR PETER SANDISON MA CertEd DipLib — Lynhurst, Abbotsview Drive, Galashiels TD1 3SL, petersandison@me.com — 01896 758634, 07805 637709

Ashkirk (W) linked with Selkirk (F H W)
Margaret D.J. Steele (Miss) BSc BD — 2000 2011 — office@selkirkparish.church, 1 Loanside, Selkirk TD7 4DJ, MSteele@churchofscotland.org.uk — 01750 22078, 01750 23308

Bowden (H) and Melrose (F H W)
Rosemary Frew (Mrs) MA BD — 1988 2017 — bowden.melrosepc@btinternet.com, The Manse, Tweedmount Road, Melrose TD6 9ST, RFrew@churchofscotland.org.uk — 01896 823339, 01896 822217

Broughton, Glenholm and Kilbucho (F H W) linked with Skirling (F W) linked with Stobo and Drumelzier (F W) linked with Tweedsmuir (F H W)
Vacant
Secretary to the Upper Tweed Parishes: Isobel Hunter — info@uppertweeddale.org.uk, isobel@skirlinghouse.com — 01899 860274

Caddonfoot (HW) linked with Galashiels: Trinity (HW)
Vacant
Session Clerk, Caddonfoot: Anne Grieve (Mrs)
Session Clerk, Galashiels: Trinity: Edward Martin — office@caddonfootgalatrinity.org.uk, 8 Mossilee Road, Galashiels TD1 1NF, anne@blakehope.co.uk, edwrd984@aol.com — 01896 752967, 01896 758485, 01896 850344, 01896 752252

Carlops (W) linked with Kirkurd and Newlands (F H) linked with West Linton: St Andrew's (F H W)
Vacant
The Manse, Main Street, West Linton   EH46 7EE   01968 660221
Session Clerk, Carlops: Murray Campbell (Prof)
sessionclerk@carlopschurch.org   01968 660530

Channelkirk and Lauder
Vacant
The Manse, Brownsmuir Park, Lauder   TD2 6QD   01578 718996
Session Clerk: William Anderson
wdanderson0709@hotmail.com   01578 722848

Earlston (F W)
Vacant
The Manse, High Street, Earlston   TD4 6DE   01896 849236
Session Clerk: Robert Turnbull
rgtapoth@btinternet.com   01896 848515

Eddleston (F H) linked with Peebles: Old (F H W)
Vacant
admin@topcop.org.uk   **01721 723986**
Pamela D. Strachan (Lady) MA (Cantab)   2015
7 Clement Gunn Square, Peebles   EH45 8LW   01721 720568
(Ordained Local Minister)
Glenhighton, Broughton, Biggar   ML12 6JF   01899 830423
PStrachan@churchofscotland.org.uk   07837 873688
Session Clerk, Eddleston: Vacant
Session Clerk, Peebles: Old: Vivien Aitchison
vivaitchison@btinternet.com   01721 722197

Ettrick and Yarrow (F W)
Vacant
Session Clerk: Nora Hunter
nhunter.ettrickyarrow@btinternet.com   01750 52349

Galashiels: Old and St Paul's (H W) linked with Galashiels: St John's (H)
Vacant
Session Clerk, Old and St Paul's: David Leckey
dl28133@aol.com   01896 757631
Session Clerk, St John's: Andrew T. Bramhall
andrewtbramhall@gmail.com   01896 755326

Galashiels: St John's See Galashiels: Old and St Paul's
Galashiels: Trinity See Caddonfoot

Innerleithen (H), Traquair and Walkerburn (W)
Vacant
The Manse, 1 Millwell Park, Innerleithen, Peebles   EH44 6JF   01896 830309
Session Clerk: Jim Borthwick
james.borthwick@btinternet.com   01721 720483

Kirkurd and Newlands See Carlops

Lyne and Manor (W) linked with Peebles: St Andrew's Leckie (F H W) office@standrewsleckie.co.uk   **01721 723121**
Malcolm S. Jefferson   2012   Mansefield, Innerleithen Road, Peebles EH45 8BE   01721 725148
MJefferson@churchofscotland.org.uk

Maxton and Mertoun (F W) linked with Newtown (F W) linked with St Boswells (F W) web4churches@gmail.com
Sheila W. Moir (Ms) MTheol   2008   7 Strae Brigs, St Boswells, Melrose TD6 0DH   01835 822255
SMoir@churchofscotland.org.uk

Newtown See Maxton and Mertoun
Peebles: Old See Eddleston
Peebles: St Andrew's Leckie See Lyne and Manor
St Boswells See Maxton and Mertoun
Selkirk See Ashkirk
Skirling See Broughton, Glenholm and Kilbucho
Stobo and Drumelzier See Broughton, Glenholm and Kilbucho

Stow: St Mary of Wedale and Heriot (W)
Victoria J. Linford (Mrs) LLB BD   2010   20 Wedale View, Stow, Galashiels TD1 2SJ   01578 730237
VLinford@churchofscotland.org.uk

Tweedsmuir See Broughton, Glenholm and Kilbucho
West Linton: St Andrew's See Carlops

C. Demitted

Name			(Charge)	Address	Phone
Arnott, A. David K. MA BD	1971	2010	(St Andrews: Hope Park with Strathkinness)	53 Whitehaugh Park, Peebles EH45 9DB adka53@btinternet.com	01721 725979 07759 709205
Devenny, Robert P.	2002	2017	(Head of Spiritual Care, NHS Borders)	Blakeburn Cottage, Wester Housebyres, Melrose TD6 9BW	01896 822350
Dick, J. Ronald BD	1973	2012	(Hospital Chaplain)	1 Viewfield Terrace, Leet Street, Coldstream TD12 4BL ron.dick180@yahoo.co.uk	01890 882206
Dobie, Rachel J.W. (Mrs) LTh	1991	2008	(Broughton, Glenholm and Kilbucho with Skirling with Stobo and Drumelzier with Tweedsmuir)	20 Moss Side Crescent, Biggar ML12 6GE revracheldobie@gmail.com	01899 229244
Dodd, Marion E. (Miss) MA BD LRAM	1988	2010	(Kelso: Old and Sprouston)	Esdaile, Tweedmount Road, Melrose TD6 9ST mariondodd@btinternet.com	01896 822446
Donaldson, David MA BD DMin	1969	2018	(Manish-Scarista)	13 Rose Park, Peebles EH45 8HP davidandjeandonaldson@gmail.com	07817 479866
Faris, Janice M. (Mrs) BSc BD	1991	2018	(Innerleithen, Traquair and Walkerburn)	Overdale Cottage, Grange Park Road, Orton Grange, Carlisle CA5 6LT revjfaris@gmail.com	07427 371239
Harley, Elspeth S. BA MTh	1991	2020	(Caddonfoot with Galashiels: Trinity)	eharley@hotmail.co.uk	07950 076528

Name	Ord.	App.	(Former charge / Role)	Address	Tel.
Hogg, Thomas M. BD	1986	2007	(Tranent)	22 Douglas Place, Galashiels TD1 3BT	01896 759381
Kellet, John M. MA	1962	1995	(Edinburgh: Leith South)	4 High Cottages, Walkerburn EH43 6AZ	01896 870351
Lawrie, Bruce B. BD	1974	2012	(Duffus, Spynie and Hopeman)	5 Thorncroft, Scotts Place, Selkirk TD7 4LN thorncroft54@gmail.com	01750 725427
Levison, Chris L. MA BD	1972	2010	(Health Care Chaplaincy Training and Development Officer)	Gardenfield, Nine Mile Burn, Penicuik EH26 9LT chrislevison@hotmail.com	01968 674566
Macdonald, Finlay A.J. MA BD PhD DD	1971	2010	(Principal Clerk)	8 St Ronan's Way, Innerleithen EH44 6RG finlay_macdonald@btinternet.com	01896 831631
Macdougall, Malcolm M. BD MTh DipCE	1981	2019	(Eddleston with Peebles: Old)	2 Woodilee, Broughton, Biggar ML12 6GB MMacdougall@churchofscotland.org.uk	
Milloy, A. Miller DPE LTh DipTrMan LHD	1979	2012	(General Secretary: United Bible Societies)	18 Kittlegairy Crescent, Peebles EH45 9NJ ammilloy@aol.com	01721 723380
Moore, W. Haisley MA	1966	1996	(Secretary: The Boys' Brigade)	1/2 Dovecot Court, Peebles EH45 8FG jillandhaisley@outlook.com	01721 720837
Munson, Winnie (Ms) BD	1996	2006	(Delting with Northmavine)	6 St Cuthbert's Drive, St Boswells, Melrose TD6 0DF wabsmith@btinternet.com	01835 823375
Norman, Nancy M. (Miss) BA MDiv MTh	1988	2012	(Lyne and Manor)	25 March Street, Peebles EH45 8EP nancy.norman1@googlemail.com	01721 721699
Rennie, John D. MA	1962	1996	(Broughton, Glenholm and Kilbucho with Skirling with Stobo and Drumelzier with Tweedsmuir)	29/1 Rosetta Road, Peebles EH45 8HJ tworennies@talktalk.net	01721 720963
Riddell, John A. MA BD	1967	2006	(Jedburgh: Trinity)	Orchid Cottage, Gingham Row, Earlston TD4 6ET c/o Hopeview House, Yarrow, Selkirk TD7 5LB	01896 848784
Siroky, Samuel BA MTh	2003	2017	(Ettrick and Yarrow)	25 Bardfield Road, Colchester CO2 8LW lms@hotmail.co.uk	0206 621939 07786 797974
Steele, Leslie M. MA BD	1973	2013	(Galashiels: Old and St Paul's)		
Wallace, James H. MA BD	1973	2011	(Peebles: St Andrew's Leckie)	52 Waverley Mills, Innerleithen EH44 6RH jimwallace121@btinternet.com	01896 831637

(5) DUNS (W)

Meets at Duns, in the Parish Church hall at 7pm on the first Tuesday of September and of December; and at venues to be announced on the first Saturday of February, the first Tuesday of May and the last Tuesday of June. It also meets throughout the year for developmental activities.

Clerk:	**MR DAVID S. PHILP**			**Sea View, West Winds, Upper Burnmouth TD14 5SL duns@churchofscotland.org.uk**	**01890 781568**

Ayton (H) and District Churches (F)

Norman R. Whyte BD MTh DipMin	1982	2006		The Manse, Beanburn, Ayton, Eyemouth TD14 5QY NWhyte@churchofscotland.org.uk	01890 781333

Berwick-upon-Tweed: St Andrew's Wallace Green (H) and Lowick (F W)
Adam J.J. Hood MA BD DPhil   1989   2012   3 Meadow Grange, Berwick-upon-Tweed TD15 1NW   01289 332787
AHood@churchofscotland.org.uk

Chirnside (F) linked with Hutton and Fishwick and Paxton
Michael A. Taylor DipTh MPhil   2006   2018   The New Manse, The Glebe, Chirnside, Duns TD11 3XE   01890 819947
MTaylor@churchofscotland.org.uk   07479 985075

Coldingham and St Abbs (F W) linked with Eyemouth (F W)
Andrew N. Haddow BEng BD   2012   The Manse, Victoria Road, Eyemouth TD14 5JD   01890 750327
AHaddow@churchofscotland.org.uk

Coldstream and District Parishes (H) linked with Eccles and Leitholm
David J. Taverner MCIBS ACIS BD   1996   2011   36 Bennecourt Drive, Coldstream TD12 4BY   01890 883387
DTaverner@churchofscotland.org.uk

Duns and District Parishes (F W)
Andrew J. Robertson BD   2008   2019   The Manse, Castle Street, Duns TD11 3DG   **01361 884502**
ARobertson@churchofscotland.org.uk   01361 883496

Eccles and Leitholm See Coldstream
Eyemouth See Coldingham and St Abbs

Fogo (F W)
H. Dane Sherrard BD DMin   1971   2019   Mount Pleasant Granary, Mount Pleasant Farm, Duns TD11 4HU   01361 882254
(Non-Stipendiary)   dane@mountpleasantgranary.net   07801 939138

Gordon: St Michael's (F) linked with Greenlaw (H) linked with Legerwood linked with Westruther
Vacant   The Manse, Todholes, Greenlaw, Duns TD10 6XD   01361 810316
Interim Moderator: H. Dane Sherrard   dane@mountpleasantgranary.net   07801 939138

Greenlaw See Gordon: St Michael's
Hutton and Fishwick and Paxton See Chirnside
Legerwood See Gordon: St Michael's
Westruther See Gordon: St Michael's

C. Demitted

Cartwright, Alan C.D. BSc BD	1976 2016	(Fogo and Swinton with Ladykirk and Whitsome with Leitholm)	Drumgray, Edrom, Duns TD11 3PX alan@cartwright-family.org.uk	01890 819191
Gaddes, Donald R.	1961 1994	(Kelso: North and Ednam)	2 Teindhill Green, Duns TD11 3DX drgaddes@btinternet.com	01361 883172
Hope, Geraldine H. (Mrs) MA BD	1986 2007	(Foulden and Mordington with Hutton and Fishwick and Paxton)	4 Well Court, Chirnside, Duns TD11 3UD geraldine.hope@virgin.net	01890 818134
Landale, William S.	2005 2016	(Auxiliary Minister)	Green Hope Guest House, Ellemford, Duns TD11 3SG WLandale@churchofscotland.org.uk	01361 890242
Neill, Bruce F. MA BD	1966 2007	(Maxton and Mertoun with Newtown with St Boswells)	18 Brierydean, St Abbs, Eyemouth TD14 5PQ bneill@phonecoop.coop	01890 771569
Paterson, William BD	1977 2001	(Bonkyl and Preston with Chirnside with Edrom Allanton)	Benachie, Gavinton, Duns TD11 3QT billdm.paterson@btinternet.com	01361 882727
Shields, John M. MBE LTh	1972 2007	(Channelkirk and Lauder)	12 Eden Park, Ednam, Kelso TD5 7RG john.shields118@btinternet.com	01573 229015
Walker, Kenneth D.F. MA BD PhD	1976 2008	(Athelstaneford with Whitekirk and Tyninghame)	Allanbank Kothi, Allanton, Duns TD11 3PY walkerkenneth49@gmail.com	01890 817102
Walker, Veronica (Mrs) BSc BD		(Licentiate)	Allanbank Kothi, Allanton, Duns TD11 3PY walkerkenneth49@gmail.com	01890 817102

(6) JEDBURGH

Meets at Denholm Church on the first Wednesday of February, March, May, September (this meeting in the out-going Moderator's church), October, November and December and on the last Wednesday of June.

Clerk	REV. LISA-JANE RANKIN BD CPS	4 Wilton Hill Terrace, Hawick TD9 8BE jedburgh@churchofscotland.org.uk	01450 370744

Ale and Teviot United (F H W)
Vacant

Session Clerk: John Rogerson	22 The Glebe, Ancrum, Jedburgh TD8 6UX B166ESS@yahoo.co.uk	01835 830318 07813 367533

Cavers and Kirkton (W) linked with Hawick: Trinity (H W)
Vacant

Interim Moderator: Alistair Cook	trinityhawick@outlook.com Trinity Manse, Howdenburn, Hawick TD9 8PH ACook@churchofscotland.org.uk	01450 378248 01450 616352

Cheviot Churches (H W)

Colin D. Johnston MA BD	1986	2019	The Old Police House, Main Street, Morebattle, Kelso TD5 8QG CDJohnston@churchofscotland.org.uk	01573 440539

Hawick: Burnfoot (F T W)
Vacant
Session Clerk: Marion Webb (Ms)
29 Wilton Hill, Hawick TD9 8BA
bpcsessionclerk@gmail.com
01450 373181
07843 794247

Hawick: St Mary's and Old (F H W) linked with Hawick: Teviot (H) and Roberton (F W)   info@smop-tero.org
Alistair W. Cook BSc CA BD   2008   2017
4 Heronhill Close, Hawick TD9 9RA
ACook@churchofscotland.org.uk
01450 378175
07802 616352

Hawick: Teviot and Roberton See Hawick: St Mary's and Old
Hawick: Trinity See Cavers and Kirkton

Hawick: Wilton linked with Teviothead
Lisa-Jane Rankin BD CPS   2003
4 Wilton Hill Terrace, Hawick TD9 8BE
LRankin@churchofscotland.org.uk
01450 370744

Hobkirk and Southdean (F W) linked with Ruberslaw (F W)
Rachel Wilson BA MTh   2018
The Manse, Leydens Road, Denholm, Hawick TD9 8NB
RWilson@churchofscotland.org.uk
01450 870874

Jedburgh: Old and Trinity (F W)
Stewart M. McPherson BD CertMin   1991   2020
(Interim Minister)
The Manse, Honeyfield Drive, Jedburgh TD8 6LQ
SMcPherson@churchofscotland.org.uk
01835 863417
07814 901429

Kelso Country Churches (W)
Stephen Manners MA BD   1989   2019
1 The Meadow, Stichill TD5 7TG
SManners@churchofscotland.org.uk
01573 470663

Kelso: North (H) and Ednam (F H W)   office@kelsonorthandednam.org.uk
Anna S. Rodwell BD DipMin   1998   2016
The Manse, 24 Forestfield, Kelso TD5 7BX
ARodwell@churchofscotland.org.uk
01573 224154
01573 224248
07765 169826

Kelso: Old and Sprouston (F)
Vacant
Session Clerk: Frances Gordon
The Manse, Glebe Lane, Kelso TD5 7AU
francesgordon38@btinternet.com
01573 348749
07966 435484

Oxnam
Guardianship of the Presbytery
Session Clerk: Morag McKeand (Mrs)
mh.mckeand@btinternet.com
01835 840284

Ruberslaw See Hobkirk and Southdean
Teviothead See Hawick: Wilton

C. Demitted

Combe, Neil R. BSc MSc BD	1984	2015	(Hawick: St Mary's and Old with Hawick: Teviot and Roberton)	2 Abbotsview Gardens, Galashiels TD1 3ER neil.combe@btinternet.com	01896 755869
McNicol, Bruce	1967	2006	(Jedburgh: Old and Edgerston)	42 Dounehill, Jedburgh TD8 6LJ mcnicol1942@gmail.com	01835 862991
Stewart, Una B. (Ms) BD DipEd	1995	2014	(Law)	10 Inch Park, Kelso TD5 7BQ rev.ubs@virgin.net	01573 219231
Young, Alexander W. BD DipMin	1988	2017	(Kelso: Old and Sprouston)	9 Towerburn, Denholm TD9 8TB sandy.young45@yahoo.com	07849 241344

HAWICK ADDRESSES

	St Mary's and Old	Kirk Wynd	
	Teviot	St George's Lane	
	Trinity	Central Square	
Burnfoot	Fraser Avenue	Wilton	Princes Street

(7) ANNANDALE AND ESKDALE

Meets on the first Tuesday of September, October, December, February and June and the second Tuesday of April. The September meeting is held in the Moderator's charge. The other meetings are held in Dryfesdale Church Hall, Lockerbie, except for the June meeting, which is separately announced.

Clerk:	**VERY REV. WILLIAM HEWITT BD DipPS**	Presbytery Office, Dryfesdale Parish Church, High Street, Lockerbie DG11 2AA annandaleeskdale@churchofscotland.org.uk	07769 625321

Annan: Old (F H W) linked with Dornock (F)

David Whiteman BD	1998	12 Plumdon Park Avenue, Annan DG12 6EY DWhiteman@churchofscotland.org.uk	01461 392048

Annan: St Andrew's (H W) linked with Brydekirk (W)

John G. Pickles BD MTh MSc	2011	1 Annerley Road, Annan DG12 6HE JPickles@churchofscotland.org.uk	01461 202626

Applegarth, Sibbaldbie (H) and Johnstone (F) linked with Lochmaben (H W)
Paul R. Read BSc DipEd MA(Th)   2000   2013   The Manse, Barrashead, Lochmaben, Lockerbie DG11 1QF
                                                        PRead@churchofscotland.org.uk   01387 810640

Brydekirk See Annan: St Andrew's

Canonbie United (F H W) linked with Liddesdale (F H W)
Vacant   churchoffice@liddesdalechurch.org.uk
Session Clerks, Canonbie United: Ruth Gilbert,   23 Langholm Street, Newcastleton TD9 0QX
  Leoniek van Belzen and Lois Lane   canonbiechurch@gmail.com   01387 375242
Session Clerk, Liddesdale: lpctreasurer1@gmail.com   01387 375488
  Glynis Cambridge (Mrs)

        Canonbie United is a Local Ecumenical Partnership with the United Free Church

Dalton and Hightae (F) linked with St Mungo (F)
Vacant   The Manse, Hightae, Lockerbie DG11 1JL   01387 811499
Session Clerk, Dalton: Isobel Tinning (Mrs)   isobel.tinning@gmail.com   01387 269133
Session Clerk, St Mungo: Annie Hutchon (Mrs)   anniehutchon45@gmail.com   01576 510280

Dornock See Annan: Old

Gretna: Old (H), Gretna: St Andrew's (H), Half Morton and Kirkpatrick Fleming (F)
Eleanor J. McMahon BEd BD   1994   2020   81 Moorpark Square, Renfrew PA4 8DB
  (Interim Minister)   EMcMahon@churchofscotland.org.uk   07974 116539

Hoddom, Kirtle-Eaglesfield and Middlebie (F W)
Christopher Wallace BD DipMin   1988   The Manse, Main Road, Ecclefechan, Lockerbie DG11 3BU
                                                           Christopher.Wallace@churchofscotland.org.uk   01576 300108

Kirkpatrick Juxta (F) linked with Moffat: St Andrew's (F H W) linked with Wamphray (F)   standrewsmoffat@gmail.com
Vacant   The Manse, 1 Meadowbank, Moffat DG10 9LR   01683 220128
Session Clerk, Kirkpatrick Juxta: Mary Brown (Mrs)   marybrown591@gmail.com   01683 300451
Session Clerk, Moffat: Donald Walker   donaldann66@gmail.com   01683 220707
Session Clerk, Wamphray: Helen Braid (Mrs)   r.braid557@btinternet.com   01576 470637

Langholm Eskdalemuir Ewes and Westerkirk (W)   leewparishchurch@outlook.com
Robert G. D. W. Pickles BD MPhil ThD   1984   2019   The Manse, Thomas Telford Road, Langholm DG13 0BL
                                                             RPickles@churchofscotland.org.uk   01387 380252

Liddesdale See Canonbie United
Lochmaben See Applegarth, Sibbaldbie and Johnstone

Lockerbie: Dryfesdale, Hutton and Corrie (F W)

Štěpán Janča Mgr   1998   2019   Dryfesdale Manse, 5 Carlisle Road, Lockerbie DG11 2DW   01576 204188
SJanca@churchofscotland.org.uk

Eric T. Dempster   2016   2018   Annanside, Wamphray, Moffat DG10 9LZ   01576 470496
(Ordained Local Minister)   EDempster@churchofscotland.org.uk

Moffat: St Andrew's See Kirkpatrick Juxta
St Mungo See Dalton and Hightae

The Border Kirk (F W)   **Chapel Street, Carlisle CA1 1JA**   **01228 591757**
David G. Pitkeathly LLB BD   1996   2007   95 Pinecroft, Carlisle CA3 0DB   01228 593243
DPitkeathly@churchofscotland.org.uk

Tundergarth
Guardianship of the Presbytery
Session Clerk: David Paterson   jilljoe@tiscali.co.uk   07982 037029

Wamphray See Kirkpatrick Juxta

B. In other appointments

Brydson, Angela (Mrs) DCS   2015 2014   Deacon, Lochmaben, Moffat and Lockerbie Grouping   52 Victoria Park, Lockerbie DG11 2AY   07543 796820
ABrydson@churchofscotland.org.uk

Campbell, Neil G. MA BD   1988 2018   Chaplain, HM Prison Dumfries and HMP Greenock   12 Charles Street, Annan DG12 5AJ
neil.campbell2@sps.pnn.gov.uk

Harvey, P. Ruth (Ms) MA BD   2009 2020   Leader, Iona Community   Croslands, Beacon Street, Penrith CA11 7TZ   01768 840749
leadershipteam@iona.org.uk   07403 638339

Macpherson, Duncan J. BSc BD   1993 2002   Deputy Assistant Chaplain General: Army   HQ 51 Infantry Brigade and HQ Scotland, Forthside, Stirling FK7 7RR

Steenbergen, Pauline (Ms) MA BD   1996 2018   Locum Minister, Presbytery   locum.ae@gmail.com   07743 927182

C. Demitted

Annand, James M. MA BD   1955 1995   (Lockerbie: Dryfesdale)   Dere Cottage, 48 Main Street, Newstead, Melrose TD6 9DX

Beveridge, S. Edwin P. BA   1959 2004   (Brydekirk with Hoddom)   19 Rothesay Terrace, Edinburgh EH3 7RY   0131 225 3393

Gibb, J. Daniel M. BA LTh   1994 2006   (Aberfoyle with Port of Menteith)   1 Beechfield, Newton Aycliffe DL5 7AX
dannygibb@hotmail.co.uk

Seaman, Ronald S. MA   1967 2007   (Dornock)   1 Springfield Farm Court, Springfield, Gretna DG16 5EH   01461 337228

(8) DUMFRIES AND KIRKCUDBRIGHT

Meets at Dumfries on the last Wednesday of February, April, June, September and November.

Clerk: REV. DONALD CAMPBELL BD   St George's Church, 50 George Street, Dumfries DG1 1EJ   **01387 252965**
dumfrieskirkcudbright@churchofscotland.org.uk

Balmaclellan, Kells (H) and Dalry (H) linked with Carsphairn (H)
David S. Bartholomew BSc MSc PhD BD   1994   The Manse, Dalry, Castle Douglas DG7 3PJ   01644 430380
DBartholomew@churchofscotland.org.uk

Caerlaverock (F) linked with Dumfries: St Mary's-Greyfriars' (F H W)
Vacant   4 Georgetown Crescent, Dumfries DG1 4EQ   01387 270128
Session Clerk, Caerlaverock: Sheila Wilson   wilson.glencaple@btopenworld.com   01387 770327
Interim Moderator: Fiona A. Wilson   FWilson@churchofscotland.org.uk   01556 610708

Carsphairn See Balmaclellan, Kells and Dalry

Castle Douglas (H W) linked with The Bengairn Parishes (W)
Alison H. Burnside (Mrs) MA BD   1990   2018   1 Castle View, Castle Douglas DG7 1BG   01556 505983
ABurnside@churchofscotland.org.uk

Closeburn linked with Kirkmahoe
Vacant   The Manse, Kirkmahoe, Dumfries DG1 1ST   01387 710572
Session Clerk, Closeburn: Jack Tait   jacktait1941@gmail.com   01848 331700
Session Clerk, Kirkmahoe: Alexander Fergusson   alexanderfergusson@btinternet.com   01387 253014

Colvend, Southwick and Kirkbean (W)
Vacant   The Manse, Colvend, Dalbeattie DG5 4QN   01556 630255
Interim Moderator: John R. Notman   JNotman@churchofscotland.org.uk   01387 253043

Corsock and Kirkpatrick Durham (W) linked with Crossmichael, Parton and Balmaghie (W)
Sally M.F. Russell BTh MTh   2006   Knockdrocket, Clarebrand, Castle Douglas DG7 3AH   01556 503645
SRussell@churchofscotland.org.uk

Crossmichael, Parton and Balmaghie See Corsock and Kirkpatrick Durham

Cummertrees, Mouswald and Ruthwell (H W)
Vacant
Interim Moderator: William Holland — The Manse, Ruthwell, Dumfries DG1 4NP — billholland55@btinternet.com — 01387 870217 / 01387 256131

Dalbeattie and Kirkgunzeon (F H W) linked with Urr (H W)
Fiona A. Wilson (Mrs) BD   2008   2014 — 36 Mill Street, Dalbeattie DG5 4HE — FWilson@churchofscotland.org.uk — 01556 610708

Dumfries: Maxwelltown West (H W)
Vacant
Session Clerk: Drew Crossan — Maxwelltown West Manse, 11 Laurieknowe, Dumfries DG2 7AH — andrew@ahrcrossan.co.uk — **01387 255900** / 01387 247538 / 01387 255265

Dumfries: Northwest (F T)
Vacant — c/o Church Office, Dumfries Northwest Church, Lochside Road, Dumfries DG2 0DZ. — 01387 249964
Session Clerk: Clara Jackson — sessionclerk.dumfriesnorthwest@gmail.com — 01387 249964

Dumfries: St George's (F H W)
Donald Campbell BD   1997 — office@saint-georges.org.uk — 9 Nunholm Park, Dumfries DG1 1JP — DCampbell@churchofscotland.org.uk — **01387 267072** / 01387 252965

Dumfries: St Mary's-Greyfriars' See Caerlaverock

Dumfries: St Michael's and South (W)
Vacant
Session Clerk: Esther Preston — 39 Cardoness Street, Dumfries DG1 3AL — prestoncraigavon@supanet.com — 01387 253849 / 01387 263402

Dumfries: Troqueer (F H W)
John R. Notman BSc BD   1990   2015 — secretary@troqueerparishchurch.com — Troqueer Manse, Troqueer Road, Dumfries DG2 7DF — JNotman@churchofscotland.org.uk — 01387 253043

Dunscore (F W) linked with Glencairn and Moniaive (F W)
Mark R. S. Smith BSc CertMin   1990   2020 — The Manse, Wallaceton, Auldgirth, Dumfries DG2 0TJ — Mark.Smith@churchofscotland.org.uk — 01387 820245

Durisdeer linked with Penpont, Keir and Tynron linked with Thornhill (H)
J. Stuart Mill MA MBA BD DipEd   1974   2013 — The Manse, Manse Park, Thornhill DG3 5ER — JMill@churchofscotland.org.uk — 01848 331191

Gatehouse and Borgue linked with Tarff and Twynholm
Valerie J. Ott (Mrs) BA BD   2002   The Manse, Planetree Park, Gatehouse of Fleet, Castle Douglas DG7 2EQ   01557 814233
VOtt@churchofscotland.org.uk

Glencairn and Moniaive See Dunscore

Irongray, Lochrutton and Terregles
Gary J. Peacock MA BD MTh   2015   The Manse, Shawhead, Dumfries DG2 9SJ   01387 730759
GPeacock@churchofscotland.org.uk

Kirkconnel (H) linked with Sanquhar: St Bride's (F H)
Vacant
Session Clerk, Kirkconnel: Fay Rafferty   fayrafferty1957@gmail.com   01659 67650
Session Clerk, Sanquhar: Duncan Close   dunruth@btinternet.com   01659 50596

Kirkcudbright (H W)
James F. Gatherer BD   1984   2020   church@kirkcudbrightparishchurch.org.uk   01557 339108
6 Bourtree Avenue, Kirkcudbright DG6 4AU
JGatherer@churchofscotland.org.uk

Kirkmahoe See Closeburn

Kirkmichael, Tinwald and Torthorwald (W)
Vacant
Mhairi Wallace (Mrs)   2013   2017   Manse of Tinwald, 6 Sundew Lane, Dumfries DG1 3TW   07701 375064
(Ordained Local Minister)   5 Dee Road, Kirkcudbright DG 4HQ
MWallace@churchofscotland.org.uk

Lochend and New Abbey
Vacant
Elizabeth A. Mack (Miss) DipPE   1994   2018   New Abbey Manse, 32 Main Street, New Abbey, Dumfries DG2 8BY   01387 850490
(Auxiliary Minster)   24 Roberts Crescent, Dumfries DG2 7RS   01387 264847
mackliz@btinternet.com

Penpont, Keir and Tynron See Durisdeer
Sanquhar: St Bride's See Kirkconnel
Tarff and Twynholm See Gatehouse and Borgue
The Bengairn Parishes See Castle Douglas
Thornhill See Durisdeer
Urr See Dalbeattie and Kirkgunzeon

C. Demitted

Bond, Maurice S. BA DipEd MTh PhD	1983	2019	(Dumfries: St Michael's and South)	15 Pleasance Avenue, Dumfries DG2 7JJ	01644 460595
Burns, John H. BSc BD	1985	2019	(Inch with Portpatrick with Stranraer: Trinity)	The Cabin, Dundeugh, Dalry DG7 3SY	01556 620001
Dee, Oonagh	2014	2019	(Ordained Local Minister)	Kendoon, Merse Way, Kippford, Dalbeattie DG5 4LL ODee@churchofscotland.org.uk	
du Plessis, Joachim J.H. BA BD MTh	1976	2019	(Dunscore with Glencairn and Moniaive)	Postnet Suite 283, Private Suite 283, Elardus Park, South Africa 0047	01557 620123
Finch, Graham S. MA BD	1977	2015	(Cadder)	32a St Mary Street, Kirkcudbright DG6 4DN gsf231@gmail.com	
Hammond, Richard J. BA BD	1993	2007	(Kirkmahoe)	3 Marchfield Mount, Marchfield, Dumfries DG1 1SE libby.hammond@virgin.net	07764 465783
Hogg, William T. MA BD	1979	2018	(Kirkconnel with Sanquhar St Bride's)	30 Castle Street, Kirkcudbright DG6 4JD WHogg@churchofscotland.org.uk	07515 102776
Holland, William MA	1967	2009	(Lochend and New Abbey)	Ardshean, 55 Georgetown Road, Dumfries DG1 4DD billholland55@btinternet.com	01387 256131 / 07766 531732
Hutcheson, Norman M. MA BD	1973	2013	(Dalbeattie with Urr)	66 Maxwell Park, Dalbeattie DG5 4LS norman.hutcheson@gmail.com	01556 610102
Irving, Douglas R. LLB BD WS	1984	2016	(Kirkcudbright)	17 Galla Crescent, Dalbeattie DG5 4JY douglas.irving@outlook.com	01556 610156
Kelly, William W. BSc BD	1994	2014	(Dumfries: Troqueer)	6 Vitality Way, Craigie, Perth, WA 6025, Australia ww.kelly@yahoo.com	
McKay, David M. MA BD	1979	2007	(Kirkpatrick Juxta with Moffat: St Andrew's with Wamphray)	20 Auld Brig View, Auldgirth, Dumfries DG2 0XE davidmckay20@tiscali.co.uk	01387 740013
McKenzie, William M. DA	1958	1993	(Dumfries: Troqueer)	41 Kingholm Road, Dumfries DG1 4SR mckenzie.dumfries@btinternet.com	01387 253688
McLauchlan, Mary C. (Mrs) LTh	1997	2013	(Mochrum)	3 Ayr Street, Moniaive, Thornhill DG3 4HP mary@revmother.co.uk	01848 200786
Owen, John J.C. LTh	1967	2001	(Applegarth and Sibbaldbie with Lochmaben)	5 Galla Avenue, Dalbeattie DG5 4JZ jj.owen@onetel.net	01556 612125
Sutherland, Colin A. LTh	1995	2007	(Blantyre: Livingstone Memorial)	71 Caulstran Road, Dumfries DG2 9FJ colin.csutherland@btinternet.com	01387 279954
Wotherspoon, Robert C. LTh	1976	1998	(Corsock and Kirkpatrick Durham with Crossmichael and Parton)	5 Goddards Green Cottages, Goddards Green, Beneden, Cranbrook TN17 4AW	01580 243091

DUMFRIES ADDRESSES

Maxwelltown West	Laurieknowe
Northwest	Lochside Road
St George's	George Street
St Mary's-Greyfriars	St Mary's Street
St Michael's and South	St Michael's Street
Troqueer	Troqueer Road

(9) WIGTOWN AND STRANRAER

Meets at Glenluce, in the church hall, on the first Tuesday of March, October and December for ordinary business; on the first Tuesday of September for formal business followed by meetings of committees; on the first Tuesday of November, February and May for worship followed by meetings of committees; and at a church designated by the Moderator on the first Tuesday of June for Holy Communion followed by ordinary business.

Clerk:	MR SAM SCOBIE		40 Clenoch Parks Road, Stranraer DG9 7QT wigtownstranraer@churchofscotland.org.uk	01776 703975

Ervie Kirkcolm (H W) linked with Leswalt (W)
Guardianship of the Presbytery
Session Clerk, Ervie Kirkcolm:

Jennifer Comery (Mrs)			Skellies Knowe West, Leswalt, Stranraer DH9 0RY	01776 854277
Session Clerk, Leswalt: Fiona McColm (Mrs)			sessionclerk@leswaltparishchurch.org.uk	01776 870555

Glasserton and Isle of Whithorn linked with Whithorn: St Ninian's Priory (F W)

Alexander I. Currie BD CPS	1990		The Manse, Whithorn, Newton Stewart DG8 8PT ACurrie@churchofscotland.org.uk	01988 500267

Inch linked with Luce Valley (F W)

Stephen Ogston MPhys MSc BD	2009	2017	Ladyburn Manse, Main Street, Glenluce, Newton Stewart DG8 0PU SOgston@churchofscotland.org.uk	01581 300316

Kirkcowan (H) linked with Wigtown (F H W)

Eric Boyle BA MTh	2006		Seaview Manse, Church Lane, Wigtown, Newton Stewart DG8 9HT EBoyle@churchofscotland.org.uk	01988 402314

Kirkinner linked with Mochrum linked with Sorbie (H)

Jeffrey M. Mead BD	1978	1986	The Manse, Kirkinner, Newton Stewart DG8 9AL JMead@churchofscotland.org.uk	01988 840643

Kirkmabreck (W) linked with Monigaff (H W)

Stuart Farmes	2011	2014	Creebridge, Newton Stewart DG8 6NR SFarmes@churchofscotland.org.uk	01671 403361

Kirkmaiden (F H W) linked with Stoneykirk
Vacant
Session Clerk, Kirkmaiden:
Maureen Graham (Mrs)   Church Road, Sandhead, Stranraer DG9 9JJ   01776 830757
                        maureen.grahamm@btinternet.com   01776 840209
Session Clerk, Stoneykirk: Gillian Lynn (Mrs)   randglynn@btinternet.com   01776 860665

Leswalt See Ervie Kirkcolm
Luce Valley See Inch
Mochrum See Kirkinner
Monigaff See Kirkmabreck

Penninghame (F H)
Edward D. Lyons BD MTh   2007   The Manse, 1A Corvisel Road, Newton Stewart DG8 6LW   01671 404425
                                   ELyons@churchofscotland.org.uk

Portpatrick linked with Stranraer (F H W)
Vacant
Session Clerk, Portpatrick: D. Maxwell (Mr)   Stoneleigh, Whitehouse Road, Stranraer DG9 0JB   01776 700616
                                               maxwell@supanet.com   01776 704045
Session Clerks, Stranraer: Isobel Irving (Mrs)   irvingisobel217@gmail.com   01776 820643
                           Louise McCandlish (Mrs)   lmccandlish27@gmail.com   01776 704916

Stranraer is a new congregation formed by the union of Stranraer: High Kirk and Stranraer: Trinity

Sorbie See Kirkinner
Stoneykirk See Kirkmaiden
Stranraer See Portpatrick
Whithorn: St Ninian's Priory See Glasserton and Isle of Whithorn
Wigtown See Kirkcowan

B. In other appointments
Bellis, Pamela A. BA   2004   Ordained Local Minister   Mayfield, Dunragit, Stranraer DG9 8PG   01581 400378
                                                           PBellis@churchofscotland.org.uk   07751 379249

C. Demitted
Baker, Carolyn M. (Mrs) BD   1997 2008   (Ochiltree with Stair)   Clanary, 1 Maxwell Drive, Newton Stewart DG8 6EL   01671 404292
                                                                       cncbaker@btinternet.com
Cairns, Alexander B. MA   1957 2009   (Turin)   Beechwood, Main Street, Sandhead, Stranraer DG9 9JG   01776 830389
                                                     dorothycairns@aol.com
Sheppard, Michael J. BD   1997 2016   (Ervie Kirkcolm with Leswalt)   4 Mill Street, Drummore, Stranraer DG9 9PS   01776 840369
                                                                          michaelsheppard00@gmail.com

(10) AYR

Meets in the Carrick Centre, Maybole (except as shown), on the first Tuesday of September, the fourth Tuesday of October (at a designated location), the first Tuesday of December, the first Tuesday of March, the first Tuesday of May, and the third Tuesday of June (in the Moderator's church). A conference is held in January.

Clerk:	REV. KENNETH C. ELLIOTT BD BA CertMin	68 St Quivox Road, Prestwick KA9 1JF ayr@churchofscotland.org.uk	01292 478788
Presbytery Office:		Prestwick South Parish Church, 50 Main Street, Prestwick KA9 1NX ayroffice@cofscotland.org.uk	01292 678556

Alloway (F H W)
Neil A. McNaught BD MA   1987 1999
secretary.allowaypc@gmail.com
1A Parkview, Alloway, Ayr KA7 4QG
NMcNaught@churchofscotland.org.uk
01292 **442083**
01292 441252

Annbank (H W) linked with Tarbolton (F W)
Mandy R. Ralph RGN   2013 2019
The Manse, Tarbolton, Mauchline KA5 5QJ
MRalph@churchofscotland.org.uk
01292 541452

Auchinleck (F H) linked with Catrine (F)
Stephen F. Clipston MA BD   1982 2006
28 Mauchline Road, Auchinleck KA18 2BN
SClipston@churchofscotland.org.uk
01290 424776

Ayr: Auld Kirk of Ayr (St John the Baptist) (H L W)
David R. Gemmell MA BD   1991 1999
auldkirkayr@hotmail.co.uk
20 Seafield Drive, Ayr KA7 4BQ
DGemmell@churchofscotland.org.uk
01292 **262938**
01292 864140

Ayr: Castlehill (F H W)
Paul R. Russell MA BD   1984 2019
office@castlehillchurch.org
3 Old Hillfoot Road, Ayr KA7 3LW
PRussell@churchofscotland.org.uk
01292 **267520**
01292 261464

Ayr: Newton Wallacetown (F H W)
Vacant
Session Clerk: John Bell
newtonwallacetownchurch@gmail.com
9 Nursery Grove, Ayr KA7 3PH
johnbell31@gmail.com
01292 **611371**
01292 264251

Ayr: St Andrew's (F H W)
Stanley Okeke BA MSc   2012   2020

info@standrewsayr.org.uk
17 Whiteford View, Ayr KA7 3LL
SOkeke@churchofscotland.org.uk

01292 261472

Ayr: St Columba (F H W)
Scott S. McKenna BA BD MTh MPhil PhD   1994   2019

irene@ayrstcolumba.co.uk
3 Upper Crofts, Alloway, Ayr KA7 4QX
SMcKenna@churchofscotland.org.uk

01292 265794
01292 226075

Ayr: St James' (F H W)
Barbara V. Suchanek-Seitz   CertMin DTh   2016

admin@stjamesayr.plus.com
1 Prestwick Road, Ayr KA8 8LD
BSuchanek-Seitz@churchofscotland.org.uk

01292 266993
01292 262420

Ayr: St Leonard's (F H W) linked with Dalrymple (F)
Brian R. Hendrie BD   1992   2015

st_leonards@btinternet.com
35 Roman Road, Ayr KA7 3SZ
BHendrie@churchofscotland.org.uk

01292 611117
01292 283825

Ayr: St Quivox (F H W)
John McCutcheon BA BD(Min)   2014   2019

11 Springfield Avenue, Prestwick KA9 2HA
JMcCutcheon@churchofscotland.org.uk

01292 861641

Ballantrae (H W) linked with St Colmon (Arnsheen Barrhill and Colmonell) (W)
Theodore L. Corney BA MTh GDipTh   2006   2019

The Manse, 1 The Vennel, Ballantrae, Girvan KA26 0NH
TCorney@churchofscotland.org.uk

01465 831252

Barr linked with Dailly linked with Girvan: South
Vacant
Session Clerk, Barr: Sharon Trotter (Mrs)
Session Clerk, Dailly: Ronald Turnbull
Session Clerk, Girvan: South: Lorna Dunn (Mrs)

30 Henrietta Street, Girvan KA26 9AL
sharontrotter26@gmail.com
janron2012@yahoo.com
lornadunn73@aol.com

01465 713370
07875 523752
01465 811424
01465 713063

Catrine See Auchinleck

Coylton (F W) linked with Drongan: The Schaw Kirk (W)
Alwyn Landman BTh MDiv MTh DMin   2005   2019

4 Hamilton Place, Coylton, Ayr KA6 6JQ
ALandman@churchofscotland.org.uk

01292 571287

Craigie Symington (W) linked with Prestwick South (H W) 1989
Kenneth C. Elliott BD BA Cert Min
office@pwksouth.plus.com
68 St Quivox Road, Prestwick KA9 1JF
KElliott@churchofscotland.org.uk
01292 **678556**
01292 478788

Tom McLeod 2014 2015
(Ordained Local Minister)
3 Martnaham Drive, Coylton KA6 6JE
TMcleod@churchofscotland.org.uk
01292 570100

Crosshill (H) linked with Maybole (F W)
Vacant
Interim Moderator: Paul R. Russell
Session Clerk, Maybole: Lynne Rankin (Mrs)
74A Culzean Road, Maybole KA19 8AH
PRussell@churchofscotland.org.uk
lynnerankin21@gmail.com
01655 889454
01292 261464
07947 482238

Dailly See Barr

Dalmellington (F) linked with Patna Waterside (F)
Vacant
Interim Moderator: Bill Mackie
4 Carsphairn Road, Dalmellington, Ayr KA6 7RE
bill.ayr1304@outlook.com
01292 551503
01292 281163

Dalrymple See Ayr: St Leonard's
Drongan: The Schaw Kirk See Coylton

Dundonald (H W) 2019
Lynsey J. Brennan BSc MSc BA
64 Main Street, Dundonald, Kilmarnock KA2 9HG
LBrennan@churchofscotland.org.uk
01563 850243

Fisherton (H) linked with Kirkoswald (H W) 1990 2016
Ian R. Stirling BSc BD MTh MSc DPT
The Manse, Kirkoswald, Maybole KA19 8HZ
IStirling@churchofscotland.org.uk
01655 760532

Girvan: North (F H W)
churchoffice12@btconnect.com
Vacant
Interim Moderator: James Anderson (Dr)
38 The Avenue, Girvan KA26 9DS
jc.anderson2@talktalk.net
01465 **712672**
01465 713203
01465 710059

Girvan: South See Barr

Kirkmichael linked with Straiton: St Cuthbert's 1984 1985
W. Gerald Jones MA BD ThM
The Manse, Patna Road, Kirkmichael, Maybole KA19 7PJ
WJones@churchofscotland.org.uk
01655 750286

Kirkoswald See Fisherton

Lugar linked with Old Cumnock: Old (H)
John W. Paterson BSc BD DipEd   1994   33 Barrhill Road, Cumnock KA18 1PJ   01290 420769
JPaterson@churchofscotland.org.uk

Mauchline (H W) linked with Sorn
Vacant   1991   2011   mauchlineparish@yahoo.com   01290 518528
Session Clerk, Mauchline: Kristy Murray (Mrs)   4 Westside Gardens, Mauchline KA5 5DJ   01290 552465
Session Clerk, Sorn: Christeen Dunlop (Mrs)   cmurray@murrayireland.freeonline.co.uk   01290 552629
christeen.dunlop@ymail.com

Maybole See Crosshill

Monkton and Prestwick: North (F H T W)
Vacant   office@mpnchurch.org.uk   01292 678810
Session Clerk: Lesley Keenan (Mrs)   40 Monkton Road, Prestwick KA9 1AR   01292 471379
lesleykeenan@tkinternet.com   07754 327561

Muirkirk (H W) linked with Old Cumnock: Trinity (F W)
Vacant   46 Ayr Road, Cumnock KA18 1DW   01290 422145
Session Clerk, Muirkirk: Sylvia McGlynn (Miss)   hiddendepths@hotmail.com
Session Clerk, Trinity: Kay Mitchell (Mrs)   kaymitch14@sky.com

New Cumnock (F H W)
Helen E. Cuthbert MA MSc BD   2009   37 Castle, New Cumnock, Cumnock KA18 4AG   01290 338296
HCuthbert@churchofscotland.org.uk

Ochiltree (W) linked with Stair (F W)
Morag V. Garrett (Mrs) BD   2011   2017   (temporary) 89 South Beach, Troon KA10 6EQ   01292 318929
MGarrett@churchofscotland.org.uk

Old Cumnock: Old See Lugar
Old Cumnock: Trinity See Muirkirk
Patna Waterside See Dalmellington

Prestwick: Kingcase (F H W)
Ian Wiseman BTh DipHSW   1993   2015   office@kingcase.freeserve.co.uk   01292 479571
15 Bellrock Avenue, Prestwick KA9 1SQ
IWiseman@churchofscotland.org.uk

Prestwick: St Nicholas' (H W)
Vacant
Session Clerk: Margaret McIntosh

office@stnicholasprestwick.org.uk
3 Bellevue Road, Prestwick KA9 1NW
mwmcin@mwmcinfowoodlea.plus.com

01292 671547

Prestwick: South See Craigie Symington
St Colmon (Arnsheen Barrhill and Colmonell) See Ballantrae
Sorn See Mauchline
Stair See Ochiltree
Straiton: St Cuthbert's See Kirkmichael
Tarbolton See Annbank

Troon: Old (F H W)
David B. Prentice-Hyers BA MDiv   2003   2013

office@troonold.org.uk
85 Bentinck Drive, Troon KA10 6HZ
DPrentice-Hyers@churchofscotland.org.uk

01292 **313520**
01292 313644

Troon: Portland (F H W)
Vacant
Session Clerk: John Reid

office@troonportlandchurch.org.uk
89 South Beach, Troon KA10 6EQ
session@troonportlandchurch.org.uk

01292 **317929**
01292 318929

Troon: St Meddan's (F H T W)
Vacant
Session Clerk: Elaine Rodger

stmeddanschurch@gmail.com
27 Bentinck Drive, Troon KA10 6HX
stmeddansclerk@gmail.com

01292 **317750**
01292 319163
01292 315623

B. In other appointments
Blackshaw, Christopher J. BA(Theol)   2015   2017   Pioneer Minister, Farming Community
Chris Blackshaw is a Methodist Minister
Crossan, Morag BA   2016   Ordained Local Minister

Hogg, James   2018   Ordained Local Minister

Livestock Auction Mart, Whitefordhill, Ayr KA6 5TW
CBlackshaw@churchofscotland.org.uk
1A Church Hill, Dalmellington KA26 9AN
MCrossan@churchofscotland.org.uk
JHogg@churchofscotland.org.uk

01292 262241
07989 100818
07861 736071

C. Demitted
Aitken, Fraser R. GCSJ MA BD   1978   2019   (Ayr: St Columba)

Anderson, Robert A. MA BD DPhil   1984   2017   (Blackburn and Seafield)

Birse, G. Stewart CA BD BSc   1980   2013   (Ayr: Newton Wallacetown)

Sandringham, 38 Coylebank, Prestwick KA9 2DH
FAitken@churchofscotland.org.uk
Aiona, 8 Old Auchans View, Dundonald KA2 9EX
robertanderson307@btinternet.com
9 Calvinston Road, Prestwick KA9 2EL
stewart.birse@gmail.com

01292 225087

01563 850554
07484 206190
01292 474556

Name	Dates	Charge	Address / Email	Phone
Bogle, Thomas C. BD	1983 2003	(Fisherton with Maybole: West)	38 McEwan Crescent, Mossblown, Ayr KA6 5DR	01292 521215
Brown, Jack M. BSc BD	1977 2012	(Applegarth, Sibbaldbie and Johnstone with Lochmaben)	69 Berelands Road, Prestwick KA9 1ER jackm.brown@tiscali.co.uk	01292 477151
Crichton, James MA BD MTh	1969 2010	(Crosshill with Dalrymple)	60 Kyle Court, Ayr KA7 3AW crichton.james@btinternet.com	07549 988643
Dickie, Michael M. BSc	1955 1993	(Ayr: Castlehill)	8 Noltmire Road, Ayr KA8 9ES	01292 618512
Fiddes, George R. BD	1979 2019	(Prestwick: St Nicholas')	14 Crawford Avenue, Prestwick KA9 2BN fidkid@hotmail.co.uk	07925 004062
Geddes, Alexander J. MA BD	1960 1998	(Stewarton: St Columba's)	2 Gregory Street, Mauchline KA5 6BY sandy270736@gmail.com	01290 518597
Glencross, William M. LTh	1968 1999	(Bellshill: Macdonald Memorial)	1 Lochay Place, Troon KA10 7HH	01292 317097
Guthrie, James A.	1969 2005	(Corsock and Kirkpatrick Durham with Crossmichael and Parton)	2 Barthill Road, Pinwherry, Girvan KA26 0QE p.h.m.guthrie@btinternet.com	01465 841236
Harper, David L. BSc BD	1972 2012	(Troon: St Meddan's)	19 Calder Avenue, Troon KA10 7JT d.l.harper@btinternet.com	01292 312626
Jackson, Nancy	2009	(Auxiliary Minister)	35 Auchentrae Crescent, Ayr KA7 4BD nancyjaxon@btinternet.com	01292 262034
Keating, Glenda K. (Mrs) MTh	1996 2015	(Craigie Symington)	8 Wardlaw Gardens, Irvine KA11 2EW kirkglen@btinternet.com	01294 218820
Laing, Iain A. MA BD	1971 2009	(Bishopbriggs: Kenmuir)	9 Annfield Road, Prestwick KA9 1PP iandrlaing@yahoo.co.uk	01292 471732
Lennox, Lawrie I. MA BD DipEd	1991 2006	(Cromar)	7 Carwinshoch View, Ayr KA7 4AY lennox127@btinternet.com	01292 288658
Lochrie, John S. BSc BD MTh PhD	1967 2008	(St Colmon)	Cosgylen, Kilkerran, Maybole KA19 8LS	01465 811262
McGurk, Andrew F. BD	1983 2011	(Largs: St John's)	15 Fraser Avenue, Troon KA10 6XF afmcg.largs@talk21.com	01292 676008
McNidder, Roderick H. BD	1987 2007	(Chaplain: NHS Ayrshire and Arran Trust)	6 Hollow Park, Alloway, Ayr KA7 4SR roddymcnidder@sky.com	01292 442554
McPhail, Andrew M. BA	1968 2002	(Ayr: Wallacetown)	25 Maybole Road, Ayr KA7 2QA	01292 282108
MacPherson, Gordon C. MA BD MTh	1963 1988	(Associate, Kilmarnock: Henderson)	6 Crosbie Place, Troon KA10 6EY ggmacpherson@btinternet.com	01292 679146
Matthews, John C. MA BD OBE	1992 2010	(Glasgow: Ruchill Kelvinside)	12 Arrol Drive, Ayr KA7 4AF mejohnmatthews@gmail.com	01292 264382
Mayes, Robert BD	1982 2017	(Dundonald)	Garfield Cottage, Sorn Road, Mauchline KA5 6HQ bobmayes3@gmail.com	01290 519869
Moore, Douglas T.	2003 2019	(Auxiliary Minister)	9 Midton Avenue, Prestwick KA9 1PU DMoore@churchofscotland.org.uk	01292 671352
Morrison, Alistair H. BTh DipYCS	1985 2004	(Paisley: St Mark's Oldhall)	92 St Leonard's Road, Ayr KA7 2PU alistairhmorrison@gmail.com	01292 266021
Ness, David T. LTh	1972 2008	(Ayr: St Quivox)	17 Winston Avenue, Prestwick KA9 2EZ dtness@gmail.com	01292 471625
Ogston, Edgar J. BSc BD	1976 2017	(North West Lochaber)	14 North Park Avenue, Girvan KA26 9DH edgar.ogston@macfish.com	01465 713081

Name	Years	(Previous charge)	Address	Phone / Email
Paterson, John L. MA BD STM	1964 2003	(Linlithgow: St Michael's)	9 The Pines, Murdoch's Lane, Alloway, Ayr KA7 4WD lip38rev@gmail.com	01292 443615
Rae, Scott M. MBE BD CPS	1976 2016	(Muirkirk with Old Cumnock: Trinity)	2 Primrose Place, Kilmarnock KA1 2RR scottrae1@btopenworld.com	01563 532711
Sanderson, Alastair M. BA LTh	1971 2007	(Craigie with Symington)	26 Main Street, Monkton, Prestwick KA9 2QL alel@sanderson29.fsnet.co.uk	01292 475819
Simpson, Edward V. BSc BD	1972 2009	(Glasgow: Giffnock South)	8 Paddock View, Thorntoun, Crosshouse, Kilmarnock KA2 0BH eddie.simpson3@talktalk.net	01563 522841
Symington, Alastair H. MA BD	1972 2012	(Troon: Old)	1 Cavendish Place, Troon KA10 6JG revdahs@virginmedia.com	01292 312556
Whitecross, Jeanette BD	2002 2019	(Kilwinning: Old)	4 Fir Bank, Ayr KA7 3SX jeanettewx@yahoo.com	07803 181150
Wilson, Muriel (Miss) MA BD DCS	1997 2011	(Deacon)	28 Bellevue Crescent, Ayr KA7 2DR me.wilson@btinternet.com	01292 264039
Young, Rona M. (Mrs) BD DipEd	1991 2015	(Ayr: St Quivox)	16 Macintyre Road, Prestwick KA9 1BE revronyoung@hotmail.com	01292 471982
Yorke, Kenneth B.	1982 2009	(Dalmellington with Patna Waterside)	13 Annfield Terrace, Prestwick KA9 1PS kenyorke@yahoo.com	01292 670476

AYR ADDRESSES

Ayr

Church	Address
Auld Kirk	Kirkport (116 High Street)
Castlehill	Castlehill Road x Hillfoot Road
Newton Wallacetown	Main Street
St Andrew's	Park Circus
St Columba	Midton Road x Carrick Park
St James'	Prestwick Road x Falkland Park Road
St Leonard's	St Leonard's Road x Monument Road

Girvan

Church	Address
North	Montgomerie Street
South	Stair Park

Prestwick

Church	Address
Kingcase	Waterloo Road

Monkton and Prestwick North

Church	Address
St Nicholas	Monkton Road
South	Main Street

Troon

Church	Address
Old	Main Street
Portland	Ayr Street
St Meddan's	St Meddan's Street

(11) IRVINE AND KILMARNOCK (W)

The Presbytery meets at 7:00pm in the Howard Centre, Portland Road, Kilmarnock, on the first Tuesday in September, December and March and on the fourth Tuesday in June for ordinary business, and at different locations on the first Tuesday in October, November, February and May for mission. The September meeting commences with the celebration of Holy Communion.

| Clerk: | MR I. STEUART DEY LLB | 72 Dundonald Road, Kilmarnock KA1 1RZ
steuart.dey@btinternet.com | 01563 521686 (Home) |
| Presbytery Office: | | Howard Centre, 5 Portland Road, Kilmarnock KA1 2BT
irvinekilmarnock@churchofscotland.org.uk | 01563 526295 (Office) |

The Presbytery office is staffed each Tuesday, Wednesday and Thursday from 9am until 12:30pm.

Ayrshire Mission to the Deaf
Richard C. Durno DSW CQSW 1989 2013 31 Springfield Road, Bishopbriggs, Glasgow G64 1PJ richard.durno@btinternet.com 0141 772 1052 (Voice/Text/Fax) 07748 607721 (Voice/Text/Voicemail) (Mbl)

Caldwell (F) linked with Dunlop (W)
Alison McBrier MA BD 2011 2017 4 Dampark, Dunlop, Kilmarnock KA3 4BZ AMcBrier@churchofscotland.org.uk 01560 673686

Crosshouse (F H W)
Vacant
Interim Moderator: C. Blair Gillon 27 Kilmarnock Road, Crosshouse, Kilmarnock KA2 0EZ charlesgillon21@gmail.com 07490 495936

Darvel (F W)
Vacant
Session Clerk: John Grier
Interim Moderator: Margaret A. Hamilton (Mrs) 46 West Main Street, Darvel KA17 0AQ johngrier46@btinternet.com mahamilton1@outlook.com **01560 322924** 01560 322924 01560 321355 01563 534431

Dreghorn and Springside (T W)
Jamie W. Milliken BD 2005 2020 7 Sycamore Wynd, Perceton, Irvine KA11 2FA JMilliken@churchofscotland.org.uk 01294 211893

Dunlop See Caldwell

Fenwick (F H W) linked with Kilmarnock: Riccarton (F H W)
Colin A. Strong BSc BD 1989 2007 2 Jasmine Road, Kilmarnock KA1 2HD CStrong@churchofscotland.org.uk 01563 549490

Galston (F H W)
Kristina I. Hine BS MDiv
2011   2016
19 Manse Gardens, Galston KA4 8DX
KHine@churchofscotland.org.uk
01563 820136
01563 257172

Hurlford (F H W)
Vacant
Session Clerk: Elizabeth F.G. Lauchlan
Interim Moderator: Colin G.F. Brockie
12 Main Road, Crookedholm, Kilmarnock KA3 6JT
elizabeth.lauchlan@btinternet.com
revcolin@uwclub.net
01563 539739
01563 537381
01563 559960

Irvine: Fullarton (F H T W)
Neil Urquhart BD DipMin DipSC
1989
secretary@fullartonchurch.co.uk
48 Waterside, Irvine KA12 8QJ
NUrquhart@churchofscotland.org.uk
01294 273741
01294 279909

Irvine: Girdle Toll (F H) linked with Irvine: St Andrew's (H)
Ian W. Benzie BD
1999   2008
St Andrew's Manse, 206 Bank Street, Irvine KA12 0YD
Ian.Benzie@churchofscotland.org.uk
01294 276051
01294 216139

Irvine: Mure (F H) linked with Irvine: Relief Boutreehill (F H W)
Vacant
Interim Moderator: George K. Lind
9 West Road, Irvine KA12 8RE
gklind@talktalk.net
01294 279916
01560 428732

Irvine: Old (F H)
Vacant
Interim Moderator: Kim Watt
22 Kirk Vennel, Irvine KA12 0DQ
KWatt@churchofscotland.org.uk
01294 273503
01294 279265
01560 482267

Irvine: Relief Bourtreehill See Irvine: Mure
Irvine: St Andrew's See Irvine: Girdle Toll

Kilmarnock: Kay Park (F H W)
Fiona E. Maxwell BA BD
2004   2018
1 Glebe Court, Kilmarnock KA1 3BD
FMaxwell@churchofscotland.org.uk
01563 574106
01563 521762

Kilmarnock: New Laigh Kirk (F H W)
David S. Cameron BD
2001   2009
1 Holmes Farm Road, Kilmarnock KA1 1TP
David.Cameron@churchofscotland.org.uk
01563 525416

Kilmarnock: Riccarton See Fenwick

Kilmarnock: St Andrew's and St Marnock's (F W)
James McNaughtan BD DipMin — 1983 — 35 South Gargieston Drive, Kilmarnock KA1 1TB / JMcNaughtan@churchofscotland.org.uk — 01563 521665

Kilmarnock: St John's Onthank (F H W)
Allison E. Becker BA MDiv — 2015 2008 — 84 Wardneuk Drive, Kilmarnock KA3 2EX / ABecker@churchofscotland.org.uk — 07716 162380

Kilmarnock: St Kentigern's (F W)
Vacant — hub@stkentigern.org.uk
Interim Moderator: Anne McAllister — AMcAllister@churchofscotland.org.uk — 01560 483191

Kilmarnock: South (F H)
H. Taylor Brown BD CertMin — 1997 2002 — 14 McLelland Drive, Kilmarnock KA1 1SE / HBrown@churchofscotland.org.uk — 01563 529920

Kilmaurs: St Maur's Glencairn (H)
John A. Urquhart BD — 1993 — 9 Standalane, Kilmaurs, Kilmarnock KA3 2NB / John.Urquhart@churchofscotland.org.uk — 01563 538289

Newmilns: Loudoun (F H T W)
Vacant — Loudoun Manse, 116A Loudoun Road, Newmilns KA16 9HH
Interim Moderator: James McNaughtan — JMcNaughtan@churchofscotland.org.uk — 01560 320174 / 01563 521665

Stewarton: John Knox (F T W)
Gavin A. Niven BSc MSc BD — 2010 — getconnected@johnknox.org.uk / 27 Avenue Street, Stewarton, Kilmarnock KA3 5AP / GNiven@churchofscotland.org.uk — **01560 484560** / 01560 482418

Stewarton: St Columba's (H W)
Vacant — 1 Kirk Glebe, Stewarton, Kilmarnock KA3 5BJ
Interim Moderator: T. Alan W. Garrity — alangarrity@btinternet.com — 01560 485113 / 01560 486879

B. In other appointments
Clancy, P. Jill (Mrs) BD DipMin — 2000 2017 — Prison Chaplain, HMP Barlinnie — 27 Cross Street, Galston KA4 8AA / JClancy@churchofscotland.org.uk

Huggett, Judith A. (Miss) BA BD — 1990 1998 — Lead Chaplain, NHS Ayrshire and Arran — 4 Westmoor Crescent, Kilmarnock KA1 1TX / judith.huggett@aapct.scot.nhs.uk — 07956 557087

Name	Ordained	Status	Description	Address / Email	Phone
Watt, Kim	2015		(Ordained Local Minister, Presbytery)	Reddans Park Gate, The Crescent, Stewarton, Kilmarnock KA3 5AY / KWatt@churchofscotland.org.uk	01560 482267
C. Demitted					
Brockie, Colin G.F. BSc(Eng) BD SOSc	1967	2007	(Kilmarnock Grange)	36 Brachead Court, Kilmarnock KA3 7AB / colin@brockie.org.uk	01563 559960
Burgess, Paul C.J. MA	1970	2003	(World Mission Partner, Gujranwala Theological Seminary, Pakistan)	Springvale, Halket Road, Lugton, Kilmarnock KA4 3EE / paulandcathie@gmail.com	01505 850254
Cant, Thomas M. MA BD	1964	2004	(Paisley: Laigh Kirk)	3 Meikle Cutstraw, Stewarton, Kilmarnock KA3 5HU / revtmcant@aol.com	01560 480566
Christie, Robert S. MA BD ThM	1964	2000	(Kilmarnock: West High)	24 Homeroyal House, 2 Chalmers Crescent, Edinburgh EH9 1TP	
Davidson, James BD DipAFH	1989	2002	(Wishaw: Old)	13 Redburn Place, Irvine KA12 9BQ	01294 312515
Garrity, T. Alan W. BSc BD MTh	1969	2008	(Bermuda)	17 Solomon's View, Dunlop, Kilmarnock KA3 4ES / alangarrity@btinternet.com	01560 486879
Gillon, C. Blair BD	1975	2007	(Glasgow: Ibrox)	East Muirshiel Farmhouse, Dunlop, Kilmarnock KA3 4EJ / charlesgillon21@gmail.com	01560 483778
Godfrey, Linda BSc BD	2012	2014	(Ayr: St Leonard's with Dalrymple)	9 Taybank Drive, Ayr KA7 4RL / godfreykayak@aol.com	07825 663866
Hall, William M. BD	1972	2010	(Kilmarnock: Old High Kirk)	33 Cairns Terrace, Kilmarnock KA1 2JG / revwillie@talktalk.net	01563 525080
Hewitt, William C. BD DipPS	1977	2017	(Presbytery Clerk: Glasgow)	60 Woodlands Grove, Kilmarnock KA3 1TZ / WHewitt@churchofscotland.org.uk	01563 533312
Horsburgh, Gary E. BA	1977	2015	(Dreghorn and Springside)	1 Woodlands Grove, Kilmarnock KA3 1TY / garyhorsburgh@hotmail.co.uk	01563 624508
Lacy, David W. DL BA BD DLitt	1976	2017	(Kilmarnock: Kay Park)	4 Cairns Terrace, Kilmarnock KA1 2JG / DLacy@churchofscotland.org.uk	01563 624034 / 07974 760272
Lamarti, Samuel H. BD MTh PhD	1979	2006	(Stewarton: John Knox)	7 Dalwhinnie Crescent, Kilmarnock KA3 1QS / samlamar@pobroadband.co.uk	01563 529632
Lind, George K. BD MCIBS	1998	2017	(Stewarton: St. Columba's)	Endrig, 98 Loudoun Road, Newmilns KA16 9HQ / gklind@talktalk.net	01560 428732
Marshall, T. Edward BD	1987	2020	(Crosshouse)	20 Alloway Drive, Paisley PA2 7DS	
McAllister, Anne C. BSc DipEd CCS	2013	2016	(Ordained Local Minister)	39 Bowes Rigg, Stewarton, Kilmarnock KA3 5EN / AMcAllister@churchofscotland.org.uk	01560 483191
McCulloch, James D. BD MIOP MIP3 FSAScot	1996	2016	(Hurlford)	18 Edradour Place, Dunsmuir Park, Kilmarnock KA3 1US / mccullochmanse1@btinternet.com	01563 535833
MacLeod, Malcolm (Calum) BA BD	1979	2018	(Rutherglen: Old)	12 Main Road, Crookedholm, Kilmarnock KA3 6JT	01563 539739
Scott, Thomas T.	1968	1989	(Kilmarnock: St Marnock's)	6 North Hamilton Place, Kilmarnock KA1 2QN / tomtscott@btinternet.com	01563 531415
Shaw, Catherine A.M. MA	1998	2006	(Auxiliary Minister)	40 Merrygreen Place, Stewarton, Kilmarnock KA3 5EP / catherine.shaw@tesco.net	01560 483352

Urquhart, Barbara (Mrs) DCS	1986 2017	(Deacon)	9 Standalane, Kilmaurs, Kilmarnock KA3 2NB barbaraurquhart1@gmail.com	01563 538289
Wark, Alexander C. MA BD STM	1982 2017	(Mid Deeside)	43 Mure Avenue, Kilmarnock KA3 1TT alecwark@yahoo.co.uk	01563 559581
Welsh, Alex M. MA BD	1979	(Hospital Chaplain, NHS Ayrshire and Arran)	8 Greenside Avenue, Prestwick KA9 2HB alexandevelyn@hotmail.com	01292 475341

IRVINE and KILMARNOCK ADDRESSES

Irvine

Dreghorn and Springside	Townfoot x Station Brae
Fullarton	Marress Road x Church Street
Girdle Toll	Bryce Knox Court
Mure	West Road
Old	Kirkgate
Relief Bourtreehill	Crofthead, Bourtreehill
St Andrew's	Caldon Road x Oaklands Ave

Kilmarnock

Ayrshire Mission to the Deaf	10 Clark Street
Kay Park	London Road
New Laigh Kirk	John Dickie Street
Riccarton	Old Street
St Andrew's and St Marnock's	St Marnock Street
St John's Onthank	84 Wardneuk Street
St Kentigern's	Dunbar Drive
South	Whatriggs Road

(12) ARDROSSAN (F W)

Meets at Ardrossan and Saltcoats: Kirkgate, on the first Tuesday of February, March, May, September, October, November and December, and on the second Tuesday of June.

Clerk:	MRS JEAN C. Q. HUNTER BD		The Manse, Shiskine, Isle of Arran KA27 8EP ardrossan@churchofscotland.org.uk	01770 **860380** 07961 **299907**

Ardrossan: Park (W)
Vacant

Session Clerk: Moira Crocker (Mrs)			35 Ardneil Court, Ardrossan KA22 7NQ moirafcrocker@yahoo.co.uk	01294 **463711** 01294 468683

Ardrossan and Saltcoats: Kirkgate (F H W)
Vacant

Session Clerk: Vivien Bruce (Mrs)			10 Seafield Drive, Ardrossan KA22 8NU andrew_bruce2@sky.com	01294 **472001** 01294 605113

Beith (F H W)

Roderick I.T. MacDonald BD CertMin	1992	2005	beithchurch@btinternet.com 2 Glebe Court, Beith KA15 1ET RMacDonald@churchofscotland.org.uk	01505 **502686** 01505 503858
Fiona Blair DCS	1994	2015	9 Powgree Crescent, Beith KA15 1ES FBlair@churchofscotland.org.uk	07368 696550

Brodick (W) linked with Corrie linked with Lochranza and Pirnmill (W) linked with Shiskine (F H W)
brodickchurch@gmail.com;
info@lochranzachurch.org.uk; stmolios@gmail.com — **01770 870228**

R. Angus Adamson BD — 2006
Otterburn, Corriecravie, Isle of Arran KA27 8EP
RAdamson@churchofscotland.org.uk — 01770 870228

Corrie See Brodick

Cumbrae (F W) linked with Largs: St John's (F H W) Cumbrae: **01475 531198** St John's: **01475 674468**
Jonathan C. Fleming MA BD — 2012 2017
1 Newhaven Grove, Largs KA30 8NS
JFleming@churchofscotland.org.uk — 01475 329933

Dalry: St Margaret's (F W) — stmargaret@talktalk.net — **01294 832264**
David A. Albon BA MCS — 1991 2019
33 Templand Crescent, Dalry KA24 5ED
DAlbon@churchofscotland.org.uk — 01294 832747

Dalry: Trinity (F H W)
Martin Thomson BSc DipEd BD — 1988 2004
Trinity Manse, West Kilbride Road, Dalry KA24 5DX
MThomson@churchofscotland.org.uk — 01294 832363

Fairlie (F H W) linked with Largs: St Columba's (F W) — secretary@largscolumba.org — **01475 686212**
Graham McWilliams BSc BD DMin — 2005 2019
14 Fairlieburne Gardens, Fairlie, Largs KA29 0ER
GMcWilliams@churchofscotland.org.uk — 01475 568515

Kilbirnie: Auld Kirk (F H)
Vacant
49 Holmhead, Kilbirnie KA25 6BS — 01505 682342
Session Clerk: Archie Currie — archiecurrie@yahoo.co.uk — 01505 681474

Kilbirnie: St Columba's (H W) — **01505 685239**
Fiona C. Ross (Miss) BD DipMin — 1996 2004
Manse of St Columba's, Dipple Road, Kilbirnie KA25 7JU
FRoss@churchofscotland.org.uk — 01505 683342

Kilmory (F W) linked with Lamlash (W)
Lily F. H. McKinnon (Mrs) MA BD PGCE — 1993 2015
The Manse, Margnaheglish Road, Lamlash, Isle of Arran KA27 8LL
LMcKinnon@churchofscotland.org.uk — 01770 600074

Kilwinning: Abbey (W)
Vacant
Isobel Beck BD DCS   2014   2016   54 Dalry Road, Kilwinning KA13 7HE   **01294 552606**
16 Patrick Avenue, Stevenston KA20 4AW   01294 552606
IBeck@churchofscotland.org.uk   07919 193425

Session Clerk: Fiona Silver (Mrs)   fionamfrew@aol.com   01294 556297

Kilwinning: Mansefield Trinity (F W)
Hilary J. Beresford BD   2000   2018   Mansefield Trinity Church, West Doura Way, Kilwinning KA13 6DY   **01294 550746**
HBeresford@churchofscotland.org.uk   01294 550746

Lamlash See Kilmory

Largs: Clark Memorial (H W)
T. David Watson BSc BD   1988   2014   31 Douglas Street, Largs KA30 8PT   **01475 675186**
DWatson@churchofscotland.org.uk   01475 672370

Largs: St Columba's See Fairlie
Largs: St John's See Cumbrae
Lochranza and Pirnmill See Brodick

Saltcoats: North (W)
Vacant
Session Clerk: Rosann McLean (Mrs)   25 Longfield Avenue, Saltcoats KA21 6DR   **01294 464679**
01294 604923
01294 467106

Saltcoats: St Cuthbert's (H W)
Sarah E.C. Nicol (Mrs) BSc BD MTh   1985   2018   10 Kennedy Road, Saltcoats KA21 5SF   01294 696030
SNicol@churchofscotland.org.uk

Shiskine See Brodick

Stevenston: Ardeer (F W) linked with Stevenston: Livingstone (F H W)
David A. Sutherland BD   2001   2017   27 Cuninghame Drive, Stevenston KA20 4AB   01294 608993
DSutherland@churchofscotland.org.uk

Stevenston: High (F H W)
M. Scott Cameron MA BD   2002   9 Schoolwell Street, Stevenston KA20 3DL   01294 463356
Scott.Cameron@churchofscotland.org.uk

Stevenston: Livingstone See Stevenston: Ardeer

West Kilbride (F T H W)
James J. McNay MA BD   2008   office@westkilbrideparishchurch.org.uk   **01294 829902**
The Manse, Goldenberry Avenue, West Kilbride KA23 9LJ   01294 823186
JMcNay@churchofscotland.org.uk

Whiting Bay and Kildonan
Elizabeth R.L. Watson (Miss) BA BD   1981 1982   The Manse, Whiting Bay, Brodick, Isle of Arran KA27 8RE   01770 700289
EWatson@churchofscotland.org.uk

C. Demitted

Black, Andrew R. BD	1987 2018	(Irvine: Relief Bourtreehill)	4 Nursery Wynd, Kilwinning KA13 6ER 01294 673090
			andrewblack@tiscali.co.uk
Cruickshank, Norman BA BD	1983 2006	(West Kilbride: Overton)	24D Faulds Wynd, Seamill, West Kilbride KA23 9FA 01294 822239
Davidson, Amelia (Mrs) BD	2004 2011	(Coatbridge: Calder)	11 St Mary's Place, Saltcoats KA21 5NY
Drysdale, James H. LTh	1987 2006	(Blackbraes and Shieldhill)	10 John Clark Street, Largs KA30 9AH 01475 674870
Falconer, Alan D. MA BD DLitt DD	1972 2011	(Aberdeen: St Machar's Cathedral)	18 North Crescent Road, Ardrossan KA22 8NA 07491 484800
			alanfalconer@gmx.com
Finlay, William P. MA BD	1969 2000	(Glasgow: Townhead Blochairn)	High Corrie, Brodick, Isle of Arran KA27 8JB 01770 810689
Ford, Alan A. BD	1977 2013	(Glasgow: Springburn)	14 Corsankell Wynd, Saltcoats KA21 6HY 01294 465740
			alan.andy@btinternet.com
Hebenton, David J. MA BD	1958 2002	(Ayton and Burnmouth with Grantshouse and Houndwood and Reston)	22B Faulds Wynd, Seamill, West Kilbride KA23 9FA 01294 829228
Howie, Marion L.K. (Mrs) MA ARCS	1992 2016	(Auxiliary Minister)	51 High Road, Stevenston KA20 3DY 01294 466571
			MHowie@churchofscotland.org.uk
McCallum, Alexander D. BD	1987 2005	(Saltcoats: New Trinity)	59 Woodcroft Avenue, Largs KA30 9EW 01475 670133
			sandyandjose@madasafish.com
Mackay, Marjory H. (Mrs) BD DipEd CCE	1998 2008	(Cumbrae)	4 Golf Road, Millport, Isle of Cumbrae KA28 0HB 01475 530388
			marjory.mackay@gmail.com
MacKinnon, Ronald M. DCS	1996 2012	(Deacon)	32 Strathclyde House, Shore Road, Skelmorlie PA17 5AN 01475 521333 / 07594 427960
			ronnie@ronniemac.plus.com
MacLeod, Ian LTh BA MTh PhD	1969 2006	(Brodick with Corrie)	Cromla Cottage, Corrie, Isle of Arran KA27 8JB 01770 810237
			i.macleod829@btinternet.com
Mitchell, D. Ross BA BD	1972 2007	(West Kilbride: St Andrew's)	11 Dunbar Gardens, Saltcoats KA21 6GJ 01294 474375
			ross.mitchell@virgin.net
Noble, Alexander B. MA BD ThM	1982 2020	(Saltcoats: North)	93 Snipe Street, Ellon AB41 9FW
Paterson, John H. BD	1977 2000	(Kirkintilloch: St David's Memorial Park)	Creag Bhan, Golf Course Road, Whiting Bay, Isle of Arran KA27 8QT 01770 700569
Roy, Iain M. MA BD	1960 1997	(Stevenston: Livingstone)	2 The Fieldings, Dunlop, Kilmarnock KA3 4AU 01560 483072
Taylor, Andrew S. BTh FPhS	1959 1992	(Greenock: The Union)	9 Raillies Avenue, Largs KA30 8QY 01475 674709
			andrew.taylor_123@btinternet.com

| Travers, Robert BA BD | 1993 | 2015 | (Irvine: Old) | 74 Caledonian Road, Stevenson KA20 3LF roberttravers@live.co.uk | 01294 279265 |
| Ward, Alan H. MA BD | 1978 | 2015 | (Interim Minister) | 47 Meadowfoot Road, West Kilbride KA23 9BU | 01475 822244 07709 906130 |

(13) LANARK (W)

Meets on the first Tuesday of February, March, May, September, October, November and December; and on the third Tuesday of June.

Presbytery Office:				Greyfriars Parish Church, Bloomgate, Lanark ML11 9ET administrator@lanarkpresbytery.org	**01555 437050**
Clerk:	**REV. BRYAN KERR BA BD**			Greyfriars Manse, 3 Bellefield Way, Lanark ML11 7NW lanark@churchofscotland.org.uk	**01555 437050** 01555 663363
Depute Clerk:	**REV. GEORGE C. SHAND MA BD**			16 Abington Road, Symington, Biggar ML12 6JX George.Shand@churchofscotland.org.uk	**01899 309400**

Biggar (F H W) linked with Black Mount

| Mike D. Fucella BD MTh | 1997 | 2013 | **biggarkirk09@gmail.com** 'Candlemas', 6C Leafield Road, Biggar ML12 6AY MFucella@churchofscotland.org.uk | **01889 229291** 01899 229291 |

Black Mount See Biggar

Cairngryffe (F W) linked with Libberton and Quothquan (F H W) linked with Symington (F W) (The Tinto Parishes)

| George C. Shand MA BD | 1981 | 2014 | **contactus@symingtonkirk.com** 16 Abington Road, Symington, Biggar ML12 6JX George.Shand@churchofscotland.org.uk | **01899 309400** |

Carluke: Kirkton (H W)

| Iain D. Cunningham MA BD | 1979 | 1987 | **kirktonchurch@btconnect.com** 9 Station Road, Carluke ML8 5AA ICunningham@churchofscotland.org.uk | **01555 750778** 01555 771262 |

Carluke: St Andrew's (H W)

| Helen E. Jamieson (Mrs) BD DipEd | 1989 | | **standrewscarluke@btinternet.com** 120 Clyde Street, Carluke ML8 5BG HJamieson@churchofscotland.org.uk | **01555 771218** |

Carluke: St John's (F H W)
Elijah O. Obinna BA MTh PhD
2002 2016
18 Old Bridgend, Carluke ML8 4HN
EObinna@churchofscotland.org.uk
01555 751730
01555 752389

Carnwath (H) linked with Carstairs (W)
Vacant
Session Clerk, Carnwath: Betty McLeod
Session Clerk, Carstairs: Ruth Campbell
11 Range View, Cleghorn, Carstairs, Lanark ML11 8TF
williemcleod913@btinternet.com
ruth25c@aol.com
01555 840736
01555 870441

Carstairs See Carnwath

Coalburn and Lesmahagow (F H W)
Vacant
Session Clerk: Douglas Walsh
9 Elm Bank, Lesmahagow, Lanark ML11 0EA
lopc@btinternet.com
dougandwilma1@btinternet.com
01555 892425
01555 892848

New charge formed by the union of Coalburn and Lesmahagow: Old and Lesmahagow: Abbeygreen

Crossford (H) linked with Kirkfieldbank
Steven Reid BAcc CA BD
1989 1997
74 Lanark Road, Crossford, Carluke ML8 5RE
SReid@churchofscotland.org.uk
01555 860415

Douglas Valley (F W)
Guardianship of the Presbytery
Session Clerk: Andy Robinson
office.tdvc@yahoo.co.uk
The Manse, Douglas, Lanark ML11 0RB
gavdrewandjoe@aol.com
01555 850000
01555 851246

Forth: St Paul's (F H W)
Elspeth J. MacLean (Mrs) BVMS BD
2011 2016
22 Lea Rig, Forth, Lanark ML11 8EA
EMacLean@churchofscotland.org.uk
01555 728837

Kirkfieldbank See Crossford

Kirkmuirhill (F H W)
Andrew D. Rooney BSc BD
2019
kirkmuirhillchurch@btinternet.com
The Manse, 82 Vere Road, Kirkmuirhill, Lanark ML11 9RP
ARooney@churchofscotland.org.uk
01555 895593
01555 892409

Lanark: Greyfriars (F H T W)
Bryan Kerr BA BD
2002 2007
office@lanarkgreyfriars.com
Greyfriars Manse, 3 Bellefield Way, Lanark ML11 7NW
BKerr@churchofscotland.org.uk
01555 437050
01555 663363

Lanark: St Nicholas' (F H W)
Louise E. Mackay BSc BD — 2017 — lanarkstnicholas@outlook.com — **01555 666220**
2 Kairnhill Court, Lanark ML11 9HU — 01555 661936

Law (F W)
Paul G.R. Grant BD MTh — 2003 2018 — info@lawparishchurch.org
3 Shawgill Court, Law, Carluke ML8 5SJ — 01698 373180
PGrant@churchofscotland.org.uk

Libberton and Quothquan See Cairngryffe
Symington See Cairngryffe

Upper Clyde (F W)
Nikki M. Macdonald BD MTh PhD — 2014 — 31 Carlisle Road, Crawford, Biggar ML12 6TP — 01864 502139
NMacdonald@churchofscotland.org.uk

B. In other appointments
Clelland, Elizabeth B. (Mrs) BD — 2002 2012 — Resident Chaplain, Divine Healing Fellowship (Scotland) — Brachead House Christian Healing and Retreat Centre, Braidwood Road, Crossford, Carluke ML8 5NQ — 01555 860716
liz_clelland@yahoo.co.uk

C. Demitted

Buchan, William BD DipTheol	1987	2001	(Kilwinning: Abbey)	9 Leafield Road, Biggar ML12 6AY billbuchan3@btinternet.com	01899 229253
Cowell, Susan G. (Miss) BA BD	1986	1998	(Budapest)	3 Gavel Lane, Regency Gardens, Lanark ML11 9FB	01555 665509
Cutler, James S.H. BD CEng MIStructE	1986	2011	(Black Mount with Cutler with Libberton and Quothquan)	12 Kittlegairy Place, Peebles EH45 9LW revjimc@outlook.com	01721 723950
Findlay, Henry J.W. MA BD	1965	2005	(Wishaw: St Mark's)	2 Alba Gardens, Carluke ML8 5US henryfindlay@btinternet.com	01555 759995
Houston, Graham R. BSc BD MTh PhD	1978	2011	(Cairngryffe with Symington)	3 Alder Lane, Beechtrees, Lanark ML11 9FT gandih6156@btinternet.com	01555 678004
Young, David A.	1972	2003	(Kirkmuirhill)	110 Carlisle Road, Blackwood, Lanark ML11 9RT youngdavid@aol.com	01555 893357

(14) CLYDE (W)

New presbytery formed by the union of the Presbytery of Dumbarton and the Presbytery of Greenock and Paisley on 1 September 2020
Meets on 1 September 2020 at Inchinnan and thereafter as decided.

Clerk to be appointed. Pro tem: REV. ALISTAIR N. SHAW MA BD MTh PhD   The Presbytery Office (see below)
clyde@churchofscotland.org.uk

Presbytery Office: 'Homelea', Faith Avenue, Quarrier's Village, Bridge of Weir   Tel **01505 615033**
PA11 3SX   Fax **01505 615088**

1 Arrochar (F W) linked with Luss (F W)
Interim Moderator: Grace Rogerson (Dr)
ggrogerson@btinternet.com

2 Baldernock (H) linked with Milngavie: St Paul's (F H W)   1982   1988
Fergus C. Buchanan MA BD MTh
stpauls@btconnect.com
8 Buchanan Street, Milngavie, Glasgow   G62 8DD   **0141 956 4405**
Fergus.Buchanan@churchofscotland.org.uk   0141 956 1043

3 Barrhead: Bourock (F H W)   2006
Pamela Gordon BD
14 Maxton Avenue, Barrhead, Glasgow   G78 1DY   **0141 881 9813**
PGordon@churchofscotland.org.uk   0141 881 8736

4 Barrhead: St Andrew's (F H W)
Vacant
Interim Moderator: Ann C. McCool
10 Arthurlie Avenue, Barrhead, Glasgow   G78 2BU   **0141 881 8442**
AMcCool@churchofscotland.org.uk   0141 881 3457
                                                      01505 320006

5 Bearsden: Baljaffray (F H W)   2008
Ian K. McEwan BSc PhD BD FRSE
5 Fintry Gardens, Bearsden, Glasgow   G61 4RJ   **0141 942 5304**
IMcEwan@churchofscotland.org.uk   0141 942 0366

6 Bearsden: Cross (F H W)   2006   2013
Graeme R. Wilson MCIBS BD ThM DMin
secretary@bearsdencross.org
61 Drymen Road, Bearsden, Glasgow   G61 2SU   **0141 942 0507**
GWilson@churchofscotland.org.uk   0141 942 0507

7 Bearsden: Killermont (F H W)   2003
Alan J. Hamilton LLB BD PhD
8 Clathic Avenue, Bearsden, Glasgow   G61 2HF
AHamilton@churchofscotland.org.uk   0141 942 0021

8 Bearsden: New Kilpatrick (F H W)
Roderick G. Hamilton MA BD   1992   2011
mail@nkchurch.org.uk
51 Manse Road, Bearsden, Glasgow   G61 3PN
Roddy.Hamilton@churchofscotland.org.uk
0141 942 8827
0141 942 0035

9 Bearsden: Westerton Fairlie Memorial (H W)
Christine M. Goldie LLB BD MTh DMin   1984   2008
westertonchurch@talktalk.net
3 Canniesburn Road, Bearsden, Glasgow   G61 1PW
CGoldie@churchofscotland.org.uk
0141 942 6960
0141 942 2672

10 Bonhill (H W) linked with Renton: Trinity (H)
Barbara A. O'Donnell BD PGSE   2007   2016
bonhillchurchoffice@gmail.com
Ashbank, 258 Main Street, Alexandria   G83 0NU
BODonnell@churchofscotland.org.uk
Bonhill: 01389 756516
01389 752356
07889 251912

11 Bishopton (F H W)
Yvonne Smith BSc BD   2017
office@bishoptonkirk.org.uk
The Manse, Newton Road, Bishopton   PA7 5JP
YSmith@churchofscotland.org.uk
01505 862583
01505 862161

12 Bridge of Weir: Freeland (F H W)
Kenneth N. Gray BA BD   1988
15 Lawmarnock Crescent, Bridge of Weir PA11 3AS
aandkgray@btinternet.com
01505 612610
01505 690918

13 Bridge of Weir: St Machar's Ranfurly (F W)
Hanneke A.S. Marshall (Mrs) MTh MA   2017
PGCE CertMin
9 St Andrew's Drive, Bridge of Weir PA11 3SH
Hanneke.Marshall@churchofscotland.org.uk
01505 612975
01505 612975

14 Cardross (F H W)
Margaret McArthur BD DipMin   1995   2015
16 Bainfield Road, Cardross G82 5IQ
MMcArthur@churchofscotland.org.uk
01389 841322
01389 849329
07799 556367

15 Clydebank: Faifley (F W)
Gregor McIntyre BSc BD   1991
Kirklea, Cochno Road, Hardgate, Clydebank   G81 6PT
Gregor.McIntyre@churchofscotland.org.uk
01389 876836

16 Clydebank: Kilbowie St Andrew's (F) linked with Clydebank: Radnor Park (H)
Vacant
Session Clerk, Kilbowie St Andrew's: Derek W. Smith
11 Tiree Gardens, Old Kilpatrick, Glasgow   G60 5AT
ann.smith@live.co.uk
01389 875599
0141 952 8425
Session Clerk, Radnor Park: Mabel Baillie (Mrs)
r.baillie1@ntlworld.com
07703 185423
0141 579 5957

17 Clydebank: Radnor Park   See Clydebank: Kilbowie St Andrew's

18 Clydebank: Waterfront (F W) linked with Dalmuir: Barclay (F W)   **Dalmuir Barclay: 0141 941 3988**
Ruth H.B. Morrison MA BD PhD   2009   2014   16 Parkhall Road, Dalmuir, Clydebank G81 3RJ   0141 941 3317
RMorrison@churchofscotland.org.uk

19 Craigrownie (F W) linked with Garelochhead (F W) linked with Rosneath: St Modan's (F H W)   **Garelochhead: 01436 810589**
Christine M. Murdoch BD   1999   2015   The Manse, Argyll Road, Kilcreggan, Helensburgh G84 0JW   01436 842274
CMurdoch@churchofscotland.org.uk   07973 331890
Ian J. Millar BA   2020   Lochfada House, Succoth, Arrochar G83 7AL   01301 702133
(Ordained Local Minister)   IMillar@churchofscotland.org.uk

20 Dalmuir: Barclay See Clydebank: Waterfront

21 Dumbarton: Riverside (F H W) linked with Dumbarton: St Andrew's (H W) linked with Dumbarton: West Kirk (F H W)   **Riverside: 01389 742551**
office@dumbartonriverside.org.uk
administration@standrewsdumbarton.co.uk
C. Ian W. Johnson MA BD   1997   2014   18 Castle Road, Dumbarton G82 1JF   01389 726685
CJohnson@churchofscotland.org.uk

22 Dumbarton: St Andrew's See Dumbarton: Riverside
23 Dumbarton: West Kirk See Dumbarton: Riverside

24 Duntocher: Trinity (F H L T W)   info@duntochertrinitychurch.co.uk
Vacant   The Manse, Roman Road, Duntocher, Clydebank G81 6BT   01389 380038
Session Clerk: Colin G. Dow   colin.g.dow@ntlworld.com

25 Elderslie Kirk (F H W)   **01505 323348**
G. Gray Fletcher BSc BD   1989   2019   282 Main Road, Elderslie, Johnstone PA5 9EF   01505 321767
GFletcher@churchofscotland.org.uk

26 Erskine (F T W)   **0141 812 4620**
David Nicolson BA   2019   The Manse, 7 Leven Place, Linburn, Erskine PA8 6AS   0141 570 8103
DNicolson@churchofscotland.org.uk

27 Garelochhead See Craigrownie

28 Gourock: Old Gourock and Ashton (H W)
David W.G. Burt BD DipMin MTh — 1989   2014
secretary@ogachurch.org.uk
331 Eldon Street, Greenock PA16 7QN
DBurt@churchofscotland.org.uk
01475 633914

29 Gourock: St John's (F H T W)
Teri C. Peterson MDiv BMus — 2006   2018
office@stjohns-gourock.org.uk
6 Barrhill Road, Greenrock PA19 1JX
TPeterson@churchofscotland.org.uk
01475 632143

30 Greenock: East End (F) linked with Greenock: Mount Kirk (F W)
Francis E. Murphy BEng DipDSE BD — 2006
info@themountkirk.org.uk
76 Finnart Street, Greenock PA16 8HJ
FMurphy@churchofscotland.org.uk
01475 722338

31 Greenock: Lyle Kirk (F T W)
Vacant
Interim Moderator: David W.G. Burt
office@lylekirk.org
39 Fox Street, Greenock PA16 8PD
DBurt@churchofscotland.org.uk
01475 727694
01475 717229
01475 633914

32 Greenock: Mount Kirk See Greenock: East End

33 Greenock: St Margaret's (F W)
Guardianship of the Presbytery
Interim Moderator: Teri C. Peterson
TPeterson@churchofscotland.org.uk
01475 781953

34 Greenock: St Ninian's
Vacant
Eileen Manson (Mrs) DipCE — 1994   2017
(Auxiliary Minister)
Interim Moderator: Karen Harbison
1 Cambridge Avenue, Gourock PA19 1XT
EManson@churchofscotland.org.uk
KHarbison@churchofscotland.org.uk
01475 632401
01475 721048

35 Greenock: Wellpark Mid Kirk (F)
Alan K. Sorensen DL BD MTh — 1983   2000
DipMin FSAScot
101 Brisbane Street, Greenock PA16 8PA
ASorensen@churchofscotland.org.uk
01475 721741

36 Greenock: Westburn (F W)
Karen E. Harbison (Mrs) MA BD — 1991   2014
50 Ardgowan Street, Greenock PA16 8EP
KHarbison@churchofscotland.org.uk
01475 720257
01475 721048

37 Helensburgh (F W) linked with Rhu and Shandon (F W)

David T. Young BA BD MTh   2007   2015
35 East Argyle Street, Helensburgh G84 8UP
DYoung@churchofscotland.org.uk

Tina Kemp MA   2005   2017
(Auxiliary Minister)
12 Oaktree Gardens, Dumbarton G82 1EU
TKemp@churchofscotland.org.uk

Helensburgh: 01436 676880
Rhu and Shandon: 01436 820605
01436 673365
07508 628133
01389 730477
hello@helensburghcos.org

38 Houston and Killellan (F H W)

Gary D. Noonan BA   2018
The Manse of Houston, Main Street, Houston, Johnstone PA6 7EL
GNoonan@churchofscotland.org.uk

01505 612569

39 Howwood (W) linked with Johnstone: St Paul's (F H W)

Alistair N. Shaw MA BD MTh PhD   1982   2003
9 Stanley Drive, Brookfield, Johnstone PA5 8UF
Alistair.Shaw@churchofscotland.org.uk

St Paul's: 01505 321632
01505 320060

40 Inchinnan (F H W)

Ann Knox BD Cert.Health.Chap   2017
51 Old Greenock Road, Inchinnan, Renfrew PA4 9PH
AKnox@churchofscotland.org.uk

0141 812 1263
0141 389 1724
07534 900065

41 Inverkip (H W) linked with Skelmorlie and Wemyss Bay (W)

Archibald Speirs BD   1995   2013
admin@inverkip.org.uk
3a Montgomery Terrace, Skelmorlie PA17 5DT
ASpeirs@churchofscotland.org.uk

01475 529320

42 Johnstone: High (F H W)

Ann C. McCool (Mrs) BD DSD IPA ALCM 1989   2001
76 North Road, Johnstone PA5 8NF
AMcCool@churchofscotland.org.uk

01505 336303
01505 320006

43 Johnstone: St Andrew's Trinity

Charles M. Cameron BA BD PhD   1980   2013
45 Woodlands Crescent, Johnstone PA5 0AZ
Charles.Cameron@churchofscotland.org.uk

01505 337827
01505 672908

44 Johnstone: St Paul's See Howwood

45 Kilbarchan (F T W)

Stephen J. Smith BSc BD   1993   2015
The Manse, Church Street, Kilbarchan, Johnstone PA10 2JQ
SSmith@churchofscotland.org.uk

01505 702621

46 Kilmacolm: Old (F H W)
Vacant
Interim Moderator: Gary D. Noonan

The Old Kirk Manse, Glencairn Road, Kilmacolm PA13 4NJ   **01505 873911**
GNoonan@churchofscotland.org.uk   01505 873174
                                                           01505 612569

47 Kilmacolm: St Columba (F H)
Vacant
Interim Moderator: William R. Armstrong

6 Churchill Road, Kilmacolm PA13 4LH   01505 873271
w.armstrong@btinternet.com   01475 520891

48 Kilmaronock Gartocharn linked with Lomond (W)
Vacant
Session Clerk, Kilmaronock Gartocharn: Mark Smith   kilgartoch@gmail.com   01389 830785
                                                                                                      07796 938318
Session Clerks, Lomond: Linda Cust (Miss)   lindaccust@btinternet.com   01389 754502
Robert M. Kinloch   rkinloch@blueyonder.co.uk   07760 276505
                  Lomond is a new congregation formed by the union of Alexandria and Jamestown

49 Langbank (F T W)   **info@langbankparishchurch.co.uk**
Guardianship of the Presbytery
Elizabeth Geddes (Mrs)   2013   2019   9 Shillingworth Place, Bridge of Weir PA11 3DY   01505 612639
   (Ordained Local Minister)   EGeddes@churchofscotland.org.uk

50 Linwood (F H)
Eileen M. Ross (Mrs) BD MTh   2005   2008   1 John Neilson Avenue, Paisley PA1 2SX   **01505 328802**
                                                           ERoss@churchofscotland.org.uk   0141 887 2801

51 Lomond See Kilmaronock Gartocharn
52 Luss See Arrochar

53 Milngavie: Cairns (H W)   **office@cairnschurch.org.uk**
Andrew Frater BA BD MTh   1987   1994   4 Cairns Drive, Milngavie, Glasgow G62 8AJ   **0141 956 4868**
                                                          AFrater@churchofscotland.org.uk   0141 956 1717

54 Milngavie: St Luke's (W)
Ramsay B. Shields BA BD   1990   1997   70 Hunter Road, Milngavie, Glasgow G62 7BY   **0141 956 4226**
                                                          RShields@churchofscotland.org.uk   Tel 0141 577 9171
                                                                                                    Fax 0141 577 9181

55 Milngavie: St Paul's See Baldernock

No.	Charge / Minister	Year(s)	Address / Email	Telephone
56	**Neilston (F W)** Vacant Interim Moderator: Maureen Leitch		The Manse, Neilston Road, Neilston, Glasgow G78 3NP maureen.leitch@ntl.world	0141 881 9445 0141 258 0805 0141 580 2927
57	**Old Kilpatrick Bowling** Scott McCrum BD	2015 2018	The Manse, Old Kilpatrick, Glasgow G60 5JQ SMcCrum@churchofscotland.org.uk	08005 668242
58	**Paisley: Abbey (F H W)** Vacant Interim Moderator: E. Lorna Hood		info@paisleyabbey.org.uk 15 Main Road, Castlehead, Paisley PA2 6AJ revlornahood@gmail.com	0141 889 7654; Fax 0141 887 3929 0141 889 3587 0141 384 9516
59	**Paisley: Glenburn (F T W)** Vacant Interim Moderator: Maureen Leitch		10 Hawick Avenue, Paisley PA2 9LD maureen.leitch@ntl.world	0141 884 2602 0141 884 4903 0141 580 2927
60	**Paisley: Martyrs' Sandyford** Vacant Interim Moderator: Philip Wallace		27 Acer Crescent, Paisley PA2 9LR PWallace@churchofscotland.org.uk	0141 889 6603 0141 884 7400 0141 570 3502
61	**Paisley: Oakshaw Trinity (F H W)** Gordon B. Armstrong BD FIAB BRC CertCS	1998 2012	The Manse, 52 Balgonie Drive, Paisley PA2 9LP GArmstrong@churchofscotland.org.uk	0141 887 4647; Fax 0141 848 5139 0141 587 3124

Oakshaw Trinity is a Local Ecumenical Partnership with the United Reformed Church

No.	Charge / Minister	Year(s)	Address / Email	Telephone
62	**Paisley: St Columba Foxbar (H)** Vacant Interim Moderator: Gordon Armstrong		13 Corsebar Drive, Paisley PA2 9QD GArmstrong@churchofscotland.org.uk	01505 812377 0141 884 5826 0141 587 3124
63	**Paisley: St Mark's Oldhall (F H L W)** A. Sonia Blakesley MB ChB BD	2020	office@stmarksoldhall.org.uk 36 Newtyle Road, Paisley PA1 3JX SBlakesley@churchofscotland.org.uk	0141 882 2755 0141 889 4279
64	**Paisley: Sherwood Greenlaw (F H W)** John Murning BD	1988 2014	5 Greenlaw Drive, Paisley PA1 3RX JMurning@churchofscotland.org.uk	0141 889 7060 0141 316 2678

65 Paisley: South (F H W)
Vacant
Interim Moderator: Kenneth N. Gray   aandkgray@btinternet.com   **0141 561 7139**
01505 690918

New charge formed by the union of Paisley: Lylesland and Paisley: St Luke's

66 Paisley: Stow Brae Kirk (F W)
Vacant   stowbraekirk@gmail.com   **0141 889 4335**
Mhairi M. Breingan   2011   2019   290 Glasgow Road, Paisley PA1 3DP   0141 576 1710
(Ordained Local Minister)   6 Park Road, Inchinnan, Renfrew PA4 4QJ   0141 812 1425
mhairi.b@btinternet.com

67 Paisley: Wallneuk North (F W)
Peter G. Gill MA BA   2008   wallneuknorthchurch@gmail.com   **0141 889 9265**
5 Glenville Crescent, Paisley PA2 8TW   0141 884 4429
PGill@churchofscotland.org.uk

68 Port Glasgow: Hamilton Bardrainney (F)
Guardianship of the Presbytery   80 Bardrainney Avenue, Port Glasgow PA14 6HD   01475 701213
Interim Moderator: Francis Murphy   FMurphy@churchofscotland.org.uk   01475 722338

69 Port Glasgow: New (F H W)
William A. Boyle BA   2020   St Andrew's Manse, Barr's Brae, Port Glasgow PA14 5QA   01475 741486
WBoyle@churchofscotland.org.uk

New charge formed by the union of Port Glasgow: St Andrew's and Port Glasgow: St Martin's

70 Renfrew: North (F T W)
Philip D. Wallace BSc BTh DTS   1998   2018   contact@renfrewnorth.org.uk   **0141 530 1308**
1 Alexandra Drive, Renfrew PA4 8UB   0141 570 3502
PWallace@churchofscotland.org.uk

71 Renfrew: Trinity (F H W)
Stuart C. Steell BD CertMin   1992   2015   25 Paisley Road, Renfrew PA4 8JH   **0141 885 2129**
SSteell@churchofscotland.org.uk   0141 387 2464

72 Renton: Trinity See Bonhill
73 Rhu and Shandon See Helensburgh
74 Roseneath: St Modan's See Craigrownie
75 Skelmorlie and Wemyss Bay See Inverkip

B. In other appointments

Dalton, Mark BD DipMin RN	2002		Chaplain: Royal Navy	Royal Naval Air Station Culdrose, Helston, Cornwall TR12 7RH mark.dalton242@mod.gov.uk	07717 503059
Davidson, Stuart BD	2008	2017	Pioneer Minister, Paisley North End	25H Cross Road, Paisley PA2 9QJ SDavidson@churchofscotland.org.uk	
Nutter, Margaret A.E. BA BD MFPh	2014	2019	Ordained Local Minister: Presbytery-wide	Kilmorich, 14 Balloch Road, Balloch, Alexandria G83 8SR MNutter@churchofscotland.org.uk	01389 754505
Stevenson, Stuart	2011		Ordained Local Minister	143 Springfield Park, Johnstone PA5 8JT SStevenson@churchofscotland.org.uk	0141 886 2131

C. Demitted

Name			(Charge)	Address / Email	Tel
Armstrong, William R. BD	1979	2008	(Skelmorlie and Wemyss Bay)	25A The Lane, Skelmorlie PA17 5AR w.armstrong@btinternet.com	01475 520891
Bell, Ian W. LTh	1990	2011	(Erskine)	40 Brueacre Drive, Wemyss Bay PA18 6HA revianbell@gmail.com	01475 529312
Bell, May (Mrs) LTh	1998	2012	(Johnstone: St Andrew's Trinity)	40 Brueacre Drive, Wemyss Bay PA18 6HA revmaybell22@gmail.com	01475 529312
Birss, Alan D. MA BD	1979	2020	(Paisley: Abbey)	36 Marquis Drive, Aboyne AB34 5FD alan.birss@btinternet.com	07411 088786
Black, Janette M.K. (Mrs) BD	1993	2006	(Assistant: Paisley: Oakshaw Trinity)	5 Craigiehall Avenue, Erskine PA8 7DB	0141 812 0794
Booth, Frederick M. LTh	1970	2005	(Helensburgh: St Columba)	Achnashie Coach House, Clynder, Helensburgh G84 0QD boothef@btinternet.com	01436 831858
Cameron, Ann J. (Mrs) CertCS	2005	2019	(Auxiliary Minister)	Water's Edge, Ferry Road, Rosneath, Helensburgh G84 0RS ACameron@churchofscotland.org.uk	01436 831800
Campbell, Donald BD	1998	2016	(Houston and Killellan)	15 Garshake Road, Dumbarton G82 3LH	01389 739353
Christie, John C. BSc BD CBiol MRSB	1990	2012	(Interim Minister)	10 Cumberland Avenue, Helensburgh G84 8QG JChristie@churchofscotland.org.uk	01436 674078 07711 336392
Clark, David W. MA BD	1975	2014	(Helensburgh: St Andrew's Kirk with Rhu and Shandon)	3 Ritchie Avenue, Cardross, Dumbarton G82 5LL clarkdw@talktalk.net	01389 849319
Coull, Morris C. BD	1974	2018	(Greenock St Margaret's)	14 Kelvin Gardens, Largs KA30 8SY	01475 338674
Currie, Ian S. MBE BD	1975	2010	(The United Church of Bute)	26 Old Bridge of Weir, Houston PA6 7EB ianscurrie@tiscali.co.uk	07764 254300
Easton, Lilly C. (Mrs)	1999	2012	(Renfrew: Old)	Flat 0/2, 90 Beith Street, Glasgow G11 6DG revlillyeaston@hotmail.co.uk	0141 586 7628
Fraser, Ian C. BA BD	1982	2008	(Glasgow: St Luke's and St Andrew's)	62 Kingston Avenue, Neilston, Glasgow G78 3JG ianandlindafraser@gmail.com	0141 563 6794
Gray, Greta (Miss) DCS	1992	2014	(Deacon)	67 Crags Avenue, Paisley PA3 6SG greta.gray@ntlworld.com	0141 884 6178
Hamilton, David G. MA BD	1971	2004	(Braes of Rannoch with Foss and Rannoch)	79 Finlay Rise, Milngavie, Glasgow G62 6QL davidhamilton40@googlemail.com	0141 956 4202
Harris, John W.F. MA	1967	2012	(Bearsden: Cross)	68 Mitre Road, Glasgow G14 9LL jwfh@sky.com	0141 321 1061

Hood, E. Lorna OBE MA BD DD	1978	2016	(Renfrew: North)	4 Thornly Park Drive, Paisley PA2 7RR / revlornahood@gmail.com	0141 384 9516
Houston, Elizabeth W. MA BD DipEd	1985	2018	(Alexandria)	Croftengea, 25 Honeysuckle Lane, Jamestown, Alexandria G83 8PL / Cleric2@hotmail.com	01389 721165
Kay, David BA BD MTh	1974	2008	(Paisley: Sandyford: Thread Street)	36 Donaldswood Park, Paisley PA2 8RS / david.kay500@o2.co.uk	0141 884 2080
Lees, Andrew P. BD	1984	2017	(Baldernock)	58 Lindores Drive, Stepps G33 6PD / andrew.lees@yahoo.co.uk	0141 389 5840
Leitch, Maureen (Mrs) BA BD	1995	2011	(Barrhead: Bourock)	Rockfield, 92 Paisley Road, Barrhead G78 1NW / maureen.leitch@ntlworld.com	0141 580 2927
MacColl, James C. BSc BD	1966	2002	(Johnstone: St Andrew's Trinity)	20 Dunrobin Avenue, Johnstone PA5 9NW / hamishmaccoll@gmail.com	01505 227439
Macdonald, Alexander MA BD	1966	2006	(Neilston)	35 Lochore Avenue, Paisley PA3 4BY / alexsmacdonald42@aol.com	0141 889 0066
McFarlane, Robert G. BD	2001	2018	(Paisley St Mark's Oldhall)	990 Crookston Road, Glasgow G53 7DY / jamcintyre@hotmail.com	0141 942 5143
McIntyre, J. Ainslie MA BD	1963	1984	(University of Glasgow)	60 Bonnaughton Road, Bearsden, Glasgow G61 4DB	07826 013266
Mayne, Kenneth A.L. BA MSc CertEd	1976	2018	(Paisley Martyrs' Sandyford)	300 Glasgow Road, Paisley PA1 3DP	
Miller, Ian H. BA BD	1975	2012	(Bonhill)	Derand, Queen Street, Alexandria G83 0AS / revianmiller@btinternet.com	01389 753039
Moore, Norma MA BD	1995	2017	(Jamestown)	25 Miller Street, Dumbarton G82 2JA / norma-moore@sky.com	01475 723235
Nicol, Joyce M. (Mrs) BA DCS	1974	2006	(Deacon)	93 Brisbane Street, Greenock PA16 8NY / joycenicol@hotmail.co.uk	07957 642709
Ramsden, Iain R. MStJ BTh	1999	2013	(Killearnan with Knockbain)	Flat 1/1, 15 Cardon Square, Renfrew PA4 8BY / s4rev@sky.com	07795 972560
Robertson, Ishbel A. R. MA BD	2013	2018	(Ordained Local Minister)	Oakdene, 81 Bonhill Road, Dumbarton G82 2DU / ssornacnud@hotmail.com	01389 763436
Ross, Duncan DCS	1996	2015	(Deacon)	1 John Neilson Avenue, Paisley PA1 2SX	0141 887 2801
Simpson, James H. BD LLB	1964	2004	(Greenock: Mount Kirk)	82 Harbourside, Inverkip, Greenock PA16 0BF / jameshsimpson@yahoo.co.uk	01475 520582
Smillie, Andrew M. LTh	1990	2005	(Langbank)	7 Turnbull Avenue, West Freeland, Erskine PA8 7DL / andrewsmillie@talktalk.net	0141 812 7030
Steven, Harold A.M. MStJ LTh FSA Scot	1970	2001	(Baldernock)	9 Cairnhill Road, Bearsden, Glasgow G61 1AT / harold.allison.steven@gmail.com	0141 942 1598
Stewart, David MA DipEd BD MTh	1977	2013	(Howwood)	72 Glen Avenue, Largs KA30 8QQ / revdavidst@aol.com	01475 675159
Taylor, Jane C. BD DipMin	1990	2013	(Insch-Leslie-Premnay-Oyne)	Timbers, Argyll Road, Kilcreggan G84 0JW / jane.c.taylor@btinternet.com	01436 842336
Watson, Valerie G.C. MA BD STM	1987	2018	(North and West Islay)	Flat 0/1, 38 Brougham Street, Greenock PA16 8AH / vgcwatson@btinternet.com	01475 726102
Webster, Peter BD	1977	2014	(Edinburgh: Portobello St James')	51 Kempock Street, Gourock PA19 1NF	
Whiteford, Alexander LTh	1996	2013	(Ardersier with Petty)	Cumbrae, 17 Netherburn Gardens, Houston, Johnstone PA6 7NG / alex.whiteford@hotmail.co.uk	01505 229611
Whyte, Margaret A. (Mrs) BA BD	1988	2011	(Glasgow: Pollokshaws)	4 Springhill Road, Barrhead G78 2AA / mawhyte@hotmail.co.uk	0141 881 4942

Wilson, John BD	1985	2010	(Glasgow: Temple Anniesland)	4 Carron Crescent, Bearsden, Glasgow G61 1HJ revjwilson@btinternet.com	0141 931 5609
Wright, Malcolm LTh	1970	2003	(Craigrownie with Rosneath: St Modan's)	30 Clairinsh, Drumkinnon Gate, Balloch, Alexandria G83 8SE malcolmcatherine@msn.com	01389 720338
Yule, Margaret J.B. BD	1992	2019	(Clydebank: Kilbowie St Andrew's with Radnor Park)	4 Overtoun Road, Clydebank G81 3QY mjbyule@yahoo.co.uk	0141 390 3243

CLYDE ADDRESSES

Bearsden
Baljaffray — Grampian Way
Cross — Drymen Road
Killermont — Rannoch Drive
New Kilpatrick — Manse Road
Westerton — Crarae Avenue

Clydebank
Faifley — Faifley Road
Kilbowie St Andrew's — Kilbowie Road
Radnor Park — Radnor Street
Waterfront — Town Centre

Dumbarton
Riverside — High Street
St Andrew's — Aitkenbar Circle
West Kirk — West Bridgend

Gourock
Old Gourock and Ashton — 41 Royal Street
St John's — Bath Street x St John's Road

Greenock
East End — Crawfurdsburn Community Centre
Lyle Kirk — Newark Street x Bentinck Street
Mount Kirk — Dempster Street at Murdieston Park
St Margaret's — Finch Road x Kestrel Crescent
St Ninian's — Warwick Road, Larkfield
Wellpark Mid Kirk — Cathcart Square
Westburn — 9 Nelson Street

Helensburgh — Colquhoun Square

Milngavie
Cairns — Buchanan Street
St Luke's — Kirk Street
St Paul's — Strathblane Road

Paisley
Abbey — Town Centre
Glenburn — Nethercraigs Drive off Glenburn Road
Martyrs' — King Street
Sandyford — Montgomery Road
Oakshaw Trinity — Churchill
St Columba Foxbar — Amochrie Road, Foxbar
St Mark's Oldhall — Glasgow Road, Ralston
Sherwood Greenlaw South — Glasgow Road
Stow Brae Kirk — Rowan Street off Neilston Road
Wallneuk North — Causeyside Street
  off Renfrew Road

Port Glasgow
Hamilton Bardrainney — Bardrainney Avenue x Auchenbothie Road
New — Princes Street

(16) GLASGOW (F W)

Meets at 7pm on the second Tuesday of every month apart from June when it is the third Tuesday and July, August and January when it does not meet. Details of the venue are displayed on the Presbytery website.

Clerk:	REV. GEORGE S. COWIE BSc BD	260 Bath Street, Glasgow G2 4JP glasgow@churchofscotland.org.uk	0141 332 6606 Fax 0141 352 6646
Depute Clerk:	REV. HILARY N. McDOUGALL MA PGCE BD	HMcDougall@churchofscotland.org.uk	
Treasurer:	MRS ALISON WHITELAW	treasurer@presbyteryofglasgow.org.uk	

1   **Banton (F W) linked with Twechar (W)**
Guardianship of the Presbytery
Session Clerk, Banton: Mary Dixon (Mrs)   magicmaria67@gmail.com   01236 822055
Session Clerk, Twechar: Gena Whyte (Mrs)   whyteg@live.co.uk   0141 777 7704

2   **Bishopbriggs: Kenmure (F W)**
Vacant
Interim Moderator: John B. MacGregor   100 Kenmure Avenue, Bishopbriggs, Glasgow G64 2DB   **0141 762 4242**
JMacGregor@churchofscotland.org.uk   0141 390 3598
0141 576 7127

3   **Bishopbriggs: Springfield Cambridge (F W)**
Ian Taylor BD ThM DipPSRP   1995   2006   **springfieldcamb@btconnect.com**   **0141 772 1596**
64 Miller Drive, Bishopbriggs, Glasgow G64 1FB   0141 772 1540
ITaylor@churchofscotland.org.uk

4   **Broom (W)**
James A.S. Boag BD CertMin   1992   2007   **office@broomchurch.org.uk**   Tel   **0141 639 3528**
3 Laigh Road, Newton Mearns, Glasgow G77 5EX   0141 639 2916
JBoag@churchofscotland.org.uk   Fax   0141 639 3528

5   **Burnside Blairbeth (F W)**
William T.S. Wilson BSc BD   1999   2006   **theoffice@burnsideblairbeth.church**   **0141 634 7383**
59 Blairbeth Road, Burnside, Glasgow G73 4JD   0141 583 6470
WWilson@churchofscotland.org.uk

6   **Busby (F W)**
Jeremy C. Eve BSc BD   1995   1998   17A Carmunnock Road, Busby, Glasgow G76 8SZ   **0141 644 2073**
JEve@churchofscotland.org.uk   0141 644 3670

7   **Cadder (W)**
John B. MacGregor BD   1999   2017   231 Kirkintilloch Road, Bishopbriggs, Glasgow G64 2JB   **0141 772 7436**
JMacGregor@churchofscotland.org.uk   0141 576 7127

8   **Cambuslang (F W)**
Peter W. Nimmo BD ThM   1996   2020   **office@churchofscotland.org.uk**   **0141 642 9271**
74 Stewarton Drive, Cambuslang, Glasgow G72 8DG   0141 641 2028
PNimmo@churchofscotland.org.uk
Karen M. Hamilton (Mrs) DCS   1995   2014   6 Beckfield Gate, Glasgow G33 1SW   0141 558 3195
KHamilton@churchofscotland.org.uk   07514 402612

9   **Cambuslang: Flemington Hallside (F W)**
Ian A. Cathcart BSc BD   1994   2018   59 Hay Crescent, Cambuslang, Glasgow G72 6QA   0141 641 1049
ICathcart@churchofscotland.org.uk   07758 441895

10 Campsie (F W)
Jane M. Denniston MA BD MTh   2002   2016
DPT DipPSRP
campsieparishchurch@gmail.com   **01360 310939**
Campsie Parish Church, 130 Main Street, Lennoxtown,   07738 123101
Glasgow G66 7DA
Jane.Denniston@churchofscotland.org.uk

11 Chryston (H T W)
Mark Malcolm MA BD   1999   2008
chrystonchurch@hotmail.com   **0141 779 4188**
The Manse, 109 Main Street, Chryston, Glasgow G69 9LA   0141 779 1436
MMalcolm@churchofscotland.org.uk   07731 737377
Mark W.J. McKeown   2013   2014
MEng MDiv DipMin (Associate Minister)   01236 263406
6 Glenapp Place, Moodiesburn, Glasgow G69 0HS
MMcKeown@churchofscotland.org.uk

12 Eaglesham (F W)
Vacant
Interim Moderator: John L. McPake
office@eagleshamparishchurch.co.uk   **01355 302087**
The Manse, Cheapside Street, Eaglesham, Glasgow G76 0NS   01355 303495
JMcPake@churchofscotland.org.uk   0131 240 2208

13 Fernhill and Cathkin (F W)
Aquila R. Singh BA PGCE BD   2017
20 Glenlyon Place, Rutherglen, Glasgow G73 5PL   0141 389 3599
ASingh@churchofscotland.org.uk

14 Gartcosh (F H T W) linked with Glenboig (F T W)
David G. Slater BSc BA DipThRS   2011
26 Inchnock Avenue, Gartcosh, Glasgow G69 8EA   Gartcosh: **01236 872274**
DSlater@churchofscotland.org.uk   07722 876616

15 Giffnock: Orchardhill (F W)
S. Grant Barclay LLB DipLP BD MSc PhD 1995   2016
23 Huntly Avenue, Giffnock, Glasgow G46 6LW   **0141 638 3604**
GBarclay@churchofscotland.org.uk   0141 387 8254

16 Giffnock: South (F W)
Catherine J. Beattie (Mrs) BD   2008   2011
164 Ayr Road, Newton Mearns, Glasgow G77 6EE   **0141 638 2599**
CBeattie@churchofscotland.org.uk   0141 258 7804

17 Giffnock: The Park (F W)
Calum D. Macdonald BD   1993   2001
contact@parkchurch.org.uk   **0141 620 2204**
41 Rouken Glen Road, Thornliebank, Glasgow G46 7JD   0141 638 3023
CMacdonald@churchofscotland.org.uk

18 Glenboig See Gartcosh

19 **Greenbank (F H W)**
Jeanne N. Roddick BD
2003
greenbankoffice@tiscali.co.uk
Greenbank Manse, 38 Eaglesham Road, Clarkston,
Glasgow G76 7DJ
JRoddick@churchofscotland.org.uk
0141 644 1841
0141 644 1395

20 **Kilsyth: Anderson (F T W)**
Allan S. Vint BSc BD MTh PhD
1989   2013
Anderson Manse, 1 Kingston Road, Kilsyth, Glasgow G65 0HR
AVint@churchofscotland.org.uk
01236 822345
07795 483070

21 **Kilsyth: Burns and Old (F W)**
Robert Johnston BD MSc FSAScot
2017
boldchurch@hotmail.com
(temporary) 32 Newlands Road, Glasgow G71 5QP
RJohnston@churchofscotland.org.uk
07810 377582

22 **Kirkintilloch: Hillhead (W)**
Guardianship of the Presbytery
Bill H. Finnie BA PgDipSW CertCRS
(Ordained Local Minister)
2015
hillheadparish@gmail.com
27 Hallside Crescent, Cambuslang, Glasgow G72 7DY
BFinnie@churchofscotland.org.uk
07518 357138

23 **Kirkintilloch: St Columba's (H W)**
Philip A. Wright BSc MSc PhD BTh
2017
6 Glenwood Road, Lenzie, Glasgow G66 4DS
PWright@churchofscotland.org.uk

24 **Kirkintilloch: St David's Memorial Park (F H W)**
Adam J. Dillon BD ThM
2003   2018
sdmp2@outlook.com
2 Roman Road, Kirkintilloch, Glasgow G66 1EA
ADillon@churchofscotland.org.uk
0141 776 4989
0141 588 3570

25 **Kirkintilloch: St Mary's (W)**
Vacant
Session Clerk: Gordon Morrison
office.stmarys@btconnect.com
0141 775 1166
0141 775 1166

26 **Lenzie: Old (H W)**
Louise J.E. McClements BD
2008
41 Kirkintilloch Road, Lenzie, Glasgow G66 4LB
LMcClements@churchofscotland.org.uk
0141 573 5006

27 **Lenzie: Union (F H W)**
Daniel J.M. Carmichael MA BD
1994   2003
office@lenzieunion.org
1 Larch Avenue, Lenzie, Glasgow G66 4HX
DCarmichael@churchofscotland.org.uk
0141 776 1046
0141 776 3831

Tel/Fax

28 Maxwell Mearns Castle (W)
Scott R.M. Kirkland BD MAR DMin 1996
office@maxwellmearns.org.uk
122 Broomfield Avenue, Newton Mearns, Glasgow G77 5JR
SKirkland@churchofscotland.org.uk
0141 639 5169
0141 560 5603

29 Mearns (F H W)
Joseph A. Kavanagh BD DipPTh MTh MTh 1992 1998
office@mearnskirk.church
11 Belford Grove, Newton Mearns, Glasgow G77 5FB
JKavanagh@churchofscotland.org.uk
0141 639 6555
0141 384 2218

30 Milton of Campsie (F H W)
Julie H.C. Moody BA BD PGCE 2006
16 Cannerton Park, Milton of Campsie, Glasgow G66 8HR
JMoody@churchofscotland.org.uk
01360 310548

31 Moodiesburn (F W)
Vacant
Interim Moderator: Mark Malcolm
info@moodiesburn.church
MMalcolm@churchofscotland.org.uk
New charge formed by disjunction from Chryston
01236 870515
0141 779 1436

32 Netherlee and Stamperland (F H W)
Scott Blythe BSc BD MBA 1997 2017
office@netherleechurch.org.uk
stamperland@tiscali.org.uk
25 Ormonde Avenue, Netherlee, Glasgow G44 3QY
SBlythe@churchofscotland.org.uk
0141 637 2503
0141 637 4999
0141 533 7147
07706 203786

33 Newton Mearns (F H W)
Stuart J. Crawford BD MTh 2017
office@churchatthecross.org.uk
28 Waterside Avenue, Newton Mearns, Glasgow G77 6TJ
SCrawford@churchofscotland.org.uk
0141 639 7373
07912 534280

34 Rutherglen: Old (F H T W)
Vacant
Session Clerk: Hugh Millar
31 Highburgh Drive, Rutherglen, Glasgow G73 3RR
sessionclerk@rutherglenold.com
0141 534 7477
0141 634 4355

35 Rutherglen: Stonelaw (F T W)
Vacant
Session Clerk: David McTaggart
info@stonelawchurch.org
80 Blairbeth Road, Rutherglen, Glasgow G73 4JA
sessionclerk@stonelawchurch.org
0141 647 5113
0141 583 0157
07825 137168

36 Rutherglen: West and Wardlawhill (F W)
Malcolm Cuthbertson BA BD 1984 2017
info@westandwardlawhill.org
12 Albert Drive, Rutherglen, Glasgow G73 3RT
MCuthbertson@churchofscotland.org.uk
0844 736 1470
07864 820612

37	**Stepps (F H W)**				
	Gordon MacRae BD MTh	1985	2014	112 Jackson Drive, Crowwood Grange, Stepps, Glasgow G33 6GF	0141 779 5742
				GMacRae@churchofscotland.org.uk	
38	**Thornliebank (F H W)**				
	Mike R. Gargrave BD	2008	2014	12 Parkholm Quadrant, Thornliebank, Glasgow G53 7ZH	0141 880 5532
				MGargrave@churchofscotland.org.uk	
39	**Torrance**				
	Nigel L. Barge BSc BD	1991		1 Atholl Avenue, Torrance, Glasgow G64 4JA	**01360 620970**
				NBarge@churchofscotland.org.uk	01360 622379
40	**Twechar** See Banton				
41	**Williamwood (F W)**				
	Janet S. Mathieson MA BD	2003	2015	125 Greenwood Road, Clarkston, Glasgow G76 7LL	**0141 638 2091**
				JMathieson@churchofscotland.org.uk	0141 579 9997

42   Glasgow: Baillieston Mure Memorial (F W) linked with Glasgow: Baillieston St Andrew's (F W)   Mure Memorial: **0141 773 1216**

	Sandra Black BSc BD	1988	2019	36 Glencairn Drive, Glasgow G41 4PW	07703 822057
	(Interim Minister)			SBlack@churchofscotland.org.uk	
	Ann Lyall DCS	1980	2019	117 Barlia Drive, Glasgow G45 0AY	0141 631 3643
				ALyall@churchofscotland.org.uk	

43   Glasgow: Baillieston St Andrew's See Glasgow: Baillieston Mure Memorial

44	**Glasgow: Balshagray Victoria Park (W)**				
	Vacant				
	Interim Moderator: Jonathan A. Keefe			20 St Kilda Drive, Glasgow G14 9JN	0141 954 9780
				JKeefe@churchofscotland.org.uk	0141 558 2952
45	**Glasgow: Barlanark Greyfriars (W)**			enquiries@barlanark-greyfriars.co.uk	
	Vacant			4 Rhindmuir Grove, Baillieston, Glasgow G69 6NE	**0141 771 6477**
	Session Clerk: Jemima Bell (Mrs)			jemima.bell@ntlworld.com	0141 771 7103
					0141 771 3468
46	**Glasgow: Blawarthill (F T W)**				
	G. Melvyn Wood MA BD	1982	2009	46 Earlbank Avenue, Glasgow G14 9HL	0141 579 6521
				GMelvynWood@churchofscotland.org.uk	

47 Glasgow: Bridgeton St Francis in the East (F H L W)   0141 556 2830 (Church House: 0141 554 8045)
Howard R. Hudson MA BD   1982 1984   bridgetonstfrancis@gmail.com
10 Albany Drive, Rutherglen, Glasgow G73 3QN   0141 587 8667
HHudson@churchofscotland.org.uk

48 Glasgow: Broomhill Hyndland (F W)   info@broomhillhyndlandchurch.org   0141 334 2540
George C. Mackay   1994 2014   27 St Kilda Drive, Glasgow G14 9LN   0141 959 8697
BD CertMin DipPC   GMackay@churchofscotland.org.uk   07711 569127

49 Glasgow: Calton Parkhead   0141 554 3866
Alison E.S. Davidge MA BD   1990 2008   98 Drumover Drive, Glasgow G31 5RP   07843 625059
ADavidge@churchofscotland.org.uk

50 Glasgow: Cardonald (F W)   0141 882 6264
Gavin McFadyen BEng BD   2006 2018   133 Newtyle Road, Paisley PA1 3LB   0141 576 6818
GMcFadyen@churchofscotland.org.uk   07960 212106

51 Glasgow: Carmunnock   0141 644 0655
Vacant   The Manse, 161 Waterside Road, Carmunnock,   Tel/Fax   0141 644 1578
Glasgow G76 9AJ
Session Clerk: George Dow   george.dow@macmic.co.uk   0141 644 0689
07801 613 127

52 Glasgow: Carmyle (W) linked with Glasgow: Kenmuir Mount Vernon (F W)
Murdo MacLean BD CertMin   1997 1999   3 Meryon Road, Glasgow G32 9NW   0141 778 2625
Murdo.MacLean@churchofscotland.org.uk
Roland Hunt BSc PhD CertEd   2016   4 Flora Gardens, Bishopbriggs, Glasgow G64 1DS   0141 563 3257
(Ordained Local Minister)   RHunt@churchofscotland.org.uk

53 Glasgow: Carntyne   0141 778 4186
Joan Ross BSc BD PhD   1999 2016   163 Lethamhill Road, Glasgow G33 2SQ   0141 770 9247
JRoss@churchofscotland.org.uk

54 Glasgow: Carnwadric (F L W)   0141 638 5884
James Gemmell BD MTh   1999 2020   62 Loganswell Road, Thornliebank, Glasgow G46 8AX
JGemmell@churchofscotland.org.uk
Mary S. Gargrave (Mrs) DCS   1989 2007   12 Parkholm Quadrant, Thornliebank, Glasgow G53 7ZH   0141 880 5532
Mary.Gargrave@churchofscotland.org.uk   07896 866618

No.	Congregation / Minister	Year	Year	Address / Email	Telephone
55	**Glasgow: Castlemilk (F H W)**				**0141 634 7113**
	Sarah A. Brown (Ms)	2012		156 Old Castle Road, Glasgow G44 5TW	0141 637 5451
	MA BD ThM DipYW/Theol PDCCE			Sarah.Brown@churchofscotland.org.uk	
	John Paul Cathcart DCS	2000	2017	9 Glen More, East Kilbride, Glasgow G74 2AP	01355 243970
				Paul.Cathcart@churchofscotland.org.uk	07708 396074
56	**Glasgow: Cathcart Old (F)**				**0141 637 4168**
	Neil W. Galbraith BD CertMin	1987		21 Courthill Avenue, Cathcart, Glasgow G44 5AA	0141 633 5248 Tel/Fax
				NGalbraith@churchofscotland.org.uk	
57	**Glasgow: Cathcart Trinity (F H W)**			**office@cathcarttrinity.org.uk**	**0141 637 6658**
	Alasdair MacMillan LLB BD	2015		21 Muirhill Avenue, Glasgow G44 3HP	0141 391 9102
				Alasdair.MacMillan@churchofscotland.org.uk	
58	**Glasgow: Cathedral (High or St Mungo's) (F W)**				**0141 552 8198**
	Mark E. Johnstone DL MA BD	1993	2019	41 Springfield Road, Bishopbriggs, Glasgow G64 1PL	07515 285374
				Mark.Johnstone@churchofscotland.org.uk	
59	**Glasgow: Causeway (Tollcross) (F)**				0141 778 2413
	Monica Michelin-Salomon BD	1999	2007	228 Hamilton Road, Glasgow G32 9QU	
				MMichelin-Salomon@churchofscotland.org.uk	
60	**Glasgow: Clincarthill (F H W)**				**0141 632 4206**
	Stuart Love BA MTh	2016		90 Mount Annan Drive, Glasgow G44 4RZ	0141 632 2985
				SLove@churchofscotland.org.uk	
61	**Glasgow: Colston Milton**				**0141 772 1922**
	Christopher J. Rowe BA BD	2008		118 Birsay Road, Milton, Glasgow G22 7QP	0141 564 1138
				CRowe@churchofscotland.org.uk	
62	**Glasgow: Colston Wellpark (F H W)**				**0141 772 8672**
	Guardianship of the Presbytery			23 Hertford Avenue, Kelvindale, Glasgow G12 0LG	07813 255052
	Leslie E.T. Grieve BSc BA	2014		LGrieve@churchofscotland.org.uk	
	(Ordained Local Minister)				
63	**Glasgow: Cranhill (F H W)**				**0141 774 3344**
	Muriel B. Pearson (Ms) MA BD PGCE	2004		31 Lethamhill Crescent, Glasgow G33 2SH	0141 770 6873
				MPearson@churchofscotland.org.uk	07951 888860

No.	Charge	Minister	Ord.	Ind.	Address / Email	Telephone
64	**Glasgow: Crofftfoot (F H W)** Robert M. Silver BA BD		1995	2011	4 Inchmurrin Gardens, High Burnside, Rutherglen, Glasgow G73 5RU RSilver@churchofscotland.org.uk	**0141 637 3913** 0141 258 7268
65	**Glasgow: Dennistoun New (F H W)** Ian M.S. McInnes BD DipMin		1995	2008	31 Pencaitland Drive, Glasgow G32 8RL IMcInnes@churchofscotland.org.uk	**0141 554 1350** 0141 564 6498
66	**Glasgow: Drumchapel St Andrew's (F W)** John S. Purves LLB BD		1983	1984	6 Firdon Crescent, Old Drumchapel, Glasgow G15 6QQ JPurves@churchofscotland.org.uk	**0141 944 3758** 0141 944 4566
67	**Glasgow: Drumchapel St Mark's (F)** Audrey J. Jamieson BD MTh		2004	2007	146 Garscadden Road, Glasgow G15 6PR AJamieson@churchofscotland.org.uk	0141 944 5440
68	**Glasgow: Easterhouse (F W)** Derek W. Hughes BSc BD DipEd		1990	2018	3 Barony Gardens, Springhill, Glasgow G69 6TS DHughes@churchofscotland.org.uk	**0141 771 8810** 0141 771 8810 07723 578573
69	**Glasgow: Eastwood (F W)** James R. Teasdale BA BD		2009	2016	54 Mansewood Road, Eastwood, Glasgow G43 1TL JTeasdale@churchofscotland.org.uk	0141 571 7648
70	**Glasgow: Gairbraid (F H W)** Donald Michael MacInnes BD		2002	2011	4 Blackhill Gardens, Summerston, Glasgow G23 5NE DMacInnes@churchofscotland.org.uk	0141 946 0604
71	**Glasgow: Gallowgate** Peter L.V. Davidge BD MTh		2003	2009	98 Drumover Drive, Glasgow G31 5RP	07765 096599
72	**Glasgow: Garthamlock and Craigend (F W)** I. Scott McCarthy BD		2010	2018	9 Craigievar Court, Garthamlock, Glasgow G33 5DJ ISMcCarthy@churchofscotland.org.uk	07725 037394
73	**Glasgow: Gorbals** Ian F. Galloway BA BD		1977	1996	6 Stirlingfauld Place, Gorbals, Glasgow G5 9QF IGalloway@churchofscotland.org.uk	07753 686603

74 Glasgow: Govan and Linthouse (F T W)
Vacant
Ann Lyall DCS 1980 2019
glpcglasgow@googlemail.com **0141 445 2010**
44 Forfar Avenue, Glasgow G52 3JQ 0141 631 3643
117 Barlia Drive, Glasgow G45 0AY
ALyall@churchofscotland.org.uk

75 Glasgow: Hillington Park (F H W)
Robert Craig BA BD DipRS PGCertHC 2008 2019
81 Raeswood Road, Glasgow G53 7HH 0141 463 3203
RCraig@churchofscotland.org.uk

76 Glasgow: Ibrox (F H W)
Tara P. Granados (Ms) BA MDiv 2018
ibroxparishchurch@gmail.com **07380 830030**
59 Langhaul Road, Glasgow G53 7SE 07475 128128
TGranados@churchofscotland.org.uk

77 Glasgow: John Ross Memorial Church for Deaf People (W) 1989 1998
Richard C. Durno DSW CQSW
Voice/Text 0141 420 1391; Fax 0141 420 3778
31 Springfield Road, Bishopbriggs, Voice/Text/Fax 0141 772 1052
Glasgow G64 1PJ Voice/Text/Voicemail 07748 607721
RDurno@churchofscotland.org.uk

78 Glasgow: Jordanhill (F W)
Bruce H Sinclair BA BD 2009 2015
12 Priorwood Gardens, Academy Park, Glasgow G13 1GD **0141 959 2496**
BSinclair@churchofscotland.org.uk 0141 959 1310

79 Glasgow: Kelvinbridge (F W)
Gordon Kirkwood BSc BD MTh 1987 2003
MPhil PGCE
Flat 2/2, 94 Hyndland Road, Glasgow G12 9PZ **0141 339 1750**
GKirkwood@churchofscotland.org.uk 0141 334 5352

80 Glasgow: Kelvinside Hillhead (F W)
Vacant
Roger D. Sturrock (Prof.) BD MD FCRP 2014
(Ordained Local Minister)
36 Thomson Drive, Bearsden, Glasgow G61 3PA **0141 334 2788**
RSturrock@churchofscotland.org.uk 0141 942 7412

81 Glasgow: Kenmuir Mount Vernon See Glasgow: Carmyle

82 Glasgow: King's Park (F H W)
Vacant
Interim Moderator: Thomas L. Pollock
office@kingspark.church.co.uk **0141 636 8688**
1101 Aikenhead Road, Glasgow G44 5SL 0141 427 2094
TPollock@churchofscotland.org.uk

83 Glasgow: Kinning Park (W)
Margaret H. Johnston BD 1988 2000
168 Arbroath Avenue, Cardonald, Glasgow G52 3HH 0141 810 3782
MHJohnston@churchofscotland.org.uk

84   Glasgow: Knightswood St Margaret's (H W)
Vacant
Session Clerk: David Adams
26 Airthrey Avenue, Glasgow G14 9LJ
dp.adams@btinternet.com
0141 959 7075
0141 958 0404

85   Glasgow: Langside (F T W)
David N. McLachlan BD — 1985 — 2004
langsidechurch@gmail.com
36 Madison Avenue, Glasgow G44 5AQ
DMcLachlan@churchofscotland.org.uk
0141 632 7520
0141 637 0797

86   Glasgow: Maryhill (F H W)
Stuart C. Matthews BD MA — 2006 — 2010
251 Milngavie Road, Bearsden, Glasgow G61 3DQ
SMatthews@churchofscotland.org.uk
James Hamilton DCS — 1997 — 2000
6 Beckfield Gate, Glasgow G33 1SW
James.Hamilton@churchofscotland.org.uk
0141 946 3512
0141 942 0804
0141 558 3195
07584 137314

87   Glasgow: Merrylea (F W)
Vacant
Session Clerk: Ralph P. Boettcher
4 Pilmuir Avenue, Glasgow G44 3HX
merryleasessionclerk@outlook.com
0141 637 2009
07806 453724

88   Glasgow: Newlands South (H T W)
R. Stuart M. Fulton BA BD — 1991 — 2017
secretary@newlandschurch.org.uk
24 Monreith Road, Glasgow G43 2NY
SFulton@churchofscotland.org.uk
0141 632 3055
0141 632 2588

89   Glasgow: Partick South (F H W)
James Andrew McIntyre BD — 2010
3 Branklyn Crescent, Glasgow G13 1GJ
Andy.McIntyre@churchofscotland.org.uk
0141 339 8816
0141 959 3732

90   Glasgow: Partick Trinity (F H T W)
Timothy D. Sinclair MA MDiv — 2018
enquiry@particktrinity.org.uk
99 Balshagray Avenue, Glasgow G11 7EQ
TSinclair@churchofscotland.org.uk
0141 563 6424

91   Glasgow: Pollokshaws (F)
Roy J.M. Henderson MA BD DipMin — 1987 — 2013
33 Mannering Road, Glasgow G41 3SW
RHenderson@churchofscotland.org.uk
0141 649 1879
0141 632 8768

92   Glasgow: Pollokshields (F H T W)
David R. Black MA BD — 1986 — 1997
36 Glencairn Drive, Glasgow G41 4PW
DBlack@churchofscotland.org.uk
0141 423 4000

93 Glasgow: Possilpark (F)
Rosalind (Linda) E. Pollock (Miss)   2001   2014
BD ThM ThM
1262 Balmuildy Road, Glasgow G23 5HE
RPollock@churchofscotland.org.uk
0141 336 8028
07470 052618

94 Glasgow: Queen's Park Govanhill (F W)
David W. Denniston BD DipMin   1981   2019
(Interim Minister)
officeQPG@btinternet.com
c/o Campsie Parish Church, 130 Main Street, Lennoxtown,
Glasgow G66 7DA
DDenniston@churchofscotland.org.uk
0141 423 3654
07903 926727

95 Glasgow: Robroyston (F W)
Jonathan A. Keefe BSc BD   2009
info@robroystonchurch.org.uk
7 Beckfield Drive, Glasgow G33 1SR
JKeefe@churchofscotland.org.uk
0141 558 8414
0141 558 2952

96 Glasgow: Ruchazie (F)
Guardianship of the Presbytery
Session Clerk: Margaret Dott
0141 774 2759
0141 572 0451

97 Glasgow: Ruchill Kelvinside (W)
Mark Lowey BD DipTh   2012   2013
ruchill.kelvinside@gmail.com
41 Mitre Road, Glasgow G14 9LE
MLowey@churchofscotland.org.uk
0141 533 2731
0141 959 6718

98 Glasgow: St Andrew and St Nicholas (F W)
Lyn M. Peden (Mrs) BD   2010   2015
80 Tweedsmuir Road, Glasgow G52 2RX
LPeden@churchofscotland.org.uk
0141 882 3601
0141 883 9873

99 Glasgow: St Andrew's East (F W)
Vacant
Session Clerk: Elizabeth McIvor
43 Broompark Drive, Glasgow G31 2JB
emcivor@talktalk.net
0141 554 1485
0141 556 4838

100 Glasgow: St Andrew's West (F W)
Kleber Machado BD MTh   1998   2019
BTh MSc PhD
info@rsschurch.org.uk
101 Hill Street, Glasgow G3 6TY
KMachado@churchofscotland.org.uk
Tel: 0141 332 4293; Fax: 0141 332 8482
0141 353 6551

101 Glasgow: St Christopher's Priesthill and Nitshill (W)
Douglas M. Nicol BD CA   1987   1996
36 Springkell Drive, Glasgow G41 4EZ
DNicol@churchofscotland.org.uk
0141 881 6541
0141 427 7877

102 Glasgow: St Columba (F GE W)
Vacant
Session Clerk: Duncan Mitchell
dpm@addapt.org.uk
0141 221 3305
0141 339 9679

103 Glasgow: St David's Knightswood (F)
Graham M. Thain LLB BD   1988   1999
60 Southbrae Drive, Glasgow G13 1QD
GThain@churchofscotland.org.uk
0141 954 1081
0141 959 2904

104 Glasgow: St Enoch's Hogganfield (F H W)
Elaine H. MacRae (Mrs) BD   1985   2017
church@st-enoch.org.uk   Tel 0141 770 5694; Fax 08702 840084
112 Jackson Drive, Crowwood Grange, Stepps, Glasgow G33 6GF   0141 779 5742
EMacRae@churchofscotland.org.uk   07834 269487

105 Glasgow: St George's Tron (F W)
Alastair S. Duncan MA BD   1989   2013
info@sgt.church
29 Hertford Avenue, Glasgow G12 0LG
ADuncan@churchofscotland.org.uk
0141 229 5746
07968 852083

106 Glasgow: St James' (Pollok)
Vacant
Session Clerk: David T. Arbuckle
30 Ralston Avenue, Glasgow G52 3NA
davidtarbuckle@outlook.com
0141 882 4984
07469 878303

107 Glasgow: St John's Renfield (W)
D. Stewart Gillan BSc MDiv PhD   1985   2018
secretary@sjrchurch.plus.com
26 Leicester Avenue, Glasgow G12 0LU
SGillan@churchofscotland.org.uk
0141 334 0782
0141 339 4637

108 Glasgow: St Paul's (F T W)
Vacant
Interim Moderator: Rhona E. Graham
38 Lochview Drive, Glasgow G33 1QF
RGraham@churchofscotland.org.uk
0141 770 8559
0141 770 1561
0141 389 8816

109 Glasgow: St Rollox (F W)
Jane M. Howitt MA BD   1996   2016
(Transition Minister)
inbox@strollox.co.uk
42 Melville Gardens, Bishopbriggs, Glasgow G64 3DE
JHowitt@churchofscotland.org.uk
0141 558 1809
0141 581 0050

110 Glasgow: Sandyford Henderson Memorial (F H L T W)
Vacant
Session Clerk: Noel Peacock (Prof.)
enquiries@sandyfordhenderson.net
66 Woodend Drive, Glasgow G13 1TG
noel.peacock@glasgow.ac.uk
0141 226 3696
0141 954 9013
0141 334 1611

111 Glasgow: Sandyhills (W)
Norman A. Afrin BA MRes — 2018
60 Wester Road, Glasgow G32 9JJ
NAfrin@churchofscotland.org.uk
0141 778 3415
0141 778 1213

112 Glasgow: Scotstoun (W)
Richard Cameron BD DipMin — 2000
15 Northland Drive, Glasgow G14 9BE
RCameron@churchofscotland.org.uk
0141 959 4637

113 Glasgow: Shawlands Trinity (F)
Valerie J. Duff (Miss) DMin — 1993   2014
29 St Ronan's Drive, Glasgow G41 3SQ
VDuff@churchofscotland.org.uk
0141 258 6782

114 Glasgow: Sherbrooke Mosspark (F H W)
Thomas L. Pollock
BA BD MTh FSAScot JP — 1982   2003
114 Springkell Avenue, Glasgow G41 4EW
TPollock@churchofscotland.org.uk
0141 427 1968
0141 427 2094

115 Glasgow: Shettleston New (F W)
W. Louis T. Reddick MA BD — 2017
211 Sandyhills Road, Glasgow G32 9NB
LReddick@churchofscotland.org.uk
0141 778 4769
0141 230 7365
07843 083548

116 Glasgow: Springburn (F H T W)
Brian M. Casey MA BD — 2014
springburnparishchurch@btconnect.com
c/o Springburn Parish Church, 180 Springburn Way,
Glasgow G21 1TU
BCasey@churchofscotland.org.uk
0141 557 2345
07703 166772

117 Glasgow: Temple Anniesland (F W)
Fiona M.E. Gardner (Mrs) BD MA MLitt — 1997   2011
info@tachurch.org.uk
76 Victoria Park Drive North, Glasgow G14 9PJ
FGardner@churchofscotland.org.uk
Ruth Forsythe (Mrs) MCS — 2017   2018
(Ordained Local Minister)
Flat 1/2, 41 Bellwood Street, Glasgow G41 3EX
RForsythe@churchofscotland.org.uk
0141 530 9745
0141 959 5647
07824 641212

118 Glasgow: Toryglen (F H T W)
Vacant
toryglenparish@gmail.com
toryglensession@gmail.com
Session Clerk: Ina Cole (Mrs)
07587 207981
0141 562 4807

119 Glasgow: Trinity Possil and Henry Drummond (W)
Richard G. Buckley BD MTh DMin — 1990   1995
tphdcofs@yahoo.com
50 Highfield Drive, Glasgow G12 0HL
RBuckley@churchofscotland.org.uk
0141 339 2870

120 Glasgow: Tron St Mary's (F)
Rhona E. Graham BA BD 2015
30 Louden Hill Road, Robroyston, Glasgow G33 1GA
RGraham@churchofscotland.org.uk
0141 558 1011
0141 389 8816

121 Glasgow: Wallacewell (New Charge Development) (F T W)
Daniel L. Frank BA MDiv DMin 1984 2011
info@wallacewell.org
8 Streamfield Gate, Glasgow G33 1SJ
DFrank@churchofscotland.org.uk
0141 558 4466
0141 585 0283

122 Glasgow: Wellington (F H T W)
Vacant
Roger D. Sturrock (Prof.) BD MD FCRP 2014
(Ordained Local Minister)
wellingtonchurch@btinternet.com
31 Hughenden Gardens, Glasgow G12 9YH
36 Thomson Drive, Bearsden, Glasgow G61 3PA
RSturrock@churchofscotland.org.uk
0141 339 0454
0141 334 2343
0141 942 7412

123 Glasgow: Whiteinch (F W)
Vacant
Session Clerk: Shona Campbell
65 Victoria Park Drive South, Glasgow G14 9NX
shona.campbell@whiteinchchurch.org
0141 959 9317
0141 576 9020
0141 587 0179

124 Glasgow: Yoker (F T)
Karen E. Hendry BSc BD 2005
15 Coldingham Avenue, Glasgow G14 0PX
KHendry@churchofscotland.org.uk
0141 952 3620

B. In other appointments

Bell, John L. MA BD FRSCM DUniv 1978 1988 Iona Community
148 West Princes Street, Glasgow G4 9DA
0141 387 7628

Cowie, George S. BSc BD 1991 2017 Presbytery Clerk: Glasgow
260 Bath Street, Glasgow G2 4JP
GCowie@churchofscotland.org.uk
0141 332 6066

Forrest, Martin R. BA MA BD 1988 2012 Chaplain: HM Prison Low Moss
4/1. 7 Blochairm Place, Glasgow G21 2EB
martinrforrest@gmail.com
0141 552 1132

Forsyth, Sandy O. LLB BD DipLP 2009 2018 University of Edinburgh, Lecturer,
MTh PhD   New College
48 Kerr Street, Kirkintilloch, Glasgow G66 1IZ
AForsyth@churchofscotland.org.uk
0141 777 8194
07739 639037

Foster-Fulton, Sally BA BD 1999 2016 Head of Christian Aid Scotland
24 Monreith Road, Glasgow G43 2NY
sallyfulton01@gmail.com
07850 937226

Gardner, Peter M. MA BD 1988 2016 Pioneer Minister, Glasgow Arts Community
Flat 3/2. 10 Haggswood Avenue, Glasgow G41 4RE
PGardner@churchofscotland.org.uk
07743 539654

Gay, Douglas C. MA BD PhD 1998 2005 University of Glasgow: Trinity College
4 Copland Place, Glasgow G51 2RS
douggay@mac.com
0141 330 2073
07971 321452

Herbert, Claire DCS 2019 Chaplain, Lodging House Mission,
                                Glasgow
35 East Campbell Street, Glasgow G51 5DT
CHerbert@churchofscotland.org.uk
0141 552 0285

Name	Years	Role / Charge	Address	Phone
Kelly, Ewan R. MB ChB PhD	1994 2019	Spiritual Care and Wellbeing Lead, Dumfries and Galloway NHS	Flat 1/2, 17 Overdale Street, Glasgow G42 9PZ / ewan.kelly1@nhs.net	0141 649 2714
Love, Joanna R. (Ms) BSc DCS	1992 2009	Iona Community: Wild Goose Resource Group	92 Everard Drive, Glasgow G21 1XQ (Office) / jo@wildgoose.scot	0141 429 7281
MacDonald, Anne (Miss) BA DCS	1980 2002	Healthcare Chaplain	Chaplaincy Office, Glasgow Royal Infirmary G4 0SF	0141 211 4661
McDougall, Hilary N. (Mrs) MA PGCE BD	2004 2013	Depute Clerk & Congregational Facilitator: Presbytery of Glasgow	16 Central Court, Central Avenue, Cambuslang G72 8DJ / HMcdougall@churchofscotland.org.uk	0141 641 8574 / 07539 321832
McPake, John L. BA BD PhD	1987 2017	Ecumenical Officer, Church of Scotland	121 George Street, Edinburgh EH2 4YN / JMcPake@churchofscotland.org.uk	0131 240 2208
Maxwell, David	2014	Ordained Local Minister	248 Old Castle Road, Glasgow G44 5EZ / DMaxwell@churchofscotland.org.uk	0141 569 6379
Peat, Derek A. BA BD MTh	2013 2019	Local Church Review Co-ordinator, Presbytery of Glasgow	20 Rannoch Drive, Glasgow G61 2JH / DPeat@churchofscotland.org.uk	07561 427802
Walker, Linda	2008 2013	Auxiliary Minister, Presbytery	18 Valeview Terrace, Glasgow G42 9LA / LWalker@churchofscotland.org.uk	0141 649 1340

C. Demitted

Name	Years	Charge	Address	Phone
Alexander, Eric J. MA BD	1958 1997	(Glasgow: St George's Tron)	77 Norwood Park, Bearsden, Glasgow G61 2RZ	0141 942 4404
Alston, William G.	1961 2009	(Glasgow: North Kelvinside)	Flat 0/2, 5 Knightswood Court, Glasgow G13 2XN / williamalston@hotmail.com	0141 959 3113
Beaton, Margaret S. (Miss) DCS	1989 2015	(Deacon)	64 Gardenside Grove, Carmyle, Glasgow G32 8EZ / margaretbeaton54@hotmail.com	0141 646 2297 / 07796 642382
Birch, James PgDip FRSA FIOC	2001 2007	(Auxiliary Minister)	1 Kirkhill Grove, Cambuslang, Glasgow G72 8EH	0141 583 1722
Black, William B. MA BD	1970 2011	(Stornoway: High)	33 Tankerland Road, Glasgow G44 4EN / revwillieblack@gmail.com	0141 637 4717
Blount, A. Sheila (Mrs) BD BA	1978 2010	(Cupar: St John's and Dairsie United)	28 Alcaig Road, Mosspark, Glasgow G52 1NH / asheilablount@gmail.com	0141 419 0746
Blount, Graham K. LLB BD PhD	1976 2017	(Presbytery Clerk: Glasgow)	28 Alcaig Road, Mosspark, Glasgow G52 1NH / Graham.Blount@churchofscotland.org.uk	0141 419 0746
Campbell, A. Iain MA DipEd	1961 1997	(Busby)	430 Clarkston Road, Glasgow G44 3QF / iaingillian@talktalk.net	0141 637 7460
Campbell, John MA BA BSc	1973 2009	(Caldwell)	96 Boghead Road, Lenzie, Glasgow G66 4EN / johncampbell.lenzie@gmail.com	0141 776 0874
Carruth, Patricia A. (Mrs) BD	1998 2012	(Coatbridge: Blairhill Dundyvan)	38 Springhill Farm Road, Baillieston, Glasgow G69 6GW	0141 771 3758
Cartlidge, Graham R.G. MA BD STM	1977 2015	(Glasgow: Eastwood)	5 Briar Grove, Newlands, Glasgow G43 2TG	0141 637 3228
Cherry, Alastair J. BA BD FPLD	1982 2009	(Glasgow: Penilee St Andrew's)	8 Coruisk Drive, Clarkston, Glasgow G76 7NG / ajcherry133@gmail.com	0141 571 6052
Clark, Douglas W. LTh	1993 2015	(Lenzie: Old)	2 Poplar Drive, Lenzie, Glasgow G66 4DN / douglaswclark@hotmail.com	0141 776 1298
Cowie, Marian (Mrs) MA BD MTh	1990 2012	(Aberdeen: Midstocket)	120e Southbrae Drive, Glasgow G12 1TZ / mcowieou@aol.com	07740 174969
Cunningham, Alexander MA BD	1961 2002	(Presbytery Clerk: Glasgow)	18 Lady Jane Gate, Bothwell, Glasgow G71 8BW	01698 811051

Name	Ord.	App.	Charge / Position	Address	Tel.
Cunningham, James S.A. MA BD BLitt PhD	1992	2000	(Glasgow: Barlanark Greyfriars)	'Kirkland', 5 Inveresk Place, Coatbridge ML5 2DA	01236 421541
Drummond, John W. MA BD	1971	2011	(Rutherglen: West and Wardlawhill)	25 Kingsburn Drive, Rutherglen, Glasgow G73 2AN	0141 571 6002
Duff, T. Malcolm F. MA BD MTh	1985	2009	(Glasgow: Queen's Park)	54 Hawkhead Road, Paisley PA1 3NB	0141 570 0614 / 07846 926584
Dunsmore, Barry W. MA BD	1982	2019	(Aberdeen: St Machar's Cathedral)	25H Hughenden Gardens, Hyndland, Glasgow G12 9XZ / barrydunsmore@gmail.com	07951 588912
Dutch, Morris M. BD BA Dip BTI	1998	2013	(Costa del Sol)	41 Baronald Drive, Glasgow G12 OHN / mnmdutch@yahoo.co.uk	0141 357 2286
Easton, David J.C. MA BD	1965	2005	(Burnside Blairbeth)	6 Peveril Court, Burnside, Glasgow G73 4RE / deaston@btinternet.com	0141 634 9775
Farrington, Alexandra LTh	2003	2015	(Campsie)	'Glenburn', High Banton, Kilsyth G65 0RA / revsfarrington@aol.co.uk	01236 824516
Ferguson, James B. LTh	1972	2002	(Lenzie: Union)	3 Bridgeway Place, Kirkintilloch, Glasgow G66 3HW	0141 588 5868
Fleming, Alexander F. MA BD	1966	1995	(Strathblane)	11 Bankwood Drive, Kilsyth, Glasgow G65 0GZ	01236 821461
Fraser, Alexander M. BD DipMin	1985	2019	(Glasgow: Knightswood St Margaret's)	3 Moor Road, Eaglesham G76 0BA / AFraser@churchofscotland.org.uk	0141 942 9281
Haley, Derek BD DPS	1960	1999	(Chaplain: Gartnavel Royal Hospital)	9 Kinnaird Crescent, Bearsden, Glasgow G61 2BN	
Hood, David P. BD CertMin DiplOB(Scot)	1997	2019	(Chaplain: Marie Curie Hospice)	Flat 1/2, 32 Giffnock Park Avenue, Giffnock G46 6AY / DHood@churchofscotland.org.uk	
Hope, Evelyn P. (Miss) BA BD	1990	1998	(Wishaw: Thornlie)	Flat 0/1, 48 Moss Side Road, Glasgow G41 3UA	0141 649 1522
Hughes, Helen (Miss) DCS	1977	2008	(Deacon)	2/2, 43 Burnbank Terrace, Glasgow G20 6UQ / helhug35@gmail.com	0141 333 9459 / 07752 604817
Hunter, Alastair G. MSc BD	1976	2010	(University of Glasgow)	13 Kilmardinny Crescent, Bearsden, Glasgow G61 3NP	0141 931 5862
Johnston, Robert W.M. MA BD STM MTh PhD	1964	1999	(Glasgow: Temple Anniesland)		0141 636 5819
Johnstone, H. Martin J. MA BD	1989	2020	(Secretary: Church and Society Council)	3/1, 952 Pollokshaws Road, Glasgow G41 2ET / MJohnstone@churchofscotland.org.uk	
Lang, I. Pat (Miss) BSc	1996	2003	(Dunoon: The High Kirk)	37 Crawford Drive, Glasgow G15 6TW	0141 944 2240
Lloyd, John M. BD CertMin	1984	2009	(Glasgow: Croftfoot)	17 Acacia Way, Cambuslang, Glasgow G72 7ZY	07879 812816
Lunan, David W. MA BD DLitt DD	1970	2009	(Presbytery Clerk: Glasgow)	30 Mill Road, Banton, Glasgow G65 0RD	01236 824110 / 0141 943 1103
MacDonald, Kenneth MA BA	2001	2006	(Auxiliary Minister)	5 Henderland Road, Bearsden, Glasgow G61 1AH	
MacFadyen, Anne M. (Mrs) BSc BD FSAScot	1995	2003	(Auxiliary Minister)	295 Mearns Road, Glasgow G77 5LT	0141 639 3605
Mackenzie, Gordon R. BSc-Agr BD	1977	2014	(Chapelhall)	16 Crowhill Road, Bishopbriggs, Glasgow G64 1QY / rev-g.mackenzie@btopenworld.com	0141 772 6052
MacKinnon, Campbell BSc BD	1982	2019	(Glasgow: Balshagray Victoria Park)	36 Hilton Terrace, Bishopbriggs, Glasgow G64 3HB / cm.ccmackinnon@gmail.com	0141 772 3811
MacKinnon, Charles M. BD	1989	2009	(Kilsyth: Anderson)		
McLachlan, Eric BD MTh	1978	2005	(Glasgow: Cardonald)	16 Kinpurnie Road, Paisley PA1 3HH / eric.janis@btinternet.com	0141 810 5789
McLachlan, T. Alastair BSc	1972	2009	(Craignish with Kilbrandon and Kilchattan with Kilninver and Kilmelford)	9 Alder Road, Milton of Campsie, Glasgow G66 8HH / talastair@btinternet.com	01360 319861

McLaren, D. Muir MA BD MTh PhD	1971	2001	(Glasgow: Mosspark)	House 44, 145 Shawhill Road, Glasgow G43 1SX muir44@yahoo.co.uk	07931 155779
McLaughlin, Cathie H. (Mrs)	2014	2018	(Ordained Local Minister)	8 Lamlash Place, Glasgow G33 3XH	0141 774 2483
Macleod, Donald BD LRAM DRSAM	1987	2008	(Blairgowrie)	9 Millersneuk Avenue, Lenzie G66 5HJ donmac2@sky.com	0141 776 6235
McLellan, Margaret DCS	1986	2018	(Deacon)	18 Broom Road East, Newton Mearns, Glasgow G77 5SD margaretdmclellan@outlook.com	0141 639 6853
MacQuarrie, Stuart JP BD BSc MBA	1984	2020	(Chaplain: University of Glasgow)		
McWilliam, Alan BD MTh	1993	2019	(Glasgow: Whiteinch)	1 Springbank Gardens, Glasgow G31 4QD	
Manastireanu, Daniel BA MTh	2010	2020	(Glasgow: St Paul's)	61 Vancouver Walk, Glasgow G40 4TP	
Miller, John D. BA BD DD	1971	2007	(Glasgow: Castlemilk East)	98 Kirkcaldy Road, Glasgow G41 4LD rev.john.miller@btinternet.com	0141 423 0221
Moffat, Thomas BSc BD	1976	2008	(Culross and Torryburn)	Flat 8/1, 8 Cranston Street, Glasgow G3 8GG tom@gallus.org.uk	0141 248 1886
Nelson, Thomas BSc BD	1992	2002	(Netherlee)	11a Crosshill Drive, Rutherglen, Glasgow G73 3QU	0141 534 7834
Ninian, Esther J. (Miss) MA BD	1993	2015	(Newton Mearns)	21 St Ronan's Drive, Rutherglen, Rutherglen G73 3SR estherninian5914@btinternet.com	0141 647 9720
Paciti, Stephen A. MA	1963	2003	(Black Mount with Culter with Libberton and Quothquan)	157 Nithsdale Road, Glasgow G41 5RD	0141 423 5792
Pearson, Wilma (Mrs) BD	2004	2018	(Associate, Glasgow: Cathcart Trinity)	90 Newlands Road, Glasgow G43 2R WPearson@churchofscotland.org.uk	0141 632 2491
Raeburn, Alan C. MA BD	1971	2010	(Glasgow: Battlefield East)	3 Orchard Gardens, Strathaven ML10 6UN acraeburn@hotmail.com	01357 522924
Ramsay, W.G.	1967	1999	(Glasgow: Springburn)	53 Kelvinvale, Kirkintilloch, Glasgow G66 1RD billram@btopenworld.com	0141 776 2915
Reid, Iain M.A. BD CQSW	1990	2017	(Paisley Glenburn)	16 Walker Court, Glasgow G16 6QP ireid@churchofscotland.org.uk	0141 577 1200
Ross, Donald M. MA	1953	1993	(Industrial Mission Organiser)	14 Cartsbridge Road, Busby, Glasgow G76 8DH	0141 644 2220
Shackleton, William	1960	1996	(Greenock: Wellpark West)	3 Tynwald Avenue, Burnside, Glasgow G73 4RN	0141 569 9407
Smith, G. Stewart MA BD STM	1966	2006	(Glasgow: King's Park)	33 Brent Road, Stewartfield, East Kilbride, Glasgow G74 4RA Tel/Fax stewartandmary@googlemail.com	01355 226718
Spencer, John MA BD	1962	2001	(Dumfries: Lincluden with Holywood)	10 Kinkell Gardens, Kirkintilloch, Glasgow G66 2HJ	0141 777 8935
Stewart, Diane E. BD	1988	2006	(Milton of Campsie)	4 Miller Gardens, Bishopbriggs, Glasgow G64 1FG destewart@givemail.co.uk	0141 762 1358
Stewart, Norma D. (Miss) MA MEd MTh	1977	2000	(Glasgow: Strathbungo Queen's Park)	127 Nether Auldhouse Road, Glasgow G43 2YS	0141 637 6956
Thomson, Andrew BA	1976	2007	(Airdrie: Broomknoll)	3 Laurel Wynd, Drumsagard Village, Cambuslang, Glasgow G72 7BH AThomson@churchofscotland.org.uk	0141 641 2936 07772 502774
Tuton, Robert M. MA	1957	1995	(Glasgow: Shettleston Old)	6 Holmwood Gardens, Uddingston, Glasgow G71 7BH	01698 321108
White, C. Peter BVMS BD	1974	2011	(Glasgow: Sandyford Henderson Memorial)	2 Hawthorn Place, Torrance, Glasgow G64 4EA revcpw@gmail.com	01360 622680
White, David M. BA BD DMin	1988	2016	(Kirkintilloch St Columba's)	9 Lapwing Avenue, Lenzie, Glasgow G66 3DJ drdavidmwhite@btinternet.com	0141 578 4357

Whiteford, John D. MA BD	1989 2016	(Glasgow: Newlands South)	42 Maxwell Drive, East Kilbride, Glasgow G74 4HJ JWhiteford@churchofscotland.org.uk	07809 290806
Whyte, James BD	1981 2011	(Fairlie)	32 Torburn Avenue, Giffnock, Glasgow G46 7RB jameswhyte89@btinternet.com	0141 620 3043
Wilson, Phyllis M. (Mrs) DipCom DipRE	1985 2006	(Motherwell: South Dalziel)	Glasgow thomas.wilson38@btinternet.com	
Younger, Adah (Mrs) BD	1978 2004	(Glasgow: Dennistoun Central)	7 Gartocher Terrace, Glasgow G32 0HE	0141 774 6475

GLASGOW ADDRESSES

Banton	Kelvinhead Road, Banton
Bishopbriggs	
Kenmure	Viewfield Road, Bishopbriggs
Springfield Cambridge	The Leys, off Springfield Road
Broom	Mearns Road, Newton Mearns
Burnside Blairbeth	Church Avenue, Burnside
	Kirkriggs Avenue, Blairbeth
Busby	Church Road, Busby
Cadder	Cadder Road, Bishopbriggs
Cambuslang	Arnott Way
Flemington Hallside	Hutchinson Place
Campsie	Main Street, Lennoxtown
Chryston	Main Street, Chryston
Eaglesham	Montgomery Street, Eaglesham
Fernhill and Cathkin	Neilvaig Drive
Gartcosh	113 Lochend Road, Gartcosh
Giffnock	
Orchardhill	Church Road
South	Eastwood Toll
The Park	Ravenscliffe Drive
Glenboig	Main Street, Glenboig
Greenbank	Eaglesham Road, Clarkston
Kilsyth	
Anderson	Kingston Road, Kilsyth
Burns and Old	Church Street, Kilsyth
Kirkintilloch	
Hillhead	Newdyke Road, Kirkintilloch
St Columba's	Waterside Road nr Auld Aisle Road
St David's Mem Pk	Alexandra Street
St Mary's	Cowgate

Lenzie	
Old	Kirkintilloch Road x Garngaber Ave
Union	65 Kirkintilloch Road
Maxwell	Waterfoot Road
Mearns Castle	
Mearns	Mearns Road, Newton Mearns
Milton of Campsie	Locheil Drive, Milton of Campsie
Moodiesburn	20 Blackwoods Crescent, Moodiesburn
Netherlee	Ormonde Drive x Ormonde Avenue
and Stamperland	Stamperland Gardens, Clarkston
Newton Mearns	Ayr Road, Newton Mearns
Rutherglen	
Stonelaw	Main Street at Queen Street
West and Wardlawhill	Stonelaw Road x Dryburgh Avenue
	3 Western Avenue
Stepps	Whitehill Avenue
Thornliebank	61 Spiersbridge Road
Torrance	School Road, Torrance
Twechar	Main Street, Twechar
Williamwood	4 Vardar Avenue, Clarkston
Glasgow	
Baillieston	
Mure Memorial	Maxwell Drive, Garrowhill
St Andrew's	Bredisholm Road
Balshagray Victoria Pk	218–230 Broomhill Drive
Barlanark Greyfriars	Edinburgh Rd x Hallhill Rd (365)
Blawarthill	Millbrix Avenue

Bridgeton St Francis in the East	26 Queen Mary Street
Broomhill Hyndland	64–66 Randolph Rd (x Marlborough Ave)
Calton Parkhead	122 Helenvale Street
Cardonald	2155 Paisley Road West
Carmunnock	Kirk Road, Carmunnock
Carmyle	155 Carmyle Avenue
Carntyne	358 Carntynehall Road
Carnwadric	556 Boydstone Road, Thornliebank
Castlemilk	1 Dougrie Road
Cathcart	
Old	119 Carmunnock Road
Trinity	90 Clarkston Road
Cathedral	Cathedral Square, 2 Castle Street
Causeway, Tollcross	1134 Tollcross Road
Clincarthill	1216 Cathcart Road
Colston Milton	Egilsay Crescent
Colston Wellpark	1378 Springburn Road
Cranhill	109 Bellrock St (at Bellrock Cr)
Croftfoot	Croftpark Ave x Crofthill Road
Dennistoun New	9 Armadale Street
Drumchapel	
St Andrew's	153 Garscadden Road
St Mark's	281 Kinfauns Drive
Easterhouse	
Eastwood	Boyndie Street
	Mansewood Road
Gairbraid	1517 Maryhill Road
Gallowgate	Calton Parkhead halls
	122 Helenvale Street
Garthamlock and Craigend	46 Porchester Street
Gorbals	1 Errol Gardens

Govan and Linthouse	Govan Cross
Hillington Park	24 Berryknowes Road
Ibrox	Carillon Road x Clifford Street
John Ross Memorial	100 Norfolk Street
Jordanhill	28 Woodend Drive (x Munro Road)
Kelvinbridge	Belmont Street at Belmont Bridge
Kelvinside Hillhead	Observatory Road
Kenmuir Mount Vernon	2405 London Road, Mount Vernon
King's Park	242 Castlemilk Road
Kinning Park	Eaglesham Place
Knightswood St Margaret's	2000 Great Western Road
Langside	167–169 Ledard Road (x Lochleven Road)
Maryhill	1990 Maryhill Road
Merrylea	78 Merrylee Road
Newlands South	Riverside Road x Langside Drive
Partick South	259 Dumbarton Road
Trinity	20 Lawrence Street x Elie Street
Pollokshaws	223 Shawbridge Street
Pollokshields	Albert Drive x Shields Road
Possilpark	124 Saracen Street
Queen's Park Govanhill	170 Queen's Drive
Robroyston	34 Saughs Road
Ruchazie	4 Elibank Street (x Milncroft Road)
Ruchill Kelvinside	Shakespeare Street nr Maryhill Rd
St Andrew and St Nicholas	224 Hartlaw Crescent
St Andrew's East	681 Alexandra Parade
St Andrew's West	260 Bath Street
St Christopher's Priesthill and Nitshill	100 Priesthill Rd (x Muirshiel Cr)
St Columba	300 St Vincent Street
St David's Knightswood	66 Boreland Drive (nr Lincoln Avenue)
St Enoch's Hogganfield	860 Cumbernauld Road
St George's Tron	163 Buchanan Street
St James' (Pollok)	Lyoncross Road x Byrebush Road
St John's Renfield	22 Beaconsfield Road
St Paul's	30 Langdale St (x Greenrig St)
St Rollox	70 Fountainwell Road
Sandyford Henderson Memorial	Kelvinhaugh Street at Argyle Street
Sandyhills	28 Baillieston Rd nr Sandyhills Rd
Scotstoun	Earlbank Ave x Ormiston Ave
Shawlands Trinity	Shawlands Cross (1114 Pollokshaws Road)
Sherbrooke Mosspark	Nithsdale Rd x Sherbrooke Avenue
Shettleston New	679 Old Shettleston Road
Springburn	180 Springburn Way
Temple Anniesland	869 Crow Road
Toryglen	Glenmore Ave nr Prospecthill Road
Trinity Possil and Henry Drummond	2 Crowhill Street (x Broadholm Street)
Tron St Mary's	128 Red Road
Wallacewell	57 Northgate Rd.. Balornock
Wellington	University Ave x Southpark Ave
Whiteinch	1a Northinch Court
Yoker	10 Hawick Street

(17) HAMILTON (F W)

Meets at Motherwell: Dalziel St Andrew's Parish Church on the first Tuesday of February, March, May, September, October, November and December, and on the third Tuesday of June.

Presbytery Office: Rex House, 103 Bothwell Road, Hamilton ML3 0DW   01698 285672
hamilton@churchofscotland.org.uk

Clerk: REV. GORDON A. McCRACKEN BD CertMin DMin   c/o The Presbytery Office

Depute Clerk: Vacant

Presbytery Treasurer: MR DAVID J. WATT BAcc CA CPFA   c/o The Presbytery Office   01698 285672
david.j.watt@btinternet.com

1	Airdrie: Cairnlea (F H W) linked with Calderbank (F T)			**Cairnlea: 01236 762101**
	Peter H. Donald MA PhD BD	1991 2018	31 Victoria Place, Airdrie ML6 9BU	01236 753159
			PDonald@churchofscotland.org.uk	

2 Airdrie: Clarkston (F W)
Hanna I. Rankine BA BD — 2018
enquiries@airdrieclarkstonparishchurch.org.uk
66 Wellhall Road, Hamilton ML3 9BY
HRankine@churchofscotland.org.uk
01236 756862

3 Airdrie: High (W) linked with Caldercruix and Longriggend (H)
Ian R.W. McDonald BSc BD PhD — 2007
17 Etive Drive, Airdrie ML6 9QL
IMcDonald@churchofscotland.org.uk
High: **01236 779620**
01236 760023

4 Airdrie: Jackson (W)
Kay Gilchrist (Miss) BD — 1996 2008
48 Dunrobin Road, Airdrie ML6 8LR
KGilchrist@churchofscotland.org.uk
01236 597649

5 Airdrie: New Monkland (F H W) linked with Greengairs (F W)
William Jackson BD CertMin — 1994 2015
3 Dykehead Crescent, Airdrie ML6 6PU
WJackson@churchofscotland.org.uk
01236 761723

6 Airdrie: St Columba's
Margaret F. Currie BEd BD — 1980 1987
52 Kennedy Drive, Airdrie ML6 9AW
MCurrie@churchofscotland.org.uk
01236 763173

7 Airdrie: The New Wellwynd (W)
Robert A. Hamilton BA BD — 1995 2001
72 Inverlochy Road, Airdrie ML6 9DJ
RHamilton@churchofscotland.org.uk
01236 748646
01236 763022

8 Bargeddie (H W)
Vacant
Interim Moderator: Michael G. Lyall
The Manse, Manse Road, Bargeddie, Baillieston, Glasgow G69 6UB
MLyall@churchofscotland.org.uk
0141 771 1322
01698 813113

9 Bellshill: Central (F T W)
Kevin M. de Beer BTh — 1995 2016
32 Adamson Street, Bellshill ML4 1DT
KdeBeer@churchofscotland.org.uk
01698 841176
07555 265609

10 Bellshill: West (F H W)
Calum Stark LLB BD — 2011 2015
16 Croftpark Street, Bellshill ML4 1EY
CStark@churchofscotland.org.uk
01698 747581
01698 842877

11 Blantyre: Livingstone Memorial (F W) linked with Blantyre St Andrew's (F) info@livingstonechurch.org.uk
Murdo C. Macdonald MA BD — 2002 2017
332 Glasgow Road, Blantyre, Glasgow G72 9LQ
Murdo.Macdonald@churchofscotland.org.uk
01698 769699

12 Blantyre: Old (F H T W)
Sarah L. Ross (Mrs) BD MTh PGDip   2004   2013
The Manse, Craigmuir Road, High Blantyre, Glasgow G72 9UA   01698 769046
SRoss@churchofscotland.org.uk

13 Blantyre: St Andrew's See Blantyre: Livingstone Memorial

14 Bothwell (F H W)
Vacant
bothwellparishchurch@yahoo.com   **01698 854903**
Manse Avenue, Bothwell, Glasgow G71 8PQ   Tel 01698 853189 / 01698 854903
Fax 01698 854998
Session Clerk: David Craig   craigdavid241@gmail.com

15 Calderbank See Airdrie: Cairnlea
16 Caldercruix and Longriggend See Airdrie: High

17 Chapelhall (F H W) linked with Kirk o' Shotts (F H W)
Vacant
The Manse, Russell Street, Chapelhall, Airdrie ML6 8SG   01236 763439
Session Clerk, Chapelhall: Elizabeth Millar (Mrs)   millarelizabeth@btconnect.com   01698 870205

18 Cleland (F H) linked with Wishaw: St Mark's (F)
Graham Austin BD   1997   2008
3 Laburnum Crescent, Wishaw ML2 7EH   01698 384596
GAustin@churchofscotland.org.uk

19 Coatbridge: Blairhill Dundyvan (H W) linked with Coatbridge: Middle (W)   **Blairhill Dundyvan: 01236 435198**
Vacant
1 Nelson Terrace, East Kilbride, Glasgow G74 2EY   01355 520093
Session Clerk, Blairhill Dundyvan: Myra Fraser   myrafraser@hotmail.co.uk   01236 421728

20 Coatbridge: Calder (F H W) linked with Coatbridge: Old Monkland (F W)
Vacant
26 Bute Street, Coatbridge ML5 4HF   01236 421516
Session Clerk, Calder:
Session Clerk, Old Monkland: Alison McGowan (Mrs)   alisonrobertsonmcgowan@gmail.com   07798 644253

21 Coatbridge: Middle See Coatbridge: Blairhill Dundyvan

22 Coatbridge: New St Andrew's (W)
Fiona M. Nicolson BA BD CQSW   1996   2005
77 Eglinton Street, Coatbridge ML5 3JF   01236 437271
FNicolson@churchofscotland.org.uk

23 Coatbridge: Old Monkland See Coatbridge: Calder

24 Coatbridge: Townhead (F H)
Ecilo Selemani LTh MTh — 1993 — 2004
Crinan Crescent, Coatbridge ML5 2LH
ESelemani@churchofscotland.org.uk
01236 702914

25 Dalserf (F H)
Vacant
Session Clerk: Joan Pollok
Manse Brae, Dalserf, Larkhall ML9 3BN
joan.pollok@btinternet.com
01698 882195
07728 337212

26 East Kilbride: Claremont (F H W)
Gordon R. Palmer MA BD STM — 1986 — 2003
office@claremontparishchurch.co.uk
17 Deveron Road, East Kilbride, Glasgow G74 2HR
GPalmer@churchofscotland.org.uk
01355 238088
01355 248526

27 East Kilbride: Greenhills
John Brewster MA BD DipEd — 1988
21 Tumberry Place, East Kilbride, Glasgow G75 8TB
JBrewster@churchofscotland.org.uk
01355 221746
01355 242564

28 East Kilbride: Moncreiff (F H W)
Vacant
Session Clerk: William McDougall MBE
theoffice@moncrieffparishchurch.co.uk
16 Almond Drive, East Kilbride, Glasgow G74 2HX
mcdougall204@btinternet.com
01355 223328
01355 238639
01355 238075
07715 369757

29 East Kilbride: Mossneuk (F)
Vacant
Jim Murphy — 2014 — 2017
(Ordained Local Minister)
30 Eden Grove, Mossneuk, East Kilbride, Glasgow G75 8XU
10 Hillview Crescent, Bellshill ML4 1NX
JMurphy@churchofscotland.org.uk
01355 260954
01355 234196
01698 740189

30 East Kilbride: Old (H W)
Anne S. Paton BA BD — 2001
ekopc.office@btconnect.com
40 Maxwell Drive, East Kilbride, Glasgow G74 4HJ
APaton@churchofscotland.org.uk
01355 279004
01355 220732

31 East Kilbride: South (F H W)
Terry Ann Taylor BA MTh — 2005 — 2017
7 Clamps Wood, St Leonard's, East Kilbride, Glasgow G74 2HB
TTaylor@churchofscotland.org.uk
01355 902758

32 East Kilbride: Stewartfield (New Charge Development) (W)
Vacant
Session Clerk: Colin C. Russell
russellc56@gmail.com
07912 554291

No.	Name			Address / Email	Telephone
33	**East Kilbride: West (F H W)**				
	Mahboob Masih BA MDiv MTh	1999	2008	4 East Milton Grove, East Kilbride, Glasgow G75 8FN MMasih@churchofscotland.org.uk	01355 224469
34	**East Kilbride: Westwood (H W)**				
	Kevin Mackenzie BD DPS	1989	1996	16 Inglewood Crescent, East Kilbride, Glasgow G75 8QD Kevin.MacKenzie@churchofscotland.org.uk	**01355 245657** 01355 223992
35	**Greengairs** See Airdrie: New Monkland				
36	**Hamilton: Cadzow (F H W)**				
	W. John Carswell BS MDiv DPT	1996	2009	**contact@cadzowchurch.org.uk** 3 Carlisle Road, Hamilton ML3 7BZ JCarswell@churchofscotland.org.uk	**01698 428695** 01698 426682
37	**Hamilton: Gilmour and Whitehill (H W) linked with Hamilton: West (H W)**				**West: 01698 284670**
	Vacant				
	Session Clerk, Gilmour: Ann Paul			annepaul.gandw@gmail.com	01698 284670 01698 421697
	Session Clerk, West: Ian Hindle			ianmarilyn.hindle@googlemail.com	01698 429080
38	**Hamilton: Hillhouse (F W)**				
	Christopher A. Rankine MA MTh PgDE	2016		66 Wellhall Road, Hamilton ML3 9BY CRankine@churchofscotland.org.uk	01698 327579
39	**Hamilton: Old (F H W)**				
	I. Ross Blackman BSc MBA BD	2015		**office@hamiltonold.co.uk** 1 Chateau Grove, Hamilton ML3 7DS RBlackman@churchofscotland.org.uk	**01698 281905** 01698 640185
40	**Hamilton: St John's (H W)**				
	Joanne C. Hood (Miss) MA BD	2003	2012	9 Shearer Avenue, Ferniegair, Hamilton ML3 7FX JHood@churchofscotland.org.uk	**01698 283492** 01698 425002
41	**Hamilton: South (F H) linked with Quarter (F)**				**South: 01698 281014**
	Vacant				
	Session Clerk, South: Joanne Kennedy			The Manse, Limekilnburn Road, Quarter, Hamilton ML3 7XA hamiltonsouthchurch@outlook.com	01698 424511 07828 504176
	Session Clerk, Quarter: Louise Ross			louise.ross7@btinternet.com	01698 424458
42	**Hamilton: Trinity**				
	S. Lindsay A. Turnbull BSc BD	2014		69 Buchan Street, Hamilton ML3 8JY Lindsay.Turnbull@churchofscotland.org.uk	**01698 284254** 01698 284919

43 Hamilton: West See Hamilton: Gilmour and Whitehill

44 Holytown (W) linked with New Stevenston: Wrangholm Kirk (W)
Caryl A.E. Kyle (Mrs) BD DipEd   2008
The Manse, 260 Edinburgh Road, Holytown, Motherwell ML1 5RU   01698 832622
CKyle@churchofscotland.org.uk

45 Kirk o' Shotts (H) See Chapelhall

46 Larkhall: Chalmers (F H)
Vacant
Interim Moderator: Lorna I. MacDougall
Quarry Road, Larkhall ML9 1HH   01698 882238
L.MacDougall@churchofscotland.org.uk   01698 352090

47 Larkhall: St Machan's (F H W)
Alastair G. McKillop BD DipMin   1995   2004
2 Orchard Gate, Larkhall ML9 1HG   01698 321976
AMcKillop@churchofscotland.org.uk

48 Larkhall: Trinity
Vacant
Session Clerk: Wilma Gilmour (Miss)
13 Machan Avenue, Larkhall ML9 2HE   01698 881401
gilmourgilmour@btinternet.com   01698 883002

49 Motherwell: Crosshill (F H W) linked with Motherwell: St Margaret's (F W)
Vacant
Session Clerk, Crosshill: Willie Talbot   talbottally@aol.com   01698 269598
Session Clerk, St Margaret's:

50 Motherwell: Dalziel St Andrew's (F H T W)
Alistair S. May LLB BD PhD   2002   2020
4 Pollock Street, Motherwell ML1 1LP   **01698 264097**
AMay@churchofscotland.org.uk   01698 263414

51 Motherwell: North (F W) linked with Wishaw: Craigneuk and Belhaven (H)
Derek H.N. Pope BD   1987   1995
35 Birrens Road, Motherwell ML1 3NS   01698 266716
DPope@churchofscotland.org.uk

52 Motherwell: St Margaret's See Motherwell: Crosshill

53 **Motherwell: St Mary's (H T W)**
Bryce Calder MA BD   1995   **office@stmarysmotherwell.org.uk**
19 Orchard Street, Motherwell ML1 3JE
BCalder@churchofscotland.org.uk   **01698 268854**
07986 144834

54 **Motherwell: South (F H T)**
Alan W. Gibson BA BD   2001   2016   62 Manse Road, Motherwell ML1 2PT
Alan.Gibson@churchofscotland.org.uk   01698 239279

55 **Newarthill and Carfin (F W)**
Elaine W. McKinnon MA BD   1988   2014   Church Street, Newarthill, Motherwell ML1 5HS
EMcKinnon@churchofscotland.org.uk   01698 296850

56 **Newmains: Bonkle (F H W) linked with Newmains: Coltness Memorial (F H W)**
Graham Raeburn MTh   2004   5 Kirkgate, Newmains, Wishaw ML2 9BT
GRaeburn@churchofscotland.org.uk   **01698 344001**
01698 383858

57 **Newmains: Coltness Memorial** See Newmains: Bonkle
58 **New Stevenston: Wrangholm Kirk** See Holytown

59 **Overtown (F W)**
Lorna I. MacDougall MA DipGC BD   2003   2017   The Manse, 146 Main Street, Overtown, Wishaw ML2 0QP
LMacDougall@churchofscotland.org.uk   **01698 358727**
01698 352090

60 **Quarter** See Hamilton: South

61 **Shotts: Calderhead Erskine**
Vacant
Session Clerk: Liam T. Haggart SSC   The Manse, 9 Kirk Road, Shotts ML7 5ET
a2lth@hotmail.com   01501 823204
07896 557687

62 **Stonehouse: St Ninian's (F H T W)**
Stewart J. Cutler BA Msc DipHE   2017   **info@st-ninians-stonehouse.org.uk**
4 Hamilton Way, Stonehouse, Larkhall ML9 3PU
revstewartcutler@gmail.com   01698 791508
Stonehouse: St Ninian's is a Local Ecumenical Partnership with the United Reformed Church

63 **Strathaven: Avendale Old and Drumclog (F H W)**
Alan B. Telfer BA BD   1983   2010   **avendale_office@btconnect.com**
4 Fortrose Gardens, Strathaven ML10 6SH
ATelfer@churchofscotland.org.uk   **01357 529748**
01357 523031

			Tel	Fax
64	**Strathaven: Trinity (F H W)** Shaw J. Paterson BSc BD MSc	1991		15 Lethame Road, Strathaven ML10 6AD SPaterson@churchofscotland.org.uk	01357 520019 01357 529316
65	**Uddingston: Burnhead (F H W)** Les N. Brunger BD	2010		90 Laburnum Road, Uddingston, Glasgow G71 5DB LBrunger@churchofscotland.org.uk	01698 813716
66	**Uddingston: Old (F H W)** Fiona L.J. McKibbin (Mrs) MA BD	2011		1 Belmont Avenue, Uddingston, Glasgow G71 7AX FMcKibbin@churchofscotland.org.uk	**01698 814015** 01698 814757
67	**Uddingston: Viewpark (F H W)** Michael G. Lyall BD	1993	2001	14 Holmbrae Road, Uddingston, Glasgow G71 6AP MLyall@churchofscotland.org.uk	**01698 810478** 01698 813113
68	**Wishaw: Cambusnethan North (F H W)** Mhorag Macdonald (Ms) MA BD	1989		350 Kirk Road, Wishaw ML2 8LH Mhorag.Macdonald@churchofscotland.org.uk	01698 381305
69	**Wishaw: Cambusnethan Old and Morningside (W)** Vacant Session Clerk: Graeme Vincent			22 Coronation Street, Wishaw ML2 8LF gvincent@theiet.org	01698 384235 01555 752166
70	**Wishaw: Craigneuk and Belhaven** See Motherwell North				
71	**Wishaw: Old (F H)** Vacant Session Clerk: Thomas W. Donaldson			130 Glen Road, Wishaw ML2 7NP tomdonaldson@talktalk.net	**01698 376080** 01698 375134 01698 357605
72	**Wishaw: St Mark's** See Cleland				
73	**Wishaw: South Wishaw (F H W)** Terence C. Moran BD CertMin	1995	2015	**southwishaw@tiscali.co.uk** 3 Walter Street, Wishaw ML2 8LQ TMoran@churchofscotland.org.uk	**01698 375306** 01698 767459

B. In other appointments

Buck, Maxine	2007	2015	Auxiliary Minister, Presbytery	Brownlee House, Mauldslie Road, Carluke ML8 5HW MBuck@churchofscotland.org.uk	01555 759063
Gilroy, Lorraine (Mrs) DCS	1988		Deacon	68 Clement Drive, Airdrie ML16 7FB lorraine.gilroy@sky.com	07923 540602
McCracken, Gordon A. BD CertMin DMin	1988	2015	Presbytery Clerk: Hamilton	1 Kenilworth Road, Lanark ML11 7BL	07918 600720
Pandian, Ali R. BA BD PGCertHC DipPS	2017		Healthcare Chaplain: University Hospital Wishaw	50 Netherton Street, Wishaw ML2 0DP APandian@churchofscotland.org.uk	01698 366779 07966 368344

C. Demitted

Barrie, Arthur P. LTh	1973	2007	(Hamilton: Cadzow)	30 Airbles Crescent, Motherwell ML1 3AR elizabethbarrie@ymail.com	01698 261147
Baxendale, Georgina M. DipEd BD DMin	1981	2014	(Motherwell: South)	32 Meadowhead Road, Plains, Airdrie ML6 7HG georgiebaxendale@btinternet.com	01236 842752
Buchanan, Neil BD	1991	2019	(East Kilbride: Moncrieff)	40 Links View, Port Seton, Prestonpans EH32 0EZ NBuchanan@churchofscotland.org.uk	01875 814632
Collard, John K. MA BD	1986	2019	(Interim Minister)	1 Nelson Terrace, East Kilbride G74 2EY JCollard@churchofscotland.org.uk	01355 520093
Colvin, Sharon E.F. (Mrs) BD LRAM LTCL	1985	2008	(Airdrie: Jackson)	25 Balblair Road, Airdrie ML6 6GQ dibleycol@hotmail.com	01236 590796
Cook, J. Stanley BD Dip PSS	1974	2001	(Hamilton: West)	Mansend, 137A Old Manse Road, Netherton, Wishaw ML2 0EW stancook@blueyonder.co.uk	01698 299600
Donaldson, George M. MA BD	1984	2015	(Caldercruix and Longriggend)	4 Toul Gardens, Motherwell ML1 2FE g.donaldson505@btinternet.com	01698 239477
Doyle, David W. MA BD	1977	2015	(Motherwell: St Mary's)	76 Kethers Street, Motherwell ML1 3HN revamore2@tiscali.co.uk	01698 263472
Fuller, Agnes A. (Mrs) BD	1987	2014	(Bellshill: West)	14 Croftpark Street, Bellshill ML14 1EY	01698 748244
Gibson, James M. TD LTh LRAM	1978	2019	(Bothwell)	22 Kirklands Crescent, Bothwell, Glasgow G71 8HU JGibson@churchofscotland.org.uk	01698 854907
Grier, James BD	1991	2005	(Coatbridge: Middle)	14 Love Drive, Bellshill ML4 1BY	01698 742545
Jessamine, Alistair L. MA BD	1979	2011	(Dunfermline: Abbey)	11 Gallowhill Farm Cottages, Strathaven ML10 6BZ	01357 520934
Jones, Robert BSc BD	1990	2017	(Rosskeen)	3 Grantown Avenue, Airdrie ML6 8HH rob2jones@btinternet.com	07761 782714
Kent, Robert M. MA BD	1973	2011	(Hamilton: St John's)	48 Fyne Crescent, Larkhall ML9 2UX robertmkent@talktalk.net	01698 769244
McDonald, John A. MA BD	1978	1997	(Cumbernauld: Condorrat)	17 Thomson Drive, Bellshill ML4 3ND	
McKee, Norman B. BD	1987	2010	(Uddingston: Old)	148 Station Road, Blantyre, Glasgow G72 9BW normanmckee946@btinternet.com	01698 827358
MacKenzie, Ian C. MA BD	1970	2011	(Interim Minister)	21 Wilson Street, Motherwell ML1 1NP iancmac@blueyonder.co.uk	01698 301230
Munton, James G. BA	1969	2002	(Coatbridge: Old Monkland)	2 Moorcroft Drive, Airdrie ML6 8ES revjgm1@gmail.com	01236 754848

Murdoch, Iain C. MA LLB DipEd BD	1995	2017	(Wishaw: Cambusnethan Old and Morningside)	2 Pegasus Avenue, Carluke ML8 5TN / iaincmurdoch@btopenworld.com	01555 773891
Ogilvie, Colin BA DCS	1998	2015	(Deacon)	21 Neilsland Drive, Motherwell ML1 3DZ / colinogilvie2@gmail.com	01698 321836 / 07837 287804
Price, Peter O. CBE QHC BA FPhS	1957	1996	(Blantyre: Old)	22 Old Bothwell Road, Bothwell, Glasgow G71 8AW / peteroprice@sky.com	01698 854032
Salmond, James S. BA BD MTh ThD	1979	2003	(Holytown)	165 Torbothie Road, Shotts ML7 5NE	01698 817582
Stevenson, John LTh	1998	2006	(Cambuslang: St Andrew's)	20 Knowehead Gardens, Uddingston, Glasgow G71 7PY / therev20@sky.com	
Stewart, William T. BD	1980	2018	(Glassford with Strathaven: East)	8 Cot Castle Grove, Stonehouse ML9 3RQ	01698 793979
Tait, Agnes (Mrs) DCS	1995		(Deacon)	10 Carnoustie Crescent, Greenhills, East Kilbride, Glasgow G75 8TE	01355 243095
Thomson, John M.A. TD JP BD ThM	1978	2014	(Hamilton: Old)	8 Skylands Place, Hamilton ML3 8SB / jt@john1949.plus.com	01698 422511
Waddell, Elizabeth A. (Mrs) BD	1999	2014	(Hamilton: West)	114 Branchalfield, Wishaw ML2 8QD / elizabethwaddell@tiscali.co.uk	01698 382909
Wallace, Douglas W. MA BD	1981	2019	(East Kilbride: Stewartfield)	11 Cromalt Avenue, East Kilbride, Glasgow G75 GQ / DWallace@churchofscotland.org.uk	
Wilson, James H. LTh	1970	1996	(Cleland)	21 Austine Drive, Hamilton ML3 7YE / wilsonjh@blueyonder.co.uk	01698 457042
Wyllie, Hugh R. MA DD FCIBS	1962	2000	(Hamilton: Old)	18 Chantinghall Road, Hamilton ML3 8NP	01698 420002
Zambonini, James LIADip	1997	2015	(Auxiliary Minister)	100 Old Manse Road, Netherton, Wishaw ML2 0EP	01698 350889

HAMILTON ADDRESSES

Airdrie
Cairnlea — 89 Graham Street
Clarkston — Forrest Street
High — North Bridge Street
Jackson — Glen Road
New Monkland — Glenmavis
St Columba's — Thrashbush Road
The New Wellwynd — Wellwynd

Coatbridge
Blairhill Dundyvan — Blairhill Street
Calder — Calder Street
Middle — Bank Street
New St Andrew's — Church Street
Old Monkland — Woodside Street
Townhead — Crinan Crescent

East Kilbride
Claremont — High Common Road, St Leonard's
Greenhills — Greenhills Centre
Moncreiff — Calderwood Road
Mossneuk — Eden Drive
Old — Montgomery Street
South — Baird Hill, Murray
Stewartfield — Stewartfield Community Centre
West — Kittoch Street
Westwood — Belmont Drive, Westwood

Hamilton
Cadzow — Woodside Walk
Gilmour and Whitehill — Glasgow Road, Burnbank
Hillhouse — Clerkwell Road
Old — Leechlee Road
St John's — Duke Street
South — Strathaven Road
Trinity — Neilsland Square off Neilsland Road
West — Burnbank Road

Motherwell
Crosshill — Windmillhill Street x Airbles Street
Dalziel St Andrew's — Merry Street and Muir Street
North — Chesters Crescent
St Margaret's — Shields Road
St Mary's — Avon Street
South — Gavin Street

Uddingston
Burnhead — Laburnum Road
Old — Old Glasgow Road
Viewpark — Old Edinburgh Road

Wishaw
Cambusnethan North — Kirk Road
Old — Kirk Road
Craigneuk and Belhaven — Craigneuk Street
Old — Main Street
St Mark's — Coltness Road
South Wishaw — East Academy Street

(19) ARGYLL (F W)

Meets in the Village Hall, Tarbert, Loch Fyne, Argyll on the first Tuesday or Wednesday of March, June, September and December. For details, contact the Presbytery Clerk.

| Clerk: | MR W. STEWART SHAW DL BSC | 59 Barone Road, Rothesay, Isle of Bute PA20 0DZ
argyll@churchofscotland.org.uk | 07470 520240 |
| Treasurer: | REV. DAVID CARRUTHERS BD | The Manse, Park Road, Ardrishaig, Lochgilphead PA30 8HE
DCarruthers@churchofscotland.org.uk | 01546 603269 |

Appin (F) linked with Lismore

Vacant — An Mansa, Appin, Argyll PA38 4DS — Appin 01631 730435 / Lismore 01631 760077

Interim Moderator: Thomas W. Telfer — TTelfer@churchofscotland.org.uk — 01866 822204

Ardchattan (H W) linked with Coll (W) linked with Connel (W)

Willem J. Bezuidenhout BA BD MHEd MEd 1977 2019 — St Oran's Manse, Connel, Oban PA37 1PJ — WBezuidenhout@churchofscotland.org.uk — 01631 710214 / 07484 333923 / Coll 01879 230366

Ardrishaig (H) linked with South Knapdale

David Carruthers BD 1998 — The Manse, Park Road, Ardrishaig, Lochgilphead PA30 8HE — DCarruthers@churchofscotland.org.uk — 01546 603269

Barra (GD) linked with South Uist (GD)

Lindsay Schluter ThE CertMin PhD 1995 2016 — The Manse, Cuithir, Isle of Barra HS9 5XU — LSchluter@churchofscotland.org.uk — 01871 810230 / 07835 913963

Bute, United Church of (F W)

John Owain Jones MA BD FSAScot 1981 2011 — 10 Bishop Terrace, Rothesay, Isle of Bute PA20 9HF — JJones@churchofscotland.org.uk — 01700 504502

Campbeltown: Highland (H) linked with Sadell and Carradale (H) linked with Southend (F H)

Stephen Fulcher BA MA 1993 2012 — St Blaan's Manse, Southend, Campbeltown PA28 6RQ — SFulcher@churchofscotland.org.uk — 01586 830504

Campbeltown: Lorne and Lowland (F H)
Vacant
William Crossan   2014   2018   Lorne and Lowland Manse, Castlehill, Campbeltown PA28 6AN   01586 552468
(Ordained Local Minister)   Gowanbank, Kilkerran Road, Campbeltown PA28 6JL   01586 553543

Coll   See Ardchattan

Colonsay and Oronsay (W)
Guardianship of the Presbytery
Session Clerk: Kevin Bryne   colonsaybryne@gmail.com   01950 200320

Connel   See Ardchattan

Craignish
Vacant
Interim Moderator: David Carruthers   DCarruthers@churchofscotland.org.uk   01546 603269

Dunoon: St John's linked with Kirn and Sandbank (H W) (Central Cowal)
Vacant   The Manse, 13 Dhailling Park, Hunter Street, Kirn, Dunoon PA23 8FB   01369 702256
Interim Moderator: Alison Hay (Mrs)   AHay@churchofscotland.org.uk   01546 886213 / 07887 760086
Session Clerk, Kirn and Sandbank: James Anderson   j_anderson@btinternet.com   01369 705104

Dunoon: The High Kirk (H W) linked with Innellan (H) linked with Toward (H W) (South-East Cowal)
Vacant   7A Mathieson Lane, Innellan, Dunoon PA23 7SH   01369 830276
Interim Moderator: Alison Hay (Mrs)   AHay@churchofscotland.org.uk   01546 886213 / 07887 760086

Gigha and Cara (H) (GD) linked with Kilcalmonell linked with Killean and Kilchenzie (H)
Scott E. Burton BD DipMin   1999   2019   The Manse, Muasdale, Tarbert, Argyll PA29 6XD   01583 421086
   SBurton@churchofscotland.org.uk   07776 212726

Glassary, Kilmartin and Ford linked with North Knapdale (W)
Vacant   The Manse, Kilmichael Glassary, Lochgilphead PA31 8QA   01546 606926
Session Clerk, Glassary, Kilmartin and Ford: Linda Tighe   chalin@tiscali.co.uk   01546 600330
Session Clerk, North Knapdale: David Logue   sessionclerk@northknapdale.org   01546 870647

Glenorchy and Innishael (W) linked with Strathfillan (W)
Vacant
Session Clerk, Strathfillan: Mary Anderson   m.anderson53@btinternet.com   01838 300253

Innellan See Dunoon: The High Kirk

Iona (W) linked with Kilfinichen and Kilvickeon and the Ross of Mull (W)
Jenny Earl MA BD   2007   2018   1 The Steadings, Achavaich, Isle of Iona PA76 6SW   07769 994680
JEarl@churchofscotland.org.uk

Jura (GD) linked with North and West Islay (GD) linked with South Islay (GD H W) (Islay and Jura)
Vacant   The Manse, Bowmore, Isle of Islay PA43 7LH
Session Clerk, Jura: Heather Cameron   h.cameronjura@btinternet.com   01496 810271
Session Clerk, North and West Islay: marsalithomson@outlook.com   01496 820371
Marsali Thomson   01496 810236
Session Clerk, South Islay: Sue Hind   eddieandsue2000@yahoo.co.uk   01496 311494

Kilbrandon and Kilchattan linked with Kilninver and Kilmelford (Netherlorn FW)
Vacant   The Manse, Kilmelford, Oban PA34 4XA
Session Clerk, Kilbrandon and Kilchattan: jandjalex@gmail.com   01852 200565
Jean Alexander   01852 314242
Session Clerk, Kilninver and Kilmelford: sallyinglis12@gmail.com   01852 316271
Sally Inglis

Kilcalmonell See Gigha and Cara

Kilchrenan and Dalavich (W) linked with Muckairn (W)
Thomas W. Telfer BA MDiv   1986   2018   Muckairn Manse, Taynuilt PA35 1HW   01866 822204
TTelfer@churchofscotland.org.uk

Kilfinan linked with Kilmodan and Colintraive linked with Kyles (H) (West Cowal)
David Mitchell BD DipP'Theol MSc   1988   2006   West Cowal Manse, Kames, Tighnabruaich PA21 2AD   01700 811045
DMitchell@churchofscotland.org.uk

Kilfinichen and Kilvickeon and the Ross of Mull See Iona
Killean and Kilchenzie See Gigha and Cara
Kilmodan and Colintraive See Kilfinan

Kilmore and Oban (GD W)
Dugald J. Cameron BD DipMin MTh   1990   2007   obancofs@btinternet.com   **01631 562405**
Kilmore and Oban Manse, Ganavan Road, Oban PA34 5TU   01631 566253
Dugald.Cameron@churchofscotland.org.uk

Kilmun, Strone and Ardentinny: The Shore Kirk (H)
Vacant — The Manse, Blairmore, Dunoon PA23 8TE — 01369 840313
Janet K. MacKellar BSc ProfCertMgmt 2019 — Laurel Bank, 23 George Street, Dunoon PA23 8TE — 01369 705549
FCMI (Ordained Local Minister) — JMackellar@churchofscotland.org.uk
Session Clerk: James Ritchie — jamesgibbritchie@gmail.com — 01369 706949

Kilninver and Kilmelford See Kilbrandon and Kilchattan
Kirn and Sandbank See Dunoon: St John's
Kyles See Kilfinan
Lismore See Appin

Lochgilphead (F W) 1992 2005
Hilda C. Smith (Miss) MA BD MSc — Parish Church Manse, Manse Brae, Lochgilphead PA31 8QZ — 01546 602238
HSmith@churchofscotland.org.uk

Lochgoilhead (H) and Kilmorich linked with Strachur and Strathlachlan (Upper Cowal)
Robert K. Mackenzie MA BD PhD 1976 1998 — The Manse, Strachur, Cairndow PA27 8DG — 01369 860246
RKMackenzie@churchofscotland.org.uk

Muckairn See Kilchrenan and Dalavich
North and West Islay See Jura
North Knapdale See Glassary, Kilmartin and Ford

North Mull (F GD H W)
Vacant
Contact: Elizabeth Gibson — The New Manse, Gruline Road, Salen, Aros, Isle of Mull PA72 6JF — 01680 812541
New charge formed by the union of Kilninian and Kilmore, Salen and Ulva, Tobermory and Torosay and Kinlochspelvie
egibson@churchofscotland.org.uk

Rothesay: Trinity (H W) 2018
Sibyl A. Tchaikovsky BA BD MLitt — 12 Crichton Road, Rothesay, Isle of Bute PA20 9JR — 01700 504047
STchaikovsky@churchofscotland.org.uk

Saddell and Carradale See Campbeltown: Highland
Salen and Ulva See Kilninian and Kilmore

Skipness (F) linked with Tarbert, Loch Fyne and Kilberry (F H W)
Vacant
Session Clerk, Tarbert, Loch Fyne and Kilberry: Janne Leckie (Ms)   The Manse, Campbeltown Road, Tarbert, Argyll PA29 6SX   01880 821012
Janne.Leckie@argyll-bute.gov.uk   01880 820481

Southend See Campbeltown: Highland
South Islay See Jura
South Knapdale See Ardrishaig
South Uist See Barra
Strachur and Strathlachlan See Lochgoilhead and Kilmorich
Strathfillan See Glenorchy and Innishael
Tarbert, Loch Fyne and Kilberry See Skipness

Tiree (GD)
Vacant   The Manse, Scarinish, Isle of Tiree PA77 6TN   01879 220377
Interim Moderator: Douglas Allan   douglas.allan423@gmail.com   01700 502331
                                                                                            07478 134946

Toward See Dunoon: The High Kirk

West Lochfyneside: Cumlodden, Inveraray and Lochgair (F W)
Vacant
Interim Moderator: Margaret Jacobsen   mjacobsen@churchofscotland.org.uk   01546 606914
                                                                                 07833 177862
New charge formed by the union of Cumlodden, Lochfyneside, Lochgair and Glenaray and Inveraray

B. In other appointments

Anderson, David P. BSc BD	2002 2007	Senior Army Chaplain	Infantry Training Centre, Vimy Barracks, Catterick DL9 3PS padre.anderson180@mod.gov.uk	
Fulcher, Christine P. BEd	2012 2018	Ordained Local Minister, Team Minister, South Argyll	St Blaan's Manse, Southend, Campbeltown PA28 6SX CFulcher@churchofscotland.org.uk	01586 830504
Gibson, Elizabeth A. (Mrs) MA MLitt BD	2003 2013	Locum Minister, North Mull	Mo Dhachaidh, Lochdon, Isle of Mull PA64 6AP egibson@churchofscotland.org.uk	01680 812541
Ross, Kenneth R. OBE BA BD PhD	1982 2019	Theological Educator, Africa	Zomba Theological College, PO Box 130, Zomba, Malawi kross@thinkingmission.org	

C. Demitted

Acklam, Clifford R. BD MTh	1997	2018	(Glassary, Kilmartin and Ford with North Knapdale)	4 Knoll View Terrace, Westtown, New York 10998, United States of America	
Bell, Douglas W. MA LLB BD	1975	1993	(Alexandria: North)	3 Cairnbaan Lea, Cairnbaan, Lochgilphead PA31 8BA	01546 606815
Campbell, Roderick D.M. OStJ TD BD DMin FSAScot	1975	2019	(Cumlodden, Lochfyneside and Lochgair with Glenaray and Inveraray)	Windy Ridge, Glen Loanan, Taynuilt PA35 1EY Roderick.Campbell@churchofscotland.org.uk	01866 822623
Cringles, George G. BD	1981	2017	(Coll with Connel)	The Moorings, Ganavan Road, Oban PA34 5TU george.cringles@gmail.com	01631 564215
Dunlop, Alistair J. MA	1965	2004	(Saddell and Carradale)	8 Pipers Road, Cairnbaan, Lochgilphead PA31 8UF dunrevn@btinternet.com	01546 600316
Gray, William LTh	1971	2006	(Kilberry with Tarbert)	Lochnagar, Longsdale Road, Oban PA34 5DZ gray98@hotmail.com	01631 567471
Griffiths, Ruth I. (Mrs)	2004	2020	(Auxiliary Minister)	Kirkwood, Mathieson Lane, Innellan, Dunoon PA23 7TA	01369 830145
Henderson, Grahame McL. BD	1974	2008	(Kirn)	6 Gerhallow, Bullwood Road, Dunoon PA23 7QB ghende5884@aol.com	01369 702433
Hood, H. Stanley C. MA BD	1966	2000	(London: Crown Court)	10 Dalriada Place, Kilmichael Glassary, Lochgilphead PA31 8QA	01546 606168
Lamont, Archibald MA	1952	1992	(Kilcalmonell with Skipness)	22 Bonnyton Drive, Eaglesham, Glasgow G76 0LU	01349 865932
Lind, Michael J. LLB BD	1984	2012	(Campbeltown: Highland)	Maybank, Station Road, Conon Bridge, Dingwall IV7 8BJ mijylind@gmail.com	
Macfarlane, James PhD	1991	2011	(Lochgoilhead and Kilmorich)	'Lindores', 11 Bullwood Road, Dunoon PA23 7QJ mac.farlane@btinternet.com	01369 710626
McIvor, Anne (Miss) SRD BD	1996	2013	(Gigha and Cara)	20 Albyn Avenue, Campbeltown PA28 6LY annemcivor@btinternet.com	07901 964825
MacLeod, Roderick MBE MA BD PhD(Edin) PhD(Open)	1966	2011	(Cumlodden, Lochfyneside and Lochgair)	Creag-nam-Barnach, Furnace, Inveraray PA32 8XU mail@revroddy.co.uk	01499 500629
Marshall, Freda (Mrs) BD FCII	1993	2005	(Colonsay and Oronsay with Kilbrandon and Kilchattan)	Allt Mhaluidh, Glenview, Dalmally PA33 1BE mail@freda.org.uk	01838 200693
Mill, David GCSJ MA BD	1978	2018	(Kilmun, Strone and Ardentinny: The Shore Kirk)	The Hebrides, 107 Bullwood Road, Dunoon PA23 7QN revandevmill@aol.com	01369 707544
Millar, Margaret R.M. (Miss) BTh	1977	2008	(Kilchrenan and Dalavich with Muckairn)	Fearnoch Cottage, Fearnoch, Taynuilt PA35 1JB macoje@aol.com	01866 822416
Morrison, Angus W. MA BD	1959	1999	(Kildalton and Oa)	1 Livingstone Way, Port Ellen, Isle of Islay PA42 7EP	01496 300043
Park, Peter B. BD MCIBS	1997	2014	(Fraserburgh: Old)	Hillview, 24 McKelvie Road, Oban PA34 4GB peterpark9@btinternet.com	01631 565849
Ritchie, Walter M.	1973	1999	(Uphall: South)	Hazel Cottage, Barr Mor View, Kilmartin, Lochgilphead PA31 8UN	01546 510343
Scott, Randolph MA BD	1991	2013	(Jersey: St Columba's)	18 Lochan Avenue, Kirn, Dunoon PA23 8HT rev.rs@hotmail.com	01369 703175
Stewart, Joseph LTh	1979	2011	(Dunoon: St John's with Sandbank)	7 Glenmorag Avenue, Dunoon PA23 7LG	01369 703438
Taylor, Alan T. BD	1980	2005	(Isle of Mull Parishes)	25 Munro Gate, Bridge of Allan FK9 4DJ	01688 302496
Wilkinson, W. Brian MA BD	1968	2007	(Glenaray and Inveraray)	3 Achlonan, Taynuilt PA35 1JJ williambrian35@btinternet.com	01866 822036

(22) FALKIRK (W)

Meets at Falkirk Trinity Parish Church on the first Tuesday of September, December, March and May, on the fourth Tuesday of October and January and on the third Tuesday of June.

Clerk: REV. ANDREW SARLE BSc BD — 114 High Station Road, Falkirk FK1 5LN / **falkirk@churchofscotland.org.uk** — **07565 362074**

Depute Clerk and Treasurer: MR CHRISTOPHER DUNN — 3b Afton Road, Cumbernauld G67 2DS / **depclerk@falkirkpresbytery.org.uk** — **01236 720874** / **07799 478880**

Airth (F H)
James F. Todd BD CPS — 1984 2012 — The Manse, Airth, Falkirk FK2 8LS / JTodd@churchofscotland.org.uk — 01324 831120

Blackbraes and Shieldhill (W) linked with Muiravonside (F W)
Vacant
Interim Moderator: Scott W. Burton — 81 Stevenson Avenue, Polmont, Falkirk FK2 0GU / Scott.Burton@churchofscotland.org.uk — 01324 717757 / 01324 712062

Bo'ness: Old (F H T W)
Amanda J. MacQuarrie MA PGCE MTh — 2014 2016 — 10 Dundas Street, Bo'ness EH51 0DG / A.MacQuarrie@churchofscotland.org.uk — 01506 828504

Bo'ness: St Andrew's (F W)
Vacant
Interim Moderator: David Wandrum — St Andrew's Manse, 11 Erngath Road, Bo'ness EH51 9DP / DWandrum@churchofscotland.org.uk — **01506 825803** / 01506 822195 / 01236 723288

Bonnybridge: St Helen's (H W)
George MacDonald BTh — 1996 2009 — The Manse, 32 Reilly Gardens, High Bonnybridge FK4 2BB / GMacDonald@churchofscotland.org.uk — 01324 874807

Bothkennar and Carronshore (W)
Andrew J. Moore BSc BD — 2007 — 11 Hunter Place, Greenmount Park, Carronshore, Falkirk FK2 8QS / AMoore@churchofscotland.org.uk — 01324 570525

Brightons (F H T W)
Scott W. Burton BA BA — 2018 — **info@brightonschurch.org.uk** / The Manse, Maddiston Road, Brightons, Falkirk FK2 0JP / Scott.Burton@churchofscotland.org.uk — **01324 713855** / 01324 712062

Carriden (H W)
Vacant
David C. Wandrum 1993 2017 The Spires, Foredale Terrace, Carriden, Bo'ness EH51 9LW 01506 822141
(Auxiliary Minister) 5 Cawder View, Carrickstone Meadows, Cumbernauld, 01236 723288
Glasgow G68 0BN
DWandrum@churchofscotland.org.uk

Cumbernauld: Abronhill (H W)
Joyce A. Keyes (Mrs) BD 1996 2003 26 Ash Road, Cumbernauld, Glasgow G67 3ED 01236 723833
JKeyes@churchofscotland.org.uk

Cumbernauld: Condorrat (H W)
Grace I.M. Saunders BSc BTh 2007 2011 11 Rosehill Drive, Cumbernauld, Glasgow G67 4EQ 01236 452090
GSaunders@churchofscotland.org.uk

Cumbernauld: Kildrum (H W) linked with Cumbernauld St Mungo's (W)
Vacant 18 Fergusson Road, Balloch, Cumbernauld, Glasgow G67 1LS 01236 721513
David Nicholson DCS 1994 1993 2D Doonside, Kildrum, Cumbernauld, Glasgow G67 2HX 01236 732260
DNicholson@churchofscotland.org.uk

Cumbernauld: Old (H W)
Elspeth M. McKay LLB LLM PGCert BD 2014 2017 The Manse, 23 Baronhill, Cumbernauld, Glasgow G67 2SD 01236 728853
EMckay@churchofscotland.org.uk
Valerie S. Cuthbertson (Miss) DipTMus DCS 2003 2 Muirhill Court, Hamilton ML3 6DR 01698 429232
VCuthbertson@churchofscotland.org.uk

Cumbernauld: St Mungo's See Cumbernauld: Kildrum

Denny: Old (W) linked with Haggs (H W)
Raheel Arif BA 2019 haggschurch1@yahoo.co.uk 01324 819149
31 Duke Street, Denny FK6 6NR
RArif@churchofscotland.org.uk

Denny: Westpark (F H W)
D. I. Kipchumba Too BTh MTh MSc 2017 13 Baxter Crescent, Denny FK6 5EZ 01324 882220
KToo@churchofscotland.org.uk 07340 868067

Dunipace (F H)
Jean W. Gallacher (Mrs) 1989 The Manse, 239 Stirling Street, Dunipace, Denny FK6 6QJ 01324 824540
BD CMin CTheol DMin JGallacher@churchofscotland.org.uk

Falkirk: Bainsford (F H T W)
Vacant
Andrew Sarle BSc BD   2013   1 Valleyview Place, Newcarron Village, Falkirk FK2 7JB   07743 726013
(Ordained Local Minister)   114 High Station Road, Falkirk FK1 5LN
ASarle@churchofscotland.org.uk

Falkirk: Camelon (F W)
Vacant
G.F. (Erick) du Toit BTh   2016   2018   30 Cotland Drive, Falkirk FK2 7GE   **01324 870011**
(Associate Minister)   30 Cotland Drive, Falkirk FK2 7GE   01324 623631
EduToit@churchofscotland.org.uk   01324 623631

Falkirk: Grahamston United (F H T W)
Vacant   16 Cromwell Road, Falkirk FK1 1SF   01324 624461
Anne W. White BA DipTh   2018   94 Craigleith Road, Grangemouth FK3 0BA   01324 880864
(Ordained Local Minister)   Anne.White@churchofscotland.org.uk
Grahamston United is a Local Ecumenical Partnership with the Methodist and United Reformed Churches

Falkirk: Laurieston (W) linked with Redding and Westquarter (W)
Vacant   11 Polmont Road, Laurieston, Falkirk FK2 9QQ   01324 621196
Interim Moderator: Deborah L. van Welie   DLVanWelie@churchofscotland.org.uk   01324 713427

Falkirk: St Andrew's West (H W)
Alastair M. Horne BSc BD   1989   1997   1 Maggiewood's Loan, Falkirk FK1 5SJ   **01324 622091**
AHorne@churchofscotland.org.uk   01324 623308

Falkirk: Trinity (F H T W)
Robert S.T. Allan LLB DipLP BD   1991   2003   office@falkirktrinity.org.uk   **01324 611017**
9 Major's Loan, Falkirk FK1 5QF   01324 625124
RAllan@churchofscotland.org.uk

Grangemouth: Abbotsgrange (F T W)
Aftab Gohar MA MDiv PgDip   1996   2010   8 Naismith Court, Grangemouth FK3 9BQ   01324 482109
AGohar@churchofscotland.org.uk   07528 143784

Grangemouth: Kirk of the Holy Rood (W)
Ronald Matandakufa BTh MA   2014   2019   The Manse, Bowhouse Road, Grangemouth FK3 0EX   01324 337885
RMatandakufa@churchofscotland.org.uk

Grangemouth: Zetland (F H W)
Alison A. Meikle (Mrs) BD   1999   2014   Ronaldshay Crescent, Grangemouth FK3 9JH   01324 336729
AMeikle@churchofscotland.org.uk

Haggs See Denny: Old

Larbert: East (F W) Melville D. Crosthwaite BD DipEd DipMin	1984	1995	1 Cortachy Avenue, Carron, Falkirk FK2 8DH MCrosthwaite@churchofscotland.org.uk	01324 562402
Larbert: Old (F H) Guardianship of the Presbytery Session Clerk: Eric Appelbe			The Manse, 38 South Broomage Avenue, Larbert FK5 3ED larbertoldcontact@gmail.com	01324 872760 01324 556551
Larbert: West (H W) Julie M. Rennick (Mrs) BTh	2005	2019	27 Drysdale Avenue, Kinnaird, Larbert FK2 8RE JRennick@churchofscotland.org.uk	07368 198182
Muiravonside See Blackbraes and Shieldhill				
Polmont: Old (F W) Deborah L. van Welie (Ms) MTheol	2015		3 Orchard Grove, Polmont, Falkirk FK2 0XE DLVanWelie@churchofscotland.org.uk	**01324 715995** 01324 713427
Redding and Westquarter See Falkirk: Laurieston				
Sanctuary First (F T W) Albert O. Bogle BD MTh (Pioneer Minister)	1981	2016	49a Kenilworth Road, Bridge of Allan FK9 4RS AlbertBogle@churchofscotland.org.uk **Sanctuary First is a Presbytery Mission Initiative**	07715 374557
Slamannan Vacant Monica J. MacDonald (Mrs) (Ordained Local Minister)	2014		32 Reilly Gardens, High Bonnybridge, Bonnybridge FK4 2BB Monica.MacDonald@churchofscotland.org.uk	01324 874807
Stenhouse and Carron (F H) William Thomson BD	2001	2007	The Manse, 21 Tipperary Place, Stenhousemuir, Larbert FK5 4SX WThomson@churchofscotland.org.uk	01324 416628

B. In other appointments

Christie, Helen F. (Mrs) BD	1998	2015	Chaplain: (part-time) Forth Valley Hospitals	4B Glencairn Road, Cumbernauld G67 2EN / andychristie747@yahoo.com	01236 611583
Goodison, Michael J. BSc BD	2013		Chaplain: Army	40 Comyn Drive, Wallacestone, Falkirk FK2 7FH	07833 028256
McPherson, William BD DipEd	1994	2003	Chief Executive, The Vine Trust	83 Laburnum Road, Port Seton, Prestonpans EH32 0UD	01875 812252

C. Demitted

Black, Ian W. MA BD	1976	2013	(Grangemouth: Zetland)	Flat 1R, 2 Carrickvale Court, Carrickstone, Cumbernauld, Glasgow G68 0LA / iwblack@hotmail.com	01236 453370
Brown, Kathryn I. (Mrs)	2014	2019	(Ordained Local Minister)	1 Callendar Park Walk, Callendar Grange, Falkirk FK1 1TA / kaybrown1cpw@talktalk.net	01324 617352
Brown, T. John MA BD	1995	2006	(Tullibody: St Serf's)	1 Callendar Park Walk, Callendar Grange, Falkirk FK1 1TA / johnbrown1cpw@talktalk.net	01324 617352
Chalmers, George A. MA BD MLitt	1962	2002	(Catrine with Sorn)	3 Cricket Place, Brightons, Falkirk FK2 0HZ	01324 712030
Cowan, James S.A. BD DipMin	1986	2019	(Barrhead: St Andrew's)	30 Redding Road, Falkirk FK2 9XJ / jim_cowan@ntlworld.com	07966 489609
Gunn, F. Derek BD	1986	2017	(Airdrie: Clarkston)	6 Yardley Place, Falkirk FK2 7FH / RevDerekGunn@hotmail.com	01324 624938
Job, Anne J. BSc BD	1993	2010	(Kirkcaldy: Viewforth with Thornton)	5 Carse View, Airth, Falkirk FK2 8NY / aj@ajjob.co.uk	01324 832094
McDowall, Ronald J. BD	1980	2001	(Falkirk: Laurieston with Redding and Westquarter)	'Kailas', Windsor Road, Falkirk FK1 5EJ	01324 871947
Mathers, Alexena (Sandra)	2015	2018	(Ordained Local Minister)	10 Ercall Road, Brightons, Falkirk FK2 0RS / SMathers@churchofscotland.org.uk	01324 872253
Miller, Elsie M. (Miss) DCS	1974	2001	(Deacon)	30 Swinton Avenue, Rowanbank, Baillieston, Glasgow G69 6JR	0141 771 0857
Morrison, Iain C. BA BD	1990	2003	(Linlithgow: St Ninian's Craigmailen)	Whaligoe, 53 Eastcroft Drive, Polmont, Falkirk FK2 0SU / iain@kirkweb.org	01324 713249
Ross, Evan J. LTh	1986	1998	(Cowdenbeath: West with Mossgreen and Crossgates)	5 Arneil Place, Brightons, Falkirk FK2 0NJ	01324 719936
Smith, Richard BD	1976	2002	(Denny: Old)	Easter Wayside, 46 Kennedy Way, Airth, Falkirk FK2 8GB / richards@uklinux.net	01324 831386

FALKIRK ADDRESSES

Blackbraes and Shieldhill	Main St x Anderson Cr	
Bo'ness:		
Old	Panbrae Road	
St Andrew's	Grahamsdyke Avenue	
Carriden	Carriden Brae	
Cumbernauld:		
Abronhill	Larch Road	
Condorrat	Main Road	
Kildrum	Clouden Road	
Old	Baronhill	
St Mungo's	St Mungo's Road	

Denny:		
Old	Duke Street	
Westpark	Stirling Street	
Dunipace	Denny Cross	
Falkirk:		
Bainsford	Hendry Street, Bainsford	
Camelon	Dorrator Road	
Grahamston United	Bute Street	
Laurieston	Polmont Road	
St Andrew's West	Newmarket Street	
Trinity	Kirk Wynd	
Grangemouth:		
Abbotsgrange	Abbot's Road	

Kirk of the Holy Rood	Bowhouse Road
Zetland	Ronaldshay Crescent
Haggs	Glasgow Road
Larbert:	
East	Kirk Avenue
Old	Denny Road x Stirling Road
West	Main Street
Muiravonside	off Vellore Road
Polmont: Old	Kirk Entry/Bo'ness Road
Redding and Westquarter	Main Street
Slamannan	opposite Manse Place
Stenhouse and Carron	Church Street

(23) STIRLING (F W)

Meets at the Moderator's church on the first Thursday of December, and at Bridge of Allan Parish Church on the first Thursday of February, March, May, June and November; and for conference on the first Thursday of April and October.

Clerk:	REV. ALAN F. MILLER BA MA BD	7 Windsor Place, Stirling FK8 2HY AMiller@churchofscotland.org.uk	01786 465166
			07535 949258
Depute Clerk:	MR EDWARD MORTON	22 Torry Drive, Alva FK12 5LN edmort@aol.com	01259 760861
			07525 005028
Treasurer:	MR MARTIN DUNSMORE	60 Brookfield Place, Alva FK12 5AT m.dunsmore53@btinternet.com	01259 762262
Presbytery Office:		Park Church, Park Terrace, Stirling FK8 2NA stirling@churchofscotland.org.uk	01786 447575

Aberfoyle (H) linked with Port of Menteith (H)

Vacant

Interim Moderator: Dan Gunn — The Manse, Lochard Road, Aberfoyle, Stirling FK8 3SZ — degunn@hotmail.co.uk

01877 382391
01786 823798

Alloa: Ludgate (F W)

Dawn A. Laing BEd PGCertPD BD   2020   28 Alloa Park Drive, Alloa FK10 1QY — DLaing@churchofscotland .org.uk

01259 213134

Alloa: St Mungo's (F H T W)
Sang Y. Cha BD MTh — 2011
contact@alloastmungos.org
37A Claremont, Alloa FK10 2DG
SCha@churchofscotland.org.uk
01259 **723004**
01259 213872

Alva (F W)
James N.R. McNeil BSc BD — 1990 1997
alvaparishchurch@gmail.com
34 Ochil Road, Alva FK12 5JT
JMcNeil@churchofscotland.org.uk
01259 760262

Anne F. Shearer BA DipEd — 2010 2018
(Auxiliary Minister)
10 Colsnaur, Menstrie FK11 7HG
AShearer@churchofscotland.org.uk
01259 769176

Balfron (F W) linked with Fintry (F H W)
Sigrid Marten — 1997 2013
admin@balfronchurch.org.uk
7 Station Road, Balfron, Glasgow G63 0SX
SMarten@churchofscotland.org.uk
01360 440285

Balquhidder linked with Killin and Ardeonaig (H W)
Russel Moffat BD CPS MTh PhD — 1986 2016
The Manse, Killin FK21 8TN
Russel.Moffat@churchofscotland.org.uk
01567 820247

Bannockburn: Allan (F H T W) linked with Cowie and Plean (H T) hiya@allanchurch.org
Vacant
Interim Moderator: Ian McVean
The Manse, Bogend Road, Bannockburn, Stirling FK7 8NP
ianmcvean@yahoo.co.uk
01786 814692
01360 440016

Bannockburn: Ladywell (F H W)
Elizabeth M.D. Robertson (Miss) BD CertMin — 1997
57 The Firs, Bannockburn FK7 0EG
ERobertson@churchofscotland.org.uk
01786 812467

Bridge of Allan (F H W)
Daniel (Dan) J. Harper BSc BD — 2016
office@bridgeofallanparishchurch.org.uk
29 Keir Street, Bridge of Allan, Stirling FK9 4QJ
DHarper@churchofscotland.org.uk
01786 **834155**
01786 832753

Buchanan linked with Drymen (W)
Alexander J. MacPherson BD — 1986 1997
Buchanan Manse, Drymen, Glasgow G63 0AQ
AMacPherson@churchofscotland.org.uk
01360 **660370**
01360 870212

Buchlyvie (H W) linked with Gartmore (H W)
Scott J. Brown CBE BD — 1993 2019
The Manse, 8 Culbowie Crescent, Buchlyvie FK8 3NH
SJBrown@churchofscotland.org.uk

			Tel/Fax: 01877 331409
			01877 330097

Callander (F H W)
Jeffrey A. McCormick BD DipMin   1984   2018   3 Aveland Park Road, Callander FK17 8FD
JMcCormick@churchofscotland.org.uk

Cambusbarron: The Bruce Memorial (F H W)
Graham P. Nash MA BD   2006   2012   14 Woodside Court, Cambusbarron, Stirling FK7 9PH
GPNash@churchofscotland.org.uk
01786 442068

Clackmannan (H W)
Marion A. (Rae) Clark MA BD   2014   2020   **office@clackmannankirk.org.uk**
The Manse, Port Street, Clackmannan FK10 4JH
RClark@churchofscotland.org.uk
01259 214238
07824 505211

Cowie and Plean See Bannockburn: Allan

Dollar (H W) linked with Glendevon linked with Muckhart (W)
T.A. (Tony) Foley PhD   1992   2019   **info@dollarparishchurch.org.uk   muckhartchurch@gmail.com**
2 Princes Crescent East, Dollar FK14 7BU
TFoley@churchofscotland.org.uk
01259 740286

Drymen See Buchanan

Dunblane: Cathedral (F H T W)
Colin C. Renwick BMus BD   1989   2014   **office@dunblanecathedral.org.uk**
Cathedral Manse, The Cross, Dunblane FK15 0AQ
CRenwick@churchofscotland.org.uk
01786 825388
01786 822205

Dorothy U. Anderson (Mrs) LLB DipLP BD   2006   2017   Inverteith, Stirling Road, Doune FK16 6AA
(Associate Minister)   DAnderson@churchofscotland.org.uk
01786 841706

Dunblane: St Blane's (F H W) linked with Lecropt (F H W)
Gary J. Caldwell BSc BD   2007   2015   46 Kellie Wynd, Dunblane FK15 0NR
GCaldwell@churchofscotland.org.uk
01786 825324

Fallin (F W)
Vacant
Interim Moderator: Ken Field   **info@fallinchurch.com**
5 Fincastle Place, Cowie, Stirling FK7 7DS
kenneth.field2@gmail.com
01786 818413
01259 760512

Fintry See Balfron

Gargunnock (W) linked with Kilmadock (W) linked with Kincardine-in-Menteith (W)
Vacant
Interim Moderator: Val Rose   val.rose@btinternet.com   01259 722221

Gartmore See Buchlyvie
Glendevon See Dollar

Killearn (F H W)
Stuart W. Sharp MTheol DipPA   2001 2018   2 The Oaks, Killearn G63 9SF   01360 550101
                                               SSharp@churchofscotland.org.uk

Killin and Ardeonaig See Balquhidder
Kilmadock See Gargunnock
Kincardine-in-Menteith See Gargunnock

Kippen (H W) linked with Norrieston (W)
Ellen M. Larson Davidson BA MDiv   2007 2015   The Manse, Main Street, Kippen, Stirling FK8 3DN   01786 871249
                                                   ELarsonDavidson@churchofscotland.org.uk

Lecropt See Dunblane: St Blane's

Logie (F H W)
Vacant   01786 463060
Interim Moderator: Alison E.P. Britchfield   21 Craiglea, Causewayhead, Stirling FK9 5EE   01259 750340
                                              ABritchfield@churchofscotland.org.uk

Menstrie (F H T W)
Vacant
Interim Moderator: Drew Barrie   DBarrie@churchofscotland.org.uk   01259 213326

Muckhart See Dollar
Norrieston See Kippen
Port of Menteith See Aberfoyle

Sauchie and Coalsnaughton (F)
Vacant
Session Clerk: Anne Fowler   annemfowler@yahoo.co.uk   01259 751564

Stirling: Church of the Holy Rude (F H W) linked with Stirling: Viewfield Erskine (H) holyrude@holyrude.org
Alan F. Miller BA MA BD   2000 2010   7 Windsor Place, Stirling FK8 2HY   01786 465166
AMiller@churchofscotland.org.uk

Stirling: North (F H W) info@stirlingnorth.org   01786 463376
Scott McInnes MEng BD   2016   18 Shirras Brae Road, Stirling FK7 0BA   01786 446116
SMcInnes@churchofscotland.org.uk

Stirling: Park (F H T W) parkchurchstirling@gmail.com   01786 462400
Vacant
Interim Moderator: Alan F. Miller   AMiller@churchofscotland.org.uk   01786 465166

New charge formed by the union of Stirling: Allan Park South and Stirling; St Columba's

Stirling: St Mark's (T W) stmarksstirling1@gmail.com   01786 470733
Barry J. Hughes MA BA   2011 2018   10 Laidlaw Street, Stirling FK8 1ZS   07597 386762
BHughes@churchofscotland.org.uk
Jean T. Porter (Mrs) BD DCS   2006 2008   3 Cochrie Place, Tullibody FK10 2RR   07729 316321
JPorter@churchofscotland.org.uk

Stirling: St Ninians Old (F H W) 7 Randolph Road, Stirling FK8 2AJ   01786 474421
Gary J. McIntyre BD DipMin   1993 1998   GMcIntyre@churchofscotland.org.uk

Stirling: Viewfield Erskine See Stirling: Church of the Holy Rude

Strathblane (F H T W) strathblanekirk@gmail.com   01360 770418
Murdo M. Campbell BD DipMin   1997 2017   2 Campsie Road, Strathblane, Glasgow G63 9AB   01360 770226
MCampbell@churchofscotland.org.uk

Tillicoultry (F H W)
Alison E.P. Britchfield (Mrs) MA BD   1987 2013   The Manse, 17 Dollar Road, Tillicoultry FK13 6PD   01259 750340
ABritchfield@churchofscotland.org.uk

Tullibody: St Serf's (H W) 22, The Cedars, Tullibody, Alloa FK10 2PX   01259 213326
Drew Barrie BSc BD   1984 2016   DBarrie@churchofscotland.org.uk

B. In other appointments

Name	Years	Role	Address / Email	Telephone
Allen, Valerie L. BMus MDiv DMin	1990 2015	Presbytery Chaplain	16 Pine Court, Doune FK16 6JE / VL2allen@btinternet.com	01786 842577 / 07801 291538
Begg, Richard J. MA BD	2008 2016	Army Chaplain	12 Whiteyetts Drive, Sauchie FK10 3GE / rbegg711@aol.com	07766 004292
Boyd, Ronald M.H. BD DipTheol	1993 2010	Chaplain, Queen Victoria School	6 Victoria Green, Queen Victoria School, Dunblane FK15 0JY / ron.boyd@qvs.org.uk	07899 349246
Foggie, Janet P. MA BD PhD	2003 2016	Pioneer Minister, Stirling University	Pioneer Office, Logie Kirk Halls, 15–17 Alloa Road, Stirling FK9 5LH / JFoggie@churchofscotland.org.uk	01786 826953
Jack, Alison M. MA BD PhD SFHEA	1998 2001	Assistant Principal and Senior Lecturer, New College, Edinburgh	5 Murdoch Terrace, Dunblane FK15 9JE / alisonjack809@btinternet.com	

C. Demitted

Name	Years	Role	Address / Email	Telephone
Brown, James H. BD	1977 2005	(Helensburgh: Park)	14 Gullipen View, Callander FK17 8HN / revjimhbrown@yahoo.co.uk	01877 339425
Campbell, Andrew B. BD DPS MTh	1979 2018	(Gargunnock with Kilmadock with Kincardine-in-Menteith)	Seahaven, Ganavan, Oban PA34 5TU	
Cloggie, June (Mrs)	1997 2006	(Auxiliary Minister)	11A Tulipan Crescent, Callander FK17 8AR / david.cloggie@hotmail.co.uk	01877 331021
Cochrane, James P.N. LTh	1994 2012	(Tillicoultry)	12 Sandpiper Meadow, Alloa Park, Alloa FK10 1QU / jamescochrane@pobroadband.co.uk	01259 218883
Cook, Helen K.M. (Mrs) BD	1974 2019	(Hospital Chaplain)	60 Pelstream Avenue, Stirling FK7 0BG / revhcook@btinternet.com	01786 464128
Dunnett, Alan L. LLB BD	1994 2016	(Cowie and Plean with Fallin)	9 Tulipan Crescent, Callander FK17 8AR / alan.dunnett@sky.com	01877 339640
Dunnett, Linda (Mrs) BA DCS	1976 2016	(Deacon)	9 Tulipan Crescent, Callander FK17 8AR / lindadunnett@sky.com	01877 339640 / 07838 041683
Gaston, A. Ray C. MA BD	1969 2002	(Leuchars: St Athernase)	'Hamewith', 13 Manse Road, Dollar FK14 7AL / gaston.arthur@yahoo.co.uk	01259 743202
Gilmour, William M. MA BD	1969 2008	(Lecropt)	14 Pine Court, Doune FK16 6JE	01786 842928
Goring, Iain M. BSc BD	1976 2015	(Interim Minister)	4 Argyle Grove, Dunblane FK15 9DU / imgoring@gmail.com	01786 821688
Izett, William A.F.	1968 2000	(Law)	1 Duke Street, Clackmannan FK10 4EF / william.izett@talktalk.net	01259 724203
Landels, James BD CertMin	1990 2015	(Bannockburn: Allan)	11 Ardgay Drive, Bonnybridge, Falkirk FK4 2FH / revjimlandels@icloud.com	01324 810685
Mack, Lynne (Mrs)	2013 2019	(Ordained Local Minister)	36 Middleton, Menstrie FK11 7HD / LMack@churchofscotland.org.uk	07860 944266
MacCormick, Moira G. BA LTh	1986 2003	(Buchlyvie with Gartmore)	12 Rankine Wynd, Tullibody, Alloa FK10 2UW / mgmaccormick@o2.com	01259 761465
McIntosh, Hamish N.M. MA	1949 1987	(Fintry)	Room 20, Pearson House, Erskine Home, Nursery Avenue, Bishopton PA7 5PU	01259 724619

Name	Dates	Charge	Address	Phone
McKenzie, Alan BSc BD	1988 2013	(Bellshill: Macdonald Memorial with Bellshill: Orbiston)	89 Drip Road, Stirling FK8 1RN rev.a.mckenzie@btopenworld.com	01786 430450
Malloch, Philip R.M. LLB BD	1970 2009	(Killearn)	8 Michael McParland Drive, Torrance, Glasgow G64 4EE pmalloch@mac.com	01360 620089
Mathew, J. Gordon MA BD	1973 2011	(Buckie: North)	45 Westhaugh Road, Stirling FK9 5GF jg.matthew@btinternet.com	01786 445951
Ogilvie, Catriona (Mrs)	1999 2015	(Cumbernauld: Old)	Seberham Flat, 1A Bridge Street, Dollar FK14 7DF catriona.ogilvie1@btinternet.com	01259 742155
Ovens, Samuel B. BD	1982 1992	(Slamannan)	21 Bevan Drive, Alva FK12 5PD	01259 763456
Pryde, W. Kenneth DA BD	1994 2012	(Foveran)	Corrie, 7 Alloa Road, Woodside, Cambus FK10 2NT wkpryde@hotmail.com	01259 721562
Rose, Dennis S. LTh	1996 2016	(Arbuthnott, Bervie and Kinneff)	69 Blackthorn Grove, Menstrie FK11 7DX dennis2327@aol.com	01259 692451
Russell, Kenneth G. BD CCE	1986 2020	(Prison Chaplain)	158 Bannockburn Road, Stirling FK7 0EW kenrussell1000@hotmail.com	01786 812680
Scott, James F.	1957 1997	(Dyce)	5 Gullipen View, Callander FK17 8HN	01877 330565
Sewell, Paul M.N. MA BD	1970 2010	(Berwick-upon-Tweed: St Andrew's Wallace Green and Lowick)	7 Bohun Court, Stirling FK7 7UT paulmsewell@btinternet.com	01786 489969
Thomson, Raymond BD DipMin	1992 2013	(Slamannan)	8 Rhodders Grove, Alva FK12 5ER	01259 769083
Wilson, Hazel MA BD DMS	1991 2015	(Dundee: Lochee)	2 Boe Court, Springfield Terrace, Dunblane FK15 9LU hmwilson704@gmail.com	01786 825850

STIRLING ADDRESSES

| Holy Rude | St John Street | Park | Park Terrace | St Ninians Old | Kirk Wynd, St Ninians |
| North | Springfield Road | St Mark's | Drip Road | Viewfield Erskine | Barnton Street |

(24) DUNFERMLINE (F W)

Meets at Dunfermline in St Andrew's Erskine Church, Robertson Road, on the first Thursday of September, November and Deecember 2020.

On 1 January 2021 it will unite with the Presbytery of Kirkcaldy and the Presbytery of St Andrews to form the new Presbytery of Fife. That new Presbytery shall meet on the first Saturday in February (in St Bryce Kirk, Kirkcaldy), the third Saturday in June and the third Saturday in September.

| Clerk: | REV. IAIN M. GREENSHIELDS BD DipRS ACMA MSc MTh DD | 38 Garvock Hill, Dunfermline KY12 7UU dunfermline@churchofscotland.org.uk | Office 01383 741495 Home 07427 477575 |

Aberdour: St Fillan's (H W)
Peter S. Gerbrandy-Baird
MA BD MSc FRSA FRGS
2004 — St Fillan's Manse, 36 Bellhouse Road, Aberdour, Fife KY3 0TL — 01383 861522
PGerbrandy-Baird@churchofscotland.org.uk

Beath and Cowdenbeath: North (H W)
Deborah J. Dobby (Mrs)
BA BD PGCE RGN RSCN
2014 2018 — 42 Woodside Avenue, Rosyth KY11 2LA — 01383 325520
DDobby@churchofscotland.org.uk

Cairneyhill (H W) linked with Limekilns (H W)
Norman M. Grant BD
1990 — office@limekilnschurch.org Cairneyhill: 01383 882252 Limekilns: 01383 873337
The Manse, 10 Church Street, Limekilns, Dunfermline KY11 3HT — 01383 872341
NGrant@churchofscotland.org.uk

Carnock and Oakley (H W)
Charles M.D. Lines BA
2010 2017 — The Manse, Main Street, Carnock, Dunfermline KY12 9JG — 01383 247209
CLines@churchofscotland.org.uk — 07909 762257

Cowdenbeath: Trinity (H)
Vacant
Interim Moderator: Monika R.W. Redman
2 Glenfield Road, Cowdenbeath KY4 9EL — 01383 510696
MRedman@churchofscotland.org.uk — 01383 300092

Culross and Torryburn (H)
Elizabeth A. Fisk BD
1996 2019 — 30 Masterton Road, Dunfermline KY11 8RB — 01383 730039
EFisk@churchofscotland.org.uk

Dalgety (H W)
Christine M. Sime (Miss) BSc BD
1994 2012 — office@dalgety-church.co.uk — **01383 824092**
9 St Colme Drive, Dalgety Bay, Dunfermline KY11 9LQ — 01383 822316
CSime@churchofscotland.org.uk

Dunfermline: Abbey (F H T W)
MaryAnn R. Rennie (Mrs) BD MTh
1998 2012 — dunfermline.abbey.church@gmail.com — **01383 724586**
3 Perdieus Mount, Dunfermline KY12 7XE — 01383 727311
MARennie@churchofscotland.org.uk

Dunfermline: East (F W)
Andrew A. Morrice MA BD
1999 2010 — 71 Swift Street, Dunfermline KY11 8SN — 01383 223144
AMorrice@churchofscotland.org.uk — 07815 719301

Dunfermline: Gillespie Memorial (F H W)
Michael A. Weaver BSc BD   2017
office@gillespiechurch.org
4 Killin Court, Dunfermline KY12 7XF
MWeaver@churchofscotland.org.uk
01383 621253
01383 724347
07980 492299

Dunfermline: North
Vacant
13 Barbour Grove, Dunfermline KY12 9YB
01383 733471

Dunfermline: St Andrew's Erskine (W)
Muriel F. Willoughby (Mrs) MA BD   2006   2013
staechurch@standrewserskine.org.uk
71A Townhill Road, Dunfermline KY12 0BN
MWilloughby@churchofscotland.org.uk
01383 841660
01383 738487

Dunfermline: St Leonard's (F W)
Monika R. W. Redman BA BD   2003   2014
office@slpc.org
12 Torvean Place, Dunfermline KY11 4YY
MRedman@churchofscotland.org.uk
01383 620106
01383 300092

Margaret B. Mateos   2018
(Ordained Local Minister)
43 South Street, Lochgelly KY5 9LJ
MMateos@churchofscotland.org.uk
01592 780073

Dunfermline: St Margaret's (F W)
Iain M. Greenshields
BD DipRS ACMA MSc MTh DD   1984   2007
38 Garvock Hill, Dunfermline KY12 7UU
IGreenshields@churchofscotland.org.uk
01383 723955
07427 477575

Dunfermline: St Ninian's (F W)
Carolann Erskine BD DipPSRP   2009   2018
51 St John's Drive, Dunfermline KY12 7TL
CErskine@churchofscotland.org.uk
01383 271548

Dunfermline: Townhill and Kingseat (F H W)
Jean A. Kirkwood BSc PhD BD   2015
info@townhillandkingseatchurchofscotland.org
7 Lochwood Park, Kingseat, Dunfermline KY12 0UX
JKirkwood@churchofscotland.org.uk
01383 723691

Inverkeithing (F W) linked with North Queensferry (W)
Colin M. Alston BMus BD BN RN   1975   2012
1 Dover Way, Dunfermline KY11 8HR
CAlston@churchofscotland.org.uk
01383 621050

Kelty (W)
Vacant
kelty.kirk@virgin.net
15 Arlick Road, Kelty KY4 0BH
01383 831362

Limekilns See Cairneyhill

Lochgelly and Benarty: St Serf's (F W)
Vacant

Pamela Scott (Mrs) BD DCS	2017		82 Main Street, Lochgelly KY5 9AA	01592 780435
			177 Primrose Avenue, Rosyth KY11 2TZ	01383 410530
			PScott@churchofscotland.org.uk	07548 819334
Interim Moderator: Jean A. Kirkwood			JKirkwood@churchofscotland.org.uk	01383 723691

North Queensferry See Inverkeithing

Rosyth (F W)

D. Brian Dobby MA BA	1999	2018	rpc@cos82a.plus.com	**01383 412534**
			42 Woodside Avenue, Rosyth KY11 2LA	01383 412776
			BDobby@churchofscotland.org.uk	
Morag Crawford (Miss) MSc DCS	1977	1998	118 Wester Drylaw Place, Edinburgh EH4 2TG	0131 332 2253
			MCrawford@churchofscotland.org.uk	07970 982563

Saline and Blairingone (W) linked with Tulliallan and Kincardine (F) tulliallanandkincardine@gmail.com

Alexander J. Shuttleworth MA BD	2004	2013	62 Toll Road, Kincardine, Alloa FK10 4QZ	01259 731002
			AShuttleworth@churchofscotland.org.uk	

Tulliallan and Kincardine See Saline and Blairingone

B. In other appointments

Kenny, Elizabeth S.S. BD RGN SCM	1989	2011	Chaplain: HM Prison Glenochil	5 Cobden Court, Crossgates, Cowdenbeath KY4 8AU	07831 763494
				esskenny@btinternet.com	
Paterson, Andrew E. JP	1994	2016	Auxiliary Minister, Presbytery	6 The Willows, Kelty KY4 0FQ	01383 830998
				APaterson@churchofscotland.org.uk	
Shuttleworth, Margaret MA BD	2013	2020	Chaplain, HMP Perth	62 Toll Road, Kincardine, Alloa FK10 4QZ	01259 731002
				MShuttleworth@churchofscotland.org.uk	

C. Demitted

Bjarnason, Sven S. CandTheol	1973	2011	(Tomintoul, Glenlivet and Inveraven)	14 Edward Street, Dunfermline KY12 0JW	01383 724625
				sven@bjarnason.org.uk	
Boyle, Robert P. LTh	1990	2010	(Saline and Blairingone)	23 Farnell Way, Dunfermline KY12 0SR	01383 729568
				boab.boyle@btinternet.com	
Brown, Peter MA BD FRAScot	1953	1992	(Holm)	24 Inchmickery Avenue, Dalgety Bay, Dunfermline KY11 5NF	01383 822456
Chalmers, John P. BD CPS DD	1979	2017	(Principal Clerk)	10 Liggars Place, Dunfermline KY12 7XZ	01383 739130
				JChalmers@churchofscotland.org.uk	
Christie, Arthur A. BD	1997	2018	(Anstruther and Cellardyke: St Ayle with Kilrenny)	194 Foulford Road, Cowdenbeath KY4 9AX	01383 511326
				revacc@btinternet.com	
Dick, John H.A. (Ian) MA MSc BD	1982	2012	(Aberdeen: Ferryhill)	18 Fairfield Road, Kelty KY4 0BY	01383 271147
Farquhar, William E. BA BD	1987	2006	(Dunfermline: Townhill and Kingseat)	29 Queens Drive, Middlewich, Cheshire CW10 0DG	01606 835097
Jenkins, Gordon F.C. MA BD PhD	1968	2006	(Dunfermline: North)	2 Balrymonth Court, St Andrews KY16 8XT	01335 477194
				jenkinsgordon1@sky.com	
Johnston, Thomas N. LTh	1972	2008	(Edinburgh: Priestfield)	71 Main Street, Newmills, Dunfermline KY12 8ST	01383 889240
				tomjohnston@blueyonder.co.uk	

Name	Ord.	Ind.	Notes	Address / Email	Tel
Laidlaw, Victor W.N. BD	1975	2008	(Edinburgh: St Catherine's Argyle)	9 Tern Road, Dunfermline KY11 8GA / v9wintern@hotmail.co.uk	01383 620134
Leitch, D. Graham MA BD	1974	2012	(Tyne Valley)	9 St Margaret Wynd, Dunfermline KY12 0UT / dgrahamleitch@gmail.com	01383 249245
McCulloch, William B BD	1997	2016	(Rome: St Andrew's)	81 Meldrum Court, Dunfermline KY11 4XR / revwbmcculloch@hotmail.com	01383 730305
McDonald, Tom BD	1994	2015	(Kelso: North and Ednam)	12 Woodmill Grove, Dunfermline KY11 4JR / revtomparadise12@gmail.com	01383 695365
McKay, Violet C.C. BD	1988	2017	(Rosyth)	20B Blane Crescent, Dunfermline KY11 8ZF / violetcm@gmail.com	01383 727255
McLellan, Andrew R.C. CBE MA BD STM DD	1970	2009	(HM Chief Inspector of Prisons for Scotland)	4 Liggars Place, Dunfermline KY12 7XZ / iamclellan4@gmail.com	01383 725959
Melville, David D. BD	1989	2008	(Kirkconnel)	28 Porterfield, Comrie, Dunfermline KY12 9HJ / revddm@gmail.com	01383 850075
Redmayne, David W. BSc BD	2001	2017	(Beath and Cowdenbeath: North)	10 Hawthorn Park, Dunfermline KY12 0DY	01383 738137
Reid, A. Gordon BSc BD	1982	2008	(Dunfermline: Gillespie Memorial)	7 Arkleston Crescent, Paisley PA3 4TG / reid501@fsmail.net	0141 842 1542
Reid, David MSc LTh FSAScot	1961	1992	(St Monans with Largoward)	North Lethans, Saline, Dunfermline KY12 9TE	07773 300989
Steele, Hugh D. LTh DipMin	1994	2020			
Thom, Ian G. BSc PhD BD	1990	2020	(Dunfermline: North)		01383 733144
Watt, Robert J. BD	1994	2009	(Dumbarton: Riverside)	101 Birrell Drive, Dunfermline KY11 8FA / robertwatt101@gmail.com	01383 735417 / 07753 683717
Whyte, Iain A. BA BD STM PhD	1968	2005	(Community Mental Health Chaplain)	14 Carlingnose Point, North Queensferry, Inverkeithing KY11 1ER / iainisabelwhyte@gmail.com	01383 410732
Whyte, Isabel H. (Mrs) BD	1993	2006	(Chaplain: Queen Margaret Hospital, Dunfermline)	14 Carlingnose Point, North Queensferry, Inverkeithing KY11 1ER / iainisabelwhyte@gmail.com	01383 410732

(25) KIRKCALDY (W)

Meets at Kirkcaldy, in the St Bryce Kirk Centre, on the first Tuesday of September and December 2020. It meets also on the first Tuesday of November 2020 for Holy Communion at the church of the Moderator.

On 1 January 2021 it will unite with the Presbytery of Dunfermline and the Presbytery of St Andrews to form the Presbytery of Fife. That new Presbytery shall meet on the first Saturday in February in 2021 (in St Bryce Kirk, Kirkcaldy), the third Saturday in June and the third Saturday in September.

Clerk:	REV. ALAN W.D. KIMMITT BSc BD	40 Liberton Drive, Glenrothes KY6 3PB / kirkcaldy@churchofscotland.org.uk / 57b Salisbury Street, Kirkcaldy KY2 5HP / kirkcaldy@churchofscotland.org.uk	01592 742233
Depute Clerk:	MRS. LAUREN JONES		07913 611018

Auchterderran Kinglassie (F W)
Donald R. Lawrie MA BD DipCouns 1991 2018
7 Woodend Road, Cardenden, Lochgelly KY5 0NE
DLawrie@churchofscotland.org.uk
01592 720508

Auchtertool (W) linked with Kirkcaldy: Linktown (F H W)
Catriona M. Morrison MA BD 1995 2000
16 Raith Crescent, Kirkcaldy KY2 5NN
CMorrison@churchofscotland.org.uk
01592 641080
01592 265536

Marc A. Prowe 2000 2008
16 Raith Crescent, Kirkcaldy KY2 5NN
MProwe@churchofscotland.org.uk
01592 265536

Buckhaven and Wemyss
Vacant
Jacqueline Thomson (Mrs) MTh DCS 2004 2008
16 Aitken Place, Coaltown of Wemyss, Kirkcaldy KY1 4PA
Jacqueline.Thomson@churchofscotland.org.uk
01592 715577
07806 776560

Burntisland (F H)
Vacant
Session Clerk: William Sweenie
21 Ramsay Crescent, Burntisland KY3 9JL
billsweenie01@gmail.com
01592 873567

Dysart: St Clair (H W)
Vacant
Session Clerk: Raymond Domin
42 Craigfoot Walk, Kirkcaldy KY1 1GA
raymonddomin@blueyonder.co.uk
01592 561967
01592 203620

Glenrothes: Christ's Kirk (H W)
Andrew Gardner BSc BD PhD 1997 2019
(Interim Minister)
christskirkglenrothes@yahoo.com
Christ's Kirk, Pitcoudie Avenue, Glenrothes KY7 6SU
AGardner@churchofscotland.org.uk
01592 745938
07411 989344

Glenrothes: St Columba's (F W)
Alan W.D. Kimmitt BSc BD 2013
info@st-columbas.com
40 Liberton Drive, Glenrothes KY6 3PB
Alan.Kimmitt@churchofscotland.org.uk
01592 752539
01592 742233

Glenrothes: St Margaret's (F H)
Eileen A. Miller BD MBACP (Snr. Accred.) 2014
DipCouns DipComEd
office@stmargaretschurch.org.uk
8 Alburne Park, Glenrothes KY7 5RB
EMiller@churchofscotland.org.uk
01592 328162
01592 752241

Glenrothes: St Ninian's (F H W)
David J. Smith BD DipMin 1992 2017
office@stninians.co.uk
1 Cawdor Drive, Glenrothes KY6 2HN
David.Smith@churchofscotland.org.uk
01592 610560
01592 611963

Congregation / Minister	Ordained	Admitted	Address / Email	Telephone
Kennoway, Windygates and Balgonie: St Kenneth's (F W) 2018 Allan Morton MA BD PGDip			**stkennethsparish@gmail.com** 2 Fernhill Gardens, Windygates, Leven KY8 5DZ AMorton@churchofscotland.org.uk	**01333 351372** 01333 350240
Kinghorn (F W) James Reid BD	1985	1997	17 Myre Crescent, Kinghorn, Burntisland KY3 9UB JReid@churchofscotland.org.uk	01592 890269
Kirkcaldy: Abbotshall (F H T W) Justin W. Taylor BTh MTh MTh	2018		83 Milton Road, Kirkcaldy KY1 1TP JTaylor@churchofscotland.org.uk	01592 267915
Kirkcaldy: Bennochy (F W) Robin J. McAlpine BDS BD MTh	1988	2011	25 Bennochy Avenue, Kirkcaldy KY2 5QE RMcAlpine@churchofscotland.org.uk	**01592 201723** 01592 643518
Kirkcaldy: Linktown See Auchtertool				
Kirkcaldy: Pathhead (F H W) Andrew C. Donald BD DPS	1992	2005	**pathheadchurch@btconnect.com** 73 Loughborough Road, Kirkcaldy KY1 3DB ADonald@churchofscotland.org.uk	**01592 204635** 01592 652215
Kirkcaldy: St Bryce Kirk (F H T W) J. Kenneth (Ken) Froude MA BD	1979		**office@stbrycekirk.org.uk** 44 Templars Crescent, Kinghorn KY3 9XS JFroude@churchofscotland.org.uk	**01592 640016** 01592 892512
Kirkcaldy: Templehall (H) Vacant Session Clerk: George Thomson			35 Appin Crescent, Kirkcaldy KY2 6EJ georget1955@live.co.uk	01592 260156 01592 203178
Kirkcaldy: Torbain (F W) Vacant Brian W. Porteous BSc DipCS (Ordained Local Minister)	2018		91 Sauchenbush Road, Kirkcaldy KY2 5RN Kildene, Westfield Road, Cupar KY15 5DS BPorteous@churchofscotland.org.uk	01592 263015 01334 653561

Leslie: Trinity
Guardianship of the Presbytery
Session Clerk: Alec Redpath
sessionclerk@leslietrinitychurch.co.uk
01592 742636

Leven (F)
Vacant
Session Clerk: Linda Archer
levenparish@tiscali.co.uk
5 Forman Road, Leven KY8 4HH
lindaarcher847@ymail.com
01333 423969
01333 303339
01333 329850

Markinch and Thornton (F W)
Vacant
Session Clerk: Bryan Gould
7 Guthrie Crescent, Markinch, Glenrothes KY7 6AY
monsieurgould@hotmail.com
01592 758264

Methil: Wellesley (F H)
Gillian Paterson (Mrs) BD   2010
10 Vettriano Vale, Leven KY8 4GD
GPaterson@churchofscotland.org.uk
01333 423147

Methilhill and Denbeath (F)
Elisabeth F. Cranfield (Ms) MA BD   1988
9 Chemiss Road, Methilhill, Leven KY8 2BS
ECranfield@churchofscotland.org.uk
01592 713142

B. In other appointments
Wright, Lynda BEd DCS   1979 2016
Community Chaplaincy Listening Co-ordinator, NHS Fife
71a Broomhill Avenue, Burntisland KY3 0BP
lyndawright20@gmail.com
07835 303395

C. Demitted
Adams, David G. BD   1991 2011
(Cowdenbeath: Trinity)
13 Fernhill Gardens, Windygates, Leven KY8 5DZ
adams.69@btinternet.com
01333 351214

Campbell, Reginald F. BSc BD DipChEd   1979 2015
(Daviot and Dunlichity with Moy, Dalarossie and Tomatin)
12 Alloway Drive, Kirkcaldy KY2 6DX
campbell578@talktalk.net

Collins, Mitchell BD CPS   1996 2005
(Creich, Flisk and Kilmany with Monimail)
6 Netherby Park, Glenrothes KY6 3PL
collinsmit@aol.com
01592 742915

Deans, Graham D.S. MA BD MTh MLitt DMin   1978 2017
(Aberdeen: Queen Street)
38 Sir Thomas Elder Way, Kirkcaldy KY2 6ZS
graham.deans@btopenworld.com
01592 641429

Dick, James S. MA BTh   1988 1997
(Glasgow Ruchazie)
20 Church Street, Kirkcaldy KY1 2AD
jdick63@yahoo.com
01592 369239

Elston, Ian J. BD MTh   1999 2019
(Kirkcaldy: Torbain)
65 Longbrae Gardens, Kirkcaldy KY2 5YJ
IElston@churchofscotland.org.uk
01592 592393

Elston, Peter K.   1963 1999
(Dalgety)
6 Cairngorm Crescent, Kirkcaldy KY2 5RF
peterkelston@btinternet.com
01592 205622

Ferguson, David J.   1966 2001
(Bellie with Speymouth)
4 Russell Gardens, Ladybank, Cupar KY15 7LT
01337 831406

Name			(Charge)	Address	Phone
Forester, Ian L. MA	1964	1996		8 Bennochy Avenue, Kirkcaldy KY2 5QE	01592 260251
Forsyth, Alexander R. TD BA MTh	1973	2014	(Friockheim Kinnell with Inverkeilor and Lunan) (Markinch)	49 Scaraben Crescent, Formonthills, Glenrothes KY6 3HL alex@arforsyth.com	01592 749049 07483 232581
Galbraith, D. Douglas MA BD BMus MPhil ARSCM PhD	1965	2005	(Office for Worship, Doctrine and Artistic Matters) (Markinch)	34 Balbirnie Street, Markinch, Glenrothes KY7 6DA dgalbraith@churchofscotland.org.uk	01592 752403
Gordon, Ian D. LTh	1972	2001	(Markinch)	2 Somerville Way, Glenrothes KY7 5GE	01592 742487
McDonald, Ian J.M. MA BD	1984	2018	(Lausanne: The Scots Kirk)	11 James Grove, Kirkcaldy KY1 1TN IanJMMcdonald@churchofscotland.org.uk	07421 775644
McLeod, Alistair G.	1988	2005	(Glenrothes: St Columba's)	13 Greenmantle Way, Glenrothes KY6 3QG alistairmcleod1936@gmail.com	01592 744558
McNaught, Samuel M. MA BD MTh	1968	2002	(Kirkcaldy: St John's)	6 Munro Court, Glenrothes KY7 5GD sjmcnaught@btinternet.com	01592 742352
Munro, Andrew MA BD PhD	1972	2000	(Glencaple with Lowther)	7 Dunvegan Avenue, Kirkcaldy KY2 5SG am.smm@blueyonder.co.uk	01592 566129
Nicol, George G. BD DPhil	1982	2013	(Falkland with Freuchie)	48 Fidra Avenue, Burntisland KY3 0AZ ggnicol@totalise.co.uk	01592 873258
Nisbet, Gilbert C. CA BD	1993	2019	(Leven)	Upper Flat, 2 Temple Crescent, Crail KY10 3RS gcn@insprint.co.uk	01333 450929
Paterson, Maureen (Mrs) BSc	1992	2010	(Auxiliary Minister)	91 Dalmahoy Crescent, Kirkcaldy KY2 6TA m.e.paterson@blueyonder.co.uk	01592 262300
Roy, Allistair BD DipSW PgDip	2007	2016	(Glenrothes: St Ninian's)	39 Ravenswood Drive, Glenrothes KY6 2PA minister@revroy.co.uk	
Sharp, Alan BSc BD	1980	2019	(Burntisland)	29 Cromwell Road, Burntisland KY3 9EH alansharp03@aol.com	
Templeton, James L. BSc BD	1975	2012	(Innerleven: East)	29 Coldstream Avenue, Leven KY8 5TN jamietempleton@btinternet.com	01333 427102
Thomson, John D. BD	1985	2005	(Kirkcaldy: Pathhead)	3 Tottenham Court, Hill Street, Dysart, Kirkcaldy KY1 2XY j.thomson10@sky.com	01592 655313 07885 414979
Tomlinson, Bryan L. TD	1969	2003	(Kirkcaldy: Abbotshall)	2 Duddingston Drive, Kirkcaldy KY2 6JP abbkirk@blueyonder.co.uk	01592 564843
Wilson, Tilly (Miss) MTh	1990	2012	(Dysart)	6 Citron Glebe, Kirkcaldy KY1 2NF tillywilson1@sky.com	01592 263134

KIRKCALDY ADDRESSES

Abbotshall	Abbotshall Road
Bennochy	Elgin Street x High Street
Linktown	Nicol Street x High Street
Pathhead	Harriet Street x Church Street
St Bryce Kirk	St Brycedale Avenue x Kirk Wynd
Templehall	Beauly Place
Torbain	Carron Place
Viewforth	Viewforth Street x Viewforth Terrace
(Dysart St Clair)	

(26) ST ANDREWS (W)

Meets on the first Wednesday of September, October and December 2020 at locations to be announced.

On 1 January 2021 it will unite with the Presbytery of Dunfermline and the Presbytery of Kirkcaldy to form the Presbytery of Fife. That new Presbytery shall meet on the first Saturday in February (in St Bryce Kirk, Kirkcaldy), the third Saturday in June and the third Saturday in September.

Clerk:	REV. NIGEL J. ROBB FCP MA BD ThM MTh	Presbytery Office, The Basement, 1 Howard Place, St Andrews KY16 9HL	**01334 461300**
		standrews@churchofscotland.org.uk	

Anstruther and Cellardyke: St Ayle (H W) linked with Crail (F)

John W. Murray LLB BA	2003	2020	16 Taeping Close, Cellardyke, Anstruther KY10 3YL	
			JMurray@churchofscotland.org.uk	

Balmerino (H W) linked with Wormit (F H W)

James Connolly	1982	2004	5 Westwater Place, Newport-on-Tay DD6 8NS	01382 542626
DipTh CertMin MA(Theol) DMin			JConnolly@churchofscotland.org.uk	

Boarhills and Dunino linked with St Andrews: Holy Trinity (W)

Guardianship of the Presbytery			holytrinitystandrews@gmail.com	**01334 478317**
Session Clerk, Boarhills and Dunino: Kenneth S. Morris			kensm48@gmail.com	01334 474468
Session Clerk, Holy Trinity: Michael Stewart (Dr)			htsessionclerk@gmail.com	01334 461270

Cameron (F W) linked with St Andrews: St Leonard's (F H W)

Graeme W. Beebee BD	1993	2017	stlencam@btconnect.com	**01334 478702**
			1 Cairnhill Gardens, St Andrews KY16 8QY	01334 472793
			GBeebee@churchofscotland.org.uk	

Carnbee linked with Pittenweem

Margaret E.S. Rose BD	2007	29 Milton Road, Pittenweem, Anstruther KY10 2LN	01333 312838
		MRose@churchofscotland.org.uk	

Ceres, Kemback and Springfield (W)

James W. Campbell BD	1995	2010	Almbank, Gladney, Ceres, Cupar KY15 5LT	01334 829350
			James.Campbell@churchofscotland.org.uk	

Crail See Anstruther and Cellardyke: St Ayle

Creich, Flisk and Kilmany (W)
Guardianship of the Presbytery
Reader: Graham Peacock
grahampeacock6@btinternet.com
01382 330124

Cupar: Old (H) and St Michael of Tarvit linked with Monimail
Jeffrey A. Martin BA MDiv   1991   2016
76 Hogarth Drive, Cupar KY15 5YU
JMartin@churchofscotland.org.uk
01334 656181

Cupar: St John's and Dairsie United (F W)
Gavin W.G. Black BD   2006   2019
The Manse, 23 Hogarth Drive, Cupar KY15 5YH
GBlack@churchofscotland.org.uk
01334 650751

East Neuk Trinity (H W) linked with St Monans (H)
Vacant
Session Clerk, East Neuk Trinity: Olive Weir (Mrs)
jamandlor1@gmail.com
01333 340642

Edenshead
Vacant
Session Clerk: Rodney McCall
The Manse, Kirk Wynd, Strathmiglo, Cupar KY14 7QS
rodmccall@yahoo.co.uk
01337 860256
01337 827001

Falkland (F W) linked with Freuchie (H W)
Guardianship of the Presbytery
Session Clerk, Falkland: Marion Baldie
Session Clerk, Freuchie: Margaret Cuthbert
1 Newton Road, Falkland, Cupar KY15 7AQ
sessionclerk.falkland@gmail.com
cuthbertmargaret@yahoo.co.uk
01337 858557
07951 824488
01337 830940

Freuchie See Falkland

Howe of Fife (F W)
William F. Hunter MA BD   1986   2011
The Manse, 83 Church Street, Ladybank, Cupar KY15 7ND
WHunter@churchofscotland.org.uk
01337 832717

Kilrenny (W)
Guardianship of the Presbytery
Session Clerk: Robert A.J. Moodie
robmoodie1@btinternet.com
01334 880497

Kingsbarns (F H)
Guardianship of the Presbytery
Session Clerk: John (Ian) Ramsay
johnvramsay@btinternet.com — 01333 451480

Largo (F W)
Gavin R. Boswell BTheol — 1993 — 1 Castaway Lane, Lower Largo KY8 6FA — 01333 320850
GBoswell@churchofscotland.org.uk

Largoward (H W)
Guardianship of the Presbytery
Interim Moderator: Catherine Wilson (Mrs)
catherine.wilson15@btinternet.com — 01333 310936

Leuchars: St Athernase (F)
John C. Duncan MBE BD MPhil — 1987 — 7 David Wilson Park, Balmullo, St Andrews KY16 0NP — 01334 870038
JDuncan@churchofscotland.org.uk

Lindores (F H)
Guardianship of Presbytery
Session Clerk: Rosslynn Scott (Ms)
2 Guthrie Court, Cupar Road, Newburgh, Cupar KY14 6HA — 01337 842228
rosslyn6@btinternet.com

Monimail See Cupar: Old and St Michael of Tarvit

Newport-on-Tay (F H W)
Amos B. Chewachong BTh MTh PhD — 2005 — 2017 — 17 East Station Place, Newport-on-Tay DD6 8EG — 01382 542893
AChewachong@churchofscotland.org.uk

Pittenweem See Carnbee

St Andrews: Holy Trinity See Boarhills and Dunino

St Andrews: Hope Park and Martyrs (F H W) linked with Strathkinness (W)   admin@hpmchurch.org.uk
Allan McCafferty BSc BD — 1993 — 2011 — 20 Priory Gardens, St Andrews KY16 8XX — Tel/Fax **01334 478144**
AMcCafferty@churchofscotland.org.uk — 01334 478287

St Andrews: St Leonard's See Cameron
St Monans See East Neuk Trinity
Strathkinness See St Andrews: Hope Park and Martyrs

Tayport (F W)
Guardianship of the Presbytery
Interim Moderator: Allan McCafferty

AMcCafferty@churchofscotland.org.uk

01334 478287

Wormit See Balmerino

B. In other appointments

Allardice, Michael MA MPhil PGCertTHE FHEA	2014		Ordained Local Minister	2 Station Road, Kingskettle, Cupar KY15 7PR 01337 597073 MAllardice@churchofscotland.org.uk 07936 203465
Jeffrey, Kenneth S. BA BD PhD DMin	2002	2014	University of Aberdeen	The North Steading, Dalgairn, Cupar KY15 4PH 01334 653196 ksjeffrey@btopenworld.com
MacEwan, Donald G. MA BD PhD	2001	2011	Chaplain: University of St Andrews	Chaplaincy Centre, 3A St Mary's Place, St Andrews KY16 9UY 01334 462865 dgm21@st-andrews.ac.uk 07713 322036
Robb, Nigel J. FCP MA BD ThM MTh	1981	2014	Presbytery Clerk: St Andrews	Presbytery Office, Hope Park and Martyrs' Church, The Basement, 07966 286958 1 Howard Place, St Andrews KY16 9UY

C. Demitted

Barron, Jane L. (Mrs) BA DipEd BD	1999	2013	(Aberdeen: St Machar's Cathedral)	Denhead Old Farm, St Andrews KY16 8PA 07545 904541 arthurmagnus@icloud.com
Bradley, Ian C. (Prof.) MA BD DPhil	1990	2017	(University of St Andrews)	4 Donaldson Gardens, St Andrews KY16 9DN 01334 475389 icb@st-andrews.ac.uk
Cameron, John U. BA BSc PhD BD ThD	1974	2008	(Dundee: Broughty Ferry St Stephen's and West)	10 Howard Place, St Andrews KY16 9HL 01334 474474 jucameron@yahoo.co.uk
Clark, David M. MA BD	1989	2013	(Dundee: The Steeple)	2b Rose Street, St Monans, Anstruther KY10 2BQ 01333 739034 dmclark72@gmail.com
Connolly, Daniel BD DipTheol Dip Min	1983	2015	(Army Chaplain)	2 Cairngreen, Cupar KY15 2SY 07951 078478 dannyconnolly@hotmail.co.uk
Douglas, Peter C. JP	1966	1993	(Boarhills with Dunino)	12 Greyfriars Gardens, St Andrews KY16 8DR 01334 475868
Fairlie, George BD BVMS MRCVS	1971	2002	(Crail with Kingsbarns)	41 Warrack Street, St Andrews KY16 8DR 01334 475868
Fraser, Ann G. BD CertMin	1990	2007	(Auchtermuchty)	24 Irvine Crescent, St Andrews KY16 8LG 01334 461329 anngilfraser@btinternet.com
Gordon, Peter M. MA BD	1958	1995	(Airdrie: West)	3 Cupar Road, Cuparmuir, Cupar KY15 5RH 01334 652341 machrie@madasafish.com
Hamilton, Ian W.F. BD LTh ALCM AVCM	1978	2012	(Nairn: Old)	Mossneuk, 5 Windsor Gardens, St Andrews KY16 8XL 01334 477745 reviwfh@btinternet.com
Harrison, Cameron	2006	2011	(Auxiliary Minister)	Woodfield House, Priormuir, St Andrews KY16 8LP 01334 478067 cameron@harrisonleimon.co.uk
Kesting, Sheilagh M. BA BD DD DSG	1980	2016	(Ecumenical Officer, Church of Scotland)	Restalrig, Chance Inn, Cupar KY15 5QJ 01334 829485 smkesting@btinternet.com

McGregor, Duncan J. MIFM	1982	1996	(Channelkirk with Lauder: Old)	
McKinnon, Eric BA BD MTh PhD	1983	2014	(Cargill Burrelton with Collace)	14 Mount Melville, St Andrews KY16 8NG	01334 478314
McLean, John P. BSc BPhil BD	1994	2013	(Glenrothes: St Margaret's)	14 Marionfield Place, Cupar KY15 5JN / ericmckinmon@gmail.com	01334 659650
Meager, Peter MA BD CertMgmt(Open)	1971	1998	(Elie with Kilconquhar and Colinsburgh)	72 Lawmill Gardens, St Andrews KY16 8QS / jpmclean72@gmail.com	01334 470803
Neilson, Peter MA BD MTh	1975	2016	(Mission Consultant)	7 Lorraine Drive, Cupar KY15 5DY / meager52@btinternet.com	01334 656991
Paton, Marion J. (Miss) MA BMus BD	1991	2017	(Dundee: St David's High Kirk)	Linne Bheag, 2 School Green, Anstruther KY10 3HF / neilson.peter@btinternet.com	01333 310477 / 07818 418608
Scott, David D. BSc BD	1981	2019	(Traprain)	18 Winram Place, St Andrews KY16 8XH / mjpdht@gmail.com	01334 208743
Torrance, Alan J. (Prof.) MA BD DrTheol ARCM	1984	2020	(University of St Andrews)	259 Lamond Drive, St Andrews KY16 8RR / revddd.scott@gmail.com	01334 473460
Unsworth, Ruth BA BD CertMHS PgDipCBP BABCP	1984	1987	(Glasgow Pollokshaws)	Kincaple House, Kincaple, St Andrews KY16 9SH	Home 01334 850755 / Office 01334 462843 / 07894 802119
Walker, James B. MA BD DPhil	1975	2011	(Chaplain: University of St Andrews)	5 Lindsay Gardens, St Andrews KY16 8XB / RUnsworth@churchofscotland.org.uk	
Wallace, Hugh M. MA BD	1980	2018	(Newhills)	5 Priestden Park, St Andrews KY16 8DL	01334 472839
Wotherspoon, Ian G. BA LTh	1967	2004	(Coatbridge: St Andrew's)	15 West End, St Monans KY10 2BX	
				12 Cherry Lane, Cupar KY15 5DA / wotherspoonrig@aol.com	01334 650710

(27) DUNKELD AND MEIGLE

Meets at Pitlochry on the first Tuesday of February, September and December, on the third Tuesday of April and the fourth Tuesday of October; and at the Moderator's church on the third Tuesday of June.

Clerk:	**REV. JOHN RUSSELL MA**			**Kilblaan, Gladstone Terrace, Birnam, Dunkeld PH8 0DP** dunkeldmeigle@churchofscotland.org.uk	**01350 728896**
Depute Clerk:	**REV. R. FRASER PENNY BA BD**			**Cathedral Manse, Dunkeld PH8 0AW** RPenny@churchofscotland.org.uk	**01350 727249**

Aberfeldy (H W) linked with Dull and Weem (H W) linked with Grantully, Logierait and Strathtay (F W)

Neil M. Glover	2005	2017	The Manse, Taybridge Terrace, Aberfeldy PH15 2BS / NGlover@churchofscotland.org.uk	01887 820819 / 07779 280074

Alyth (F H W)

Michael J. Erskine MA BD	1985	2012	The Manse, Cambridge Street, Alyth, Blairgowrie PH11 8AW / erskinemike@gmail.com	01828 632238

Ardler, Kettins and Meigle (F W)
Vacant
Interim Moderator: Linda Stewart
The Manse, Dundee Road, Meigle, Blairgowrie PH12 8SB
Linda.Stewart@churchofscotland.org.uk
01828 640074
01250 872462

Bendochy (W) linked with Coupar Angus: Abbey (W)
Andrew F. Graham BTh DPS 2001
Caddam Road, Coupar Angus, Blairgowrie PH13 9EF
Andrew.Graham@churchofscotland.org.uk
01828 627864

Blair Atholl and Struan linked with Braes of Rannoch linked with Foss and Rannoch (H)
Vacant
Interim Moderator: Grace M. F. Steele
The Manse, Blair Atholl, Pitlochry PH18 5SX
GSteele@churchofscotland.org.uk
01796 481213
01887 820025

Blairgowrie (F W)
Benjamin J. A. Abeledo BTh DipTh PTh 1991
The Manse, Upper David Street, Blairgowrie PH10 6HB
BAbeledo@churchofscotland.org.uk
01250 870986

Braes of Rannoch See Blair Atholl and Struan

Caputh and Clunie (H) linked with Kinclaven (H)
Peggy Ewart-Roberts BA BD 2003
Cara Beag, Essendy Road, Blairgowrie PH10 6QU
PEwart-Roberts@churchofscotland.org.uk
01250 876897

Coupar Angus: Abbey See Bendochy
Dull and Weem See Aberfeldy

Dunkeld (H W)
R. Fraser Penny BA BD 1984
Cathedral Manse, Dunkeld PH8 0AW
RPenny@churchofscotland.org.uk
01350 727249

Fortingall, Glenlyon, Kenmore (H) and Lawers (W)
Vacant
Interim Moderator: Robert D. Nicol
The Manse, Balnaskeag, Kenmore, Aberfeldy PH15 2HB
RNicol@churchofscotland.org.uk
01887 830218
01887 820242

Foss and Rannoch See Blair Atholl and Struan
Grantully, Logierait and Strathtay See Aberfeldy
Kinclaven See Caputh and Clunie

Kirkmichael, Straloch and Glenshee (W) linked with Rattray (H W)

Linda Stewart (Mrs) BD   1996 2012   The Manse, Alyth Road, Rattray, Blairgowrie PH10 7HF   01250 872462
Linda.Stewart@churchofscotland.org.uk

Pitlochry (H W)

Mary M. Haddow (Mrs) BD   2001 2012   thetryst@btconnect.com   01796 **474010**
Manse Road, Moulin, Pitlochry PH16 5EP   01796 472774
MHaddow@churchofscotland.org.uk

Rattray   See Kirkmichael, Straloch and Glenshee

Tenandry

Guardianship of the Presbytery
Interim Moderator: Neil M. Glover   NGlover@churchofscotland.org.uk   01887 820819
07779 280074

B. In other appointments

Nicol, Robert D. MA   2013   Ordained Local Minister   Rappla Lodge, Camserney, Aberfeldy PH15 2JF   01887 820242
RNicol@churchofscotland.org.uk

Russell, John MA   1959 2000   Presbytery Clerk: Dunkeld and Meigle   Kilblaan, Gladstone Terrace, Birnam, Dunkeld PH8 0DP   01350 728896

Steele, Grace M.F. MA BTh   2014   Ordained Local Minister   12a Farragon Drive, Aberfeldy PH15 2BQ   01887 820025
GSteele@churchofscotland.org.uk

C. Demitted

Campbell, Richard S. LTh   1993 2010   (Gargunnock with Kilmadock with Kincardine-in-Menteith)   3 David Farquharson Road, Blairgowrie PH10 6FD   01250 876386
revrichards@yahoo.co.uk

Dingwall, Brian BTh CQSW   1999 2020   (Arbirlot with Carmyllie)   10 New Road, Rattray, Blairgowrie PH10 7RA   07906 656847
brian.d12@btinternet.com

Ewart, William BSc BD   1972 2010   (Caputh and Clunie with Kinclaven)   Cara Beag, Essendy Road, Blairgowrie PH10 6QU   01250 876897
ewe1@btinternet.com

Knox, John W. MTheol   1992 1997   (Lochgelly: Macainsh)   2 Darroch Gate, Blairgowrie PH10 6GT   01250 872733
ian.knox.5@btinternet.com

Mackay, Kenneth D. DCS   1996 2020   (Deacon)   11F Balgowan Road, Perth PH1 2JG   01738 621169
deakendam@gmail.com   07843 883042

McLachlan, Ian K. MA BD   1999 2019   (Barr with Dailly with Girvan: South)   22 Beeches Road, Blairgowrie PH10 6PN   01250 369224
iankmclachlanyetiville53@gmail.com

MacRae, Malcolm H. MA PhD   1971 2010   (Kirkmichael, Straloch and Glenshee with Rattray)   10B Victoria Place, Stirling FK8 2QU   01786 465547
malcolm.macrae1@btopenworld.com

Mowbray, Harry BD CA   2003 2018   (Blairgowrie)   12 Isla Road, Blairgowrie PH10 6RR   01250 873479

Nelson, Robert C. BA BD   1980 2010   (Isle of Mull, Kilninian and Kilmore with Salen and Ulva with Tobermory with Torosay and Kinlochspelvie)   St Colme's, Perth Road, Birnam, Dunkeld PH8 0BH   01350 727455
rcnelson49@btinternet.com

Notman, Alison BD	2014	2020	(Ardler, Kettins and Meigle)	6 Hall Street, Kettlebridge, Cupar KY15 7QF	01828 670539
Ormiston, Hugh C. BSc BD MPhil PhD	1969	2004	(Kirkmichael, Straloch and Glenshee with Rattray)	Cedar Lea, Main Road, Woodside, Blairgowrie PH13 9NP	01887 840780
Robertson, Matthew LTh	1968	2002	(Cawdor with Croy and Dalcross)	Inver, Strathtay, Pitlochry PH9 0PG	01250 874833
Tait, Thomas W. BD MBE	1972	1997	(Rattray)	3 Rosemount Park, Blairgowrie PH10 6TZ	01796 481647
Wallace, Sheila D. (Mrs) BA BD DCS	2009	2020	(Deacon)	Little Orchard, Blair Atholl, Pitlochry PH18 5SH	07733 243046
Whyte, William B. BD	1973	2004	(Nairn: St Ninian's)	The Old Inn, Park Hill Road, Rattray, Blairgowrie PH10 7DS	01250 874401
Wilson, John M. MA BD	1967	2004	(Altnaharra and Farr)	Berbice, The Terrace, Blair Atholl, Pitlochry PH18 5SZ	01796 481619

(28) PERTH (W)

Meets at 10am on the second Saturday of February and September, and at 7pm on the second Tuesday of March, June and November in venues throughout the Presbytery.

Clerk: REV. ALEXANDER M. MILLAR MA BD MBA

Presbytery Office: 209 High Street, Perth PH1 5PB   01738 451177
perth@churchofscotland.org.uk

Aberdalgie and Forteviot (F H W) linked with Aberuthven and Dunning (F H W)

James W. Aitchison BD	1993	2015	The Manse, Aberdalgie, Perth PH2 0QD	01738 446771

JAitchison@churchofscotland.org.uk

Abernethy and Dron and Arngask (W)

Stanley Kennon BA BD	1992	2018	3 Manse Road, Abernethy, Perth PH2 9JP	01738 850194

SKennon@churchofscotland.org.uk

Aberuthven and Dunning See Aberdalgie and Forteviot

Almondbank Tibbermore linked with Methven and Logiealmond (W)

Robert J. Malloch BD	1987	2019	The Manse, Dalcrue Road, Pitcairngreen, Perth PH1 3EA	01738 583727

RMalloch@churchofscotland.org.uk

Ardoch (H W) linked with Blackford (F H W)

info@ardochparishchurch.org

Mairi Perkins BA BTh	2012	2016	Manse of Ardoch, Feddoch Road, Braco, Dunblane FK15 5RE	01786 880948

MPerkins@churchofscotland.org.uk

Auchterarder (F H T W)
Lynn M. McChlery BA BD MLitt PhD   2005   2019   22 Kirkfield Place, Auchterarder PH3 1FP   01764 662399
LMcChlery@churchofscotland.org.uk

Auchtergaven and Moneydie (F W) linked with Redgorton and Stanley (W)
Vacant   22 King Street, Stanley, Perth PH1 4ND   **01738 788017**
Interim Moderator: James C. Stewart   JStewart@churchofscotland.org.uk   01738 624167

Blackford See Ardoch

Cargill Burrelton (F) linked with Collace (F)
Steven Thomson BSc BD   2001   2016   The Manse, Manse Road, Woodside, Blairgowrie PH13 9NQ   01828 670384
SThomson@churchofscotland.org.uk

Cleish (H W) linked with Fossoway: St Serf's and Devonside (F W)
Elisabeth M. Stenhouse BD   2006   2014   Station House, Station Road, Crook of Devon, Kinross KY13 0PG   01577 842128
EStenhouse@churchofscotland.org.uk

Collace See Cargill Burrelton

Comrie (F H W) linked with Dundurn (F H)
Vacant   **strathearnkirks@btinternet.com**   **01764 679555**
Interim Moderator: John A.H. Murdoch   The Manse, Strowan Road, Comrie, Crieff PH6 2ES   01764 670076
JMurdoch@churchofscotland.org.uk   01738 628378
07578 558978

Crieff (F H W)
Andrew J. Philip BSc BD   1996   2013   8 Strathearn Terrace, Crieff PH7 3AQ   01764 218976
APhilip@churchofscotland.org.uk

Dunbarney (H) and Forgandenny (W)
Allan J. Wilson BSc MEd BD   2007   **dfpoffice@btconnect.com**   **01738 812463**
Dunbarney Manse, Manse Road, Bridge of Earn, Perth PH2 9DY   01738 812211
AWilson@churchofscotland.org.uk

Dundurn See Comrie

Errol (F H) linked with Kilspindie and Rait
Vacant   South Bank, Errol, Perth PH2 7PZ   01821 642279
Interim Moderator: James K. Wallace   jkwministry@hotmail.com   07576 071743

Fossoway: St Serf's and Devonside See Cleish
Kilspindie and Rait See Errol

Kinross (F H W)
Alan D. Reid MA BD 1989 2009
office@kinrossparishchurch.org **01577 862570**
15 Green Wood, Kinross KY13 8FG 01577 862952
AReid@churchofscotland.org.uk

Methven and Logiealmond See Almondbank Tibbermore

Mid Strathearn (H W)
Vacant
Interim Moderator: Marjorie Clark (Miss)
Beechview, Abercairney, Crieff PH7 3NF 01764 652116
marjorie.clark@btinternet.com 01738 637017

Muthill (F H W) linked with Trinity Gask and Kinkell (F W)
Klaus O.F. Buwert LLB BD DMin 1984 2013
The Manse, Station Road, Muthill, Crieff PH5 2AR 01764 681205
KBuwert@churchofscotland.org.uk

Orwell and Portmoak (F H W)
Angus Morrison MA BD PhD DD 1979 2011
orwellandportmoakchurch@gmail.com **01577 862100**
41 Auld Mart Road, Milnathort, Kinross KY13 9FR 01577 863461
AMorrison@churchofscotland.org.uk

Perth: Craigie and Moncreiffe (F W)
Vacant
Robert F. Wilkie 2011 2012
(Auxiliary Minister)
Interim Moderator: Robert J. Malloch
The Manse, 46 Abbot Street, Perth PH2 0EE 01738 623748
24 Huntingtower Road, Perth PH1 2JS 01738 628301
RWilkie@churchofscotland.org.uk
RMalloch@churchofscotland.org.uk 01738 583727

Perth: Kinnoull (F H W)
Graham C. Crawford BSc BD STM 1991 2016
1 Mount Tabor Avenue, Perth PH2 7BT 01738 626046
GCrawford@churchofscotland.org.uk 07817 504042

Perth: Letham St Mark's (H W)
James C. Stewart BD DipMin 1997
office@lethamstmarks.org.uk **01738 446377**
35 Rose Crescent, Perth PH1 1NT 01738 624167
JStewart@churchofscotland.org.uk

Perth: North (F W)
Kenneth D. Stott MA BD 1989 2017
info@perthnorthchurch.org.uk **01738 622298**
2 Cragganmore Place, Perth PH1 3GJ 01738 625728
KStott@churchofscotland.org.uk

Perth: Riverside (F W)
David R. Rankin MA BD   2009 2014   perthriverside.bookings@gmail.com   01738 622341
44 Hay Street, Perth PH1 5HS   07810 008754
DRankin@churchofscotland.org.uk

Perth: St John's Kirk of Perth (F H W) linked with Perth: St Leonard's-in-the-Fields (H)   St John's: 01738 633192   St Leonard's: 01738 632238
John A.H. Murdoch BA BD DPSS   1979 2016   Ferntower, Kinfauns Holdings, Perth PH2 7JY   01738 628378
JMurdoch@churchofscotland.org.uk   07578 558978

Alexander T. Stewart MA BD FSAScot   1975 2017   36 Viewlands Terrace, Perth PH1 1BZ   01738 566675
(Associate Minister)   alex.t.stewart@blueyonder.co.uk

Perth: St Leonard's-in-the-Fields See Perth: St John's Kirk of Perth

Perth: St Matthew's (T W)   office@stmatts.org.uk   Office: 01738 636757; Vestry: 01738 630725
Vacant   23 Kincarrathie Crescent, Perth PH2 7HH   01738 626828
Interim Moderator: Marc F. Bircham   MBircham@churchofscotland.org.uk   01738 860837

Redgorton and Stanley See Auchtergaven and Moneydie

St Madoes and Kinfauns (F W)
Marc F. Bircham BD MTh   2000   Glencarse, Perth PH2 7NF   01738 860837
MBircham@churchofscotland.org.uk

Scone and St Martins   sconeandstmartinschurch@talktalk.net   01738 553900
Maudeen I. MacDougall BA BD MTh   1978 2019   The Manse, Burnside, Scone PH2 6LP   01738 551942
Maudeen.MacDougall@churchofscotland.org.uk

Trinity Gask and Kinkell See Muthill

B. In other appointments

McCarthy, David J. BSc BD   1985 2014   Fresh Expressions Development Worker,   121 George Street, Edinburgh EH2 4YN   0131 225 5722
Faith Nurture Forum   DMcCarthy@churchofscotland.org.uk

MacLaughlan, Grant BA BD   1998 2015   Community Worker, Perth Tulloch Net   Unit 2, Tulloch Square, Perth PH1 2PW   01738 562731
grantmac.tullochnet@gmail.com   07790 518041

Michie, Margaret   2013   Ordained Local Minister: Loch Leven   3 Loch Leven Court, Wester Balgedie, Kinross KY13 9NE   01592 840602
Parish Grouping   margaretmichie@btinternet.com

Millar, Alexander M. MA BD MBA   1980 2020   Presbytery Clerk: Perth   17 Mapledene Road, Scone, Perth PH2 6NX   01738 550270
alexmillar0406@gmail.com

Millar, Jennifer M. (Mrs) BD DipMin   1986 1988   Teacher: Religious and Moral Education   17 Mapledene Road, Scone, Perth PH2 6NX   01738 550270
ajrmillar@blueyonder.co.uk

Name	Years	Role / Parish	Address / Email	Telephone
Stewart, Anne E. BD CertMin	1998 2007	Prison Chaplain: HM Prison Castle Huntly	35 Rose Crescent, Perth PH1 1NT anne.stewart2@sps.pnn.gov.uk	01738 624167
Stott, Anne M.	2019	Ordained Local Minister: Presbytery Pioneer Worker, Bertha Park	2 Cragganmore Place, Perth PH1 3GJ AStott@churchofscotland.org.uk	01738 625728
Thorburn, Susan MTh	2014	Ordained Local Minister	3 Daleally Farm Cottages, St Madoes Road, Errol, Perth PH1 7TJ SThorburn@churchofscotland.org.uk	01821 642681
Wallace, Catherine PGDipC DCS	1987 2017	Deacon: Honorary Secretary, Diaconate Council	21 Durley Dene Crescent, Bridge of Earn PH2 9RD secretary@churchofscotland.org.uk	01738 621709
Wyjie, Jonathan BSc BD MTh	2000 2015	Chaplain: Strathallan School	Strathallan School, Forgandenny, Perth PH2 9EG chaplain@strathallan.co.uk	01738 815098

C. Demitted

Name	Years	Role / Parish	Address / Email	Telephone
Ballentine, Ann M. MA BD	1981 2007	(Kirknewton and East Calder)	17 Nellfield Road, Crieff PH7 3DU annmballentine@gmail.com	01764 652567
Barr, T. Leslie LTh	1969 1997	(Kinross)	8 Fairfield Road, Kelty KY4 0BY leslie_barr@yahoo.co.uk	07727 718076 01738 730350
Bremna, Anne J. BSc BD MTh	1999 2019	(Fortingall, Glenlyon, Kenmore and Lawers)	Dunmore House, Findo Gask, Auchterarder PH3 1HS annebrennan@yahoo.co.uk	01738 552391
Brown, Elizabeth JP RGN	1996 2007	(Auxiliary Minister)	8 Viewlands Place, Perth PH1 1BS liz.brown@blueyonder.co.uk	01738 582163
Brown, Marina D. MA BD MTh	2000 2012	(Hawick: St Mary's and Old)	Moneydie School Cottage, Luncarty, Perth PH1 3HZ revmdb1711@btinternet.com	01577 863990
Cairns, Evelyn BD	2004 2012	(Chaplain: Rachel House)	15 Talla Park, Kinross KY13 8AB revelyn@btinternet.com	01738 445543
Caskie, J. Colin BA BD	1977 2012	(Rhu and Shandon)	13 Anderson Drive, Perth PH1 1JZ jcolincaskie@gmail.com	01382 645824
Coleman, Sidney H. BA BD MTh	1961 2001	(Glasgow: Merrylea)	15 Richmond Terrace, Dundee DD2 1BQ sidney.h.coleman@gmail.com	01738 626315
Corbett, Richard T. BSc MSc PhD BD	1992 2019	(Kilmallie)	Flat 309, Knights Court, 1 North William Street, Perth PH1 5NB richard.t.corbett@btinternet.com	01738 580180
Craig, Joan H. MTheol	1986 2005	(Orkney: East Mainland)	7 Jedburgh Place, Perth PH1 1SJ joanhcraig@btinternet.com	01764 655178 01764 679178
Dunn, W. Stuart LTh	1970 2006	(Motherwell: Crosshill)	10 Macrosie Gardens, Crieff PH7 4LP	
Fleming, Hamish K. MA	1966 2001	(Banchory Ternan: East)	36 Earnmuir Road, Comrie, Crieff PH6 2EY hamishnan@gmail.com	
Fletcher, Timothy E.G. BA FCMA PGDipCM MTh	1998 2019	(Auxiliary Minister)	3 Ardchoille Park, Perth PH2 7TL fletcherts495@btinternet.com	01738 638189 07747 013985
Gilchrist, Ewen J. BD DipMin DipComm	1982 2017	(Cults)	9 David Douglas Avenue, Scone PH2 6QQ ewengilchrist@btconnect.com	07747 746418
Graham, Alasdair G. BD DipMin	1981 2019	(Arbroath: West Kirk)	5 Robb Place, Perth PH2 0GB alasdairgraham704@btinternet.com	01738 626952

Name	Ord.	Ind.	Charge	Address / Email	Telephone
Graham, Sydney S. DipYL MPhil BD	1987	2009	(Iona with Kilfinichen and Kilvickeon and the Ross of Mull)	'Aspen', Milton Road, Luncarty, Perth PH1 3ES / syd@sydgraham.plus.com	01738 829350
Gregory, J.C. LTh	1968	1992	(Blantyre: St Andrew's)	2 Southlands Road, Auchterarder PH3 1BA	01764 664594
Gunn, Alexander M. MA BD	1967	2006	(Aberfeldy with Amulree and Strathbraan with Dull and Weem)	'Navarone', 12 Cornhill Road, Perth PH1 1LR / sandygunn@btinternet.com	01738 443216
Halliday, Archibald R. BD MTh	1964	1999	(Duffus, Spynie and Hopeman)	8 Turretbank Drive, Crieff PH7 4LW / roberthalliday343@btinternet.com	01764 656464
Kelly, T. Clifford	1973	1993	(Ferintosh)	20 Whinfield Drive, Kinross KY13 8UB	01577 864946
Lawson, James B. MA BD	1961	2002	(South Uist)	4 Cowden Way, Comrie, Crieff PH6 2NW / james.lawson7@btopenworld.com	01764 679180
McCormick, Alastair F.	1962	1998	(Creich with Rosehall)	14 Balmanno Park, Bridge of Earn, Perth PH2 9RJ	01738 813588
McCrum, Robert BSc BD	1982	2014	(Ayr: St James')	28 Rose Crescent, Perth PH1 1NT / robert.mccrum@virgin.net	01738 447906
MacDonald, James W. BD	1976	2012	(Crieff)	'Mingulay', 29 Hebridean Gardens, Crieff PH7 3BP / rev_up@btinternet.com	01764 654500
McFadzean, Iain MA BD	1989	2019	(Chief Executive: Work Place Chaplaincy Scotland)	2 Lowfield Crescent, Luncarty, Perth PH1 3FG / iain.mcfadzean@wpcscotland.co.uk	01738 827338 / 07969 227696
Macgregor, John BD	2001	2020	(Errol with Kilspindie and Rait)	1 Le Petit Vierzon, 16490 Hiesse, France / john_macg@hotmail.com	
McGregor, William LTh	1987	2003	(Auchtergaven and Moneydie)	'Ard Choille', 7 Taypark Road, Luncarty, Perth PH1 3FE / bill.mcgregor7@btinternet.com	01738 827866
McIntosh, Colin G. MA BD	1976	2013	(Dunblane: Cathedral)	Drumhead Cottage, Drum, Kinross KY13 0PR / colinmcintosh4@btinternet.com	01577 840012
MacMillan, Riada M. BD	1991	1998	(Perth: Craigend Moncreiffe with Rhynd)	73 Muirend Gardens, Perth PH1 1JR	01738 628867
McNaughton, David J.H. BA CA	1976	1995	(Killin and Ardeonaig)	14 Rankine Court, Wormit, Newport-on-Tay DD6 8TA	
Main, Douglas M. BD	1986	2014	(Errol with Kilspindie and Rait)	14 Madoch Road, St Madoes, Perth PH2 7TT / revdmain@sky.com	01738 860867
Malcolm, Alistair BD DPS	1976	2012	(Inverness: Insches)	11 Kinclaven Gardens, Murthly, Perth PH1 4EX / amalcolm067@btinternet.com	01738 710979
Milne, Robert B. BTh	1999	2017	(Broughton, Glenholm and Kilbucho with Skirling with Stobo and Drumelzier with Tweedsmuir)	3 Mid Square, Comrie PH6 2EG / rbmilne@aol.com	
Mitchell, Alexander B. BD	1981	2014	(Dunblane: St Blane's)	24 Hebridean Gardens, Crieff PH7 3BP / alex.mitchell6@btopenworld.com	01764 652241
Munro, Gillian BSc BD	1989	2018	(Head of Spiritual Care, NHS Tayside)	The Old Town House, 53 Main Street, Abernethy, Perth PH2 9JH / munrooh@aol.com	01738 850066
Munro, Patricia M. BSc DCS	1986	2016	(Deacon)	4 Hewat Place, Perth PH1 2UD / patmunrodcs@gmail.com	01738 443088 / 07814 836314
Paton, Iain F. BD FCIS	1980	2006	(Elie with Kilconquhar and Colinsburgh)	Muldoanich, Stirling Street, Blackford, Auchterarder PH4 1QG / iain.f.paton@btinternet.com	01764 682234
Philip, Elizabeth MA BA PGCSE DCS	2007	2018	(Deacon)	8 Strathearn Terrace, Crieff PH7 3AQ / ephilipstitch@gmail.com	01764 218976 / 07970 767851

Quigley, Barbara D. (Mrs) MTheol ThM DPS	1979	2019	(Glasgow: St Andrew's East)	33 Castle Drive, Auchterarder PH3 1FU bdquigley@aol.com	07926 064235
Redpath, James G. BD DipPTh	1988	2016	(Auchtermuchty with Edenshead and Strathmiglo)	9 Beveridge Place, Kinross KY13 8QY JRedpath@churchofscotland.org.uk	07713 919442 01821 641004
Searle, David C. MA DipTh	1965	2003	(Warden: Rutherford House)	Stonefall Lodge, 30 Abbey Lane, Grange, Errol PH2 7GB dcs@davidsearle.plus.com	
Simpson, James A. BSc BD STM DD	1960	1999	(Interim Minister, Brechin Cathedral)	'Dornoch', Perth Road, Bankfoot, Perth PH1 4ED ja@simpsondornoch.co.uk	01738 787710
Sloan, Robert P. MA BD	1968	2007	(Interim Minister, Armadale)	1 Broomhill Avenue, Perth PH1 1EN sloan12@virginmedia.com	01738 443904
Stenhouse, W. Duncan MA BD	1989	2006	(Dunbarney and Forgandenny)	32 Sandport Gait, Kinross KY13 8FB	01577 866992
Stewart, Robin J. MA BD STM	1959	1995	(Orwell with Portmoak)	'Oakbrae', Perth Road, Murthly, Perth PH1 4HF	01738 710220
Thomson, J. Bruce MA BD	1972	2009	(Scone: Old)	47 Elm Street, Errol, Perth PH2 7SQ RevBruceThomson@aol.com	01821 641039 07850 846404
Wallace, James K. MA BD STM	1988	2015	(Perth: St John's Kirk of Perth with St Leonard's-in-the-Fields)	21 Durley Dene Crescent, Bridge of Earn PH2 9RD jkwministry@hotmail.com	01738 621709

PERTH ADDRESSES

Abbot Street		Letham St Mark's	Rannoch Road	St John's	St John's Street
Craigie	Dundee Rd near Queen's Bridge	Moncreiffe	Glenbruar Crescent	St Leonard's-in-the-Fields	Marshall Place
Kinnoull		North	Mill Street near Kinnoull Street	St Matthew's	Tay Street
		Riverside	Bute Drive		

(29) DUNDEE (F W)

Meets at Dundee: The Steeple, Nethergate, on the fourth Wednesday of February, June and November, and the second Wednesday of May and September.

Clerk:	REV. JAMES L. WILSON BD CPS			dundee@churchofscotland.org.uk	07885 618659
Presbytery Office:				Whitfield Parish Church, Haddington Crescent, Dundee DD40NA	01382 503012

Abernyte (W) linked with Inchture and Kinnaird (F W) linked with Longforgan (F H W)

Marjory A. MacLean LLB BD PhD	1991	2011	The Manse, Longforgan, Dundee DD2 5HB MMacLean@churchofscotland.org.uk	01382 360238

Auchterhouse (F H W) linked with Monikie and Newbigging and Murroes and Tealing (F H W)   office@sidlawchurches.org.uk

Jean de Villiers BATheol BTh HonPsych	2003	2017	29 Oak Lane, Ballumbie Clay Estate, Dundee DD5 3UQ JdeVilliers@churchofscotland.org.uk	01382 350182 01382 351680

Dundee: Balgay (F H W)
Nardia J. Sandison BAppSc BD MLitt   2019
150 City Road, Dundee DD2 2PW
NSandison@churchofscotland.org.uk
01382 903446

Dundee: Barnhill St Margaret's (H W)
Alisa L. McDonald BA MDiv   2008   2018
church.office@btconnect.com
2 St Margaret's Lane, Barnhill, Dundee DD5 2PQ
Alisa.McDonald@churchofscotland.org.uk
01382 737294
01382 779278

Dundee: Broughty Ferry New Kirk (F H T W)
Catherine E.E. Collins (Mrs) MA BD   1993   2006
office@broughtyferrynewkirk.org.uk
New Kirk Manse, 25 Ballinard Gardens, Broughty Ferry, Dundee DD5 1BZ
CCollins@churchofscotland.org.uk
01382 738264
01382 778874

Dundee: Broughty Ferry St James' (F H)
Guardianship of the Presbytery
Session Clerks: Lyn Edwards (Mrs)   kathelyneedwards@gmail.com
David J.B. Murie   d.j.b.murie@gmail.com
01382 730552
01382 320493

Dundee: Broughty Ferry St Luke's and Queen Street (F W)
Vacant
Session Clerk: Kenneth Andrew
22 Albert Road, Broughty Ferry, Dundee DD5 1AZ
kga@scot-int.com
01382 732094
01382 779212
01382 776765

Dundee: Broughty Ferry St Stephen's and West (H W) linked with Dundee: Dundee (St Mary's) (H W)   office@dundeestmarys.co.uk
Keith F. Hall MA BD   1981   1994
33 Strathern Road, West Ferry, Dundee DD5 1PP
KHall@churchofscotland.org.uk
01382 226271
01382 778808

Dundee: Camperdown (H)
Guardianship of the Presbytery
Interim Moderator: Roderick J. Grahame
Camperdown Manse, Myrekirk Road, Dundee DD2 4SF
RGrahame@churchofscotland.org.uk
01382 561872

Dundee: Chalmers-Ardler (F H)
Jonathan W. Humphrey BSc BD PhD   2015   2018
The Manse, Turnberry Avenue, Dundee DD2 3TP
JHumphrey@churchofscotland.org.uk
07587 186424

Dundee: Coldside (F W)
Vacant
Session Clerk: Yvonne Grant (Miss)
9 Abercorn Street, Dundee DD4 7HY
yngrant@sky.com
01382 458314
01382 652705

Dundee: Craigiebank (H W) linked with Dundee: Douglas and Mid Craigie (F W)
Vacant
Interim Moderator: Kenneth Andrew   kga@scot-int.com   01382 731173
01382 776765

Dundee: Downfield Mains (H W)
Nathan S. McConnell BS MA ThM   2002   2016   downfieldmainsoffice@gmail.com   07977 042166
9 Elgin Street, Dundee DD3 8NL
NMcConnell@churchofscotland.org.uk

Dundee: Dundee (St Mary's) See Dundee: Broughty Ferry St Stephen's and West

Dundee: Fintry (F W)
Colin M. Brough BSc BD   1998   2002   4 Clive Street, Dundee DD4 7AW   01382 458629
CBrough@churchofscotland.org.uk

Catherine J. Brodie MA BA MPhil PGCE   2017   48h Cleghorn Street, Dundee DD2 2NJ   07432 513375
(Ordained Local Minister)   CBrodie@churchofscotland.org.uk

Dundee: Lochee (F H)
Roderick J. Grahame BD CPS DMin DipPSRP   1991   2018   32 Clayhills Drive, Dundee DD2 1SX   01382 561872
RGrahame@churchofscotland.org.uk

Willie D. Strachan MBA DipY&C   2013   Ladywell House, Lucky Slap, Monikie, Dundee   DD5 3QG   01382 370286
(Ordained Local Minister)   WStrachan@churchofscotland.org.uk

Dundee: Logie and St John's Cross (F H W)
David T. Gray BArch BD   2010   2014   7 Hyndford Street, Dundee DD2 1HQ   **01382 668514**
DGray@churchofscotland.org.uk   01382 668653
07789 718622

Dundee: Meadowside St Paul's (F H T W)
linked with Dundee: St Andrew's (F H T W)
Vacant   **mspdundee@outlook.com**   **01382 225420**
standrewsdundee@outlook.com   **01382 224860**
Session Clerk, Meadowside St Paul's: Margaret Adamson (Ms)   mspdundee@outlook.com   01382 668624
Session Clerk, St Andrew's: Helen Holden (Mrs)   hholdenuk@yahoo.com   01241 853242

Dundee: Menzieshill (F W)
Robert Mallinson BD   2010   The Manse, Charleston Drive, Dundee   DD2 4ED   01382 667446
RMallinson@churchofscotland.org.uk   07595 249089

Dundee: St Andrew's See Dundee: Meadowside St Paul's

Dundee: St David's High Kirk (H W)
Emma McDonald BD — 2013 — 2018
St David's High Kirk, 119A Kinghorne Road, Dundee DD3 6PW
EMcDonald@churchofscotland.org.uk
01382 322955

Dundee: The Steeple (F H T W)
Robert A. Calvert BSc BD DMin PhD — 1983 — 2014
office@thesteeplechurch.org.uk
128 Arbroath Road, Dundee DD4 7HR
RCalvert@churchofscotland.org.uk
01382 200031
01382 522837
07532 029343

Dundee: Stobswell (F H)
William McLaren MA BD — 1990 — 2007
23 Shamrock Street, Dundee DD4 7AH
WMcLaren@churchofscotland.org.uk
01382 461397
01382 459119

Dundee: Strathmartine (F H W)
Stewart McMillan BD — 1983 — 1990
19 Americanmuir Road, Dundee DD3 9AA
SMcMillan@churchofscotland.org.uk
01382 825817
01382 812423

Dundee: Trinity (H W)
Vacant
Session Clerk: Ian Main
secretary@trinitychurchdundee.org
ian-main@sky.com
01382 783783

Dundee: West (F W)
Vacant
Interim Moderator: John J. Laidlaw
enquiries@dundeewestchurch.org
jacklaidlaw@blueyonder.co.uk
07341 255354
01382 477458

Dundee: Whitfield (H)
James L. Wilson BD CPS — 1986 — 2001
53 Old Craigie Road, Dundee DD4 7JD
James.Wilson@churchofscotland.org.uk
01382 503012
07885 618659

Fowlis and Liff (F T W) linked with Lundie and Muirhead (F H T W)
Donna M. Hays (Mrs) MTheol DipEd DipTMHA — 2004
enquiries@churches-flandlm.co.uk
149 Coupar Angus Road, Muirhead of Liff, Dundee DD2 5QN
DHays@churchofscotland.org.uk
01382 580210

Inchture and Kinnaird See Abernyte

Invergowrie (H W)
Vacant
Session Clerk: Peter Mackay
hello@invergowrieparishchurch.org
2 Boniface Place, Invergowrie, Dundee DD2 5DW
peter.mackay@scottishwater.co.uk
01382 561118
01382 933867

Longforgan See Abernyte
Lundie and Muirhead See Fowlis and Liff

Monifieth (F H W)   office@monifiethparishchurch.co.uk
Fiona J. Reynolds LLB BD   2018   8 Church Street, Monifieth, Dundee DD5 4JP   01382 699183

Monikie and Newbigging and Murroes and Tealing See Auchterhouse

B. In other appointments

Campbell, Gordon MA BD CDipAF DipHSM CMgr MCMI MIHM AssocCIPD AFRIN ARSGS FRGS FSAScot	2001 2004	Auxiliary Minister: an Honorary Chaplain: University of Dundee	2 Falkland Place, Kingoodie, Invergowrie, Dundee DD2 5DY g.a.campbell@dundee.ac.uk	01382 561383
Douglas, Fiona C. MBE MA BD PhD	1989 1997	Chaplain: University of Dundee	10 Springfield, Dundee DD1 4JE f.c.douglas@dundee.ac.uk	01382 384157

C. Demitted

Allan, Jean (Mrs) DCS	1989 2011	(Deacon)	12C Hindmarsh Avenue, Dundee DD3 7LW jeannieallan45@googlemail.com	01382 827299 07709 959474
Barrett, Leslie M. BD FRICS	1991 2014	(Chaplain: University of Abertay, Dundee)	Dunelm Cottage, Logie, Cupar KY15 4SJ lesliembarrett@btinternet.com	01334 870396
Collins, David A. BSc BD	1993 2016	(Auchterhouse with Monikie and Newbigging and Murroes and Tealing)	New Kirk Manse, 25 Ballinard Gardens, Broughty Ferry, Dundee DD5 1BZ revdacollins@btinternet.com	01382 778874
Dempster, Colin J. BD CertMin	1990 2016	(Mearns Coastal)	35 Margaret Lindsay Place, Monifieth DD6 4RD Coldcoast@btinternet.com	01382 532368
Fraser, Donald W. MA	1958 2010	(Monifieth)	1 Blake Avenue, Broughty Ferry, Dundee DD5 3LH fraserdonald37@yahoo.co.uk	01382 477491 07531 863316
Jamieson, David B. MA BD STM	1974 2011	(Monifieth)	8A Albert Street, Monifieth, Dundee DD5 4JS	01382 532772
Kay, Elizabeth (Miss) DipYCS	1993 2007	(Auxiliary Minister)	1 Kintail Walk, Inchture, Perth PH14 9RY ekay007@btinternet.com	01828 686029
Laidlaw, John J. MA	1964 1996	(Adviser in Religious Education)	14 Dalhousie Road, Barnhill, Dundee DD5 2SQ jacklaidlaw@blueyonder.co.uk	01382 477458
Laing, David J.H. BD DPS	1976 2014	(Dundee: Trinity)	18 Kerrington Crescent, Barnhill, Dundee DD5 2TN david.laing@live.co.uk	01382 739586
Lillie, Fiona L. (Mrs) BA BD MLitt	1995 2017	(Glasgow: St John's Renfield)	4 McVicars Lane, Dundee DD1 4LH fionalillie@btinternet.com	01382 229082

McLeod, David C. BSc MEng BD	1969	2001	(Dundee: Fairmuir)	6 Carseview Gardens, Dundee DD2 1NE	01382 685811
McMillan, Edith F. (Mrs) MA BD	1981	2018	(Dundee: Craigiebank with Douglas and Mid Craigie)	19 Americanmuir Road, Dundee DD3 9AA wee_rev_edimac@btinternet.com	01382 812423
Mair, Michael V.A. MA BD	1968	2007	(Dundee: Craigiebank with Douglas and Mid Craigie)	48 Panmure Street, Monifieth DD5 4EH mvamair@gmail.com	01382 530538
Ramsay, Robert J. LLB NP BD	1986	2018	(Invergowrie)	50 Nethergray Road. Dundee DD2 5GT s3rjr@tiscali.co.uk	01382 562481
Reid, R. Gordon BSc BD MIET	1993	2010	(Carriden)	6 Bayview Place, Monifieth, Dundee DD5 4TN GordonReid@aol.com	01382 520519 / 07952 349884
Robertson, James H. BSc BD	1975	2014	(Culloden: The Barn)	'Far End', 35 Mains Terrace, Dundee DD4 7BZ jimrob838@gmail.com	07595 465838
Robson, George K. LTh DPS BA	1983	2011	(Dundee: Balgay)	11 Ceres Crescent, Broughty Ferry. Dundee DD5 3JN gkrobson@virginmedia.com	01382 901212
Rose, Lewis (Mr) DCS	1993	2010	(Deacon)	6 Gauldie Crescent, Dundee DD3 0RR lewis_rose48@yahoo.co.uk	01382 816580 / 07899 790466
Scott, James MA BD	1973	2010	(Drumoak-Durris)	3 Blake Place, Broughty Ferry, Dundee DD5 3LQ jimscott73@yahoo.co.uk	01382 739595
Taylor, Caroline (Mrs)	1995	2014	(Leuchars: St Athernase)	The Old Dairy, 15 Forthill Road. Broughty Ferry, Dundee DD5 3DH caro234@btinternet.com	01382 770198
Taylor, C. Graham D. BSc BD FIAB	2001	2020	(Dundee: Broughty Ferry St Luke's and Queen Street)	The Smithy. Grange, Errol, Perth PH2 7TB cgdtaylor@btinternet.com	07804 527103

DUNDEE ADDRESSES

Balgay	200 Lochee Road	Coldside	Isla Street x Main Street
Barnhill St Margaret's	10 Invermark Terrace	Craigiebank	Craigie Avenue at Greendykes Road
Broughty Ferry		Douglas and Mid Craigie	Balbeggie Place
New Kirk	370 Queen Street	Downfield Mains	Haldane Street off Strathmartine Road
St James'	5 Fort Street	Dundee (St Mary's)	Nethergate
St Luke's and Queen Street	5 West Queen Street	Fintry	Fintry Road x Fintry Drive
St Stephen's and West	96 Dundee Road	Lochee	191 High Street, Lochee
Camperdown	22 Brownhill Road	Logie and St John's Cross	Shaftesbury Rd x Blackness Ave
Chalmers-Ardler	Turnberry Avenue		

Meadowside St Paul's	114 Nethergate
Menzieshill	Charleston Drive. Menzieshill
St Andrew's	2 King Street
St David's High Kirk	119A Kinghorne Road
Steeple	Nethergate
Stobswell	170 Albert Street
Strathmartine	507 Strathmartine Road
Trinity	73 Crescent Street
West	130 Perth Road
Whitfield	Haddington Crescent

(30) ANGUS (W)

Meets at Forfar in St Margaret's Church Hall on the first Tuesday of February, March, May, September, November and December, and on the fourth Tuesday of June.

Clerk:	REV. IAN A. McLEAN BSc BD DMin	
Depute Clerk:	REV. MARGARET J. HUNT MA BD	
Presbytery Office:	angus@churchofscotland.org.uk	
	St Margaret's Church, West High Street, Forfar DD8 1BJ	01307 464224

Aberlemno (H W) linked with Guthrie and Rescobie (W) 1980 1984
Brian Ramsay BD DPS MLitt
The Manse, Guthrie, Forfar DD8 2TP 01241 828243
BRamsay@churchofscotland.org.uk

Arbirlot linked with Carmyllie
Vacant
Interim Moderator: Annette Gordon
The Manse, Arbirlot, Arbroath DD11 2NX 01241 874613
AGordon@churchofscotland.org.uk 01241 854478

Arbroath: Old and Abbey (F H W) 2003 2014
Dolly Purnell BD
church.office@old-and-abbey-church.org.uk 01241 877068 Tel/Fax
51 Cliffburn Road, Arbroath DD11 5BA 01241 872196
DPurnell@churchofscotland.org.uk

Arbroath: St Andrew's (F H W) 1992
W. Martin Fair BA BD DMin
office@arbroathstandrews.org.uk 01241 431135 Tel/Fax
92 Grampian Gardens, Arbroath DD11 4AQ 01241 873238
MFair@churchofscotland.org.uk

Arbroath: St Vigeans (F H W)
Guardianship of the Presbytery
office.stvigeans@gmail.com 01241 879567
Session Clerk: Margaret Pullar (Mrs) 01241 873206
The Manse, St Vigeans, Arbroath DD11 4RF 01241 876667
margaret.pullar@btinternet.com

Arbroath: West Kirk (H)
Vacant
Session Clerk: William Clark
1 Charles Avenue, Arbroath DD11 2EY 01241 872244
w467clark@btinternet.com

Barry (W) linked with Carnoustie (F W) 1991 2003
Michael S. Goss BD DPS
44 Terrace Road, Carnoustie DD7 7AR 01241 410194
MGoss@churchofscotland.org.uk 07787 141567

Brechin: Cathedral (H W)
Vacant
office@brechincathedral.org.uk 01356 629360
Chanonry Wynd, Brechin DD9 6JS 01356 624980

Brechin: Gardner Memorial (F H T W) linked with Farnell (W) Gardner Memorial: 01356 629191
Vacant
Session Clerk, Gardner Memorial: office@gardnermemorial.plus.com 01356 622034
Dorothy Black (Miss) 15 Caldhame Gardens, Brechin DD9 7JJ 01356 622614
dorothy.black6@btinternet.com

Carmyllie See Arbirlot
Carnoustie See Barry

Carnoustie: Panbride (F H W)
Annette Gordon BD 2017 8 Arbroath Road, Carnoustie DD7 6BL 01241 854478
AGordon@churchofscotland.org.uk

Colliston linked with Friockheim Kinnell linked with Inverkeilor and Lunan (H)
Peter A. Phillips BA 1995 2004 The Manse, Inverkeilor, Arbroath DD11 5SA 01241 830464
PPhillips@churchofscotland.org.uk

Dun and Hillside (F)
Fiona C. Bullock (Mrs) MA LLB BD 2014 4 Manse Road, Hillside, Montrose DD10 9FB 01674 830288
FBullock@churchofscotland.org.uk

Dunnichen, Letham and Kirkden (W)
Guardianship of the Presbytery
Session Clerk: Irene McGugan irene.mcgugan@btinternet.com 01307 818436

Eassie, Nevay and Newtyle
Carleen J. Robertson (Miss) BD 1992 2 Kirkton Road, Newtyle, Blairgowrie PH12 8TS 01828 650461
CRobertson@churchofscotland.org.uk

Edzell Lethnot Glenesk (F H W) linked with Fern Careston Menmuir (F W) elgparish@btconnect.com 01356 647815
A.S. Wayne Pearce MA PhD 2002 2017 19 Lethnot Road, Edzell, Brechin DD9 7TG 01356 648117
ASWaynePearce@churchofscotland.org.uk

Farnell See Brechin: Gardner Memorial
Fern Careston Menmuir See Edzell Lethnot Glenesk

Forfar: East and Old (F H W)
Barbara Ann Sweetin BD — 2011 — eando_office@yahoo.co.uk / The Manse, Lour Road, Forfar DD8 2BB / BSweetin@churchofscotland.org.uk — 01307 248228

Forfar: Lowson Memorial (F H)
Karen Fenwick BSc BD MPhil PhD — 2006 — 1 Jamieson Street, Forfar DD8 2HY / KFenwick@churchofscotland.org.uk — 01307 468585

Forfar: St Margaret's (F H W)
Margaret J. Hunt (Mrs) MA BD — 2014 — **stmargaretsforfar@gmail.com** / St Margaret's Manse, 15 Potters Park Crescent, Forfar   DD8 1HH / MHunt@churchofscotland.org.uk — **01307 464224** / 01307 462044

Friockheim Kinnell See Colliston

Glamis (H), Inverarity and Kinnettles (W)
Guardianship of the Presbytery
Session Clerk: Mary Reid (Mrs) — mmreid@btinternet.com — 01307 840999

Guthrie and Rescobie See Aberlemno
Inverkeilor and Lunan See Colliston

Montrose: Old and St Andrew's (F W)
Ian A. McLean BSc BD DMin — 1981 / 2008 — 2 Rosehill Road, Montrose DD10 8ST / IMcLean@churchofscotland.org.uk — 01674 672447
Ian Gray — 2013 / 2017 — The Mallards, 15 Rossie Island Road, Montrose   DD10 9NH / IGray@churchofscotland.org.uk — 01674 677126
(Ordained Local Minister)

Montrose: South and Ferryden (W)
Geoffrey Redmayne BSc BD MPhil — 2000 / 2016 — Inchbrayock Manse, Usan, Montrose DD10 9SD / GRedmayne@churchofscotland.org.uk — 01674 675634

Oathlaw Tannadice (F W) linked with The Glens and Kirriemuir United (F W)
John K. Orr BD MTh — 2012 — 26 Quarry Park, Kirriemuir DD8 4DR / JOrr@churchofscotland.org.uk — **01575 572819** / 01575 572610
Linda Stevens (Mrs) BSc BD PgDip — 2006 — 17 North Latch Road, Brechin DD9 6LE / LStevens@churchofscotland.org.uk — 01356 623415 / 07801 192730
(Team Minister)

The Glens and Kirriemuir United See Oathlaw Tannadice

The Isla Parishes (W)

Stephen A. Blakey BSc BD	1977	2018		Balduff House, Kilry, Blairgowrie PH11 8HS	01575 560226
				SBlakey@churchofscotland.org.uk	

C. Demitted

Buchan, Alexander MA BD PGCE	1975	1992	(North Ronaldsay with Sanday)	59 Cliffburn Road, Arbroath DD11 5BA	01241 878862
				revicbuchan@bluebucket.org	
Buchan, Isabel C. (Mrs)	1975	2019	(Buckie: North with Rathven)	59 Cliffburn Road, Arbroath DD11 5BA	01241 878862
BSc BD RE(PgCE)				revicbuchan@bluebucket.org	
Duncan, Robert F. MTheol	1986	2001	(Lochgelly: St Andrew's)	25 Rowan Avenue, Kirriemuir DD8 4TB	01575 573973
Edwards, Dougal BTh	2013	2017	(Ordained Local Minister)	25 Mackenzie Street, Carnoustie DD7 6HD	01241 852666
Gough, Ian G. MA BD MTh DMin	1974	2009	(Arbroath: Knox's with Arbroath:	23 Keptie Road, Arbroath DD11 3ED	07891 838379
			St Vigeans)	ianggough@btinternet.com	
Hastie, George I. MA BD	1971	2009	(Mearns Coastal)	23 Borrowfield Crescent, Montrose DD10 9BR	01674 672290
Morrice, Alastair M. MA BD	1968	2000	(Rutherglen: Stonelaw)	5 Brechin Road, Kirriemuir DD8 4BX	01575 574102
				ambishkek@swissmail.org	
Norrie, Graham MA BD	1967	2007	(Forfar: East and Old)	'Novar', 14A Wyllie Street, Forfar DD8 3DN	01307 468152
				grahamnorrie@hotmail.com	
Oxburgh, Brian H. BSc BD	1980	2019	(Tayport)	50 Ravensbay Park Gardens, Carnoustie DD7 7NY	01356 647322
Robertson, George R. LTh	1985	2004	(Udny and Pitmedden)	3 Slateford Gardens, Edzell, Brechin DD9 7SX	
				geomag.robertson@btinternet.com	
Rooney, Malcolm I.G. DPE BEd BD	1993	2017	(The Glens and Kirriemuir: Old)	23 Mart Lane, Northmuir, Kirriemuir DD8 4TL	01575 575334
				malc.rooney@gmail.com	07909 993233
Smith, Hamish G.	1965	1993	(Auchterless with Rothienorman)	11A Guthrie Street, Letham, Forfar DD8 2PS	01307 818973
Thomas, Martyn R.H.	1987	2002	(Fowlis and Liff with Lundie	14 Kirkgait, Letham, Forfar DD8 2XQ	01307 818084
CEng MIStructE			and Muirhead of Liff)	martyn317thomas@btinternet.com	
Watt, Alan G.N.	1996	2009	(Edzell Lethnot Glenesk	6 Pine Way, Friockheim, Arbroath DD11 4WF	01241 826018
MTh CQSW DipCommEd			with Fern Careston Menmuir)	watt455@btinternet.com	
Webster, Allan F. MA BD	1978	2013	(Workplace Chaplain)	42 McCulloch Drive, Forfar DD8 2EB	01307 464252
				allanfwebster@aol.com	07546 276725

ANGUS ADDRESSES

Arbroath: Old and Abbey	West Abbey Street	Brechin: Cathedral	Bishop's Close	St Margaret's	West High Street
St Andrew's	Hamilton Green	Gardner Memorial	South Esk Street	Kirriemuir: United	High Street
St Vigeans	St Vigeans Brae	Carnoustie:	Dundee Street	Montrose: Old and St Andrew's	High Street
West Kirk	Keptie Street	Panbride	Arbroath Road	South and Ferryden	Church Road, Ferryden
		Forfar: East and Old	East High Street		
		Lowson Memorial	Jamieson Street		

(31) ABERDEEN AND SHETLAND (F W)

New presbytery formed by the union of the Presbytery of Aberdeen and the Presbytery of Shetland on 1 June 2020.
Meets at Queen's Cross four times a year in September, November, March and June and at other times as it may determine.

Clerk:	REV. JOHN A. FERGUSON BD DipMin DMin	
Depute Clerk:	MRS CHERYL BRANKIN BA	
Treasurer:	MR ALAN MORRISON	
Presbytery Office:	Mastrick Church, Greenfern Road, Aberdeen AB16 6TR	**01224 698119**
	aberdeenshetland@churchofscotland.org.uk	

Aberdeen: Bridge of Don Oldmachar (F H W) secretary@oldmacharchurch.org

Vacant		60 Newburgh Circle, Aberdeen AB22 8QZ	**01224 709299**
Joseph K. Somevi BSc MSc PhD MRICS	2015	2018	97 Ashwood Road, Aberdeen AB22 8QX	01224 823283
MRTPI MIEMA CertCRS (Ordained Local Minister)		JSomevi@churchofscotland.org.uk	01224 826362
			07886 533259

Aberdeen: Craigiebuckler (F H W) office@craigiebuckler.org.uk

Kenneth L. Petrie MA BD	1984	1999	185 Springfield Road, Aberdeen AB15 8AA	**01224 315649**
			KPetrie@churchofscotland.org.uk	01224 315125

Aberdeen: Ferryhill (F H W) office@ferryhillparishchurch.org

J. Peter N. Johnston BSc BD	2001	2013	54 Polmuir Road, Aberdeen AB11 7RT	**01224 213093**
			PJohnston@churchofscotland.org.uk	01224 949192

Aberdeen: High Hilton (F H W)

G. Hutton B. Steel MA BD	1982	2013	24 Rosehill Drive, Aberdeen AB24 4JJ	**01224 494717**
			Hutton.Steel@churchofscotland.org.uk	01224 493552

New charge formed by the union of Aberdeen: High Hilton and Aberdeen: Middlefield

Aberdeen: Holburn West (F H W) churchoffice@holburnwestchurch.org.uk

Duncan C. Eddie MA BD	1992	1999	31 Cranford Road, Aberdeen AB10 7NJ	**01224 571120**
			DEddie@churchofscotland.org.uk	01224 325873

Aberdeen: Mannofield (F H T W) office@mannofieldchurch.org.uk

Keith T. Blackwood BD DipMin	1997	2007	21 Forest Avenue, Aberdeen AB15 4TU	**01224 310087**
			KBlackwood@churchofscotland.org.uk	01224 315748

Congregation / Minister			Contact	Telephone
Aberdeen: Mastrick (F H W) Susan J. Sutherland (Mrs) BD	2009	2017	8 Corse Wynd, Kingswells, Aberdeen AB15 8TP SSutherland@churchofscotland.org.uk	**01224 694121** 01224 279562
Aberdeen: Midstocket (H W) Tanya J. Webster BCom DipAcc BD	2011	2019	secretary@midstocketchurch.org.uk 182 Midstocket Road, Aberdeen AB15 5HS TWebster@churchofscotland.org.uk	**01224 319519** 01224 561358
Aberdeen: Northfield (F H) Scott C. Guy BD	1989	1998	28 Byron Crescent, Aberdeen AB16 7EX SGuy@churchofscotland.org.uk	**01224 692332** 01224 692332
Aberdeen: Queen's Cross (F H W) Scott M. Rennie MA BD STM	1999	2009	office@queenscrosschurch.org.uk 1 St Swithin Street, Aberdeen AB10 6XH SRennie@churchofscotland.org.uk	**01224 644742** 01224 322549
Aberdeen: Rubislaw (F H W) Robert L. Smith BS MTh PhD	2000	2013	rubislawchurch@btconnect.com 13 Oakhill Road, Aberdeen AB15 5ERR RSmith@churchofscotland.org.uk	**01224 645477** 01224 314773
Aberdeen: Ruthrieston West (F W) Benjamin D.W. Byun BS MDiv MTh PhD	1992	2008	53 Springfield Avenue, Aberdeen AB15 8JJ BByun@churchofscotland.org.uk	01224 312706
Aberdeen: St Columba's Bridge of Don (F H W) Louis Kinsey BD DipMin TD	1991		administrator@stcolumbaschurch.org.uk 151 Jesmond Avenue, Aberdeen AB22 8UG LKinsey@churchofscotland.org.uk	**01224 825653** 01224 705337
Aberdeen: St George's Tillydrone (F H W) Vacant Session Clerk: Kenneth Williamson			admin@tillydrone.church kdwllmsn@yahoo.co.uk	**01224 482204** 01224 487302
Aberdeen: St John's Church for Deaf People P. Mary Whittaker BSc BD	2011	2018	11 Templand Road, Lhanbryde, Elgin IV30 8BR MWhittaker@churchofscotland.org.uk	Text only 07501 454766 or contact Aberdeen: St Mark's
Aberdeen: St Machar's Cathedral (F H T W) Vacant Session Clerk: Alan Grant			office@stmachar.com bryce.grant@outlook.com	**01224 485988** 07801 078000

Aberdeen: St Mark's (F H W)
Vacant
Session Clerks: Helen Burr (Mrs)
                 Dianne Morrison (Miss)
office@stmarksaberdeen.org.uk   **01224 640672**
helen.burr@hotmail.co.uk   07751 851610
diannemorrison@talktalk.net   07767 140582

Aberdeen: St Mary's (F H W)
Elsie J. Fortune (Mrs) BSc BD   2003
stmaryschurch924@btinternet.com   **01224 487227**
456 King Street, Aberdeen AB24 3DE   01224 633778
EFortune@churchofscotland.org.uk

Aberdeen: St Nicholas Kincorth, South of (W)
Edward C. McKenna BD DPS   1989   2002
The Manse, Kincorth Circle, Aberdeen AB12 5NX   01224 872820
EMcKenna@churchofscotland.org.uk

Aberdeen: St Nicholas, Kirk of (F H W)
B. Ian Murray BD   2002   2020
(Interim Minister)
mither.kirk@btconnect.com   **01224 643494** (ext 21)
Kilmorie House, 6 Institution Road, Elgin IV30 1RP 01343 546265
BMurray@churchofscotland.org.uk

Aberdeen: St Stephen's (F H W)
Maggie Whyte BD   2010
6 Belvidere Street, Aberdeen AB25 2QS   **01224 624443**
Maggie.Whyte@churchofscotland.org.uk   01224 635694

Aberdeen: South Holburn (H W)
David J. Stewart BD MTh DipMin   2000   2018
54 Woodstock Road, Aberdeen AB15 5JF   **07498 781457**
DStewart@churchofscotland.org.uk   01224 317975

Aberdeen: Stockethill (W)
B. Ian M. Aitken MA BD   1999
52 Ashgrove Road West, Aberdeen AB16 5EE   01224 686929
IAitken@churchofscotland.org.uk

Aberdeen: Summerhill (F H W)
Michael R.R. Shewan MA BD CPS   1985
36 Stronsay Drive, Aberdeen AB15 6JL   01224 324669
MShewan@churchofscotland.org.uk

Aberdeen: Torry St Fittick's (F H W)
Edmond Gatima BEng BD MSc MPhil PhD   2013
11 Devanha Gardens East, Aberdeen AB11 7UN   **01224 899183**
EGatima@churchofscotland.org.uk   01224 588245

Congregation / Minister	Year(s)	Address / Email	Tel.
Aberdeen: Woodside (F H W) Markus Auffermann DipTheol ThD	1999 2006	officewpc@talktalk.net 322 Clifton Road, Aberdeen AB24 4HQ MAuffermann@churchofscotland.org.uk	01224 277249 01224 484562
Bucksburn Stoneywood (H W) Nigel Parker BD MTh DMin	1994	23 Polo Park, Stoneywood, Aberdeen AB21 9JW NParker@churchofscotland.org.uk	01224 712411 01224 712635
Cults (F H T W) Shuna M. Dicks BSc BD	2010 2018	cultsparishchurch@btinternet.com 1 Cairnlee Terrace, Bieldside, Aberdeen AB15 9AE SDicks@churchofscotland.org.uk	01224 869028 01224 861692
Dyce (F H T W) Manson C. Merchant BD CPS Joan I. Thorne BA CertCS (Ordained Local Minister)	1992 2008 2019	dyceparishchurch@outlook.com 100 Burnside Road, Dyce, Aberdeen AB21 7HA MMerchant@churchofscotland.org.uk 85 Mosside Drive, Portlethen, Aberdeen AB12 4QY JThorne@churchofscotland.org.uk	01224 771295 01224 722380 07368 390832
Kingswells (F H W) Laurene M. Lafontaine BA MDiv	1987 2019	Kingswells Manse, Lang Stracht, Aberdeen AB15 8PN LLafontaine@churchofscotland.org.uk	01224 749986
Newhills (F H W) Jonathan A. Clipston MDiv	202	office@newhillschurch.org.uk Newhills Manse, Bucksburn, Aberdeen AB21 9SS JClipston@churchofscotland.org.uk	01224 716161 01224 712594
Peterculter (F H W) John A. Ferguson BD DipMin DMin	1988 1999	secretary@culterkirk.co.uk 7 Howie Lane, Peterculter AB14 0LJ JFerguson@churchofscotland.org.uk	01224 735845 01224 735041
Shetland (F) Frances M. Henderson BA BD PhD (Transition Minister/ Minister) Irene A. Charlton (Mrs) BTh (Team Minister) Lynn Brady BD DipMin (Interim Minister)	2006 2018 1994 1997 1996 2020	ShetlandParish@churchofscotland.org.uk Tingwall Manse, 25 Hogalee, East Voe, Scalloway, Shetland ZE1 0UU FHenderson@churchofscotland.org.uk The Manse, Marrister, Symbister, Whalsay, Shetland ZE2 9AE ICharlton@churchofscotland.org.uk The North Isles Manse, Yell, Gutcher, Yell, Shetland ZE2 9DF LBrady@churchofscotland.org.uk	01585 881184 01806 566767 07815 922889

New charge formed by the union of all 13 congregations in the former Presbytery of Shetland:
Burra Isle, Delting, Dunrossness and St Ninian's including Fair Isle, Lerwick and Bressay,
Nesting and Lunnasting, Northmavine, Sandsting and Aithsting, Sandwick, Cunningsburgh and Quarff,
Tingwall, Unst and Fetlar, Walls and Sandness, Whalsay and Skerries, Yell

B. In other appointments

Name	Years	Appointment	Address / Contact	Phone
Craig, Gordon T. BD DipMin	1988 2012	Chaplain to UK Oil and Gas Industry	Shell Exploration and Production, Tullos Complex, 1 Altens Farm Road, Aberdeen AB12 3FY / gordon.craig@ukoilandgaschaplaincy.com	01224 882600
Hutchison, David S. BSc BD ThM	1991 2015	Chaplain: University of Aberdeen	The Den of Keithfield, Tarves, Ellon AB41 7NU / d.hutchison@abdn.ac.uk	01651 851501
Murray, B. Ian BD	2002 2020	Interim Minister, Aberdeen City Centre	Kilmorie House, 6 Institution Road, Elgin IV30 1RP / BMurray@churchofscotland.org.uk	01343 546265
Rodgers, D. Mark BA BD MTh	1987 2003	Head of Spiritual Care, NHS Grampian	63 Cordiner Place, Hilton, Aberdeen AB24 4SB / mrodgers@nhs.net	01224 379135
Swinton, John (Prof.) BD PhD	1999	University of Aberdeen	51 Newburgh Circle, Bridge of Don, Aberdeen AB22 8XA / j.swinton@abdn.ac.uk	01224 825637

C. Demitted

Name	Years	Appointment	Address / Contact	Phone
Gardner, Bruce K. MA BD PhD	1988 2011	(Aberdeen: Bridge of Don Oldmachar)	21 Hopetoun Crescent, Bucksburn, Aberdeen AB21 9QY / drbrueckgardner@aol.com	07891 186724
Greig, Charles H.M. MA BD	1976 2016	(Dunrossness and St Ninian's inc. Fair Isle with Sandwick, Cunningsburgh and Quarff)	6 Hayhoull Place, Bigton, Shetland ZE2 9GA / chm.greig@btinternet.com	01950 422468
Lundie, Ann V. (Miss) DCS	1972 2007	(Deacon)	20 Langdykes Drive, Cove, Aberdeen AB12 3HW / ann.lundie@btopenworld.com	01224 898416
Main, Alan (Prof.) TD MA BD STM PhD DD	1963 2001	(University of Aberdeen)	Kirkfield, Barthol Chapel, Inverurie AB51 8TD / amain@talktalk.net	01651 806773
Macintyre, Thomas MA BD	1972 2011	(Sandsting and Aithsting with Walls and Sandness)	Lappideks, South Voxter, Cunningsburgh, Shetland ZE2 9HF / the2macs.macintyre@btinternet.com	01950 477549
Montgomerie, Jean B. (Miss) MA BD	1973 2006	(Forfar: St Margaret's)	12 St Ronan's Place, Peterculter, Aberdeen AB14 0QX / revjeanb@tiscali.co.uk	01224 732350
Phillippo, Michael MTh BSc BVetMed MRCVS	2003 2011	(Auxiliary Minister)	126 St Michael's Road, Newtonhill AB39 3XW	01569 739475
Richardson, Thomas C. LTh ThB	1971 2004	(Cults: West)	19 Kinkell Road, Aberdeen AB15 8HR / tomandpatrich@gmail.com	01224 315328
Sheret, Brian S. MA BD DPhil	1982 2009	(Glasgow: Drumchapel Drumry St Mary's)	59 Airyhall Crescent, Aberdeen AB15 7QS	01224 323032
Smith, Catherine (Mrs) DCS	1964 2003	(Deacon)	21 Lingaro, Bixter, Shetland ZE2 9NN	01595 810207
Stewart, James C. MA BD STM FSAScot	1960 2000	(Aberdeen: Kirk of St Nicholas)	54 Murray Terrace, Aberdeen AB11 7SB / study@jascstewart.co.uk	01224 587071
Weir, James J.C.M. BD	1991 2018	(Aberdeen: St George's Tillydrone)	114 Hilton Heights, Woodside, Aberdeen AB24 4QF	01224 901430
Williamson, Magnus J.C.	1982 1999	(Fetlar with Yell)	Creekhaven, Houl Road, Scalloway, Shetland ZE1 0XA	01595 880023
Youngson, Elizabeth J.B. BD	1996 2015	(Aberdeen: Mastrick)	47 Corse Drive, The Links, Dubford, Aberdeen AB23 8LN / elizabeth.youngson@btinternet.com	07788 294745

ABERDEEN ADDRESSES

Bridge of Don	Rosemount Viaduct
Oldmachar	Ashwood Park
Buckburn Stoneywood	Old Meldrum Road, Buckburn
Craigiebuckler	Springfield Road
Cults	Quarry Road, Cults
Dyce	Victoria Street, Dyce
Ferryhill	Fonthill Road x Polmuir Road
High Hilton	Hilton Drive
Holburn West	Great Western Road
Kingswells	Old Skene Road, Kingswells
Mannofield	Great Western Road x Craigton Road
Mastrick	Greenfern Road

Midstocket	Mid Stocket Road
Newhills	west of Bucksburn
Northfield	Byron Crescent
Peterculter	Craigton Crescent
Queen's Cross	Albyn Place
Rubislaw	Queen's Gardens
Ruthrieston West	Broomhill Road
St Columba's Bridge of Don	Braehead Way, Bridge of Don
St George's Tillydrone	Hayton Road, Tillydrone
St John's for the Deaf	at St Mark's
St Machar's Cathedral	The Chanonry

St Mark's	Rosemount Viaduct
St Mary's	King Street
St Nicholas Kincorth, South of	Kincorth Circle
St Nicholas, Kirk of	Union Street
St Stephen's	Powis Place
South Holburn	Holburn Street
Stockethill	Cairncry Community Centre
Summerhill	Stronsay Drive
Torry St Fittick's	Walker Road
Woodside	Church Street, Woodside

Worship in the Parish of Shetland held at:

Aith	11 Wirliegert, Aith, Bixter ZE2 9NW
Baltasound St John's	Baltasound, Unst ZE2 9DX
Brae	Brae, Delting ZE2 9QW
Bridgend, Burra Isle	Freefield Road, Bridge End, Burra Isle ZE2 9LD
Cullivoe	Cullivoe, Yell ZE2 9DD
Lerwick St Columba's	Greenfield Place, Lerwick ZE1 0EQ
Ollaberry	Ollaberry, Northmavine ZE2 9QW
Sandwick	Sandwick ZE2 9HW
Scalloway	Main Street, Scalloway ZE1 0TR
Vidlin St Margaret's	Methodist Chapel, Vidlin, Lunnasting ZE2 9QE
Walls St Paul's	Pier Road, Walls ZE2 9PF
Whalsay	Church Hall, Symbister, Whalsay ZE2 9AD

(32) KINCARDINE AND DEESIDE (W)

Meets in various locations as arranged on the first Tuesday of September, October, November, December, March and May, and on the last Tuesday of June at 7pm.

Clerk: REV. HUGH CONKEY BSc BD   39 St Ternans Road, Newtonhill, Stonehaven AB39 3PF   01569 739297
kincardinedeeside@churchofscotland.org.uk

Aberluthnott (F W) linked with Laurencekirk (F H W)
Vacant   contact@parishchurchofaberluthnottandlaurencekirk.co.uk
Interim Moderator: Brian D. Smith   Aberdeen Road, Laurencekirk AB30 1AJ   01561 378838
BSmith@churchofscotland.org.uk   01561 340203

Aboyne-Dinnet (F H W) linked with Cromar (F W)
Frank Ribbons MA BD DipEd   1985   2011   49 Charlton Crescent, Aboyne AB34 5GN   01339 887267
FRibbons@churchofscotland.org.uk

Arbuthnott, Bervie and Kinneff (F T W) Andrew R. Morrison MA BA	2019		5 West Park Place, Inverbervie, Montrose DD10 0XA Andrew.Morrison@churchofscotland.org.uk	01561 362530
Banchory-Ternan: East (F H W) Alan J.S. Murray BSc BD PhD	2003	2013	**info@banchoryeastchurch.com** East Manse, Station Road, Banchory AB31 5YP AJSMurray@churchofscotland.org.uk	**01330 820380** 01330 822481
Banchory-Ternan: West (F H T W) Antony A. Stephen MA BD	2001	2011	**office@banchorywestchurch.com** The Manse, 2 Wilson Road, Banchory AB31 5UY TStephen@churchofscotland.org.uk	**01330 822006** 01330 822811
Birse and Feughside (W) Amy C. Pierce BA BD	2017	2019	The Manse, Finzean, Banchory AB31 6PB ACPierce@churchofscotland.org.uk	01330 850776 07814 194997
Braemar and Crathie (F W) Kenneth I. Mackenzie DL BD CPS	1990	2005	The Manse, Crathie, Ballater AB35 5UL KMacKenzie@churchofscotland.org.uk	01339 742208
Cromar See Aboyne-Dinnet				
Drumoak-Durris (F H W) Jean A. Boyd MSc BSc BA	2016		26 Sunnyside Drive, Drumoak, Banchory AB31 3EW JBoyd@churchofscotland.org.uk	01330 811031
Glenmuick (Ballater) (H W) David L.C. Barr	2014		The Manse, Craigendarroch Walk, Ballater AB35 5ZB DBarr@churchofscotland.org.uk	01339 756111
Laurencekirk See Aberluthnott				
Maryculter Trinity (W) Melvyn J. Griffiths BTh DipTheol DMin	1978	2014	**thechurchoffice@tiscali.co.uk** The Manse, Kirkton of Maryculter, Aberdeen AB12 5FS MGriffiths@churchofscotland.org.uk	**01224 735983** 01224 730150
Mearns Coastal (F W) Guardianship of the Presbytery Norman D. Lennox-Trewren (Ordained Local Minister)	2018		32 Haulkerton Crescent, Laurencekirk AB30 1FB NLennoxTrewren@churchofscotland.org.uk	01561 377359

Mid Deeside (W)

Holly Smith BSIS MDiv MEd	2009	2019	Lochnagar, Torphins, Banchory AB31 4JU Holly.smith@churchofscotland.org.uk	**01339 889160** 01339 882915

Newtonhill (W)

Hugh Conkey BSc BD	1987	2001	39 St Ternans Road, Newtonhill, Stonehaven AB39 3PF HConkey@churchofscotland.org.uk	01569 730143

Portlethen (F H W)

Rodolphe Blanchard-Kowal MDiv MTh (Exchange Minister)	2013	2017	**portlethenpc@btconnect.com** 18 Rowanbank Road, Portlethen, Aberdeen AB12 4NX RKowal@churchofscotland.org.uk	**01224 782883** 01224 780211

Stonehaven: Carronside (H W)

Vacant				
Interim Moderator: David Galbraith			**secretary.dunnottarchurch@outlook.com** Dunnottar Manse, Stonehaven AB39 3XL David.Galbraith@churchofscotland.org.uk	**01569 760930** 01569 762166 01561 320779

Stonehaven: Fetteresso (H W)

Vacant				
Interim Moderator: William F. Wallace			**office@fetteresso.org** williamwallace39@talktalk.net	**01569 767689** 01330 822259

West Mearns (F W)

Brian D. Smith BD	1990	2016	The Manse, Fettercairn, Laurencekirk AB30 1UE BSmith@churchofscotland.org.uk	01561 340203

C. Demitted

Blair, Fyfe BA BD DMin	1989	2019	(Stonehaven: Fetteresso)	19 Crichie Place, Fettercairn, Laurencekirk AB30 1EZ Fyfe.Blair@churchofscotland.org.uk	01561 340579
Broadley, Linda J. (Mrs) LTh DipEd	1996	2013	(Dun and Hillside)	Snaefell, Lochside Road, St Cyrus, Montrose DD10 0DB lindabroadley@btinternet.com	01674 850141
Brown, J.W.S. BTh	1960	1995	(Cromar)	10 Forestside Road, Banchory AB31 5ZH iainisobel@aol.com	01330 824353
Duncan, Rosslyn P. BD MTh	2007	2018	(Stonehaven: Dunnottar with Stonehaven: South)	Four Oaks, Broomdykes, Duns TD1 3LZ rosslynpduncan@gmail.com	07899 878427
Lamb, A. Douglas MA	1964	2002	(Dalry: St Margaret's)	9 Luther Drive, Laurencekirk AB30 1FE lamb.edzell@talk21.com	01561 376816
Purves, John P. S. MBE BSc BD	1978	2013	(Colombo, Sri Lanka: St Andrew's Scots Kirk)	Lonville Cottage, 20 Viewfield Road, Ballater AB35 5RD john@thepurves.com	01339 754081
Wallace, William F. BDS BD	1968	2008	(Wick: Pulteneytown and Thrumster)	Lachan Cottage, 29 Station Road, Banchory AB31 5XX williamwallace39@talktalk.net	01330 822259
Watson, John M. LTh	1989	2009	(Aberdeen: St Mark's)	20 Greystone Place, Newtonhill, Stonehaven AB39 3UL johnmutchwatson2065@btinternet.com	01569 730604 07733 334380

(33) GORDON (F W)

Meets at various locations on the first Tuesday of February, March, April, May, September, October, November and December; and on the last Tuesday of June.

Clerk: REV. G. EUAN D. GLEN BSc BD   The Manse, 26 St Ninians, Monymusk, Inverurie AB51 7HF   01467 651470
gordon@churchofscotland.org.uk

Barthol Chapel (F) linked with Tarves (F W)
Alison I. Swindells (Mrs) LLB BD DMin   1998   2017   8 Murray Avenue, Tarves, Ellon AB41 7LZ   01651 851295
ASwindells@churchofscotland.org.uk

Belhelvie (F H W)
Paul McKeown BSc PhD BD   2000   2005   belhelviecofs@btconnect.com   01358 742227
Belhelvie Manse, Balmedie, Aberdeen   AB23 8YR
PMcKeown@churchofscotland.org.uk

Blairdaff and Chapel of Garioch (F W)
Martyn S. Sanders BA CertEd   2013   2015   The Manse, Chapel of Garioch, Inverurie   AB51 5HE   01467 681619
MSanders@churchofscotland.org.uk   07814 164373

Cluny (F H W) linked with Monymusk (F H W)
G. Euan D. Glen BSc BD   1992   The Manse, 26 St Ninians, Monymusk, Inverurie   AB51 7HF   01467 651470
GGlen@churchofscotland.org.uk

Culsalmond and Rayne (F W) linked with Daviot (H W)
Mary M. Cranfield MA BD DMin   1989   The Manse, Daviot, Inverurie AB51 0HY   01467 671241
MCranfield@churchofscotland.org.uk

Cushnie and Tough (H)
Vacant
Session Clerk: Ronald Ferguson   The Manse, Muir of Fowlis, Alford AB33 8JU   01975 581239
ronald_ferguson@btinternet.com   01975 563404

Daviot See Culsalmond and Rayne

Echt and Midmar (F H W)
Sheila M. Mitchell BD MTh   1995   2018   The Manse, Echt, Westhill AB32 7AB   01330 860004
SMitchell@churchofscotland.org.uk

			Tel/Fax
Ellon (F T W) Alastair J. Bruce BD MTh PGCE	2015	info@ellonparishchurch.co.uk The Manse, 12 Union Street, Ellon AB41 9BA ABruce@churchofscotland.org.uk	**01358 725690** 01358 723787
Fintray Kinellar Keithhall (F W) Vacant Interim Moderator: Martyn S. Sanders		MSanders@churchofscotland.org.uk	**01224 790439** 01467 681619 07814 164373
Foveran (W) Richard M.C. Reid BSc BD MTh	1991	The Manse, Foveran, Ellon AB41 6AP RReid@churchofscotland.org.uk	01358 789288
Howe Trinity (F W) John A. Cook MA BD DMin	1986	enquiries@howetrinity.org.uk The Manse, 110 Main Street, Alford AB33 8AD John.Cook@churchofscotland.org.uk	**01975 562829** 01975 562282
Huntly Cairnie Glass Thomas R. Calder LLB BD WS	1994	The Manse, Queen Street, Huntly AB54 8EB TCalder@churchofscotland.org.uk	01466 792630
Insch-Leslie-Premnay-Oyne (F H W) Kay F. Gauld BD STM PhD	1999	66 Denwell Road, Insch AB52 6LH KGauld@churchofscotland.org.uk	01464 820404
Inverurie: St Andrew's (F W) Carl J. Irvine BA	2017	standrews@btinternet.com 1 Ury Dale, Inverurie AB51 3XW CIrvine@churchofscotland.org.uk	**01467 628740** 01467 629163
Inverurie: West (F T W) Rhona P. Cathcart BA BSc BD	2017	admin@inveruriewestchurch.org West Manse, 1 Westburn Place, Inverurie AB51 5QS RCathcart@churchofscotland.org.uk	**01647 620285** 01467 620285
Kemnay (F T W) Joshua M. Mikelson BA MDiv	2008 2015	office@kemnayparish.church 15 Kirkland, Kemnay, Inverurie AB51 5QD JMikelson@churchofscotland.org.uk	**01467 643883** 01467 642219

Charge / Minister		Ordained / Inducted	Address / Email	Telephone
Kintore (F H W) Neil W. Meyer BD MTh		2000 2014	28 Oakhill Road, Kintore, Inverurie AB51 0FH NMeyer@churchofscotland.org.uk	01467 632219
Meldrum and Bourtie (F W) Vacant Valerie A. Mitchell MA FSA (Ordained Local Minister)		2019	**info@meldrumandbourtiechurch.com** The Manse, Urquhart Road, Oldmeldrum, Inverurie AB51 0EX VMitchell@churchofscotland.org.uk	01651 872250
Methlick (F W) William A. Stalder BA MDiv MLitt PhD		2014	The Manse, Manse Road, Methlick, Ellon AB41 7DG WStalder@churchofscotland.org.uk	01651 806264
Monymusk See Cluny				
New Machar (F W) Douglas G. McNab BA BD		1999 2010	The New Manse, Newmachar, Aberdeen AB21 0RD DMcNab@churchofscotland.org.uk	01651 862278
Noth Regine U. Cheyne (Mrs) MA BSc BD		1988 2010	Manse of Noth, Kennethmont, Huntly AB54 4NP RCheyne@churchofscotland.org.uk	01464 831690
Skene (F H W) Stella Campbell MA (Oxon) BD		2012	**info.skeneparish@gmail.com** The Manse, Manse Road, Kirkton of Skene, Westhill AB32 6LX SCampbell@churchofscotland.org.uk	**01224 742512** 01224 745955
Strathbogie Drumblade Vacant Interim Moderator: Mary M. Cranfield			49 Deveron Park, Huntly AB54 8UZ MCranfield@churchofscotland.org.uk	01466 792702 01467 671241
Tarves See Barthol Chapel				
Udny and Pitmedden (F W) Vacant Interim Moderator: William A. Stalder			The Manse, Manse Road, Udny Green, Ellon AB41 7RS WStalder@churchofscotland.org.uk	01651 843794 01651 806264

Upper Donside (F H)
Vacant
Session Clerk: Margaret Thomson (Mrs)

upperdonsideparishchurch@btinternet.com

margaret.thomson9@btpenworld.com

01464 861745

B. In other appointments

Crouch, Simon A.	2019	Ordained Local Minister: Cushnie and Tough: Upper Donside	Delhandy, Corgarff, Strathdon AB36 8YB SCrouch@churchofscotland.org.uk	01975 651779 07713 101358

C. Demitted

Christie, Andrew C. LTh	1975 2000	(Banchory-Devenick and Maryculter/Cookney)	17 Broadstraik Close, Elrick, Aberdeen AB32 6JP	01224 746888
Craggs, Sheila (Mrs)	2001 2016	(Auxiliary Minister)	7 Morar Court, Ellon AB41 9GG	01358 723055
Craig, Anthony J.D. BD	1987 2009	(Glasgow: Maryhill)	4 Hightown, Collieston, Ellon AB41 8RS aacraig@btinternet.com	01358 751247
Dryden, Ian MA DipEd	1988 2001	(New Machar)	16 Glenhome Gardens, Dyce, Aberdeen AB21 7FG ian@idryden.freeserve.co.uk	01224 722820
Falconer, James B. BD	1982 2018	(Hospital Chaplain)	3 Brimmond Walk, Westhill AB32 6XH	01224 744621
Ford, Carolyn (Carol) H.M. DSD RSAMD BD	2003 2018	(Edinburgh: St Margaret's)	4 Mitchell Avenue, Huntly AB54 8DW	
Greig, Alan BSc BD	1977 2017	(Interim Minister)	1 Dunnydeer Place, Insch AB52 6HP greig@kincarr.free-online.co.uk	01464 820332
Hawthorn, Daniel MA BD DMin	1965 2004	(Belhelvie)	7 Crimond Drive, Ellon AB41 8BT danhawthorn@compuserve.com	01358 723981
Macalister, Eleanor	1994 2006	(Ellon)	Quarryview, Ythan Bank, Ellon AB41 7TH macal1ster@aol.com	01358 761402
McLeish, Robert S.	1970 2000	(Insch-Leslie-Premnay-Oyne)	19 Western Road, Insch AB52 6JR	01464 820749
Rodger, Matthew A. BD	1978 1999	(Ellon)	15 Meadowlands Drive, Westhill AB32 6EJ	01224 743184
Telfer, Iain J.M. BD DPS	1978 2018	(Chaplain: Royal Infirmary of Edinburgh)	66 High Street, Inverurie AB51 3XS iain_telfer@yahoo.co.uk	07749 993070
Thomson, Iain U. MA BD	1970 2011	(Skene)	4 Keirhill Gardens, Westhill AB32 6AZ iainuthomson@googlemail.com	01224 746743

(34) BUCHAN (W)

Meets at St Kane's Centre, New Deer, Turriff on the first Tuesday of February, May, September and November, and on the third Tuesday of June.

Clerk: REV. SHEILA M. KIRK BA LLB BD   The Manse, Abbey Street, Old Deer, Peterhead AB42 5JB   01771 623582
buchan@churchofscotland.org.uk

Aberdour linked with Pitsligo (F W)
Vacant
Interim Moderator: Ruth Mackenzie (Miss)
31 Blairmore Park, Rosehearty, Fraserburgh AB43 7NZ
ursular@tiscali.co.uk
01346 571823
01779 480680

Auchaber United (W) linked with Auchterless (W)   2012
Stephen J. Potts BA
The Manse, Auchterless, Turriff AB53 8BA
SPotts@churchofscotland.org.uk
01888 511058

Auchterless See Auchaber United

Banff (F W) linked with King Edward (F W)   2000   2012
David I.W. Locke MA MSc BD
info@banffparishchurchofscotland.org.uk
7 Colleonard Road, Banff AB45 1DZ
DLocke@churchofscotland.org.uk
01262 818211
01261 812107
07776 448301

Crimond (F W) linked with Lonmay (W)
Vacant
Session Clerk, Crimond: Irene Fowlie (Mrs)
Session Clerk, Lonmay: Roy Kinghorn
The Manse, Crimond, Fraserburgh AB43 8QJ
fowlie@hotmail.com
strathelliefarm@btinternet.com
01346 532431
01346 532436

Cruden (F H W)   1996   2019
Sean Swindells BD DipMin MTh
8 Murray Avenue, Tarves, Ellon AB41 7LZ
SSwindells@churchofscotland.org.uk
01651 851295
07791 755976

Deer (F H)   2007   2010
Sheila M. Kirk BA LLB BD
The Manse, Abbey Street, Old Deer, Peterhead AB42 5JB
SKirk@churchofscotland.org.uk
01771 623582

Fraserburgh: Old (W)
Vacant
Interim Moderator: James Givan
fraserburghopc@btconnect.com
4 Robbie's Road, Fraserburgh AB43 7AF
jim.givan@btinternet.com
01346 510139
01346 515332
01261 833318

Fraserburgh: South (H) linked with Inverallochy and Rathen: East
Vacant
Session Clerk, Fraserburgh: South: William J. Smith
15 Victoria Street, Fraserburgh   AB43 9PJ
bill.moira.smith@gmail.com
01346 518244
01346 513991

Fraserburgh: West (F H T W) linked with Rathen: West (T W)
Vacant
Session Clerk, Fraserburgh: West: Jill Smith (Mrs)
Session Clerk, Rathen: West: Ian J. Campbell
4 Kirkton Gardens, Fraserburgh   AB43 8TU
jill@fraserburgh-harbour.co.uk
cicfarmers@hotmail.co.uk
01346 513303
01346 517972
01346 532062

Fyvie linked (F W) with Rothienorman (F)
Alison Jaffrey (Mrs) MA BD FSAScot   1990   2019
The Manse, Fyvie, Turriff   AB53 8RD
AJaffrey@churchofscotland.org.uk
01651 891961

Inverallochy and Rathen: East   See Fraserburgh: South
King Edward   See Banff

Longside (W)
Robert A. Fowlie   BD   2007
The Manse, Abbey Street, Old Deer, Peterhead   AB42 5JB
RFowlie@churchofscotland.org.uk
01771 622228

Lonmay   See Crimond

Macduff (F T W)
Hugh O'Brien CSS MTheol   2001   2016
contactus@macduffparishchurch.org
10 Ross Street, Macduff   AB44 1NS
HOBrien@churchofscotland.org.uk
01261 832316

Marnoch (F W)
Alan Macgregor   BA BD PhD   1992   2013
Marnoch Manse, 53 South Street, Aberchirder, Huntly   AB54 7TS
AMacgregor@churchofscotland.org.uk
01466 781143

Maud and Savoch (F W) linked with New Deer: St Kane's (F W)
Aileen M. McFie (Mrs)   BD   2003   2018
The Manse, Fordyce Terrace, New Deer, Turriff   AB53 6TD
ARobson@churchofscotland.org.uk
01771 644097
01771 644631

Monquhitter and New Byth linked with Turriff: St Andrew's
James M. Cook BSc MBA MDiv   1999   2002
info@standrewsturriff.co.uk
St Andrew's Manse, Balmellie Road, Turriff   AB53 4SP
JCook@churchofscotland.org.uk
01888 560304

New Deer: St Kane's See Maud and Savoch

New Pitsligo linked with Strichen and Tyrie (F W)
Vacant
Interim Moderator: Hugh O'Brien — Kingsville, Strichen, Fraserburgh AB43 6SQ — 01771 637365
HOBrien@churchofscotland.org.uk — 01261 832316

Ordiquhill and Cornhill (H) linked with Whitehills
Vacant
Session Clerk, Ordiquhill and Cornhill: Frances Webster (Mrs) — 6 Craigneen Place, Whitehills, Banff AB45 2NE — 01261 861317
william.webster@btconnect.com — 01466 751230
Session Clerk, Whitehills: Jenny Abel (Mrs) — jennyabel14@hotmail.co.uk — 01261 861386

Peterhead: New (F)
Vacant
Session Clerk: Ruth Mackenzie (Miss) — 1 Hawthorn Road, Peterhead AB42 2DW — 01779 480680
ursular@tiscali.co.uk

Peterhead: St Andrew's (H W)
Guardianship of the Presbytery
Session Clerk: John Leslie — eil.ian@btinternet.com — 01779 470571

Pitsligo See Aberdour

Portsoy (W)
Vacant
Interim Moderator: Kevin R. Gruer — The Manse, 4 Seafield Terrace, Portsoy, Banff AB45 2QB — 01261 842272
KGruer@churchofscotland.org.uk — 01888 563850

Rathen: West See Fraserburgh: West
Rothienorman See Fyvie

St Fergus (F)
Jeffrey Tippner BA MDiv MCS PhD   1991   2012 — 26 Newton Road, St Fergus, Peterhead AB42 3DD — 01779 838287
JTippner@churchofscotland.org.uk

Sandhaven
Guardianship of the Presbytery
Interim Moderator: David I.W. Locke — DLocke@churchofscotland.org.uk — 01261 812107
07776 448301

Strichen and Tyrie See New Pitsligo
Turriff: St Andrew's See Monquhitter and New Byth

Turriff: St Ninian's and Forglen (H L W)

| Kevin R. Gruer BSc BA | 2011 | | info@stniniansandforglen.org.uk
4 Deveronside Drive, Turriff AB53 4SP
KGruer@churchofscotland | **01888 560282**
01888 563850 |

Whitehills See Ordiquhill and Cornhill

B. In other appointments

| Stewart, William | 2015 | 2016 | Ordained Local Minister, Presbytery-wide | Denend, Strichen, Fraserburgh AB43 6RN
billandjunes@live.co.uk | 01771 637256 |
| van Sittert, Paul BA BD | 1997 | 2011 | Chaplain: Army | 32 Engineer Regiment, Marne Barracks, Catterick Garrison DL10 7NP
padre.pvs@gmail.com | |

C. Demitted

Coutts, Fred MA BD	1973	1989	(Hospital Chaplain)	Ladebank, 1 Manse Place, Hatton, Peterhead AB42 0UQ fred.coutts@btinternet.com	01779 841320
Fawkes, G.M. Allan BA BSc JP	1979	2000	(Lonmay with Rathen: West)	3 Northfield Gardens, Hatton, Peterhead AB42 0SW afawkes@aol.com	01779 841814
Macnee, Iain LTh BD MA PhD	1975	2011	(New Pitsligo with Strichen and Tyrie)	Wardend Cottage, Alvah, Banff AB45 3TR macneeiain4@googlemail.com	01261 815647
Murray, Alistair BD	1984	2018	(Inverness: Trinity)	7 Clunie Street, Banff AB45 1HY a.murray111@btinternet.com	01261 390154
Noble, George S. DipTh	1972	2000	(Carfin with Newarthill)	Craigowan, 3 Main Street, Inverallochy, Fraserburgh AB43 8XX	01346 582749
Ross, David S. MSc PhD BD	1978	2013	(Chaplain: Scottish Prison Service)	3–5 Abbey Street, Old Deer, Peterhead AB42 5LN padsross@btinternet.com	01771 623994
Thorburn, Robert J. BD	1978	2017	(Fyvie with Rothienorman)	12 Slackadale Gardens, Turriff AB53 4UA rjthorburn@aol.com	
Verster, W. Myburgh BA BTh LTh MTh	1981	2019	(Ordiquhill and Cornhill with Whitehills)	32 Newtown Drive, Macduff AB44 1SR myburghverster@gmail.com	01888 562278

(35) MORAY (F W)

Meets at St Andrew's-Lhanbryd and Urquhart on the first Tuesday of February, March, May, September, October, November and December, and at the Moderator's church on the fourth Tuesday of June.

| Clerk: | MRS JANET WHYTE | 1 Lemanfield Crescent, Garmouth IV32 7LS | 01343 870667 |
| | | moray@churchofscotland.org.uk | |

Aberlour (F H W)
Vacant
Session Clerk: Linda Cordiner — The Manse, Mary Avenue, Aberlour AB38 9QU — 01340 871687
lwcordiner@outlook.com

Alves and Burghead (F W) linked with Kinloss and Findhorn (W)
Vacant — The Manse, 4 Manse Road, Kinloss, Forres IV36 3GH — 01309 690474
Session Clerk, Alves and Burghead: Ian Rae — abcsessionclerk@aim.com — 01343 850226
Session Clerk, Kinloss and Findhorn: Corinne Davies — cozzerdavies@gmail.com — 01309 690359

Bellie and Speymouth (F W) — bellieandspeymouth@gmail.com — **01343 823802**
Seòras I. Orr MSc MTh   2018 — 11 The Square, Fochabers IV32 7DG — 01343 820256
SOrr@churchofscotland.org.uk

Birnie and Pluscarden (W) linked with Elgin: High (W)
Vacant — The Manse, 7 Kirkton Place, Elgin IV30 6JR
Session Clerk, Birnie and Pluscarden: Alistair Farquhar — alistair.farquhar@btinternet.com — 01343 541328
Session Clerk, Elgin: High: Hazel Dickson — hazelandjohn@mypostoffice.co.uk — 01343 540949

Buckie: North (H) linked with Rathven
Vacant — The Manse, 14 St Peter's Road, Buckie AB56 1DL — 01542 832118
Session Clerk (Acting), Buckie: North: Kathryn Cowie — kgcowie@btinternet.com — 01542 833017
Session Clerk, Rathven: Ann Grant — anngrantbck@gmail.com — 01542 831607

Buckie: South and West (F H) linked with Enzie (F)
Wesley C. Brandon BA MDiv   2003   2019 — Craigendarroch, 14 Cliff Terrace, Buckie AB56 1LX — 07546 360908
WBrandon@churchofscotland.org.uk

Cullen and Deskford (F T W)
Douglas F. Stevenson BD DipMin DipHE   1991   14 Seafield Road, Cullen, Buckie AB56 4AF   01542 841963
  MCOSCA MBACP MScR   DStevenson@churchofscotland.org.uk

Dallas linked with Forres: St Leonard's (F H W) linked with Rafford (F)   stleonardsforres@gmail.com
Donald K. Prentice BSc BD   1989   St Leonard's Manse, Nelson Road, Forres IV36 1DR   01309 672380
  DipPsych MSc MLitt   DPrentice@churchofscotland.org.uk
John A. Morrison BSc BA PGCE   2013   35 Kirkton Place, Elgin IV30 6JR   01343 550199
  (Ordained Local Minister)   JMorrison@churchofscotland.org.uk

Duffus, Spynie and Hopeman (H W)
Jennifer M. Adams BEng BD   2013   The Manse, Duffus, Elgin IV30 5QP   01343 830276
                                                                   JAdams@churchofscotland.org.uk

Dyke and Edinkillie (F W)
Richard G. Moffat BD   1994   Dyke and Edinkillie Manse, Westview, Mundole, Forres IV36 2TA   01309 271321
                                                                   RMoffat@churchofscotland.org.uk

Elgin: High See Birnie and Pluscarden

Elgin: St Giles' (H) and St Columba's South (F W)   stgileselgin@gmail.com
Deon F. Oelofse BA MDiv LTh MTh   2002   18 Reidhaven Street, Elgin IV30 1QH   **01343 551501**
                                                                   DOelofse@churchofscotland.org.uk   01343 208786
Sonia Palmer RGN   2017   94 Ashgrove Park, Elgin IV30 1UT   07748 700929
  (Ordained Local Minister)   Sonia.Palmer@churchofscotland.org.uk

Enzie See Buckie: South and West

Findochty (F T W) linked with Portknockie (F T W)
Jacobus Boonzaaier BA BCom(OR) BD   1995   20 Netherton Terrace, Findochty, Buckie AB56 4QD 01542 649644
  MDiv PhD   JBoonzaaier@churchofscotland.org.uk

Forres: St Laurence (H W)
Vacant   12 Mackenzie Drive, Forres IV36 2JP   01309 672260
Interim Moderator: Peter Taylor   peteltaylor@gmail.com   01309 674806

Forres: St Leonard's See Dallas

Keith: North, Newmill, Boharm and Rothiemay (F H W)
Vacant
Session Clerk: Krista Brown (Mrs)

knnbrchurch@btconnect.com
North Manse, Church Road, Keith   AB55 5BR
k80own@gmail.com

01542 886390
01542 886840
01542 887814

Keith: St Rufus, Botriphnie and Grange (F H W)
Vacant
Session Clerk: Nicola Smith (Ms)

St Rufus' Manse, Church Road, Keith   AB55 5BR
nicolasmith1099@gmail.com

01542 882799
01542 488673

Kinloss and Findhorn See Alves and Burghead

Knockando, Elchies and Archiestown (H W) linked with Rothes (W)   info@moraykirk.co.uk
Robert J.M. Anderson BD FInstLM   1993   2000

The Manse, Rothes, Aberlour   AB38 7AF
RJMAnderson@churchofscotland.org.uk

01340 831497
01340 831381

Lossiemouth: St Gerardine's High (H W) linked with Lossiemouth: St James (F T W)
Geoffrey D. McKee BA   1997   2014

The Manse, St Gerardine's Road, Lossiemouth   IV31 6RA
GMcKee@churchofscotland.org.uk

01343 208852

Lossiemouth: St James' See Lossiemouth: St Gerardine's High

Mortlach and Cabrach (F H)
Vacant
Session Clerk: Elizabeth Cameron

Mortlach Manse, Dufftown, Keith   AB55 4AR
stevie.liz@btinternet.com

01340 820380
01340 820846

Portknockie See Findochty
Rafford See Dallas
Rathven See Buckie: North
Rothes See Knockando, Elchies and Archiestown

St Andrew's-Lhanbryd (H) and Urquhart (F W)
Vacant
Session Clerk: Alastair Rossetter

39 St Andrews Road, Lhanbryde, Elgin   IV30 8PU
alastair@rossetter.plus.com

01343 843765
07751 323975

B. In other appointments
Munro, Sheila BD   1995 2003   RAF Station Chaplain
Chaplaincy Centre, RAF Wyton, Huntingdon   PE28 2EA
sheila.munro781@mod.gov.uk

C. Demitted

Name	Ord.	Dem.	(Charge)	Address / Email	Tel
Attenburrow, Anne BSc MB ChB	2006	2018	(Auxiliary Minister)	4 Jock Inksons Brae, Elgin IV30 1QE AAttenburrow@churchofscotland.org.uk	01343 552330
Bain, Brian LTh	1980	2007	(Gask with Methven and Logiealmond)	Bayview, 13 Stewart Street, Portgordon, Buckie AB56 5QT bricoreen@gmail.com	01542 831215
Bezuidenhout, Louis C. BA MA BD DD	1978	2020	(Interim Minister)	76 East Church Street, Buckie AB56 1LQ macbez@gmail.com	01542 839493
Boyd, Barry J. LTh DPS	1993	2020	(Forres: St Laurence)	7 Kirkton Place, Elgin IV30 6JR	07778 731018
Duff, Stuart M. BA	1997	2019	(Birnie and Pluscarden with Elgin: High)	stuart.duff@gmail.com	01343 200233
King, Margaret MA DCS	2002	2012	(Deacon)	56 Murrayfield, Fochabers IV32 7EZ margaretking889@gmail.com	01343 820937
Legge, Rosemary (Mrs) BSc BD MTh	1992	2017	(Cushnie and Tough)	57 High Street, Archiestown, Aberlour AB38 7QZ revrl192@aol.com	01340 810304
Morton, Alasdair J. MA BD DipEd FEIS	1960	2000	(Bowden with Newtown)	16 St Leonard's Road, Forres IV36 1DW alasgilmor@hotmail.co.uk	01309 671719
Morton, Gillian M. (Mrs) MA BD PGCE	1983	1996	(Hospital Chaplain)	16 St Leonard's Road, Forres IV36 1DW gillianmorton@hotmail.co.uk	01309 671719
Robertson, Peter BSc BD	1988	1998	(Dallas with Forres: St Leonard's with Rafford)	17 Ferryhill Road, Forres IV36 2GY peterrobertsonforres@talktalk.net	01309 676769
Rollo, George B. BD	1974	2010	(Elgin: St Giles' and St Columba's South)	'Struan', 13 Meadow View, Hopeman, Elgin IV30 5PL rollos@gmail.com	01343 835226
Ross, William B. LTh CPS	1988	2016	(Aberdour with Pitsligo)	5 Strathlene Court, Rathven AB55 3DD williamross278@btinternet.com	01542 834418
Smith, Morris BD	1988	2013	(Cromdale and Advie with Dulnain Bridge with Grantown-on-Spey)	1 Urquhart Grove, New Elgin IV30 8TB mosmith.themanse@btinternet.com	01343 545019
Watts, Anthony BD	1999	2013	(Glenmuick (Ballater))	tonyewatts@yahoo.co.uk	01309 672418
Whyte, David LTh	1993	2011	(Boat of Garten, Duthil and Kincardine)	1 Lemanfield Crescent, Garmouth, Fochabers IV32 7LS whytedj@btinternet.com	01343 870667

(36) ABERNETHY

Meets at Boat of Garten on the first Tuesday of February, March, May, September, October, November and December, and on the last Tuesday of June.

Clerk:	REV JAMES A.I. MacEWAN MA BD	Rapness, Station Road, Nethy Bridge PH25 3DN abernethy@churchofscotland.org.uk	01479 821116

Abernethy (F H W) linked with Boat of Garten (H), Carrbridge (H) and Kincardine (F W)

Graham T. Atkinson MA BD MTh	2006	2019	The Manse, Deshar Road, Boat of Garten PH24 3BN GAtkinson@churchofscotland.org.uk	01479 831637

Alvie and Insh (H W) linked with Rothiemurchus and Aviemore (H W)
Charles J. Finnie LTh DPS   1991   2019   The Manse, 8 Dalfaber Park, Aviemore PH22 1QF   01479 810280
CFinnie@churchofscotland.org.uk

Boat of Garten, Carrbridge and Kincardine See Abernethy

Cromdale (H) and Advie (F W) linked with Dulnain Bridge (H W) linked with Grantown-on-Spey (F H W)
Gordon I. Strang BSc BD   2014   The Manse, Golf Course Road, Grantown-on-Spey PH26 3HY   01479 872084
GStrang@churchofscotland.org.uk

Dulnain Bridge See Cromdale and Advie
Grantown-on-Spey See Cromdale and Advie

Kingussie (F H W) linked with Laggan (H) and Newtonmore (H W)
Catherine A. Buchan (Mrs) MA MDiv   2002   2009   The Manse, Fort William Road, Newtonmore PH20 1DG   01540 673238
CBuchan@churchofscotland.org.uk

Laggan and Newtonmore See Kingussie
Rothiemurchus and Aviemore See Alvie and Insh

Tomintoul (H), Glenlivet and Inveraven
Guardianship of the Presbytery
Session Clerk: Margo Stewart (Mrs)   The Manse, Tomintoul, Ballindalloch AB37 9HA   01807 580239
margoandedward@hotmail.co.uk

B. In other appointments
Duncanson, Mary B. (Ms) BTh   2013   Ordained Local Minister: Presbytery Pastoral Support   3 Balmenach Road, Cromdale, Grantown-on-Spey PH26 3LJ   01479 872165
MDuncanson@churchofscotland.org.uk
Thomson, Mary Ellen (Mrs)   2013   Ordained Local Minister: Presbytery Chaplain to Care Homes   Kerrowside, 3 Hillside Avenue, Kingussie PH21 1PA   01540 661772
Mary.Thomson@churchofscotland.org.uk

C. Demitted
MacEwan, James A.I. MA BD   1973   2012   (Abernethy with Cromdale and Advie)   Rapness, Station Road, Nethy Bridge PH25 3DN   01479 821116
wurrus@hotmail.co.uk
Ritchie, Christine A.Y. (Mrs) BD DipMin   2002   2012   (Braes of Rannoch with Foss and Rannoch)   25 Beachen Court, Grantown-on-Spey PH26 3JD   01479 873419
gandcritchie70@gmail.com
Walker, Donald K. BD   1979   2018   (Abernethy with Boat of Garten, Carrbridge and Kincardine)   Jabulani, Seafield Avenue, Grantown-on-Spey PH26 3JQ   01479 870104
dwalkerjabulani@gmail.com

(37) INVERNESS (W)

Meets at Inverness, in Inverness: Inshes (2020) on the second Saturday of September, the third Tuesday of November, (2021) the second Saturday of March and the last Tuesday of June; Saturday meetings preceded by a presbytery conference.

Clerk:	**REV. TREVOR G. HUNT BA BD**		**7 Woodville Court, Culduthel Avenue, Inverness IV2 6BX** **inverness@churchofscotland.org.uk**	**01463 250355** **07753 423333**

Ardersier (H) linked with Petty

Robert Cleland	1997	2014	The Manse, Ardersier, Inverness IV2 7SX RCleland@churchofscotland.org.uk

01667 462224

Auldearn and Dalmore linked (F W) with Nairn: St Ninian's (F H W)

Thomas M. Bryson BD	1997	2015	The Manse, Auldearn, Nairn IV12 5SX TBryson@churchofscotland.org.uk

01667 451675

Cawdor (F H) linked with Croy and Dalcross (F H)

Robert E. Brookes BD	2009	2016	Hillswick, Regoul, Geddes, Nairn IV12 5SB RBrookes@churchofscotland.org.uk

01667 404686

Croy and Dalcross See Cawdor

Culloden: The Barn (F H W)

Michael A. Robertson BA	2014	admin@barnchurch.org.uk 45 Oakdene Court, Culloden IV2 7XL Mike.Robertson@churchofscotland.org.uk

01463 798946
01463 795430
07740 984395

Daviot and Dunlichity (W) linked with Moy, Dalarossie and Tomatin (W)

Vacant

Interim Moderator: Robert E. Brookes RBrookes@churchofscotland.org.uk

01667 404686

Dores and Boleskine

Vacant

Interim Moderator: Scott A. McRoberts SMcRoberts@churchofscotland.org.uk

01463 230308
07535 290092

Inverness: Crown (F H W)			**office@crown-church.co.uk**	**01463 231140**
Douglas R. Robertson BSc BD	1991	2020	39 Southside Road, Inverness IV2 4XA	01463 230537
			DRRobertson@churchofscotland.org.uk	
Inverness: Dalneigh and Bona (GD H W)			9 St Mungo Road, Inverness IV3 5AS	01463 232339
Vacant			len_cazaly@btinternet.com	01463 794469
Interim Moderator: Len Cazaly				
Inverness: East (F GD H W)			**invernesseastoffice@gmail.com**	**01463 236695**
Vacant			39 Appin Drive, Inverness IV2 7AL	01456 450231
Interim Moderator: Hugh F. Watt			HWatt@churchofscotland.org.uk	
Inverness: Hilton (F W)			**office@hiltonchurch.org.uk**	**01463 233310**
Duncan MacPherson LLB BD	1994		66 Culduthel Mains Crescent, Inverness IV2 6RG	01463 231417
			DMacPherson@churchofscotland.org.uk	
Inverness: Inshes (H W)			48 Redwood Crescent, Milton of Leys, Inverness IV2 6HB	**01463 226727**
David S. Scott MA BD	1987	2013	David.Scott@churchofscotland.org.uk	01463 772402
Farquhar A.M. Forbes MA BD	2016		The Heights, Inverarnie, Inverness IV2 6XA	01808 521450
(Associate Minister)			FForbes@churchofscotland.org.uk	
Inverness: Kinmylies (F H W)			2 Balnafettack Place, Inverness IV3 8TQ	**01463 714035**
Scott Polworth LLB BD	2009	2018	SPolworth@churchofscotland.org.uk	01463 559137
Inverness: Ness Bank (F H T W)			15 Ballifeary Road, Inverness IV3 5PJ	01463 234653
Fiona E. Smith (Mrs) LLB BD	2010		FSmith@churchofscotland.org.uk	
Inverness: Old High St Stephen's (T W)			**invernesschurch@gmail.com**	**07934 285924**
Vacant			24 Damfield Road, Inverness IV2 3HU	01463 250802
Dot L.J. Getliffe (Mrs) BA BD DipEd DCS	2006	2019	136 Ardness Place, Lochardil, Inverness IV2 4QY	01463 716051
			DGetliffe@churchofscotland.org.uk	
Inverness: St Columba (New Charge Development) (F H T W)			**info@stcolumbainverness.org**	01463 230308
Scott A. McRoberts BD MTh	2012		20 Bramble Close, Inverness IV2 6BS	07535 290092
			SMcRoberts@churchofscotland.org.uk	
Fiona S. Morrison BA	2019	2020	FMorrison@churchofscotland.org.uk	
(Ordained Local Minister)				

Inverness: Trinity (F H W)
Vacant
Interim Moderator: Fraser K. Turner
invernesstrinitychurch@yahoo.co.uk
60 Kenneth Street, Inverness IV3 5PZ
fraseratq@yahoo.co.uk
01463 **221490**
01463 234756
01463 794004

Kilmorack and Erchless (F W)
Ian A. Manson BA BD   1989   2016   'Roselynn', Croyard Road, Beauly IV4 7DJ
IManson@churchofscotland.org.uk
01463 783824

Kiltarlity (F W) linked with Kirkhill (F W)
Vacant
Interim Moderator: Seòras L. Mackenzie
Wardlaw Manse, Wardlaw Road, Kirkhill IV5 7NZ
seorenzie@gmail.com
01463 831247
01463 231487

Kirkhill See Kiltarlity

Moy, Dalarossie and Tomatin See Daviot and Dunlichity

Nairn: Old (H W)
Alison C. Mehigan   BD DPS   2003   2015   15 Chattan Gardens, Nairn IV12 4QP
AMehigan@churchofscotland.org.uk
secretary.nairnold@btconnect.com
01667 **452282**
01667 453777

Nairn: St Ninian's See Auldearn and Dalmore

Petty See Ardersier

Urquhart and Glenmoriston (H)
Hugh F. Watt BD DPS DMin   1986   1996   Blairbeg, Drumnadrochit, Inverness IV3 6UG
HWatt@churchofscotland.org.uk
01456 450231

B. In other appointments
Archer, Morven (Mrs)   2013   2020   Ordained Local Minister: Presbytery Assistant Minister   42 Firthview Drive, Inverness IV3 8QE   MArcher@churchofscotland.org.uk   01463 237840
Brown, Derek G. BD DipMin DMin   1989   1994   Lead Chaplain: NHS Highland   1 Allan Gardens, Dornoch IV25 3PD   derek.brown1@nhs.net   01862 810296
Fraser, Jonathan MA(Div) MTh ThM   2012   2019   Lecturer: Highland Theological College   9 Broom Drive, Inverness IV2 4EG   Jonathan.Fraser@uhi.ac.uk   07749 539981
MacKay, Stewart A. BA   2009   2020   Chaplain: Army   3 Eastfield Avenue, Inverness IV2 3RR   seorenzie@gmail.com
Mackenzie, Seòras L. BD   1996   1998   Chaplain: Army   39 Engr Regt (Air Support), Kinloss Barracks, Kinloss, Forres IV36 3XL   01463 231487
Morrison, Hector BSc BD MTh   1981   2009   Principal: Highland Theological College   24 Oak Avenue, Inverness IV2 4NX   Helen's Lodge, Inshes, Inverness IV2 5BG   01463 238561
Whillis, David (Dr) DipHE   2020   Ordained Local Minister: Presbytery-wide minister to over 60s community   DWhillis@churchofscotland.org.uk   01463 232304

C. Demitted

Name		(Parish)	Address	Phone
Black, Archibald T. BSc	1964 1997	(Inverness: Ness Bank)	16 Elm Park, Inverness IV2 4WN	01463 230588
Buell, F. Bart BA MDiv	1980 1995	(Urquhart and Glenmoriston)	6 Towerhill Place, Cradlehall, Inverness IV2 5FN bartbuell@talktalk.net	01463 794634
Craw, John DCS	1998 2009	(Deacon)	5 Larchfield Court, Nairn IV12 4SS johncraw607@btinternet.com	07544 761653
Hunt, Trevor G. BA BD	1986 2011	(Evie with Firth with Rendall)	7 Woodville Court, Culduthel Avenue, Inverness IV2 6BX trevorhunt@gmail.com	01463 250355 07753 423333
Lyon, B. Andrew LTh	1971 2007	(Fraserburgh: West with Rathen: West)	20 Barnview, Culloden, Inverness IV2 7EX balyon2018@hotmail.com	01463 559609
MacGregor, Neil I.M. BD	1995 2019	(Strathbogie Drumblade)	1 Abban Place, Inverness IV3 8GZ	
MacQuarrie, Donald A. BSc BD	1979 2012	(Fort William: Duncansburgh MacIntosh with Kilmonivaig)	Birch Cottage, 4 Craigrorie, North Kessock, Inverness IV1 3XH donaldmacq@gmail.com	01463 731050
McRoberts, T. Douglas BD CPS FRSA	1975 2014	(Malta)	24 Redwood Avenue, Inverness IV2 6HA doug.mcroberts@btinternet.com	01463 772594
Mitchell, Joyce (Mrs) DCS	1994 2010	(Deacon)	Sunnybank, Farr, Inverness IV2 6XG joyce@mitchell71.freeserve.co.uk	01808 521285
Rettie, James A. BTh	1981 1999	(Melness and Eriboll with Tongue)	2 Trantham Drive, Westhill, Inverness IV2 5QT	01463 798896
Ritchie, Bruce BSc BD PhD	1977 2013	(Dingwall: Castle Street)	16 Brinckman Terrace, Westhill, Inverness IV2 5BL brucezomba@hotmail.com	01463 791389
Turner, Fraser K. LTh	1994 2007	(Kiltarlity with Kirkhill)	20 Caulfield Avenue, Inverness IV2 5GA fraseratq@yahoo.co.uk	01463 794004
Younger, Alastair S. BScEcon ASCC	1969 2008	(Inverness: St Columba High)	33 Duke's View, Slackbuie, Inverness IV2 6BB younger873@btinternet.com	01463 242873

INVERNESS ADDRESSES

Inverness

Crown	Kingsmills Road x Midmills Road
Dalneigh and Bona	St Mary's Avenue
East	Academy Street x Margaret Street
Hilton	Druid Road x Tomatin Road
Inshes	Inshes Retail Park
Kinmylies	Kinmylies Way
Ness Bank	Ness Bank x Castle Road
Old High	Church Street x Church Lane
St Columba	Drummond School
St Stephen's	Old Edinburgh Road x Southside Road
Trinity	Huntly Place x Upper Kessock Street

Nairn

Old	Academy Street x Seabank Road
St Ninian's	High Street x Queen Street

(38) LOCHABER (F W)

Meets at Caol, Fort William, in Kilmallie Church Hall at 6pm, on the first Tuesday of September and December, on the last Tuesday of October and on the fourth Tuesday of March. The June meeting is held at 6pm on the second Tuesday in the church of the incoming Moderator. The Presbytery Annual Conference is held in February.

Clerk:	**REV DONALD G. B. McCORKINDALE** **BD DipMin**	**The Manse, 2 The Meadows, Strontian, Acharacle PH36 4HZ** **lochaber@churchofscotland.org.uk**	**01967 402234** **07554 176580**
Treasurer:	**MRS CONNIE ANDERSON**	**faoconnie@gmail.com**	

Acharacle (F H W) linked with Ardnamurchan (F W)

M. Fiona Ogg (Mrs) BA BD	2012	The Church of Scotland Manse, Acharacle PH36 4JU Fiona.Ogg@churchofscotland.org.uk	01967 431654

Ardgour and Kingairloch (F H T W) linked with Morvern (F H T W) linked with Strontian (F H T W)

Donald G.B. McCorkindale BD DipMin	1992	2011	The Manse, 2 The Meadows, Strontian, Acharacle PH36 4HZ DMcCorkindale@churchofscotland.org.uk	01967 402234 07554 176580

Ardnamurchan See Acharacle

Duror (F H W) linked with Glencoe: St Munda's (F H W)

Alexander C. Stoddart BD	2001	2016	9 Cameron Brae, Kentallen, Duror PA38 4BF AStoddart@churchofscotland.org.uk	01631 740285

Fort Augustus (W) linked with Glengarry (W)

Anthony M. Jones BD DPS DipTheol CertMin FRSA	1994	2018	The Manse, Fort Augustus PH32 4BH AJones@churchofscotland.org.uk	01320 366210

Fort William: Duncansburgh MacIntosh (F H W) linked with Kilmonivaig (F W)

Richard Baxter MA BD	1997	2016	The Manse, The Parade, Fort William PH33 6BA RBaxter@churchofscotland.org.uk	01397 702297 07958 541418
Morag Muirhead (Mrs) (Ordained Local Minister)	2013		6 Dumbarton Road, Fort William PH33 6UU MMuirhead@churchofscotland.org.uk	01397 703643

Glencoe: St Munda's See Duror
Glengarry See Fort Augustus

Kilmallie
Vacant
Session Clerk: Margaret Antonios — m.antonios@btinternet.com — 01397 703559

Kilmonivaig See Fort William: Duncansburgh MacIntosh

Kinlochleven (H W) linked with Nether Lochaber (H W)
Malcolm A. Kinnear MA BD PhD — 2010 — The Manse, Lochaber Road, Kinlochleven PH50 4QW / MKinnear@churchofscotland.org.uk — 01855 831227

Morvern See Ardgour
Nether Lochaber See Kinlochleven

North West Lochaber (F H W)
Stewart Goudie BSc BD — 2010 2018 — Church of Scotland Manse, Annie's Brae, Mallaig PH41 4RG / SGoudie@churchofscotland.org.uk — 01687 462514

Strontian See Ardgour

B. In other appointments
Kinnear, Marion (Mrs) BD — 2009 Auxiliary Minister — The Manse, Lochaber Road, Kinlochleven PH50 4QW / Marion.Kinnear@churchofscotland.org.uk — 01855 831227 / 07519 635976

C. Demitted
Anderson, David M. MSc FCOptom — 1984 2018 (Ordained Local Minister) — 'Mirlos', 1 Dumfries Place, Fort William PH33 6UQ / david@mirlos.co.uk — 01397 702091
Millar, John L. MA BD — 1981 1990 (Fort William: Duncansburgh with Kilmonivaig) — Flat 0/1, 12 Chesterfield Gardens, Glasgow G12 0BF / johnmillar123@btinternet.com — 0141 339 4090
Varwell, Adrian P.J. BA BD PhD — 1983 2011 (Fort Augustus with Glengarry) — 19 Enrick Crescent, Kilmore, Drumnadrochit, Inverness IV63 6TP / adrian.varwell@btinternet.com — 01456 459352
Winning, A. Ann MA DipEd BD — 1984 2006 (Morvern) — 'Westering', 13C Carnoch, Glencoe, Ballachulish PH49 4HQ / awinning009@btinternet.com — 01855 811929

(39) ROSS (W)

Meets on the first Tuesday of September in the church of the incoming Moderator, and in Dingwall: Castle Street Church on the first Tuesday of October, November, December, February, March and May, and on the last Tuesday of June.

Clerk:	MRS CATH CHAMBERS			184 Kirkside, Alness IV17 0RH ross@churchofscotland.org.uk	01349 882026
Alness					
Vacant					
Michael J. Macdonald (Auxiliary Minister)		2004	2014	27 Darroch Brae, Alness IV17 0SD 73 Firhill, Alness IV17 0RT Michael.Macdonald@churchofscotland.org.uk	01349 882238 01349 884268
Avoch (W) linked with Fortrose and Rosemarkie (W)					
Warren R. Beattie BSc BD MSc PhD		1990	2019	5 Ness Way, Fortrose IV10 8SS WBeattie@churchofscotland.org.uk	01381 620111
Contin (H W) linked with Fodderty and Strathpeffer (H W)					
Vacant					
James Bissett (Ordained Local Minister)			2016	The Manse, Contin, Strathpeffer IV14 9ES JBissett@churchofscotland.org.uk	01997 421028
Cromarty (W) linked with Resolis and Urquhart (W)					
Terrance T. Burns BA MA		2004	2017	The Manse, Culbokie, Dingwall IV7 8JN TBurns@churchofscotland.org.uk	01349 877452
Dingwall: Castle Street (F H W)					
Drausio P. Goncalves		1993	2019	16 Achany Road, Dingwall IV15 9JB DGoncalves@churchofscotland.org.uk	01349 866792
Dingwall: St Clement's (H W)					
Bruce Dempsey BD		1997	2014	8 Castlehill Road, Dingwall IV15 9PB BDempsey@churchofscotland.org.uk	01349 292055
Fearn Abbey and Nigg (W) linked with Tarbat (W)					
Vacant				Church of Scotland Manse, Fearn, Tain IV20 1WN alex@balmuchy.co.uk d.gordon123@btinternet.com	01862 832282
Session Clerk, Fearn Abbey and Nigg: Alex Gordon					
Session Clerk, Tarbat: Douglas Gordon					

Ferintosh (F W) Stephen Macdonald BD MTh	2008	2018	Ferintosh Manse, Leanaig Road, Conon Bridge, Dingwall IV7 8BE SMacdonald@churchofscotland.org.uk	01349 861275 07570 804193
Fodderty and Strathpeffer See Contin **Fortrose and Rosemarkie** See Avoch				
Invergordon (W) Vacant Session Clerk: William A. Anderson			**invergordonparishchurch@live.co.uk** The Manse, Cromlet Drive, Invergordon IV18 0BA drewandliz.aultsallan@btinternet.com	01349 852273 01349 852462
Killearnan (F H W) linked with Knockbain (F H W) Susan Cord		2016	14 First Field Avenue, North Kessock, Inverness IV1 3JB SCord@churchofscotland.org.uk	01463 731930
Kilmuir and Logie Easter (F) Vacant Session Clerk: George Morrison			The Manse, Delny, Invergordon IV18 0NW ga.morrison@virgin.net	01862 842280 01862 863297
Kiltearn (H) Donald A. MacSween BD	1991	1998	The Manse, Swordale Road, Evanton, Dingwall IV16 9UZ DMacSween@churchofscotland.org.uk	01349 830472
Knockbain See Killearnan				
Lochbroom and Ullapool (F GD) Heidi J. Hercus BA		2018	The Manse, 11 Royal Park, Mill Street, Ullapool IV26 2XT HHercus@churchofscotland.org.uk	01854 613146
Resolis and Urquhart See Cromarty				
Rosskeen (F W) Vacant Carol Rattenbury (Ordained Local Minister)		2017	Rosskeen Manse, Perrins Road, Alness IV17 0XG Balloan Farm House, Alcaig, Conon Bridge, Dingwall IV7 8HU CRattenbury@churchofscotland.org.uk	01349 882265 01349 877323

Tain (F W)

Andrew P. Fothergill BA   2012 2017   14 Kingsway Avenue, Tain IV19 1NJ   01862 892296
AFothergill@churchofscotland.org.uk

Tarbat See Fearn Abbey and Nigg

Urray and Kilchrist (F)

Vacant   The Manse, Corry Road, Muir of Ord IV6 7TL   01463 870259
fionamaclean57@gmail.com   01463 872848
Session Clerk: Fiona Maclean (Mrs)

B. In other appointments

McGowan, Andrew T. B. (Prof) BD STM PhD   1979 2019   Director, Rutherford Centre for Reformed Theology   18 Davis Drive, Alness IV17 0ZD   01340 880762
AMcGowan@churchofscotland.org.uk

Munro, Irene BA   2019   Ordained Local Minister: Presbytery-wide   1 Wyvis Crescent, Conan Bridge, Dingwall IV7 8BZ   01349 865752
IMunro@churchofscotland.org.uk

C. Demitted

Archer, Nicholas D.C. BA BD   1971 1992   (Dores and Boleskine)   2 Aldie Cottages, Tain IV19 1LZ   01862 821494
na.2ac777@btinternet.com

Bell, Graeme K. BA BD   1983 2017   (Glasgow: Carnwadric)   4 Munro Terrace, Rosemarkie, Fortrose IV10 8UR   07591 180101
graemekbell@googlemail.com

Dupar, Kenneth W. BA BD PhD   1965 1993   (Christ's College, Aberdeen)   The Old Manse. The Causeway, Cromarty IV11 8XJ   01381 600428

Forsyth, James LTh   1970 2000   (Fearn Abbey with Nigg: Chapelhill)   Rhives Lodge. Golspie, Sutherland KW10 6DD   01463 712677

Horne, Douglas A. BD   1977 2009   (Tain)   151 Holm Farm Road, Culduthel, Inverness IV2 6BF
douglas.home@talktalk.net

Lincoln, John BA BD MPhil   1986 2014   (Balquhidder with Killin and Ardeonaig)   59 Obsdale Park, Alness IV17 0TR   01349 882791
johnlincoln@minister.com

McDonald, Alan D. LLB BD MTh DLitt DD   1979 2016   (Cameron with St Andrews: St Leonard's)   7 Duke Street, Cromarty IV11 8YH   01381 600954
alan.d.mcdonald@talk21.com

MacLennan, Alasdair J. BD DCE   1979 2001   (Resolis and Urquhart)   Airdale. Seaforth Road. Muir of Ord IV6 7TA   01463 870704

McLeod, John MA   1958 1993   (Resolis and Urquhart)   'Benview', 19 Balvaird. Muir of Ord IV6 7RQ   01463 871286
sheilaandjohn@yahoo.co.uk

MacLeod, Kenneth Donald BD CPS   1989 2019   (Invergordon)   11 Dundas Avenue. Torrance G64 4BD   07808 416767
kd-macleod@tiscali.co.uk

Munro, James A. BA BD DMS   1979 2013   (Port Glasgow: Hamilton Bardrainney)   1 Wyvis Crescent, Conan Bridge, Dingwall IV7 8BZ   01349 865752
james781munro@btinternet.com

Scott, David V. BTh   1994 2014   (Fearn Abbey and Nigg with Tarbat)   29 Sunnyside. Culloden Moor, Inverness IV2 5ES   01463 795802

Smith, Russel BD   1994 2013   (Dingwall: St Clement's)   1 School Road. Conan Bridge, Dingwall IV7 8AE   01349 861011
russantwo@btinternet.com

Warwick, Ivan C. MA BD TD   1980 2014   (Paisley: St James')   Ardcruidh Croft, Heights of Dochcarty, Dingwall IV15 9UF   01349 861464
L7Orev@btinternet.com   07787 535083

(40) SUTHERLAND (F)

Meets at Lairg on the first Tuesday of March, May, September, November and December, and on the first Tuesday of June at the Moderator's church.

Clerk: REV. IAN W. McCREE BD   Tigh Ardachu, Mosshill, Brora KW9 6NG   01408 621185
sutherland@churchofscotland.org.uk

Altnaharra and Farr (W) linked with Melness and Tongue (F H)
Beverly W. Cushman MA MDiv BA PhD   1977   2017   The Manse, Bettyhill, Thurso KW14 7SS   01641 521208
BCushman@churchofscotland.org.uk

Assynt and Stoer
Iain A. MacLeod BA   2012   2020   Canisp Road, Lochinver, Lairg IV27 4LH   01571 844342
IMacleod@churchofscotland.org.uk   07795 014889

Clyne (H W) linked with Kildonan and Loth Helmsdale (H W)
Vacant   info@brorachurchofscotland.org   01408 621239
Interim Moderator: Gladys McCulloch (Mrs)   Golf Road, Brora KW9 6QS   01863 755393
glad.mac@btinternet.com

Creich (W) linked with Kincardine Croick and Edderton (W) linked with Rosehall (W)   info@kyleofsutherlandchurches.org
Vacant   The Manse, Ardgay IV24 3BG   01863 766285
Interim Moderator: John B. Sterrett   JSterrett@churchofscotland.org.uk   Tel/Fax 01408 633295

Dornoch Cathedral (F H W)
Susan M. Brown (Mrs) BD DipMin DUniv   1985   1998   1 Allan Gardens, Dornoch IV25 3PD   01862 810296
Susan.Brown@churchofscotland.org.uk

Durness and Kinlochbervie (F W)
Andrea M. Boyes (Mrs) RMN BA(Theol)   2013   2017   Manse Road, Kinlochbervie, Lairg IV27 4RG   01971 521287
ABoyes@churchofscotland.org.uk

Eddrachillis
John MacPherson BSc BD   1993   Church of Scotland Manse, Scourie, Lairg IV27 4TQ   01971 502431
JMacPherson@churchofscotland.org.uk

Golspie

| John B. Sterrett BA BD PhD | 2007 | pray@standrewgolspie.org
The Manse, Fountain Road, Golspie KW10 6TH
JSterret@churchofscotland.org.uk | Tel/Fax 01408 633295 |

Kildonan and Loth Helmsdale See Clyne
Kincardine Croick and Edderton See Creich

Lairg (F H W) linked with Rogart (H W)
Vacant

| Hilary M. Gardner (Miss)
  (Auxiliary Minister) | 2010 | 2018 | | Cayman Lodge, Kincardine Hill, Ardgay IV24 3DJ
HGardner@churchofscotland.org.uk | 01863 766107 |
| Interim Moderator: Sydney L. Barnett | | | | sydneylb43@gmail.com | 01408 621569 |

Melness and Tongue See Altnaharra and Farr
Rogart See Lairg
Rosehall See Creich

B. In other appointments

| Stobo, Mary J. (Mrs) BA | 2013 | | Ordained Local Minister; Community
  Healthcare Chaplain | Druim-an-Sgairnich, Ardgay IV24 3BG
MStobo@churchofscotland.org.uk | 01863 766868 |

C. Demitted

Chambers, S. John OBE BSc	1972	2009	(Inverness: Ness Bank)	Bannlagan Lodge, 4 Earls Cross Gardens, Dornoch IV25 3NR chambersdornoch@btinternet.com	01862 811520
Goskirk, J. Leslie LTh	1968	2010	(Lairg with Rogart)	Rathvilly, Lairgmuir, Lairg IV27 4ED leslie_goskirk@sky.com	01549 402569
McCree, Ian W. BD	1971	2011	(Clyne with Kildonan and Loth Helmsdale)	Tigh Ardachu, Mosshill, Brora KW9 6NG ianmccree@live.co.uk	01408 621185
McKay, Margaret (Mrs) MA BD MTh	1991	2003	(Auchaber United with Auchterless)	2 Mackenzie Gardens, Dornoch IV25 3RU megsie38@gmail.com	01862 811859

(41) CAITHNESS (W)

Meets alternately at Wick and Thurso on the first Tuesday of February, March, May, September, November and December, and the third Tuesday of June.

| Clerk: | REV. HEATHER STEWART | Burnthill, Thrumster, Wick KW1 5TR
caithness@churchofscotland.org.uk | 01955 651717 |

Halkirk Westerdale linked with Watten
Vacant
Session Clerk, Halkirk: Janet Mowat (Mrs) — The Manse, Station Road, Watten, Wick KW1 5YN
jsmowat25@btinternet.com — 01955 621220 / 01847 831638
Session Clerk, Watten: vacant

Latheron (W)
Vacant — Central Manse, Main Street, Lybster KW3 6BN
parish-of-latheron@btconnect.com — 01593 721706
Heather Stewart (Mrs) 2013 2017 — Burnthill, Thrumster, Wick KW1 5TR
Heather.Stewart@churchofscotland.org.uk — 01955 651717 / Work 01955 603333
(Ordained Local Minister)

North Coast (F)
David J.B. Macartney BA 2017 — Church of Scotland Manse, Reay, Thurso KW14 7RE
DMacartney@churchofscotland.org.uk — 01847 811734

Pentland
Vacant
Session Clerk: Christine Shearer (Mrs) — Scartan View, Canisbay KW1 4YS — 01955 611271

Thurso: St Peter's and St Andrew's (F H W)
David S.M. Malcolm BD 2011 2014 — The Manse, 46 Rose Street, Thurso KW14 7HN
David.Malcolm@churchofscotland.org.uk — 01847 895186

Thurso: West (H W)
Vacant
Interim Moderator: David J.B. Macartney — DMacartney@churchofscotland.org.uk — 01847 811734

Watten See Halkirk Westerdale

Wick: Pulteneytown (H) and Thrumster (W)
Andrew A. Barrie BD 2013 2017 — The Manse, Coronation Street, Wick KW1 5LS
Andrew.Barrie@churchofscotland.org.uk — 01955 606192 / 07791 663439

Wick: St Fergus (F W)
John Nugent BD 1999 2011 — Mansefield, Miller Avenue, Wick KW1 4DF
JNugent@churchofscotland.org.uk — 01955 602167 / 07511 503946

C. Demitted

Duncan, Esme (Miss) 2013 2017 (Ordained Local Minister) Avalon, Upper Warse, Canisbay, Wick KW1 4YD 01955 611455
EDuncan@churchofscotland.org.uk

Rennie, Lyall 2014 2019 (Ordained Local Minister) Ruachmarra, Lower Warse, Canisbay, Wick KW1 4YB 01955 611756
LRennie@churchofscotland.org.uk

CAITHNESS Communion Sundays

Halkirk Westerdale Apr, Jul, Oct
Latheron Apr, Jul, Sep, Nov
North Coast Mar, Easter, Jun, Sep, Dec
Pentland:
Canisbay 1st Jun, Nov
Dunnet last May, Nov
Keiss 1st May, 3rd Nov
Olrig last May, Nov
Thurso: St Peter's and
St Andrew's Mar, Jun, Sep, Dec
West 4th Mar, Jun, Nov
Watten 1st Jul, Dec
Wick: Pulteneytown and 1st Mar, Jun, Sep, Dec
Thrumster Apr, Oct
St Fergus

(42) LOCHCARRON – SKYE

Meets in conference annually and in Kyle as required normally on a Tuesday.

Clerk: REV. RODERICK A.R. MacLEOD The Manse, 6 Upper Breakish, Isle of Skye IV42 8PY **01471 822416**
MA MBA BD DMin **lochcarronskye@churchofscotland.org.uk**

Applecross, Lochcarron and Torridon (GD) 2008 2017
Anita Stutter Drs (MA) The Manse, Colonel's Road, Lochcarron, Strathcarron IV54 8YG 01520 722783
AStutter@churchofscotland.org.uk

Bracadale and Duirinish (GD)
Vacant
Interim Moderator: Alisdair T. MacLeod-Mair AMacLeod-Mair@churchofscotland.org.uk 01470 532453

Gairloch and Dundonnell (F W) 1994 2016
Stuart J. Smith BEng BD MTh Church of Scotland Manse, The Glebe, Gairloch IV21 2BT 01445 712645
Stuart.Smith@churchofscotland.org.uk

Glenelg, Kintail and Lochalsh (W)
Vacant The Manse, Main Street, Kyle of Lochalsh IV40 8DA 01599 534294
Session Clerk: (Acting): Andrew Will andy@plockton.org.uk 01599 544276

Kilmuir and Stenscholl (GD W)
Vacant
Interim Moderator: John H. Lamont — 1 Totescore, Kilmuir, Isle of Skye IV51 9YN — jhlamont@btinternet.com — 01470 542297 / 01445 731888 / 07714 720753

Portree (GD W)
Sandor Fazakas BD MTh — 1976 2007 — Viewfield Road, Portree, Isle of Skye IV51 9ES — SFazakas@churchofscotland.org.uk — 01478 611868

Snizort (GD H)
Alisdair T. MacLeod-Mair MEd DipTheol — 2001 2019 — The Manse, Kensaleyre, Snizort, Portree, Isle of Skye IV51 9XE — AMacLeod-Mair@churchofscotland.org.uk — 01470 532453

Strath and Sleat (F GD W)
Roderick A.R. MacLeod MA MBA BD DMin — 1994 2015 — The Manse, 6 Upper Breakish, Isle of Skye IV42 8PY — RMacLeod@churchofscotland.org.uk — 01471 822416

B. In other appointments
MacKenzie, Hector M. — 2008 — Chaplain: Army — 5 Regiment Royal Artillery, Marne Barracks, Catterick Garrison DL10 7NP — mackenziehector@hotmail.com

C. Demitted
Martin, George M. MA BD — 1987 2005 — (Applecross, Lochcarron and Torridon) — 8(1) Buckingham Terrace, Edinburgh EH4 3AA — 0131 343 3937
Morrison, Derek — 1995 2013 — (Gairloch and Dundonnell) — 2 Clifton Place, Poolewe, Achnasheen IV22 2JU — derekmorrison1@aol.com — 01445 781333

(43) UIST

Meets on the first Tuesday of February, March, September and November in Lochmaddy, and on the third Tuesday of June in Leverburgh.

Clerk: REV. GAVIN J. ELLIOTT MA BD — 5a Aird, Isle of Benbecula HS7 5LT — uist@churchofscotland.org.uk — 01870 602726

Benbecula (F GD H) linked with Carinish (GD H W)

Andrew (Drew) P. Kuzma BA	2007	info@carinish-church.org.uk Church of Scotland Manse, Griminish, Isle of Benbecula HS7 5QA AKuzma@churchofscotland.org.uk	01870 602180
Ishabel Macdonald (Ordained Local Minister)	2011	'Cleat Afe Ora', 18 Carinish, Isle of North Uist HS6 5HN Ishie.Macdonald@churchofscotland.org.uk	01876 580367

Berneray and Lochmaddy (GD H) linked with Kilmuir and Paible (GD)

Alen J.R. McCulloch MA BD	1990	2017	Church of Scotland Manse, Paible, Isle of North Uist HS6 5HD AMcCulloch@churchofscotland.org.uk	01876 510310

Carinish   See Benbecula

Kilmuir and Paible   See Berneray and Lochmaddy

Manish-Scarista (GD H)

Vacant	Church of Scotland Manse, Scarista, Isle of Harris HS3 3HX	01859 550200
Session Clerk: Paul Alldred	paul.alldred@outlook.com	01859 520494

Tarbert (GD H T W)

Ian Murdo M. MacDonald DPA BD	2001	2015	The Manse, Manse Road, Tarbert, Isle of Harris HS3 3DF Ian.MacDonald@churchofscotland.org.uk	01859 502231

C. Demitted

Elliott, Gavin J. MA BD	1976	2015	(Ministries Council)	5a Aird, Isle of Benbecula HS7 5LT gavkondwani@gmail.com	01870 602726
MacIver, Norman BD	1976	2011	(Tarbert)	57 Boswell Road, Wester Inshes, Inverness IV2 3EW norman@n-cmaciver.freeserve.co.uk	
Morrison, Donald John	2001	2019	(Auxiliary Minister)	22 Kyles, Tarbert, Isle of Harris HS3 3BS DMorrison@churchofscotland.org.uk	01859 502341
Petrie, Jackie G.	1989	2011	(South Uist)	7B Malaclete, Isle of North Uist HS6 5BX jackiegpetrie@yahoo.com	01876 560804
Smith, John M.	1956	1992	(Lochmaddy)	Hamersay, Clachan, Locheport, Lochmaddy, Isle of North Uist HS6 5HD	
Smith, Murdo MA BD	1988	2011	(Manish-Scarista)	Aisgeir, 15A Upper Shader, Isle of Lewis HS3 3MX	01876 580332

UIST Communion Sundays

Benbecula	2nd Mar. Sep	Carinish	4th Mar. Aug
Berneray and Lochmaddy	4th Jun, last Oct	Kilmuir and Paible	1st Jun, 3rd Nov
		Manish-Scarista	3rd Apr. 1st Oct
		Tarbert	2nd Mar. 3rd Sep

(44) LEWIS

Meets at Stornoway, in St Columba's Church Hall, on the second Tuesday of February, March, June, September and November and at other times as required.

Clerk: MR JOHN CUNNINGHAM | 1 Raven's Lane, Stornoway, Isle of Lewis HS2 0EG
lewis@churchofscotland.org.uk | 01851 709977
07789 878840

Barvas (F GD H W)
Dougie Wolf BA(Theol) | 2017 | Church of Scotland Manse, Lower Barvas, Isle of Lewis HS2 0QY
DWolf@churchofscotland.org.uk | 01851 840218

Carloway (F GD H)
Duncan M. Macaskill BA BD MPhil DMin | 1992 | 2019 | Church of Scotland Manse, Knock, Carloway, Isle of Lewis HS2 9AU
DMacaskill@churchofscotland.org.uk | **01851 643211**
01851 643255

Cross Ness (GD H T W)
John M. Nicolson BD DipMin | 1997 | 2019 | **crossnesschurch@gmail.com**
Cross Manse, 43 Habost, Ness, Isle of Lewis HS2 0TG
JNicolson@churchofscotland.org.uk | 07899 235355

Kinloch (GD H)
Iain M. Campbell BD | 2004 | 2008 | Laxay, Lochs, Isle of Lewis HS2 9LA
ICampbell@churchofscotland.org.uk | 01851 830218

Knock (GD H)
Guardianship of the Presbytery
Interim Moderator: Iain M. Campbell | ICampbell@churchofscotland.org.uk | 01851 830218

Lochs-Crossbost (GD H)
Guardianship of the Presbytery
Interim Moderator: Donald Macleod | donaldmacleod25@btinternet.com | 01851 704516

Lochs-in-Bernera (F GD H) linked with Uig (F GD H)
Hugh Maurice Stewart DPA BD | 2008 | Church of Scotland Manse, Uigen, Miavaig, Isle of Lewis HS2 9HX
HStewart@churchofscotland.org.uk | 01851 672388

Stornoway: High (GD H)
Gordon M. Macleod BA | 2017 | 2019 | Woodside, Laxdale Lane, Stornoway, Isle of Lewis HS1 0DR
GMacleod@churchofscotland.org.uk | 07717 065739

Stornoway: Martin's Memorial (F H W)

Thomas MacNeil MA BD	2002	2006	enquiries@martinsmemorial.org.uk Martin's Memorial Manse, Matheson Road, Stornoway, Isle of Lewis HS1 2LR TMacNeil@churchofscotland.org.uk	**01851 700820** 01851 704238

Stornoway: St Columba (F GD H)

William J. Heenan BA MTh	2012	St Columba's Manse, Lewis Street, Stornoway, Isle of Lewis HS1 2JF WHeenan@churchofscotland.org.uk	**01851 701546** 01851 705933 07837 770589

Uig See Lochs-in-Bernera

B. In other appointments

Shadakshari, T.K. BTh BD MTh	1998	2006	Head of Spiritual Care, Western Isles Health Board	23D Benside, Newmarket, Stornoway, Isle of Lewis HS2 0DZ tk.shadakshari@nhs.net	Home 01851 701727 Office 01851 704704 07403 697138

C. Demitted

Amed, Paul LTh DPS	1992	2015	(Barvas)	6 Scotland Street, Stornoway, Isle of Lewis HS1 2JQ paul.amed@outlook.com	01851 706450
Jamieson, Esther M.M. (Mrs) BD	1984	2002	(Glasgow: Penilee St Andrew's)	1 Redburn, Bayview, Stornoway. Isle of Lewis HS1 2UU iandejamieson@biinternet.com	01851 704789
Johnstone, Ben MA BD DMin	1973	2013	(Strath and Sleat)	Loch Alainn, 5 Breaclete, Great Bernera, Isle of Lewis HS2 9LT benonbernera@gmail.com	01851 612445
Maclean, Donald A. DCS	1988	1990	(Deacon)	8 Upper Barvas, Isle of Lewis HS2 0QX	01851 840454
Macleod, William	1957	2006	(Uig)	54 Lower Barvas, Isle of Lewis HS2 0QY	01851 840217

LEWIS   Communion Sundays

Barvas	3rd Mar, Sep	Knock	3rd Apr, 1st Nov	Stornoway: Martin's Memorial	3rd Feb, last Aug, 1st Dec, Easter
Carloway	1st Mar, last Sep	Lochs-Crossbost	4th Mar, Sep	Stornoway: St Columba	3rd Feb, last Aug
Cross Ness	2nd Mar Oct	Lochs-in-Bernera	1st Apr, 2nd Sep	Uig	3rd Jun, 4th Oct
Kinloch	3rd Mar, 2nd Jun, 2nd Sep	Stornoway: High	3rd Feb, last Aug		

(45) ORKNEY (W)

Normally meets at Kirkwall on the first Wednesday of September, November, February, April, and the third Wednesday of June.

Clerk: KAREN McKNIGHT CIMA CertBA		**8 Fletts Corner, Finstown, Orkney KW17 2EE** orkney@churchofscotland.org.uk	**01856 761554**
Depute Clerk: MS MARGARET A.B. SUTHERLAND LLB BA		**13 Cursiter Crescent, Kirkwall, Orkney KW15 1XN** mabs2@tiscali.co.uk	**01856 873747**

Birsay, Harray and Sandwick (F W)

David G. McNeish MB ChB BSc BD	2015	The Manse, North Biggings Road, Dounby, Orkney KW17 2HZ DMcNeish@churchofscotland.org.uk	01856 771599

East Mainland (W)

Wilma A. Johnston MTheol MTh	2006 2014	eastmainlandchurch@gmail.com The Manse, Holm, Orkney KW17 2SB Wilma.Johnston@churchofscotland.org.uk	01856 781797

Eday

Vacant

Session Clerk: Johan Robertson	essonquoy@btinternet.com 01857 622251

Evie (H) linked with Firth (H) linked with Rendall linked with Rousay   Firth: **01856 761117**

Vacant

Session Clerk, Firth: Janis Dickey	rbdickey@hotmail.com	01856 761396
Session Clerk, Rendall: Eileen Fraser	eileenocot@hotmail.co.uk	01856 761409
Interim Moderator: Linda Broadley	lindabroadley@btinternet.com	01856 771599

Firth See Evie

Flotta (W) linked with Hoy and Walls (F) linked with Orphir and Stenness (H W)

Vacant		Stenness Manse, Stenness, Stromness, Orkney KW16 3HH	01856 851139
Martin W.M. Prentice	2013	Cott of Howe, Cairston, Stromness, Orkney KW16 3JU	07795 817213
(Ordained Local Minister)		MPrentice@churchofscotland.org.uk	01856 701219
Session Clerk, Flotta: Isobel Smith			01856 701363
Session Clerk, Hoy and Walls: Anderson Sutherland			

Hoy and Walls See Flotta

Kirkwall: East (F H W) linked with Shapinsay (F W)
Julia M. Meason MTh MA   2013   East Church Manse, Thorns Street, Kirkwall, Orkney KW15 1PF   01856 874789
JMeason@churchofscotland.org.uk

Kirkwall: St Magnus Cathedral (F H T W)
G. Fraser H. Macnaughton MA BD   1982   2002   Cathedral Manse, Berstane Road, Kirkwall, Orkney KW15 1NA   01856 873312
FMacnaughton@churchofscotland.org.uk
June Freeth BA MA (Ordained Local Minister)   2015   2016   Cumlaquoy, Orkney KW17 2ND   01856 721449
JFreeth@churchofscotland.org.uk

North Ronaldsay
Guardianship of the Presbytery
Presbytery Clerk: Karen McKnight   orkney@churchofscotland.org.uk   01856 761554

Orphir and Stenness See Flotta

Papa Westray (W) linked with Westray (W)
Iain D. MacDonald BD   1993   The Manse, Hilldavale, Westray, Orkney KW17 2DW   Tel/Fax   01857 677357
IMacDonald@churchofscotland.org.uk   07710 443780

Rendall See Evie
Rousay See Evie

Sanday
Vacant
Interim Moderator: June Freeth   JFreeth@churchofscotland.org.uk   01856 721449

Shapinsay See Kirkwall: East

South Ronaldsay and Burray
Vacant   St Margaret's Manse, Church Road, St Margaret's Hope,   01856 831670
Orkney KW17 2SR
JButterfield@churchofscotland.org.uk
Interim Moderator: John A. Butterfield   01856 850203

Stromness (F H)
John A. Butterfield BA BD MPhil   1990   2016   5 Manse Lane, Stromness, Orkney KW16 3AP   01856 850203
JButterfield@churchofscotland.org.uk

Stronsay: Moncur Memorial (W)
Vacant
Session Clerk: Elsie Dennison   elsie.dennison@live.co.uk   01857 616238

Westray See Papa Westray

C. Demitted

Clark, Thomas L. BD	1985	2008	(Orphir with Stenness)	7 Headland Rise, Burghead, Elgin IV30 5HA toml.clark@btinternet.com	01343 830144
Graham, Jennifer D. (Mrs) BA MDiv PhD	2000	2011	(Eday with Stronsay: Moncur Memorial)	Lodge, Stronsay, Orkney KW17 2AN jdgraham67@gmail.com	01857 616487
Tait, Alexander	1967	1995	(Glasgow: St Enoch's Hogganfield)	Ingermas, Evie, Orkney KW17 2PH	01856 751477
Wishart, James BD	1986	2009	(Deer)	Upper Westshore, Burray, Orkney KW17 2TE jwishart06@btinternet.com	01856 731672

(47) ENGLAND (F)

Meets at London, in Crown Court Church, on the second Tuesday of February, and at St Columba's, Pont Street, on the second Tuesday of June and the second Saturday of October.

Clerk: REV. ALISTAIR CUMMING MSc CCS FInstLM FLPI   64 Prince George's Avenue, London SW20 8BH   07534 943986
england@churchofscotland.org.uk

Corby: St Andrew's (F H W)
Vacant
Interim Moderator: James Francis   43 Hempland Close, Corby, Northants NN18 8LR
JFrancis@churchofscotland.org.uk

Corby: St Ninian's (H W)
Vacant
Session Clerk: Ben Bruce   The Manse, 46 Glyndebourne Gardens, Corby, Northants NN18 0PZ   **01536 265245**
ben17447@gmail.com   01536 669478

Guernsey: St Andrew's in the Grange (F H W)
David G. Coulter CB OStJ QHC   1989   2019   The Manse, Le Villocq, Castel, Guernsey GY5 7SB   01481 257345
  BA BD MDA PhD   DCoulter@churchofscotland.org.uk

Jersey: St Columba's (F H T W)
Graeme M. Glover MA MBA MSc   2017   18 Claremont Avenue, St Saviour, Jersey JE2 7SF   01534 730659
GGlover@churchofscotland.org.uk

London: Crown Court (F H T W)   020 7836 5643
Philip L. Majcher BD   1982 2007   53 Sidmouth Street, London WC1H 8JX   020 7278 5022
PMajcher@churchofscotland.org.uk

London: St Columba's (F H T W) linked with Newcastle: St Andrew's (H T W)   office@stcolumbas.org.uk   **St Columba's: 020 7584 2321**
C. Angus MacLeod MA BD   1996 2012   29 Hollywood Road, Chelsea, London SW10 9HT   Office 020 7584 2321
Angus.MacLeod@churchofscotland.org.uk

B. In other appointments

Binks, Mike   2007 2015   Auxiliary Minister – Churches Together in Corby   Hollybank, 10 Kingsbrook, Corby NN18 9HY   07590 507917
MBinks@churchofscotland.org.uk

Cumming, Alistair MSc CCS FInstLM FLPI   2010 2013   Presbytery Clerk: Auxiliary Minister   64 Prince George's Avenue, London SW20 8BH   020 8540 7365
ACumming@churchofscotland.org.uk   07534 943986

Francis, James MBE BD PhD   2002 2009   Army Chaplain   37 Millburn Road, Coleraine BT52 1QT   02870 353869
JFrancis@churchofscotland.org.uk

Lancaster, Craig MA BD   2004 2011   RAF Chaplain   52 Suffolk Avenue, RAF Honington, Bury St Edmunds IP31 1LW
craig.lancaster102@mod.gov.uk

Langlands, Cameron H. BD MTh ThM PhD MInstLM   1995 2012   Head of Spiritual and Pastoral Care, South London and Maudsley NHS Foundation Trust   Maudsley Hospital, Denmark Road, London SE5 8AZ   020 3228 2815
Cameron.Langlands@slam.nhs.uk   07971 169791

Lovett, Mairi F. BSc BA DipPS MTh   2005 2013   Hospital Chaplain   Royal Brompton Hospital, Sydney Street, London SW3 6NP   020 7351 8060
m.lovett@rbht.nhs.uk

McLay, Neil BA BD MTh   2006 2012   Army Chaplain   1 R Welsh, Lucknow Barracks, Lowa Road, Tidworth SP9 7BU

McMahon, John K.S. MA BD   1998 2012   Head of Spiritual and Pastoral Care, West London NHS Trust   Broadmoor Hospital, Crowthorne, Berkshire RG45 7EG   01344 754098
john.mcmahonrev@westlondon.nhs.uk

Mather, James BA DipArch MA MBA   2010   Auxiliary Minister: University Chaplain   24 Ellison Road, Barnes, London SW13 0AD   Home 020 8876 6540
JMather@churchofscotland.org.uk   Work 020 7361 1670   Mbl 07836 715655

Middleton, Paul (Prof) BMus BD ThM PhD   2000 2017   New Testament and Early Christianity, University of Chester   10 Raymond Street, Chester CH1 4EL   01244 378766
p.middleton@chester.ac.uk

Thom, David J. BD DipMin   1999 2015   Army Chaplain   revdjt@gmail.com

Walker, R. Forbes BSc BD ThM   1987 2013   School Chaplain, Emmanuel School, London   Flat 5, 18 Northside Wandsworth Common, London SW18 2SL   020 8870 0953
revrfw@gmail.com

Ward, Michael J. BSc BD PhD MA PGCE   1983 2009   Training and Development Officer: Presbyterian Church of Wales   Apt 6, Bryn Hedd, Conwy Road, Penmaen-mawr, Gwynedd LL34 6BS   07765 599816
revmw@btopenworld.com

C. Demitted

Anderson, Andrew F. MA BD	1981 2011	(Edinburgh: Greenside)	58 Reliance Way, Oxford OX4 2FG / andrew.relianceway@gmail.com	01865 778397
Cairns, W. Alexander BD	1978 2006	(Corby: St Andrew's)	Kirkton House, Kirkton of Craig, Montrose DD10 9TB / sandy.cairns@btinternet.com	07808 588045
Cameron, R. Neil	1976 2005	(Chaplain: Army)	neilandninacameron@yahoo.co.uk	
Lunn, Dorothy I.M.	2002 2017	(Auxiliary Minister)	14 Bellerby Drive, Ouston, Co.Durham DH2 1TW / dorothylunn@hotmail.com	0191 492 0647
Macfarlane, Peter T. BA LTh	1970 1994	(Chaplain: Army)	4 rue de Rives, 37160 Abilly, France	
McIndoe, John H. MA BD STM DD	1960 2000	(London: St Columba's with Newcastle: St Andrew's)	5 Dunlin, Westerlands Park, Glasgow G12 0FE / johnandeve@mcindoe555.fsnet.co.uk	0141 579 1366
MacLeod, Rory N. BA BD	1986 2017	(Chaplain: Army)	154 Regt RLC, Bothwell House, Elgin Street, Dunfermline KY12 7SB	
Mills, Peter W. CB BD DD CPD	1984 2017	(Largoward with St Monans)	16 Pearce Drive, Lawley, Telford TF3 5IQ	
Nicoll, A. Norman BD	2003 2020	(Corby: St Andrew's)	14 Victoria Street, Forfar DD8 3BA	
Wallace, Donald S.	1950 1990	(Chaplain: Royal Caledonian Schools)	7 Dellfield Close, Watford, Herts WD1 3BL	01923 223289

ENGLAND – Church Addresses

Corby: St Andrew's	Occupation Road
Corby: St Ninian's	Beanfield Avenue
Guernsey:	The Grange, St Peter Port
Jersey:	Midvale Road, St Helier
London: Crown Court	Crown Court WC2
London: St Columba's	Pont Street SW1
Newcastle:	Sandyford Road

(48) PRESBYTERY OF INTERNATIONAL CHARGES (W)

Meets over the weekend of the second Sunday of March and October, hosted by congregations in mainland Europe.

Clerk: REV. JAMES SHARP	**102 Rue des Eaux-Vives, CH-1207 Geneva, Switzerland** clerk@internationalpresbytery.net **www.internationalpresbytery.net**	**0041 22 786 4847**
Depute Clerk: REV. DEREK G. LAWSON LLB BD	**16 Rue de la Madelaine, 22210 La Chèze, France** deputeclerk@internationalpresbytery.net	**0033 25 617 9457**

Amsterdam: English Reformed Church (F T W)

Lance B. Stone BD MTh PhD	1978	2014	Jan Willem Brouwersstraat 9, NL–1071 LH Amsterdam, The Netherlands minister@ercadam.nl Church address: Begijnhof 48, 1012WV Amsterdam	0031 20 672 2288

Bermuda: Christ Church, Warwick (F H W)
Alistair G. Bennett BSc BD   1978

christchurch@logic.bm
The Manse, 6 Manse Road, Paget PG 01, Bermuda
ABennett@churchofscotland.org.uk
Church address: Christ Church, Middle Road, Warwick, Bermuda
Mailing address: PO Box WK 130, Warwick WK BX, Bermuda
001 441 236 1882
001 441 236 0400

Bochum (Associated congregation) (W)
James M. Brown MA BD   1982   1983

Neustrasse 15, D-44787 Bochum, Germany
JBrown@churchofscotland.org.uk
Church address: Pauluskircke, Grabenstrasse 9, 44787 Bochum
0049 234 133 65

Brussels: St Andrew's (F H W)
Eric W. Foggitt MA BSc BD   1991   2020

secretary@churchofscotland.be
23 Square des Nations, B-1000 Brussels, Belgium
minister@churchofscotland.be
Church address: Chaussée de Vieurgat 181, 1050 Brussels
0032 2 649 02 19
0032 2 672 40 56

Budapest: St Columba's (F W)
Aaron C. Stevens BA MDiv MACE   2004   2006

Stefánia út 32, H-1143, Budapest, Hungary
AStevens@churchofscotland.org.uk
Church address: Vörösmarty utca 51, 1064 Budapest
0036 30 567 6356
0036 70 615 5394

Colombo, Sri Lanka: St Andrew's Scots Kirk (F W)
Vacant

Session Clerk: Chandan de Silva

churchofficer@scotskirk.lk
73 Galle Road, Colpetty, Colombo 3, Sri Lanka
minister@standrewsscotskirk.org
chandan59@yahoo.com
0094 112 323 765
0094 112 386 774
0094 112 588 687

Costa del Sol (W)
Guardianship of the Presbytery

Interim Moderator: Derek G. Lawson

Avenida Jesus Santos Rein, 24 Edf. Lindamar 4 – 3Q,
Fuengirola, 29640 Malaga, Spain
Church address: Lux Mundi Ecumenical Centre, Calle Nueva 3,
29460 Fuengirola
DLawson@churchofscotland.org.uk
0034 951 260 982
0033 256 179 457

Geneva (F W)
Laurence H. Twaddle MA BD MTh   1977   2017

6 chemin Taverney, 1218 Geneva, Switzerland
cofsg@pingnet.ch
Church address: Auditoire de Calvin, 1 Place de la Taconnerie, Geneva
0041 22 788 08 31
0041 22 788 08 31

Gibraltar: St Andrew's (W)
Ewen MacLean BA BD DipBI 1995 2009
St Andrew's Manse, 29 Scud Hill, Gibraltar
scotskirk@gibraltar.gi
Church address: Governor's Parade, Gibraltar
00350 200 77040

Lausanne: The Scots Kirk (F H W)
Gillean P. MacLean (Ms) BA BD 1994 2019
26 Avenue de Rumine, CH-1005 Lausanne, Switzerland
GMacLean@churchofscotland.org.uk
0041 21 323 98 28

Lisbon: St Andrew's (F W)
Guardianship of the Presbytery
lisbonstandrewschurch@gmail.com
Rua Coelho da Rocha, N°75 - 1°
   Campa de Ourique, 1350-073 Lisbon, Portugal
cofslx@netcabo.pt
Church address: Rua da Arriaga, Lisbon
00351 213 951 165

Session Clerk: Nina O'Donnell
sessionclerklisbon@gmail.com
00351 21 483 8750

Malta: St Andrew's Scots Church (H W)
Beata (Betsi) Thane MEd BD 2020
La Romagnola, 15 Triq is-Seiqia, Misrah Kola, Attard
   ATD 1713, Malta
minister@saintandrewsmalta.com
Church address: 210 Old Bakery Street, Valletta, Malta
Tel/Fax 00356 214 15465

Paris: The Scots Kirk (F W)
Jan J. Steyn 1988 2017
10 Rue Thimmonier, F-75009 Paris, France
Church address: 17 Rue Bayard, 75009 Paris
JSteyn@churchofscotland.org.uk
0033 1 48 78 47 94

Rome: St Andrew's (F W)
Peter McEnhill BD PhD 1992 2019
scotskirkrome@gmail.com
Via XX Settembre 7, 00187 Rome, Italy
PMcEnhill@churchofscotland.org.uk
Tel 0039 06 482 7627
Fax 0039 06 487 4370

Rotterdam: Scots International Church (F W)
Vacant
Interim Moderator: Jan J. Steyn
info@scotsintchurch.com
Schiedamse Vest 121, 3012BH Rotterdam, The Netherlands
JSteyn@churchofscotland.org.uk
Church address: Schiedamsesingel 2, Rotterdam, The Netherlands
0031 10 412 4779
0033 14 878 4794
0031 10 412 5709

Trinidad: Greyfriars St Ann's, Port of Spain (W) linked with Arouca and Sangre Grande
Vacant
Interim Moderator: Aaron C. Stevens,
50 Frederick Street, Port of Spain, Trinidad
AStevens@churchofscotland.org.uk
001 868 623 6684
0036 70 615 5394

B. In other appointments

Born, Irene M.E.	2008		Ordained Local Minister-Worship and Prayer Promoter	Bergpolderstraat 53A, NL-3038 KB Rotterdam, The Netherlands ibsalem@xs4all.nl	0031 10 265 1703
Evans-Boiten, Joanne H.G. BD	2004	2018	Retreat Centre Director	Colomba le Roc, 510 Chemin du Faurat, Belmontet, 46800 Montcuq en Quercy, France Joanne.evansboiten@gmail.com	0033 5 65 22 13 11
McGeoch, Graham G. MA BD MTh PhD	2009	2017	Theology Lecturer	Faculdade Unida de Vitoria, R.Eng. Fabio Ruschi, 161 Bento Ferreira, Vitoria ES 29050-670, Brazil graham@fuv.edu.br	
Ross, Matthew Z. LLB BD MTh FSAScot	1998	2018	Programme Executive for Diakonia and Capacity Building, World Council of Churches	World Council of Churches, Route de Ferney 150, Case Postale 2100, CH-1211 Geneva 2, Switzerland Matthew.Ross@wcc-coe.org	work 0041 22 791 6322 mob 0041 79 155 8638
Sharp, James	2005	2013	Ordained Local Minister, Presbytery Clerk	102 Rue des Eaux-Vives, 1207 Geneva, Switzerland jim.sharp@churchofscotland.org.uk	0041 22 786 4847
Sinclair, David I. BSc BD PhD DipSW	1990	2017	Ecumenical and International Officer, ECCB	Evangelical Church of the Czech Brethren, Jungmannova 9, Prague 1 DSinclair@churchofscotland.org.uk	00 420 224 999 230

C. Demitted

Herbold Ross, Kristina M.	2008	2018	(Work Place Chaplain)	c/o Rev Matthew Z. Ross (see above)	
Lawson, Derek G. LLB BD	1998	2020	(Rotterdam: Scots International Church)	16 Rue de la Madeleine, 22210 La Chèze, France DLawson@churchofscotland.org.uk	0033 2 56 17 94 57
Pitkeathly, Thomas C. MA CA BD	1984	2004	(Brussels)	77 St Thomas Road. Lytham St. Anne's FY8 1JP tpitkeathly@yahoo.co.uk	01253 789634
Reamonn, Paraic BA BD	1982	2018	(Jerusalem: St Andrew's)	395B Route de Mandement, 1281 Ruissin, Switzerland PReamonn@churchofscotland.org.uk	0041 22 776 4834

(49) JERUSALEM

Clerk:	JOANNA OAKLEY-LEVSTEIN	St Andrew's, Galilee, PO Box 104, Tiberias 14100, Israel j.oak.lev@gmail.com	00972 50 5842517

Jerusalem and Tiberias: St Andrew's (F W) jerusalem@churchofscotland.org.uk

John McCulloch BA BA (Theol) PhD	2018		St Andrew's Scots Memorial Church, 1 David Remez Street, PO Box 8619, Jerusalem 91086, Israel JMcCulloch@churchofscotland.org.uk tiberias@churchofscotland.org.uk	00972 2 673 2401
Katharine S. McDonald BA MSc BD MLitt (Associate Minister) (Scottish Episcopal Church)	2012	2015	St Andrew's, Galilee, 1 Gdud Barak Street, PO Box 104, Tiberias 14100, Israel kmcdonald@churchofscotland.org.uk	00972 54 244 6736

SECTION 6

Additional Lists of Personnel

LIST A – ORDAINED LOCAL MINISTERS

Those engaged in active service. Where only one date is given it is the year of ordination and appointment. Contact details may be found under the Presbytery in Section 5 to which an OLM belongs.

NAME	ORD	APP	APPOINTMENT	PRESBYTERY
Allardice, Michael MA MPhil PGCertTHE FHEA	2014	—	—	25 Kirkcaldy
Archer, Morven (Mrs)	2013	2020	Presbytery Assistant Minister	37 Inverness
Bellis, Pamela A. BA	2014	—	—	9 Wigtown and Stranraer
Bissett, James	2016		Contin linked with Fodderty and Strathpeffer	39 Ross
Bom, Irene M.E.	2008		Worship Resourcing	48 International Charges
Breingan, Mhairi M.	2011	2019	Paisley: Stow Brae	14 Clyde
Brodie, Catherine J. MA BA MPhil PGCE	2017		Dundee: Fintry	29 Dundee
Crossan, Morag BA	2016		—	10 Ayr
Crossan, William	2014	2018	Campbeltown: Lorne and Lowland	19 Argyll
Crouch, Simon A.	2019		Cushnie and Tough; and Upper Donside	33 Gordon
Dempster, Eric T. MBA	2016	2018	Lockerbie: Dryfesdale, Hutton and Corrie	7 Annandale and Eskdale
Don, Andrew MBA	2006	2013	Newton	3 Lothian
Duncanson, Mary B. (Ms) BTh	2013		Presbytery Pastoral Support	36 Abernethy
Finnie, Bill H. BA PgDipSW CertCRS	2015		Kirkintilloch: Hillhead	16 Glasgow
Forsythe, Ruth (Mrs) MCS	2017	2018	Glasgow: Temple Anniesland	16 Glasgow
Freeth, June BA MA	2015	2016	Kirkwall: St Magnus Cathedral	45 Orkney
Fulcher, Christine P. BEd	2012	2018	Presbytery Ministries Co-ordinator – South Argyll	19 Argyll
Geddes, Elizabeth (Mrs)	2013	2019	Langbank	14 Clyde
Gray, Ian	2013	2017	Montrose: Old and St Andrew's	30 Angus
Grieve, Leslie E.T. BSc BA	2014		Glasgow: Colston Wellpark	16 Glasgow
Hardman Moore, Susan (Prof.) MA MAR PhD	2013		New College, University of Edinburgh	1 Edinburgh
Harrison, Frederick	2013		—	3 Lothian
Henderson, Derek R.	2017		Abercorn linked with Pardovan, Kingscavil and Winchburgh	2 West Lothian
Hogg, James	2018		Troon: St Meddan's	10 Ayr
Hunt, Roland BSc PhD CertEd	2016		Glasgow: Carmyle linked with Glasgow: Mount Vernon	16 Glasgow
Johnston, June E. BSc MEd BD	2013	2020	Bilston linked with Glencorse linked with Roslin	3 Lothian
Lennox-Trewren, Norman D.	2018		Mearns Coastal	32 Kincardine and Deeside
Macdonald, Ishabel	2011		Benbecula linked with Carinish	43 Uist
MacDonald, Monica J. (Mrs)	2014		Slamannan	22 Falkirk
MacKellar, Janet K. BSc ProfCertMgmt FCMI	2019		Kilmun, Strone and Ardentinny: The Shore Kirk	19 Argyll
McKenzie, Janet R. (Mrs)	2016		Edinburgh: Tron Kirk (Gilmerton and Moredun)	1 Edinburgh
McLeod, Tom	2014	2015	Craigie Symington linked with Prestwick: South	10 Ayr

Mateos, Margaret B.	2018		Dunfermline: St Leonard's	24	Dunfermline
Maxwell, David	2014	—	—	16	Glasgow
Michie, Margaret (Mrs)	2013	—	Loch Leven Parish Grouping	28	Perth
Millar, Ian J. BA	2020		Craigrownie linked with Garelochhead linked with Rosneath: St Modan's	14	Clyde
Mitchell, Valerie A. MA FSA	2019		Meldrum and Bourtie	33	Gordon
Morrison, Fiona S. BA	2019		Inverness: St Columba	37	Inverness
Morrison, John A. BSc BA PGCE	2013	2020	Dallas linked with Forres: St Leonard's linked with Rafford	35	Moray
Muirhead, Morag Y. (Mrs)	2013		Fort William: Duncansburgh MacIntosh linked with Kilmonivaig	38	Lochaber
Munro, Irene BA	2019	2017	Presbytery-wide	39	Ross
Murphy, Jim	2014		East Kilbride: Mossneuk	17	Hamilton
Nicol, Robert D. MA	2013		—	27	Dunkeld and Meigle
Nutter, Margaret A.E. BA BD MFPh	2017	2019	Presbytery-wide	14	Clyde
Palmer, Sonia RGN	2018		Elgin: St Giles' and St Columba's South	35	Moray
Porteous, Brian W. BSc DipCS	2013		Kirkcaldy: Torbain	25	Kirkcaldy
Prentice, Martin W.M.	2018		Flotta linked with Hoy and Walls linked with Orphir and Stenness	45	Orkney
Quilter, Alison	2017	—	Polbeth Harwood linked with West Kirk of Calder	2	West Lothian
Rattenbury, Carol	2013	—	Rosskeen	39	Ross
Sarle, Andrew BSc BD	2005		Falkirk: Bainsford	22	Falkirk
Sharp, James	2015	2013	Presbytery Clerk, International Charges	48	International Charges
Somervi, Joseph K. BSc MSc PhD MRICS MRTPI MIEMA CertCRS		2018	Aberdeen: Bridge of Don Oldmachar	31	Aberdeen and Shetland
Steele, Grace M.F. MA BTh	2014	—	—	27	Dunkeld and Meigle
Stevenson, Stuart	2011	—	—	14	Clyde
Stewart, Heather (Mrs)	2013		Latheron	41	Caithness
Stewart, William	2015	2017	Presbytery-wide	34	Buchan
Stobo, Mary J. (Mrs) BA	2013	2016	Community Healthcare Chaplain	40	Sutherland
Stott, Anne M.	2019		Presbytery Pioneer Worker, Bertha Park	28	Perth
Strachan, Pamela D. (Lady) MA (Cantab)	2015		Eddleston linked with Peebles: Old	4	Melrose and Peebles
Strachan, Willie D. MBA DipY&C	2015		Dundee: Lochee	29	Dundee
Sturrock, Roger D. (Prof.) BD MD FCRP	2014		Glasgow: Kelvinside Hillhead linked with Glasgow: Wellington	16	Glasgow
Thomson, Mary Ellen (Mrs)	2014		Presbytery Chaplain to Care Homes	36	Abernethy
Thorburn, Susan (Mrs) MTh	2013		—	28	Perth
Thorne, Joan I. BA CertCS	2014	—	Dyce	31	Aberdeen and Shetland
Tweedie, Fiona J. BSc PhD	2014	2014	Mission Statistics Co-ordinator, Church Offices	1	Edinburgh
Wallace, Mhairi (Mrs)	2017	2017	Kirkmichael, Tinwald and Torthorwald	8	Dumfries and Galloway
Watson, Michael D.	2019	2019	Athelstaneford linked with Whitekirk and Tyninghame	3	Lothian
Watt, Kim	2015		Presbytery-wide	11	Irvine and Kilmarnock
Welsh, Rita M. BA PhD	2017		Edinburgh: Holy Trinity	1	Edinburgh
Whillis, David (Dr) DipHE	2020		Presbytery-wide minister to over 60s community	37	Inverness
White, Anne W. BA DipTh	2018		Falkirk: Grahamston United	22	Falkirk

ORDAINED LOCAL MINISTERS (Retired)

Those who are retired and registered under the Registration of Ministries Act (Act 2, 2017, as amended) as 'O' or 'R' (Retaining). Contact details may be found under the Presbytery in Section 5 to which an OLM belongs.

NAME	ORD	RET	PRESBYTERY
Anderson, David M. MSc FCOptom	1984	2018	38 Lochaber
Brown, Kathryn I. (Mrs)	2014	2019	22 Falkirk
Dee, Oonagh	2014	2019	8 Dumfries and Kirkcudbright
Duncan, Esme (Miss)	2013	2017	41 Caithness
Edwards, Dougal BTh	2013	2017	30 Angus
Kiehlmann, Peter BA (Dr)	2016	2018	47 England (not a member of Presbytery) PKiehlmann@churchofscotland.org.uk
Mack, Lynne (Mrs)	2013	2019	23 Stirling
Mathers, Alexena (Sandra)	2015	2018	22 Falkirk
McAllister, Anne C. (Mrs) BSc DipEd CCS	2013	2016	11 Irvine and Kilmarnock
McLaughlin, Cathie H. (Mrs)	2014	2018	16 Glasgow
Rennie, Lyall	2014	2019	41 Caithness
Robertson, Ishbel A.R. MA BD	2013	2018	14 Clyde

LIST B – AUXILIARY MINISTERS

Those engaged in active service. Contact details may be found under the Presbytery in Section 5 to which an Auxiliary Minister belongs.

NAME	ORD	APP	APPOINTMENT	PRESBYTERY
Binks, Mike	2007	2015	Churches Together in Corby	47 England
Buck, Maxine	2007	2015	Presbytery-wide	17 Hamilton
Campbell, Gordon A. MA BD CDipAF DipHSM CMgr MCMI MIHM AssocCIPD AFRIN ARSGS FRGS FSAScot	2001	2004	An Honorary Chaplain, University of Dundee	29 Dundee
Cumming, Alistair MSc CCS FInstLM FLPI	2010	2013	Presbytery Clerk, England	47 England
Gardner, Hilary M. (Miss)	2010	2018	Lairg linked with Rogart	40 Sutherland
Kemp, Tina MA	2005	2017	Helensburgh linked with Rhu and Shandon	14 Clyde
Kinnear, Marion (Mrs) BD	2009	----	----	38 Lochaber
Macdonald, Michael J.	2004	2014	Alness	39 Ross

Mack, Elizabeth A. (Miss) DipPE	1994	2018	Lochend and New Abbey	8 Dumfries and Kirkcudbright
Manson, Eileen (Mrs) DipCE	1994	2017	Greenock: St Ninian's	14 Clyde
Mather, James BA DipArch MA MBA	2010		University Chaplain	47 England
Paterson, Andrew E. JP	1994	2016	Presbytery-wide	24 Dunfermline
Riddell, Thomas S. BSc CEng FIChemE	1993	1994	Linlithgow: St Michael's	2 West Lothian
Shearer, Anne F. BA DipEd	2010	2018	Alva	23 Stirling
Walker, Linda	2008	2014	Presbytery-wide	16 Glasgow
Wandrum, David C.	1993	2017	Carriden	22 Falkirk
Wilkie, Robert F.	2011	2012	Perth: Craigie and Moncrieffe	28 Perth

AUXILIARY MINISTERS (Retired)

Those who are retired and registered under the Registration of Ministries Act (Act 2, 2017, as amended) as 'O', 'R' (Retaining) or 'I' (Inactive). Only those 'Inactive' Auxiliary Ministers who have given consent under the GDPR to publication of their details are included. Contact details may be found under the Presbytery in Section 5 to which an Auxiliary Minister belongs.

NAME	ORD	RET	PRESBYTERY
Attenburrow, Anne BSc MB ChB	2006	2018	35 Moray
Birch, James PgDip FRSA FIOC	2001	2007	16 Glasgow
Brown, Elizabeth (Mrs) JP RGN	1996	2007	28 Perth
Cameron, Ann J. (Mrs) CertCS DCE TEFL	2005	2019	14 Clyde
Cloggie, June (Mrs)	1997	2006	23 Stirling
Craggs, Sheila (Mrs)	2001	2016	33 Gordon
Fletcher, Timothy E. G. BA FCMA PGDipCM MTh	1998	2019	28 Perth
Griffiths, Ruth I. (Mrs)	2004	2020	19 Argyll
Harrison, Cameron	2006	2011	26 St Andrews
Howie, Marion L.K. (Mrs) MA ARCS	1992	2016	12 Ardrossan
Jackson, Nancy	2009	—	10 Ayr
Kay, Elizabeth (Miss) DipYCS	1993	2007	29 Dundee
Landale, William S.	2005	2016	5 Duns
Lunn, Dorothy I. M.	2002	2017	47 England
McAlpine, John BSc	1988	2004	17 Hamilton (not member of Presbytery) Braeside, 201 Bonkle Road, Newmains, Wishaw ML2 9AA 01698 384610
MacDonald, Kenneth BA MA	2001	2006	16 Glasgow
MacFadyen, Anne M. (Mrs) BSc BD FSAScot	1995	2003	16 Glasgow
Mailer, Colin M.	1996	2005	22 Falkirk (not member of Presbytery) 25 Saltcoats Drive, Grangemouth FK3 9JP 01324 712401
Moore, Douglas T.	2003	2019	10 Ayr

Morrison, Donald John	2001	2019	43 Uist
Paterson, Maureen (Mrs) BSc	1992	2010	25 Kirkcaldy
Phillippo, Michael MTh BSc BVetMed MRCVS	2003	2011	31 Aberdeen and Shetland
Pot, Joost BSc	1992	2004	48 International Charges (not member of Presbytery) joostpot@gmail.com
Robson, Brenda PhD	2005	2019	2 West Lothian (not a member of Presbytery) 22 Ratho Park Road, Ratho, Newbridge EH28 8NY BRobson@churchofscotland.org.uk 0131 281 9511
Shaw, Catherine A.M. MA	1998	2006	11 Irvine and Kilmarnock
Zambonini, James LIADip	1997	2015	17 Hamilton

LIST C – THE DIACONATE

Those engaged in active service. Contact details may be found under the Presbytery in Section 5 to which a Deacon belongs.

Prior to the General Assembly of 2002, Deacons were commissioned. In 2002 existing Deacons were ordained, as have been those subsequently.

NAME	ORD	APP	APPOINTMENT	PRESBYTERY
Beck, Isobel BD DCS	2014	2016	Kilwinning: Abbey	12 Ardrossan
Blair, Fiona (Miss) DCS	1994	2015	Beith	12 Ardrossan
Brydson, Angela (Mrs) DCS	2015	2014	Lochmaben, Moffat and Lockerbie Grouping	7 Annandale and Eskdale
Cathcart, John Paul (Mr) DCS	2000	2017	Glasgow: Castlemilk	16 Glasgow
Corrie, Margaret (Miss) DCS	1989	2013	Armadale	2 West Lothian
Crawford, Morag (Miss) MSc DCS	1977	1998	Rosyth	24 Dunfermline
Crocker, Liz (Mrs) DipComEd DCS	1985	2015	Edinburgh: Tron Kirk (Gilmerton and Moredun)	1 Edinburgh
Cuthbertson, Valerie (Miss) DipTMus DCS	2003		Cumbernauld: Old	22 Falkirk
Evans, Mark (Mr) BSc MSc DCS	1988	2006	Head of Spiritual Care and Bereavement Lead, NHS Fife	1 Edinburgh
Gargrave, Mary S. (Mrs) DCS	1989	2002	Glasgow: Carnwadric	16 Glasgow
Getliffe, Dot L.J. (Mrs) BA BD DipEd DCS	2006	2019	Inverness: Old High St Stephen's	37 Inverness
Gilroy, Lorraine (Mrs) DCS	1988		—	17 Hamilton
Hamilton, James (Mr) DCS	1997	2000	Glasgow: Maryhill	16 Glasgow
Hamilton, Karen M. (Mrs) DCS	1995	2014	Glasgow: Cambuslang	16 Glasgow
Herbert, Claire BD DCS	2019		Chaplain, Lodging House Mission, Glasgow	16 Glasgow
Love, Joanna R. (Ms) BSc DCS	1992	2009	Iona Community: Wild Goose Resource Group	16 Glasgow
Lyall, Ann (Miss) DCS	1980	2019	Glasgow: Baillieston Mure Memorial linked with Baillieston St Andrew's; and Govan and Linthouse	16 Glasgow
MacDonald, Anne (Miss) BA DCS	1980	2002	Healthcare Chaplain, Glasgow Royal Infirmary	16 Glasgow
McIntosh, Kay (Mrs) DCS	1990	2018	Edinburgh: Mayfield Salisbury	2 West Lothian
McPheat, Elspeth (Miss) DCS	1985	2001	CrossReach: Manager, St Margaret's House, Polmont	1 Edinburgh

Name	COM/ORD	RET	Charge	Presbytery
Nicholson, David (Mr) DCS	1994	1993	Cumbernauld: Kildrum	22 Falkirk
Pennykid, Gordon J. BD DCS	2015	2018	Chaplain, HM Prison Edinburgh	1 Edinburgh
Porter, Jean T. (Mrs) BD DCS	2006	2008	Stirling: St Mark's	23 Stirling
Robertson, Pauline (Mrs) BA CertTheol BD DCS	2003	2016	Port Chaplain, Sailors' Society	1 Edinburgh
Scott, Pamela (Mrs) BD DCS	2017	2017	Lochgelly and Benarty: St Serf's	24 Dunfermline
Thomson, Jacqueline (Mrs) MTh DCS	2004	2008	Buckhaven and Wemyss	25 Kirkcaldy
Wallace, Catherine (Mrs) PGDipC DCS	1987	2017	Honorary Secretary, Diaconate Council	28 Perth
Wright, Lynda (Miss) BEd DCS	1979	2016	Community Chaplaincy Listening Co-ordinator, NHS Fife	25 Kirkcaldy

THE DIACONATE (Registered as Retaining or Inactive)

Those who are retired and registered under the Registration of Ministries Act (Act 2, 2017, as amended) as 'Retaining' or 'Inactive.' Only those 'Inactive' Deacons who have given consent under the GDPR to publication of their details are included. Contact details may be found under the Presbytery in Section 5 to which a Deacon belongs. Where a retired Deacon does not have a seat on Presbytery, contact details are given here. The list is shorter than in previous years, as some have not registered under the new arrangements.

NAME	COM/ORD	RET	PRESBYTERY
Allan, Jean (Mrs) DCS	1989	2011	29 Dundee
Beaton, Margaret S. (Miss) DCS	1989	2015	16 Glasgow
Bell, Sandra L.N. (Mrs) DCS	2001		39 Ross (not a member of Presbytery) 4 Munro Terrace, Rosemarkie, Fortrose IV10 8UR
Buchanan, Marion (Mrs) MA DCS	1983	2019	3 Lothian (not a member of Presbytery) 40 Links View, Port Seton, Prestonpans EH32 0EZ 01875 814632
Craw, John (Mr) DCS	1998	2009	37 Inverness
Dunnett, Linda (Mrs) BA DCS	1976	2016	23 Stirling
Gordon, Margaret (Mrs) DCS	1998	2012	1 Edinburgh
Gray, Christine M. (Mrs) DCS	1969	2003	16 Glasgow (not a member of Presbytery) 11 Woodside Avenue, Thornliebank, Glasgow G46 7HR 0141 571 1008
Gray, Greta (Miss) DCS	1992	2014	14 Clyde
Hughes, Helen (Miss) DCS	1977	2008	16 Glasgow
Johnston, Mary (Miss) DCS	1988	2003	14 Clyde (not a member of Presbytery) 19 Lounsdale Drive, Paisley PA2 9ED 0141 849 1615
King, Margaret MA DCS	2002	2012	35 Moray
Lundie, Ann V. (Miss) DCS	1972	2007	31 Aberdeen and Shetland
McCully, M. Isobel (Miss) DCS	1974	1999	14 Clyde (not a member of Presbytery) 10 Broadstone Avenue, Port Glasgow PA14 5BB 01475 742240 mi.mccully@btinternet.com
Mackay, Kenneth D. DCS	1996	2020	27 Dunkeld and Meigle
MacKinnon, Ronald M. (Mr) DCS	1996	2012	12 Ardrossan
McLaren, Glenda M. (Ms) DCS	1990	2020	2 West Lothian

NAME			ADDRESS
Maclean, Donald A. (Mr) DCS	1988	1990	44 Lewis
McLellan, Margaret DCS	1986	2018	16 Glasgow
McNaughton, Janette (Miss) DCS	1982	2007	16 Glasgow (not a member of Presbytery) 4 Dunellan Avenue, Moodiesburn, Glasgow G69 0GB 01236 870180
Merrilees, Ann (Miss) DCS	1994	2006	1 Edinburgh (not a member of Presbytery) 7/1 Slaeside, Balerno EH14 7HL 0131 449 3325 amerrilees@gmail.com
Miller, Elsie M. (Miss) DCS	1974	2001	22 Falkirk
Mitchell, Joyce (Mrs) DCS	1994	2010	37 Inverness
Mulligan, Anne MA DCS	1974	2013	1 Edinburgh
Munro, Patricia BSc DCS	1986	2016	28 Perth
Nicol, Joyce (Mrs) BA DCS	1974	2006	14 Clyde
Ogilvie, Colin (Mr) BA DCS	1998	2015	17 Hamilton
Philip, Elizabeth (Mrs) MA BA PGCSE DCS	2007	2018	28 Perth
Rennie, Agnes M. (Miss) DCS	1974	2012	1 Edinburgh
Rose, Lewis (Mr) DCS	1993	2010	29 Dundee
Ross, Duncan (Mr) DCS	1996	2015	14 Clyde
Smith, Catherine (Mrs) DCS	1964	2003	31 Aberdeen and Shetland
Steele, Marilynn J. (Mrs) BD DCS	1999	2012	3 Lothian
Steven, Gordon R. BD DCS	1997	2012	3 Lothian
Stewart, Marion G. (Miss) DCS	1991	2019	14 Clyde (not a member of Presbytery) 34 The Shores, Skelmorlie PA17 5AZ m313stewart@btinternet.com 01475 520062
Tait, Agnes (Mrs) DCS	1995	2014	17 Hamilton
Teague, Yvonne (Mrs) DCS	1965	2002	1 Edinburgh
Urquhart, Barbara (Mrs) DCS	1986	2017	11 Irvine and Kilmarnock
Wallace, Sheila D. (Mrs) BA BD DCS	2009	2020	27 Dunkeld and Meigle
Wilson, Muriel (Miss) MA BD DCS	1997	2011	10 Ayr

LIST D – MINISTERS NOT IN PRESBYTERIES REGISTERED AS RETAINING OR EMPLOYED

Those who are not members of a Presbytery but, under the Registration of Ministries Act (Act 2, 2017, as amended), are registered as 'Retaining' and authorised to perform the functions of ministry outwith an appointment covered by Category O or Category E. This list also includes a few ministers registered as 'Employed' (or 'O' for up to 3 years) who are not members of a Presbytery. The list is shorter than in previous years, as some have not registered under the new arrangements.

NAME	ORD	ADDRESS	TEL	PRES
Aitken, Ewan R. BA BD	1992	159 Restalrig Avenue, Edinburgh EH7 6PJ	0131 467 1660	1
Anderson, David MA BD	1975	Rowan Cottage, Aberlour Gardens, Aberlour AB38 9LD maurvid@hotmail.com	01340 871906	35

Name	Year	Address / Email	Phone	No.
Anderson, Susan M. (Mrs) BD	1997	32 Murrayfield, Bishopbriggs, Glasgow G64 3DS / susanbbriggs32@gmail.com	0141 772 6338	16
Auld, A. Graeme (Prof.) MA BD PhD DLit FSAScot FRSE	1973	Nether Swanshiel, Hobkirk, Bonchester Bridge, Hawick TD9 8JU / a.g.auld@ed.ac.uk	01450 860636	6
Barclay, Neil W. BSc BEd BD	1986	4 Gibsongray Street, Falkirk FK2 7LN / neil.barclay@virginmedia.com	01324 874681	22
Bardgett, Frank D. MA BD PhD	1987	Tigh an Iasgair, Street of Kincardine, Boat of Garten PH24 3BY / iasgair1@icloud.com	01479 831751	36
Black, James S.	1976	7 Breck Terrace, Penicuik EH26 0RJ / jsb.black@btopenworld.com	01968 677559	3
Blackley, Jane M. MA BD	2009	38 Garvel Road, Milngavie, Glasgow G62 7JE	0141 931 5344	14
Bradley, Andrew W. BD	1975	Flat 1/1, 38 Cairnhill View, Bearsden, Glasgow G61 1RP / andrewwbradley@hotmail.com		16
Brown, Robert F. MA BD ThM	1971	55 Hilton Drive, Aberdeen AB24 4NJ / Bjacob546@aol.com	01224 491451	31
Cowieson, Roy J. BD	1979	22 The Paddock, Hamilton ML3 0RB / arjay1232@gmail.com	001 250 650 7568	13
Currie, David E.P. BSc BD	1983	42 Onslow Gardens, Muswell Hill, London N10 3JX / davidepcurrie@gmail.com	01355 248510	17
Davidson, Mark R. MA BD STM PhD RN	2005	The Manse, Main Street, Kippen FK8 3DN / mark.davidson122@mod.gov.uk	01786 871249	
Donaghy, Leslie G. BD DipMin PG DipPsych PhD FSAScot	1990	53 Oak Avenue, East Kilbride G75 9ED / leslie@donaghy.org.uk	07809 484812	14
Douglas, Colin R. MA BD STM	1969	34 West Pilton Gardens, Edinburgh EH4 4EQ / colin.r.douglas@gmail.com	0131 551 3808	1
Drake, Wendy F. (Mrs) BD	1978	21 William Black Place, South Queensferry EH30 9QR / revwdrake@hotmail.co.uk	0131 331 1520	1
Drummond, Norman W. (Prof.) CBE MA BD DUniv FRSE	1976	c/o Columba 1400 Ltd., Staffin, Isle of Skye IV51 9JY	01478 611400	42
Espie, Howard	2011	1 Sprucebank Avenue, Langbank, Port Glasgow PA14 6YX / howardespie.me.com	01475 540391	1
Finlay, Quintin BA BD	1975	Ivy Cottage, Greenlees Farm, Kelso TD5 8BT / ronniegall@live.com	07901 981171	6
Gall, Ronald BSc BD	1985	7 North Esk Road, Edzell, Brechin DD9 7TW	01356 647870	30
Gauld, Beverly G.D.D. MA BD	1972	7 Rowan View, Lanark ML11 9FQ / jan.gillies@yahoo.com	01555 665765	13
Gillies, Janet E. BD	1998	33 Castle Road, Stirling FK9 5JD	01786 446222	3
Gordon, Elinor J. (Miss) BD	1988	6 Balgibbon Drive, Callander FK17 8EU / elinorgordon@btinternet.com	01877 331049	23
Grainger, Alison J. BD	1995	2 Hareburn Avenue, Avonbridge, Falkirk FK1 2NR / revajgrainger@btinternet.com	01324 861632	2
Green, Alex H. MA BD	1986	44 Laburnum Drive, Milton of Campsie, Glasgow G66 8HY / lesvert@btinternet.com	01360 313001	16

Name	Year	Address / Email	Phone	
Groves, Ian B. BD CPS	1989	28 Parkhill Circle, Dyce, Aberdeen AB21 7FN ian@thegroves.me.uk	01224 774380	31
Hamilton, Helen (Miss) BD	1991	The Cottage, West Tilbouries, Maryculter, Aberdeen AB12 5GD helenhamilton125@gmail.com	01224 739632	32
Harper, Anne J.M. (Miss) BD STM MTh CertSocPsych	1979	122 Greenock Road, Bishopton PA7 5AS	01505 862466	16
Haslett, Howard J. BA BD	1972	26 The Maltings, Haddington EH41 4EF howard.haslett@btinternet.com	01620 481208	3
Henderson, J. Mary MA BD DipEd PhD	1990	8 Miller Terrace, St Monans KY10 2BB jmary.henderson1@gmail.com	01333 730138	26
Hobson, Diane L. (Mrs) BA BD	2002	Flat 3, Marldon Cross Hill, Marldon, Paignton TQ3 1NE diane.hobson@me.com	07850 962007	31
Hudson, Eric V. LTh	1971	2 Murrayfield Drive, Bearsden, Glasgow G61 1JE	0141 942 6110	14
Hutchison, Alison M. (Mrs) BD DipMin	1988	Ashfield, Drumoak, Banchory AB31 5AG ahutch@hotmail.co.uk	01330 811309	32
Kerr, Hugh F. MA BD	1968	134C Great Western Road, Aberdeen AB10 6QE	01224 580091	16
Lawrie, Robert M. BD MSc DipMin LLCM(TD) MCMI FCMI	1994	West Benview, Main Road, Langbank PA14 6XP revrmlawrie@gmail.com	01475 540240 07789 824479	14
Lusk, Alastair S. BD	1974	9 MacFie Place, Stewartfield, East Kilbride, Glasgow G74 4TY	01890 885946	17
McHaffie, Robin D. BD	1979	Shepherd's Cottage, Castle Heaton, Cornhill-on-Tweed TD12 4XQ robinmchaffie@btinternet.com		5
MacKay, Alan H. BD	1974	Flat 1/1, 18 Newburgh Street, Glasgow G43 2XR alanmackay@aol.com	0141 632 0527	16
McKay, Johnston R. MA BA PhD	1969	15 Montgomerie Avenue, Fairlie, Largs KA29 0EE johnston.mckay@btopenworld.com	01475 568802	16
McKean, Alan T. BD CertMin	1982	15 Park Road, Kirn, Dunoon PA23 8JL	01369 700016	39
MacLaine, Marilyn (Mrs) LTh	1995	37 Bankton Brae, Livingston EH54 9LA marilynmaclaine@btinternet.com	01506 400619	2
McLean, Gordon LTh	1972	Beinn Dhorain, Kinnettas Square, Strathpeffer IV14 9BD gmaclean@hotmail.co.uk	01997 421380	39
McWilliam, Thomas M. MA BD	1964	Flat 3, 13 Culduthel Road, Inverness IV2 4AG tommcw@tommcwl.plus.com	01463 718981	39
Messeder, Lee BD PgDipMin	1988	59 Miles End, Cavalry Park, Kilsyth G65 0BH lee.messeder@gmail.com	07469 965934	16
Monteith, W. Graham MA BD BPhil PhD	1974	20/3 Grandfield, Edinburgh EH6 4TL	0131 552 2564	1
Muckart, Graeme W.M. MTh MSc FSAScot	1983	Kildale, Clashmore, Dornoch IV25 3RG gw2m.kildale@gmail.com	01862 881715	40
Muir, Margaret A. (Miss) MA LLB BD	1989	59/4 South Beechwood, Edinburgh EH12 5YS	0131 313 3240	1
Munro, Flora J. BD DMin	1993	87 Gairn Terrace, Aberdeen AB10 6AY floramunro@aol.com	07762 966393	31

Name		Address / Email	Tel	No.
Murray, George M.	MTh	6 Mayfield, Lesmahagow ML11 0FH george.murray7@gmail.com	01555 895216	16
Newell, Alison M. (Mrs)	BD	1A Inverleith Terrace, Edinburgh EH3 5NS alinewell@aol.com	0131 556 3505	1
Nicholson, Thomas S.	BD DPS	Sandy Hill, St Margaret's Hope, Orkney KW17 2RN TNicholson@churchofscotland.org.uk		45
Niven, William W.	LTh	4 Obsdale Park, Alness IV17 0TP	01349 884053	39
Parker, Carol Anne (Mrs)	BEd BD	The Cottages, Dornoch Firth Caravan Park, Meikle Ferry South, Tain IV19 1JX CParker@churchofscotland.org.uk	01862 892292	39
Patterson, Philip W.	BMus BD	PPatterson@churchofscotland.org.uk	0131 664 0673	28
Penman, Iain D.	BD	33/5 Carnbee Avenue, Edinburgh EH16 6GA iainpenmanklm@aol.com	07931 993427	1
Pieterse, Ben	BA BTh LTh	15 Bakeoven Close, Seaforth Sound, Simon's Town 7975, South Africa benhp1@gmail.com		25
Provan, Iain W. (Prof.)	MA BA PhD	Regent College, 5800 University Boulevard, Vancouver BC V6T 2E4, Canada	001 604 224 3245	1
Robertson, Blair	MA BD ThM	West End Guest House, 282 High Street, Elgin IV30 1AG blair.robertson@tiscali.co.uk	01343 549629	35
Roderick, Maggie R.	BA BD FRSA FTSI	34 Craiglea, Stirling FK9 5EE MRoderick@churchofscotland.org.uk	01786 478113	23
Saunders, Keith	BD	1/2, 10 Rutherford Drive, Lenzie G66 3US revchap53@hotmail.com	0141 558 4338	16
Scouler, Michael D.	MBE BSc BD	Head of Spiritual Care, NHS Borders, Chaplaincy Centre, Borders General Hospital, Melrose TD6 9BS michael.scouler@borders.scot.nhs.uk	01896 826565	6
Shackleton, Scott J.S. (Prof.) QCVS BA BD PhD RN		Deputy Chaplain of the Fleet, Naval Command HQ, MP1.2 Leach Building, Whale Island, Portsmouth PO2 8BY scott.shackleton674@mod.gov.uk		16
Shanks, Norman J.	MA BD DD	1 Marchmont Terrace, Glasgow G12 9LT rufuski@btinternet.com	0141 339 4421	16
Smith, Albert E.	BD	25 Alloway Drive, Paisley PA2 7DS aesmith42@googlemail.com	0141 533 5879	14
Smith, Elizabeth (Mrs)	BD	smithrev44@gmail.com	01770 600961	1
Smith, Hilary W.	BD DipMin MTh PhD	oxfordsmith28@yahoo.co.nz	0064 21 0283 5435	35
Smith, Ronald W.	BA BEd BD	1F1, 2 Middlefield, Edinburgh EH7 4PF	0131 553 1174 07900 896954	1
Smith, William A.	LTh	82 Ashgrove Road West, Aberdeen AB16 5EE bill2us@aol.com	01224 681866	31
Spence, Sheila M. (Mrs)	MA BD	12 Machan Avenue, Larkhall ML9 2HE	01698 310370	17
Stewart, Charles E.	BSc BD MTh PhD	105 Sinclair Street, Helensburgh G84 9HY c.e.stewart@btinternet.com	01436 678113	14
Stewart, Fraser M.C.	BSc BD	12a Crowlista, Uig, Isle of Lewis HS2 9JF fraserstewart1955@hotmail.com	01851 672413	44

NAME	ORD	ADDRESS	TEL	PRES
Stewart, Margaret L. (Mrs) BSc MB ChB BD	1985	28 Inch Crescent, Bathgate EH48 1EU famstewart@ormail.co.uk	01506 653428	2
Storrar, William F. (Prof.) MA BD PhD	1984	Director, Center of Theological Inquiry, 50 Stockton Street, Princeton, NJ 08540, USA		1
Strachan, Alexander E. MA BD	1974	2 Leafield Road, Dumfries DG1 2DS aestrachan@aol.com	01387 279460	8
Strachan, David G. BD DPS	1978	24 Kennay Place, Aberdeen AB15 8SG	01224 324032	31
Strachan, Ian M. MA BD	1959	'Cardenwell', Glen Drive, Dyce, Aberdeen AB21 7EN	01224 772028	31
Tallach, John MA MLitt	1970	29 Firthview Drive, Inverness IV3 8NS johntallach@talktalk.net	01463 418721	39
Thomson, Alexander BSc BD MPhil PhD	1973	4 Munro Street, Dornoch IV25 3RA alexander.thomson6@btinternet.com	01862 811650	40
Thrower, Charles D. BSc	1965	Grange House, Wester Grangemuir, Pittenweem, Anstruther KY10 2RB charlesandsteph@btinternet.com	01333 312631	26
Turnbull, John LTh	1994	4 Rathmor Road, Biggar ML12 6QG john.moiraturnbull62@btinternet.com	01899 221502	13
Turnbull, Julian S. BSc BD MSc CEng MBCS	1980	39 Suthren Yett, Prestonpans EH32 9GL jules@turnbull25.plus.com	01875 818305	3
Webster, John G. BSc	1964	Plane Tree, King's Cross, Brodick, Isle of Arran KA27 8RG	01770 700747	12
Whyte, Ron C. BD CPS	1990	13 Hillside Avenue, Kingussie PH21 1PA ron4xst@btinternet.com	01540 661101 07979 026973	36
Wood, James L.K.	1967	1 Glen Drive, Dyce, Aberdeen AB21 7EN	01224 722543	31

LIST E – MINISTERS NOT IN PRESBYTERIES (REGISTERED AS INACTIVE)

Those who are not members of a Presbytery but, under the Registration of Ministries Act (Act 2, 2017, as amended), are registered as 'Inactive'. Only those who have given consent under the GDPR to publication of their details are included. The list is shorter than in previous years, as some have not registered under the new arrangements.

NAME	ORD	ADDRESS	TEL	PRES
Abernethy, William LTh	1979	120/1 Willowbrae Road, Edinburgh EH8 7HW	0131 661 0390	1
Alexander, Douglas N. MA BD	1961	West Morningside, Main Road, Langbank, Port Glasgow PA4 6XP	01475 540249	14
Beckett, David M. BA BD	1964	31/1 Sciennes Road, Edinburgh EH9 1NT davidbeckett3@aol.com	0131 667 2672	1
Beautyman, Paul H. MA BD PGCCE	1993	59 Alexander Street, Dunoon PA23 7BB paulbeautyman67@gmail.com	07572 813695	19
Black, David W. BSc BD	1968	66 Bridge Street, Newbridge EH28 8SH dw.black666@yahoo.co.uk	0131 333 2609	2

Name	Year	Address	Phone	No.
Brown, Ronald H.	1974	6 Monktonhall Farm Cottages, Musselburgh EH21 6RZ	0131 653 2531	3
Campbell, J. Ewen R. MA BD	1967	20 St Margaret's Road, North Berwick EH39 4PJ	01620 890835 07840 353887	25
Chisholm, Archibald F. MA	1957	32 Seabank Road, Nairn IV12 4EU arch32@btinternet.com	01667 452001	37
Cook, John MA BD	1967	26 Silverknowes Court, Edinburgh EH4 5NR	0131 312 8447	1
Cowie, James M. BD	1977	24 Cowdrait, Burnmouth, Eyemouth TD14 5SW jimcowie@europe.com	01890 781394	5
Davidson, Ian M.P. MBE MA BD	1954	13/8 Craigend Park, Edinburgh EH16 5XX ian.m.p.davidson@btinternet.com	0131 664 0074	1
Dickson, Graham T. MA BD	1985	43 Hope Park Gardens, Bathgate EH48 2QT gtd194@googlemail.com	01506 237597	2
Donald, Robert M. BA LTh	1969	2 Blacklaw Drive, Birkhill, Dundee DD2 5RJ robandmoiradonald@yahoo.co.uk	01382 581337	29
Donaldson, Colin V.	1982	3A Playfair Terrace, St Andrews KY16 9HX colinmarion80@gmail.com	01334 472889	3
Ferguson, Ronald MA BD ThM DUniv	1972	Vinbreck, Orphir, Orkney KW17 2RE ronbluebrazil@aol.com	01856 811353	45
Forbes, John W.A. BD	1973	Little Ennochie Steading, Finzean, Banchory AB31 4LX jr6666@icloud.com	01330 850785	32
Gale, Ronald A.A. LTh	1982	Dorset contact via Clerk, Presbytery of Duns		5
Galloway, Kathy (Mrs) BD DD	1977	20 Hamilton Park Avenue, Glasgow G12 8UU kathygalloway200@btinternet.com	0141 357 4079	16
Gillon, D. Ritchie M. BD DipMin	1994	12 Fellhill Street, Ayr KA7 3JF revgillon@hotmail.com	01292 270018	10
Gordon, Laurie Y.	1960	1 Alder Drive, Portlethen, Aberdeen AB12 4WA	01224 782703	31
Grainger, Harvey L. LTh	1975	13 St Ronan's Crescent, Peterculter, Aberdeen AB14 0RL harveygrainger@btinternet.com	01224 739824	31
Hamilton, David S.M. MA BD STM	1958	Linfield, Milton of Lawton, Arbroath DD11 4RU dandmhamilton@btinternet.com	01241 238369	30
Harvey, W. John BA BD DD	1965	501 Shields Road, Glasgow G41 2RF jonmol@phonecoop.coop	0141 429 3774 07709 651335	16
Kingston, David V.F. BD DipPTh	1993	2 Cleuch Avenue, North Middleton, Gorebridge EH23 4RP	01875 822026	3
Ledgard, J. Christopher BA CertMin	1969	Streonshalh, 8 David Hume View, Chirnside, Duns TD11 3SX	01890 817124	5
Liddiard, F:G.B. MA	1957	34 Trinity Fields Crescent, Brechin DD9 6YF bernardliddiard@btinternet.com	01356 622966	30
Lithgow, Anne R. (Mrs) MA BD	1992	13 Cameron Park, Edinburgh EH16 5JY anne.lithgow@btinternet.com		1
Logan, Thomas M. LTh	1971	3 Duncan Court, Kilmarnock KA3 7TF thomasmlogan8@gmail.com	01563 524398	11
McAlister, D.J.B. MA BD PhD	1951	2 Duff Avenue, Moulin, Pitlochry PH16 5EN	01796 473591	27
McGillivray, A. Gordon MA BD STM	1951	36 Larchfield Neuk, Balerno EH14 7NL	0131 449 3901	1
McIntyre, Allan G. BD	1985	9a Templehill, Troon KA10 6BQ agmcintyre@lineone.com	07876 445626	10

Name	Year	Address / Email	Phone	No.
McLachlan, Fergus C. BD	1982	46 Queen Square, Glasgow G41 2AZ / whitegoldfm@gmail.com	07544 721032	16
Millar, Peter W. MA BD PhD	1971	6/5 Eitrickdale, Edinburgh EH3 5JN / ionacottage@hotmail.com	0131 557 0517	
Minto, Joan E. (Mrs) MA BD	1993	1 Lochaber Cottages, Forres IV36 2RL / joanminto.123@gmail.com	07800 669074	35
Murray, Douglas R. MA BD	1965	32 Forth Park, Bridge of Allan, Stirling FK9 5NT / d-smurray@supanet.com	01786 831081	23
Newlands, George M. (Prof.) MA BD PhD DLitt FRSA FRSE	1970	49 Highsett, Cambridge CB2 1NZ / gnewlsnds@icloud.com	01223 569984 / 07786 930941	16
Plate, Maria A.G. (Miss) BA LTh CQSW DSW	1983	Flat 29, 77 Barnton Park View, Edinburgh EH4 6EL / riaplate@gmail.com	0131 339 8539	1
Poole, Ann McColl (Mrs) DipEd ACE LTh	1983	Kirkside Cottage, Dyke, Forres IV36 2TF		35
Prentice, George BA BTh	1964	46 Victoria Gardens, Corsebar Road, Paisley PA2 9AQ / g.prentice04@talktalk.net	0141 842 1585	14
Ramsay, Alan MA	1967	12 Riverside Grove, Lochyside, Fort William PH33 7RD	01397 702054	38
Shannon, W.G. MA BD	1955	19 Knockard Road, Pitlochry PH16 5HJ	01796 473533	27
Sloan, Robert BD	1997	3 Gean Grove, Blairgowrie PH10 6TL	01250 875286	27
Spowart, Mary G. (Mrs) BD	1978	Aldersyde, St Abbs Road, Coldingham, Eyemouth TD14 5NR	01890 771697	5
Stirling, G. Alan S. MA	1960	97 Lochlann Road, Culloden, Inverness IV2 7HJ	01463 798313	37
Torrance, David W. MA BD	1955	38 Forth Street, North Berwick EH39 4JQ / torrance103@btinternet.com	01620 895109	3
Warner, Kenneth BD	1981	Kileaman, Clayock, Halkirk KW12 6UZ / wrmkenn@btinternet.com	01847 831825	41
Waugh, John L. LTh	1973	58 Wyvis Drive, Nairn IV12 4TP / jswaugh31@gmail.com	01667 456397	37
Webster, Brian G. BD BSc CEng MIET	1988	3/1 Cloch Court, 57 Albert Road, Gourock PA19 1NJ / revwebby@aol.com		14
Wilson, Andrew G.N. MA BD DMin	1977	Auchintarph, Coull, Tarland, Aboyne AB34 4TT / agn.wilson@gmail.com	01339 880918	32
Wilson, John M. (Ian) MA	1964	27 Bellfield Street, Edinburgh EH15 2BR / tom54wilson@aol.com	0131 669 5257	1
Wright, David L. MA BD	1957	84 Wyvis Drive, Nairn IV12 4TP	01667 451613	35

LIST F – HEALTH AND SOCIAL CARE CHAPLAINS

LOTHIAN

Head of Spiritual Care and Bereavement
Rev. Dr Duncan MacLaren; duncan.maclaren@nhs.net; 0131 242 1991
Spiritual Care Office: The Royal Infirmary of Edinburgh, 51 Little France Crescent, Edinburgh EH16 4SA
Full details of chaplains and contacts in all hospitals: www.nhslothian.scot.nhs.uk > Services > Spiritual Care > The Team

Chaplaincy team includes from the Church of Scotland:
Rev. Lynne MacMurchie, Royal Edinburgh Hospital, Community Mental Health, Astley Ainslie Hospital; lynne.macmurchie@nhslothian.scot.nhs.uk; 0131 537 6775
Rev. Georgina Nelson, St John's Hospital, Tippethill House Hospital; georgina.nelson@nhslothian.scot.nhs.uk; 01506 522188
Rev. Alistair Ridland, Western General, Ferryfield House; alistair.ridland@nhslothian.scot.nhs.uk; 0131 537 1400

Outwith NHS
Rev. Suzie Stark, St Columba's Hospice, 15 Boswall Road, Edinburgh EH5 3RW; SStark@churchofscotland.org.uk; 0131 551 1381

BORDERS

Head of Spiritual Care
Rev. Michael Scouler; michael.scouler@borders.scot.nhs.uk; 01896 826565
Spiritual Care Department: Chaplaincy Centre, Borders General Hospital, Melrose TD6 9BS; 01896 826564
Further information: www.nhsborders.scot.nhs.uk > Patients and Visitors > Our services > Chaplaincy Centre

DUMFRIES AND GALLOWAY

Spiritual Care and Wellbeing Lead
Rev. Dr Ewan Kelly, Dumfries and Galloway Royal Infirmary; ewan.kelly1@nhs.net; 01387 246246 Ext 31544
DGRI Sanctuary Office, Cargenbridge, Dumfries DG2 8RX
Further information: www.nhsdg.scot.nhs.uk > Focus on > Search > Chaplaincy

AYRSHIRE AND ARRAN

Service Lead for Chaplaincy and Staff Care
Rev. Judith A. Huggett, Crosshouse Hospital, Kilmarnock KA2 0BE; judith.huggett@aapct.scot.nhs.uk; 01563 577301

Chaplaincy Office: Ailsa Hospital, Dalmellington Road, Ayr KA6 6AB; 01292 610556
Further information: www.nhsaaa.net > Services A-Z > Chaplaincy service

LANARKSHIRE

Head of Spiritual Care and Wellbeing
Paul Graham, paul.graham@lanarkshire.scot.nhs.uk
Spiritual Care and Wellbeing Office: Law House, Airdrie Road, Carluke ML8 5EP; spiritualcare@lanarkshire.scot.nhs.uk; 01698 377637
Further information: www.nhslanarkshire.org.uk > Our services A-Z > Spiritual care

Chaplaincy team includes from Church of Scotland:
Rev. Ali Pandian, University Hospital Wishaw; 01698 366779

GREATER GLASGOW AND CLYDE

Lead Healthcare Chaplain: Dawn Allan; chaplains@ggc.scot.nhs.uk
Spiritual Care: The Sanctuary, Queen Elizabeth University Hospital, Govan Road, Glasgow G51 4TF; 0141 211 3026
Further information: www.nhsggc.org.uk > Services Directory > Spiritual Care

Chaplaincy team includes from Church of Scotland:
Anne MacDonald DCS, Glasgow Royal Infirmary; 0141 211 4661

FORTH VALLEY

Head of Spiritual Care: Tim Bennison
Spiritual Care Centre: Forth Valley Royal Hospital, Larbert FK5 4WR; 01324 566071
Further information: www.nhsforthvalley.com > Services A-Z > Spiritual Care Centre

Chaplaincy team includes from Church of Scotland:
Rev. Helen F. Christie, Forth Valley Hospitals

FIFE

Head of Spiritual Care and Bereavement Lead
Mr Mark Evans DCS, Department of Spiritual Care, Queen Margaret Hospital, Whitefield Road, Dunfermline KY12 0SU;
mark.evans59@nhs.net; 01383 623623 ext 24136

Victoria Hospital, Kirkcaldy: Chaplain's Office: 01592 648158 or 01592 729695
Queen Margaret Hospital, Dunfermline: Department of Spiritual Care: 01383 674136
Mental Health and Community Chaplain, Adamson and Stratheden Hospitals: 07976 918909
Glenrothes Community Hospital: Chaplain's Office: 01592 729675
Cameron Community Hospital: Chaplain's Office: 01592 648158
St Andrews Community Hospital: Rev Dr James Connolly; jamesconnolly@nhs.net; 07711 177655
Community Chaplaincy Listening Co-ordinator (NHS Fife): Miss Lynda Wright DCS; lynda.wright1@nhs.net; 07835 303395
Further information: www.nhsfife.org > Spiritual Care

TAYSIDE

Head of Spiritual Care: Rev. Alan Gibbon
The Wellbeing Centre, Royal Victoria Hospital, Dundee DD2 1SP: lynne.downie@nhs.net; 01382 423110
Further information: www.nhstayside.scot.nhs.uk > Our Services A-Z > Spiritual Care

GRAMPIAN

Lead Chaplain
Rev. Mark Rodgers, Chaplains' Office, Aberdeen Royal Infirmary, Foresterhill, Aberdeen AB25 2ZN; nhsg.chaplaincy@nhs.net; 01224 553166
Further information: www.nhsgrampian.co.uk > Home > Our services > A-Z > Spiritual Care

HIGHLAND

Lead Chaplain
Rev. Dr Derek Brown, Raigmore Hospital, Old Perth Road, Inverness IV2 3UJ; derek.brown1@nhs.net; 01463 704463
Further information: www.nhshighland.scot.nhs.uk/Services/Pages/Chaplaincy-Raigmore.aspx

WESTERN ISLES HEALTH BOARD

Lead Chaplain
Rev. T. K. Shadakshari, 23D Benside, Newmarket, Stornoway, Isle of Lewis HS2 0DZ; tk.shadakshari@nhs.net; (Office) 01851 704704; (Home) 01851 701727; (Mbl) 07403 697138

NHS SCOTLAND

Head of Programme, Health & Social Care Chaplaincy & Spiritual Care, NHS Education for Scotland
Rev. Canon Dr Iain Macritchie BSc BD STM PhD; iain.macritchie@nes.scot.nhs.uk; 01463 255705
NHS Education for Scotland, Centre for Health Sciences, Old Perth Road, Inverness IV2 3JH

Spiritual Care Specialist Research Lead
Rev. Iain J.M.Telfer, iain.telfer@nes.scot.nhs.uk; 01224 805120; 07554 222232
NHS Education for Scotland, Forest Grove House, Foresterhill Road, Aberdeen AB25 2ZP

Church of Scotland Chaplains in NHS ENGLAND
Rev. Dr Cameron H. Langlands, Head of Spiritual and Pastoral Care, South London and Maudsley NHS Foundation Trust, Maudsley Hospital, Denmark Road, London SE3 8AZ; Cameron.Langlands@slam.nhs.uk; 020 3228 2815; 07971 169791
Rev. Mairi F. Lovett, Chaplain, Royal Brompton Hospital, Sydney Sydney Street, London SW3 6NP; m.lovett@rbht.nhs.uk; 020 7351 8060
Rev. John K.S. McMahon, Head of Spiritual and Pastoral Care, West London NHS Trust, Broadmoor Hospital, Crowthorne, Berkshire RG45 7EG; john.mcmahonrev@westlondon.nhs.uk; 01344 754098

LIST G – CHAPLAINS TO HM FORCES

The three columns give dates of ordination and commissioning, and branch where the chaplain is serving: Royal Navy, Army, Royal Air Force, Royal Naval Reserve, Army Reserve, Royal Air Force Reserve, or where the person is an Officiating Chaplain to the Military.

NAME	ORD	COM	BCH	ADDRESS
Anderson, David P. BSc BD	2002	2007	A	Senior Chaplain, Infantry Training Centre, Vimy Barracks, Catterick Garrison DL9 3PS
Ashley-Emery, Stephen BD DPS	2006	2019	RN	Portsmouth Flotilla, The Chaplaincy, Rodney Block, HMS Nelson, Queen Street, Portsmouth PO1 3HH Stephen.Ashley-Emery100@mod.gov.uk 02392 723000
Begg, Richard J. MA BD	2008	2016	A	29 Explosive Ordnance Disposal and Search GSU, Carver Barracks, Wimbish, Saffron Walden CB10 2YA
Berry, Geoff T. BD BSc	2009	2012	A	3 SCOTS, Fort George, Ardersier, Inverness IV2 7TE
Blakey, Stephen A. BSc BD	1977	1977	OCM	Staff Chaplain, HQ Scotland, Forthside, Stirling FK7 7RR
Cobain, Alan R. BD	2000	2017	A	HQ 20 Armoured Infantry Brigade, Wing Barracks, Bulford SP4 9NA
Craig, Gordon T. BD DipMin	1988	1988	RAFR	Reserve Chaplain, RAF gordon.craig@ukoilandgaschaplaincy.com 01224 882600
Dalton, Mark F. BD DipMin RN	2002	2003	RN	The Chaplaincy, HMS Seahawk, Royal Naval Air Station Culdrose, Helston, Cornwall TR12 7RH mark.dalton242@mod.gov.uk
Davidson, Mark R. MA BD STM PhD RN	2005	2011	RN	The Chaplaincy, HMS Neptune, HM Naval Base Clyde, Faslane, Helensburgh G84 8HL mark.davidson122@mod.gov.uk
Duncan, John C. MBE BD MPhil	1987	2001	OCM	Waterloo Lines, Leuchars Station, St Andrews KY1 0JX
Frail, Nicola BLE MBA MDiv	2000	2012	A	HQ 1st Strike Brigade, Delhi Barracks, Tidworth SP9 7DX
Francis, James MBE BD PhD	2002	2009	A	SOI Chaplains, CM Comd Sp, Army Personnel Centre MP 413. Kentigern House, 65 Brown Street, Glasgow G2 8EX
Gardner, Neil N. MA BD	1991	1991	OCM	Edinburgh Universities Officers' Training Corps, 301 Colinton Road, Edinburgh EH13 0LA
Goodison, Michael J. BSc BD	2013	2013	A	2 YORKS, Somme Barracks, Catterick Garrison DL9 4LD

Name				Appointment / Address
Kellock, Chris N. MA BD	1998	2012	A	HQ 12 Armoured Infantry Brigade, Ward Barracks, Bulford, Wiltshire SP4 9NA
Kinsey, Louis BD DipMin TD	1991	1992	AR	205 (Scottish) Field Hospital (V), Graham House, Whitefield Road, Glasgow G51 6JU
Lancaster, Craig MA BD	2004	2011	RAF	Chaplaincy Centre, RAF Honington, Bury St Edmunds, Suffolk IP31 1EE craig.lancaster102@mod.gov.uk
MacKay, Stewart A. BA	2009	2009	A	New Entrant Regular Chaplain, c/o Padre Duncan Macpherson (see below)
MacKenzie, Hector M.	2008	2008	A	5 Regiment Royal Artillery, Marne Barracks, Catterick Garrison DL10 7NP
Mackenzie, Seoras L. BD	1996	1998	A	39 Engineer Regiment (Air Support), Kinloss Barracks, Kinloss, Forres IV36 3XL
McLay, Neil BA BD MTh	2006	2012	A	1 R Welsh, Lucknow Barracks, Lowa Road, Tidworth SP9 7BU
MacLeod, Rory N. BA BD	1986	1992	AR	154 Regiment RLC, Bothwell House, Elgin Street, Dunfermline KY12 7SB
Macpherson, Duncan J. BSc BD	1993	2002	A	Deputy Assistant Chaplain General, HQ 51 Infantry Brigade and HQ Scotland, Forthside, Stirling FK7 7RR
Mair, Michael J. BD	2014	2019	AR	32 (Scottish) Signal Regiment, 21 Jardine Street, Glasgow G20 6JU
Munro, Sheila BD	1995	2003	RAF	Chaplaincy Centre, RAF Cosford, Albrighton, Wolverhampton WV7 3EX sheila.munro781@mod.gov.uk
Rankin, Lisa-Jane BD CPS	2003		OCM	2 Bn Royal Regiment of Scotland, Glencorse Barracks, Penicuik EH26 0QH
Rowe, Christopher J. BA BD	2008	2008	AR	5 Military Intelligence Battalion, Redford Barracks, Colinton Road, Edinburgh EH13 0LA
Selemani, Ecilo LTh MTh	1993		OCM	51 Infantry Brigade and HQ Scotland, Forthside, Stirling FK7 7RR
Shackleton, Scott J.S. (Prof.) QCVS BA BD PhD RN	1993	2010	RN	Deputy Chaplain of the Fleet, Naval Command HQ, MP1.2 Leach Building, Whale Island, Portsmouth PO2 8BY scott.shackleton674@mod.gov.uk
Thom, David J. BD DipMin	1999	2015	A	3 Royal Horse Artillery, Albemarle Barracks, Harlaw Hill, Newcastle upon Tyne NE15 0RF
van Sittert, Paul BA BD	1997		A	32 Engineer Regiment, Marne Barracks, Catterick Garrison DL10 7NP
Young, David T. BA BD MTh	2007	2011	RNR	HMS Dalriada, Govan, Glasgow G51 3JH

ACF: Army Cadet Force

Blackwood, Keith T. BD DipMin	Regional Chaplain, Scotland & N. Ireland
Dicks, Shuna M. BSc BD	2 Bn The Highlanders, ACF, Cadet Training Centre, Rocksley Drive, Boddam, Peterhead AB42 3BA
McCulloch, Alen J.R. MA BD	2 Bn The Highlanders, ACF, Cadet Training Centre, Rocksley Drive, Boddam, Peterhead AB42 3BA
Mackenzie, Cameron BD	1 Highlanders Bn, ACF, Gordonville Road, Inverness IV2 4SU
Selemani, Ecilo LTh MTh	Lothian and Borders Bn, ACF, Drumshoreland House, Broxburn EH52 5PF
Swindells, Sean BD DipMin MTh	Glasgow and Lanark Bn, ACF, Gilbertfield Road, Cambuslang, Glasgow G72 8YP
Wilson, Fiona A. BD	Angus and Dundee Bn, ACF, Barry Buddon, Carnoustie DD7 7RY
	West Lowland Battalion, ACF, Fusilier House, Seaforth Road, Ayr KA8 9HX

ATC: Air Training Corps

Highland Wing

Wing Chaplain & 2405 Sqn	Alistair K. Ridland RAFAC	chaplain.sni@aircadets.org
52 (Aviemore) & 832 (Wester Ross) Sqn	Russel Smith	russanntwo@yahoo.co.uk
379 (County of Ross) Sqn	Ron C. Whyte	ron4xst@btinternet.com
432DF (Speyside) Sqn	Michael J. Macdonald	Michael.Macdonald@churchofscotland.org.uk
446 (Forres) Sqn	Robert J.M. Anderson	revrjmanderson-moray@outlook.com
1796 (Thurso) Sqn	Donald K. Prentice	DPrentice@churchofscotland.org.uk

North East Scotland Wing

Wing Chaplain & 107 (Aberdeen) Sqn	David J.B. Macartney	DMacartney@churchofscotland.org.uk
102 (Aberdeen Airport) Sqn	James L.K. Wood	nescot@aircadets.org
1298 (Huntly) Sqn	Nigel Parker	NParker@churchofscotland.org.uk
	Kay F. Gauld	KGauld@churchofscotland.org.uk

South East Scotland Wing

2288 (Montrose) Sqn	Ian A. McLean	IMcLean@churchofscotland.org.uk
2367 (Banchory) Sqn	Frank Ribbons	FRibbons@churchofscotland.org.uk
Wing Chaplain & 2450 (Dudhope) Sqn	C. Graham D. Taylor	AT Corps, MOD Leuchars, KY16 0JX
132 (North Berwick) Sqn	Neil J. Dougall	NDougall@churchofscotland.org.uk
775 (Burntisland) Sqn	Alan Sharp	Unity Hall, Links Place, Burntisland KY3 9DY
859 (Dalgety) Sqn	Christine M. Sime	CSime@churchofscotland.org.uk
870 (Dreghorn) Sqn, Edinburgh	Peter Nelson	PNelson@churchofscotland.org.uk
1370 (Leven) Sqn	Jacqueline Thomson DCS	Jacqueline.Thomson@churchofscotland.org.uk
1716 (Roxburgh) Sqn	Sheila W. Moir	SMoir@churchofscotland.org.uk
2345 (Leuchars) Sqn	John C. Duncan	JDuncan@churchofscotland.org.uk
2519 (Strathmore) Sqn	Thomas W. Tait	TA Centre, Union Street, Blairgowrie PH10 6BG
2535 (Livingston) Sqn	Nelu I. Balaj	NBalaj@churchofscotland.org.uk

West Scotland Wing

Wing & 1333 (Grangemouth Spitfire) Sqn	Aftab Gohar	AGohar@churchofscotland.org.uk
49F (Greenock) Sqn	Alan K. Sorensen	ASorensen@churchofscotland.org.uk
327 (Kilmarnock) Sqn	Kristina I. Hine	KHine@churchofscotland.org.uk
396 (Paisley) Sqn	Peter G. Gill	PGill@churchofscotland.org.uk
498 (Wishaw) Sqn	Ian Douglas (Mr)	ian@paphosab.demon.co.uk
867 (Denny) Sqn	F. Derek Gunn	RevDerekGunn@hotmail.com
1138 (Ardrossan) Sqn	Jonathan C. Fleming	JFleming@churchofscotland.org.uk
2166 (Hamilton) Sqn	I. Ross Blackman	RBlackman@churchofscotland.org.uk

SC: Sea Cadets

Campbell, Gordon MA BD	Sea Cadets Dundee, East Camperdown Street, Dundee DD1 3LG
Fletcher, Suzanne G. BA MDiv MA	Sea Cadets Dunbar, ACF Building, Castle Park Barracks, 33 North Road, Dunbar EH42 1EU
MacKay, Colin (Mr)	Sea Cadets Wick, The Scout Hall, Kirkhill, Wick KW1 4PN
May, John S. (Iain) BSc MBA BD	Sea Cadets Leith, Prince of Wales Dock, Leith, Edinburgh EH6 7DX
Robertson, Pauline DCS BA CertTheol	Sea Cadets Musselburgh, 9-11 South Street, Musselburgh EH21 6AT
Templeton, James L. BSc BD	Sea Cadets Methil, Harbour View, Methil KY8 3RF
Wallace, Douglas W. MA BD	Sea Cadets East Kilbride, Army Reserve Centre, Whitemoss, East Kilbride G74 2HP

LIST H – READERS

This list comprises active Readers only.

1. EDINBURGH

Devoy, Fiona (Mrs)	196 The Murrays Brae, Edinburgh EH17 8UH	fiona.devoy@yahoo.co.uk	0131 558 8210
Farrow, Edmund	14 Brunswick Terrace, Edinburgh EH7 5PG	edmundfarrow@blueyonder.co.uk	0131 664 2366
Jackson, Kate (Ms)	3 Kedslie Road, Edinburgh EH16 6NT	katejackson1252@gmail.com	0131 554 1326
Johnston, Alan	36 Foster Road, Penicuik EH26 0FL	alanacj2@gmail.com	07901 501819

Name	Address	Email	Phone
Kerrigan, Herbert A. (Prof.) MA LLB QC	Airdene, 20 Edinburgh Road, Dalkeith EH22 1JY	kerrigan@kerriganqc.com	0131 660 3007 07725 953772
Pearce, Martin J.	4 Corbiehill Avenue, Edinburgh EH4 5DR	martin.j.pearce@blueyonder.co.uk	0131 336 4864 07801 717222
Sherriffs, Irene (Mrs)	22/2 West Mill Bank, Edinburgh EH13 0QT	reenie.sherriffs@blueyonder.co.uk	0131 466 9530
Tew, Helen (Mrs)	5/5 Moat Drive, Edinburgh EH14 1NU	helentew9@gmail.com	07986 170802

2. WEST LOTHIAN

Elliott, Sarah (Miss)	105 Seafield Rows, Seafield, Bathgate EH47 7AW	sarah.elliott6@btopenworld.com	01506 654950
Galloway, Brenda (Dr)	16 Baron's Hill Court, Linlithgow EH49 7SP	dr.b.galloway82@gmail.com	01506 842069
Holden, Louise (Mrs)	Am Batnach, Easter Breich, West Calder EH55 8PP	louise.holden@btinternet.com	01506 873030
McFadzean, John	121 South Street, Armadale, Bathgate EH48 3JT	jmcfadzean2@gmail.com	01501 730260
Middleton, Alex	19 Cramond Place, Dalgety Bay KY11 9LS	alex.middleton@btinternet.com	01383 820800
Orr, Elizabeth (Mrs)	64a Marjoribanks Street, Bathgate EH48 1AL	liz-orr@hotmail.co.uk	01596 653116
Paxton, James	5 Main Street, Longridge, Bathgate EH47 8AE	jimpaxton1950@gmail.com	01501 772192
Wilkie, David	55 Goschen Place, Broxburn EH52 5JH	david-fmu_09@tiscali.co.uk	01506 238644

3. LOTHIAN

Name	Address	Email	Phone
Evans, W. John IEng MIIE(Elec)	Waterlily Cottage, 10 Fenton Steading, North Berwick EH39 5AF	jevans7is@hotmail.com	01620 842990
Hogg, David MA	82 Eskhill, Penicuik EH26 8DQ	hogg-d2@sky.com	01968 676350 07821 693946
Millan, Mary (Mrs)	33 Polton Vale, Loanhead EH20 9DF	marymillan@gmail.com	0131 440 1624 07814 466104
Trevor, A. Hugh MA MTh	29A Fidra Road, North Berwick EH39 4NE	htrevor@talktalk.net	01620 894924
Waugh, Jacqueline (Mrs)	15 Garleton Drive, Haddington EH41 3BL	jacqueline.waugh@yahoo.com	01620 825007
Yeoman, Edward T.N. FSAScot	75 Newhailes Crescent, Musselburgh EH21 6EF	edwardyeoman6@aol.com	0131 653 2291 07896 517666

4. MELROSE AND PEEBLES

Selkirk, Frances (Mrs)	21 Park Crescent, Newtown St Boswells, Melrose TD6 0QR	f.selkirk@hillview2selkirk.plus.com	01835 823669

5. DUNS

Landale, Alison (Mrs)	Green Hope Guest House, Ellemford, Duns TD11 3SG	alison@greenhope.co.uk	01361 890242

6. JEDBURGH

Findlay, Elizabeth (Mrs)	7e Rose Lane, Kelso TD5 7AP	findlay290@gmail.com	01573 226641
Knox, Dagmar (Mrs)	3 Stichill Road, Ednam, Kelso TD5 7QQ	dagmar.knox.riding@btinternet.com	01573 224883

7. ANNANDALE AND ESKDALE

Boncey, David	Redbrae, Beattock, Moffat DG10 9RF	david.boncey613@btinternet.com	01683 300613
Brown, Martin J.	Lochhouse Farm, Beattock, Moffat DG10 9SG	martin.j.brown1967@gmail.com	01683 300451

Name	Address	Email	Telephone
Brown, S. Jeffrey BA	Skara Brae, Holm Park, 8 Ballplay Road, Moffat DG10 9JU	sjbrown@btinternet.com	01683 220475
Dodds, Alan	Trinco, Battlehill, Annan DG12 6SN	alanandjen46@talktalk.net	01461 201235
Jackson, Susan (Mrs)	48 Springbells Road, Annan DG12 6LQ	peter-jackson24@sky.com	07498 714675
Morton, Andrew A. BSc	19 Sherwood Park, Lockerbie DG11 2DX	andrew_morton@mac.com	01576 203164

8. DUMFRIES AND KIRKCUDBRIGHT

Name	Address	Email	Telephone
Corson, Gwen (Mrs)	7 Sunnybrae, Borgue, Kirkcudbright DG46 4SJ	gwendolyn@hotmail.com	01557 870328
Matheson, David	44 Auchenkeld Avenue, Heathhall, Dumfries DG1 3QY	davidh.matheson44@btinternet.com	01387 252042
Monk, Geoffrey	Hilbre Cottage, Laurieston, Castle Douglas DG7 2PW		01644 450679

9. WIGTOWN AND STRANRAER

Name	Address	Email	Telephone
Cash, Marlane (Mrs)	5 Maxwell Drive, Newton Stewart DG8 6EL	marlaneg690@btinternet.com	01671 401375
McQuistan, Robert	Old Schoolhouse, Carsluith, Newton Stewart DG8 7DT	mcquistan@mcquistan.plus.com	01671 820327

10. AYR

Name	Address	Email	Telephone
Anderson, James (Dr) BVMS PhD DVM FRCPath FIBiol MRCVS	67 Henrietta Street, Girvan KA26 9AN	jc.anderson2@talktalk.net	01465 710059
Jamieson, Ian A.	2 Whinfield Avenue, Prestwick KA9 2BH	ian4189.jamieson@gmail.com	07952 512720 / 01242 476898
Morrison, James	27 Monkton Road, Prestwick KA9 1AP	jim.morrison@talktalk.net	01292 479313
Murphy, Ian	56 Lamont Crescent, Netherthird, Cumnock KA18 3DU	ianm_cumnock@yahoo.co.uk	07773 287852 / 01290 423675
Ogston, Jean (Mrs)	14 North Park Avenue, Girvan KA26 9DH	jeanogston@gmail.com	01465 713081
Ronald, Glenn	188 Prestwick Road, Ayr KA8 8NP	glennronald@btinternet.com	01292 286861
Stewart, Christine (Mrs)	52 Kilford Drive, Dundonald KA2 9ET	christiestewart@btinternet.com	01563 850486

11. IRVINE AND KILMARNOCK

Name	Address	Email	Telephone
Bircham, James F.	8 Holmlea Place, Kilmarnock KA1 1UU	james.bircham@sky.com	01563 532287
Cooper, Fraser	5 Balgray Way, Irvine KA11 1RP	frasercooper1560@gmail.com	01294 211235
Crosbie, Shona (Mrs)	4 Campbell Street, Darvel KA17 0DA	fawltytowersdarvel@yahoo.co.uk	01560 322229
Dempster, Ann (Mrs)	20 Graham Place, Kilmarnock KA3 7JN	ademp99320@aol.com	01563 529361 / 07729 152945
Gillespie, Janice (Miss)	12 Jeffrey Street, Kilmarnock KA1 4EB	janice.gillespie@tiscali.co.uk	01563 540009
Graham, Barbara (Miss) MA MLitt MPhil CertChSt	42 Annanhill Avenue, Kilmarnock KA1 2LQ	barbara.graham74@btinternet.com	01563 522108
Hamilton, Margaret A. (Mrs)	59 South Hamilton Street, Kilmarnock KA1 2DT	mahamilton1@outlook.com	01563 534431
Jamieson, John H. (Dr) BSc DEP DEdPsy AFBPsS CPsychol	22 Moorfield Avenue, Kilmarnock KA1 1TS	johnhjamieson@tiscali.co.uk	01563 534065

Name	Email	Address	Phone
McGeever, Gerard	mcgeege1@gmail.com	23 Kinloch Avenue, Stewarton, Kilmarnock KA3 3HQ	01560 484331
MacLean, Donald	donannmac@yahoo.co.uk	1 Four Acres Drive, Kilmaurs, Kilmarnock KA3 2ND	01563 538475
Mills, Catherine (Mrs)	cfmills5lib@hotmail.com	59 Crossdene Road, Crosshouse, Kilmarnock KA2 0IU	01563 535305
Raleigh, Gavin	gavin.raleigh@lineone.net	21 Landsborough Drive, Kilmarnock KA3 1RY	01563 539377
Whitelaw, David	whitelawfarn@talktalk.net	9 Kirkhill, Kilwinning KA13 6NB	01294 551695

12. ARDROSSAN

Barclay, Elizabeth (Mrs)	mfiz98@dsl.pipex.com	2 Jacks Road, Saltcoats KA21 5NT	01294 471855
Brookens, Aileen J. (Mrs)	aileenbrokens@gmail.com	Willow Cottage, Glenashdale, Whiting Bay, Isle of Arran KA27 8QW	01770 700535
Bruce, Andrew J.	andrew_bruce2@sky.com	57 Dockers Gardens, Ardrossan KA22 8GB	01294 605113
Clarke, Elizabeth (Mrs)	lizahclarke@gmail.com	Swallowbrae, Torbeg, Isle of Arran KA27 8HE	01770 860219 07780 574367
Currie, Archie BD	Archie.Currie@churchofscotland.org.uk	55 Central Avenue, Kilbirnie KA25 6JP	01505 681474 07881 452115
McCool, Robert		17 McGregor Avenue, Stevenston KA20 4BA	01294 466548
MacLeod, Sharon (Mrs)	macleodsharon@hotmail.com	Creag Dhubh, Golf Course Road, Whiting Bay, Isle of Arran KA27 8QT	01770 700353
Murray, Brian	brian.murray100@btinternet.com	19 Snowdon Terrace, Seamill KA23 9HN	01294 822272
Robertson, William	willie.robert@yahoo.co.uk	1 Archers Avenue, Irvine KA11 2GB	01294 203577
Ross, Magnus M.B. BA MEd	m.b.ross@btinternet.com	39 Beachway, Largs KA30 8QH	01475 689572

13. LANARK

Grant, Alan	amgrant25@aol.com	25 Moss-side Avenue, Carluke ML8 5UG	01555 771419
Love, William	janbill30@tiscali.co.uk	30 Barmore Avenue, Carluke ML8 4PE	01555 751243

14. CLYDE

Banks, Russell	margaret.banks2@ntlworld.com	18 Aboyne Drive, Paisley PA2 7SJ	0141 884 6925
Bird, Mary Jane (Miss)	mjbird55@gmail.com	Greenhill Farm, Barochan Road, Houston PA6 7HS	
Boag, Jennifer (Miss)	jenniferboag@hotmail.com	11 Madeira Street, Greenock PA16 7UJ	01475 720125
Davey, Charles L.	charlesdavey16@hotmail.co.uk	16 Divert Road, Gourock PA19 1DT	01475 631544
Galbraith, Iain B. MA MPhil MTh ThD FTCL	iainbg@icloud.com	Beechwood, Overton Road, Alexandria G83 0LJ	01389 753563
Hood, Eleanor (Mrs)	eleanor.hood.kilbarchan@ntlworld.com	12 Clochoderick Avenue, Kilbarchan, Johnstone PA10 2AY	01505 704208
MacDonald, Christine (Ms)	christine.macdonald10@ntlworld.com	33 Collier Street, Johnstone PA5 8AG	01505 355779
McEwan, Alex	aleximcewan@gmail.com	1/1 The Riggs, Milngavie G62 8LX	0141 384 0274
McFarlan, Elizabeth (Miss)	elizabeth.mcfarlan@ntlworld.com	20 Fauldswood Crescent, Paisley PA2 9PA	01505 358411
McHugh, Jack	jackmchugh1@btinternet.com	Earlshaugh, Earl Place, Bridge of Weir PA11 3HA	01505 612789
Marshall, Leon M.	lm@stevenson-kyles.co.uk	Glenisla, Gryffe Road, Kilmacolm PA13 4BA	01505 872417

Name	Address	Email	Phone
Maxwell, Margaret A. (Sandra) (Mrs) BD	2 Grants Avenue, Paisley PA2 6AZ	sandra@maxwellmail.co.uk	0141 884 3710
Morgan, Richard	Annandale, School Road, Rhu, Helensburgh G84 8RS	themorgans@hotmail.co.uk	01436 821269
Rankin, Kenneth	20 Bruntsfield Gardens, Glasgow G53 7QJ	krankin@hotmail.co.uk	0141 880 7474
Spooner, John R. BSc PGC(Mgt)	Onslow, Uplawmoor Road, Neilston, Glasgow G78 3LB	jrspooner@btopenworld.com	0141 881 5182 / 07481 008033
Theaker, Philip D. (Dr)	17 Kilmory Gardens, Skelmorlie PA17 5EX	ptheaker48@gmail.com	07904 919776

16. GLASGOW

Name	Address	Email	Phone
Allan, Phillip	34 Muirhead Way, Bishopbriggs, Glasgow G64 1YG	hampdenhorror@gmail.com	07954 497930
Dickson, Hector M.K.	61 Whitton Drive, Giffnock, Glasgow G46 6EF	hectordickson@hotmail.com	0141 637 0080
Fullarton, Andrew	2/2, 2263 Paisley Road West, Glasgow G52 3QA		0141 883 9518
Grant, George	8 Erskine Street, Stirling FK7 0QN	georgegrant@gmail.com	01786 609594 / 07921 168057
Horner, David J.	20 Ledi Road, Glasgow G43 2AJ	djhorner@btinternet.com	0141 637 7369
Joansson, Tordur (Todd)	1/2, 18 Eglinton Court, Glasgow G5 9NE	to41jp@yahoo.co.uk	0141 429 6733
Kelly, George	25 Westerton, Lennoxtown G66 7LR	geojkelly@btinternet.com	01360 311739
Kilpatrick, Joan (Mrs)	39 Brent Road, Regent's Park, Glasgow G46 8JG	je-kilpatrick@sky.com	0141 621 1809
McColl, John	25 Avenel Road, Glasgow G13 2PB	solfolly11@gmail.com	07757 303195
McFarlane, Robert	10 Melville Gardens, Bishopbriggs, Glasgow G64 3DF	robertmcfrln@yahoo.co.uk	0141 954 5540
McInally, Gordon	55 Culzean Crescent, Newton Mearns, Glasgow G77 5SW	gmcinally@sky.com	0141 563 2685
Mackenzie, Norman	18 Greenwood Grove West, Stewarton Road Glasgow G77 6ZF		07935 861530
Millar, Kathleen (Mrs)	1/1, 40 Gardner Street, Glasgow G11 5DF		07793 203045
Morrison, Graham	3b Lennox Court, 16 Stockiemuir Avenue, Bearsden G61 3JL		0141 579 4772 / 0141 942 3024
Morrison, Katie (Miss)	2 Lindsaybeg Court, Chryston, Glasgow G69 9DD	katiemorrison2003@hotmail.co.uk	07852 373840
Nicolson, John C.	2/3, 30 Handel Place, Glasgow G5 0TP	john.c.nicolson@btinternet.com	0141 779 2447
Phillips, John B.	2 Greenhill, Bishopbriggs, Glasgow G64 1LE	johnphillips@fish.co.uk	0141 429 7716
Robertson, Lynne M. (Mrs) MA MEd	81 Busby Road, Clarkston, Glasgow G76 8BD	emrobertsonmed@btinternet.com	0141 772 1323 / 07720 053981
Roy, Shona (Mrs)	52 Robslee Road, Thornliebank, Glasgow G46 7BX	theroyfamily@yahoo.co.uk	0141 644 3713
Smith, Ann	9A Carrick Drive, Mount Vernon, Glasgow G32 0RW		0141 621 0638
Stead, May (Mrs)		maystead@hotmail.co.uk	07917 785109
Stewart, James	45 Airthrey Avenue, Glasgow G14 9LY	jmstewart325@btinternet.com	0141 959 5814
Tindall, Maragret (Mrs)	23 Ashcroft Avenue, Lennoxtown, Glasgow G65 7EN	margarettindall@aol.com	01360 310911

17. HAMILTON

Name	Address	Email	Phone
Allan, Angus J.	Blackburn Mill, Chapelton, Strathaven ML10 6RR	angus.allan@hotmail.com	01357 300916
Beattie, Richard	4 Bent Road, Hamilton ML3 6QB	richardbeattie1958@hotmail.com	01698 420806
Codona, Joy (Mrs)	Dykehead Farm, 300 Dykehead Road, Airdrie ML6 7SR	jcodona772@btinternet.com	01236 767063 / 07810 770609
Douglas, Ian	24 Abbotsford Crescent, Strathaven ML10 6EQ	IDouglas@churchofscotland.org.uk	07742 022423
Fyfe, Lorna K.	8b Glenavon Court, Larkhall ML9 2WA	lorna.fyfe@yahoo.com	07929 031068
Haggarty, Francis	46 Glen Road, Caldercruix ML6 7PZ	frank_h@fsmail.com	01236 842182
Hastings, William Paul	186 Glen More, East Kilbride, Glasgow G74 2AN	wphastings@hotmail.co.uk	01355 521228 / 07954 167158
Hislop, Eric	1 Castlegait, Strathaven ML10 6FF	eric.hislop@tiscali.co.uk	01357 520003
Jardine, Lynette	1 Hume Drive, Uddingston, Glasgow G71 4DW	lpjardine@blueyonder.co.uk	01698 812404
Leckie, Elizabeth	8 Montgomery Place, Larkhall ML9 2EZ	elizleckie@blueyonder.co.uk	01698 325625
McCleary, Isaac	719 Coatbridge Road, Bargeddie, Glasgow G69 7PH	isaacmccleary@gmail.com	07908 547040
Preston, Steven J.	24 Glen Prosen, East Kilbride, Glasgow G74 3TA	steven.preston1@btinternet.com	01355 237359 / 07752 120536
Stevenson, Thomas	34 Castle Wynd, Quarter, Hamilton ML3 7XD	weetamgtr@gmail.com	01698 282263 / 07860 477344
White, Ian T.	4 Gilchrist Walk, Lesmahagow ML11 0FQ	iantwhite@aol.com	01555 890704

19. ARGYLL

Name	Address	Email	Phone
Alexander, John	11 Cullipool Village, Isle of Luing, Oban PA34 4UB	jandjalex@gmail.com	01852 314242
Allan, Douglas	1 Camplen Court, Rothesay, Isle of Bute PA20 0NL	douglasallan984@btinternet.com	
Binner, Aileen (Mrs)	Ailand, North Connel, Oban PA37 1QX England	binners@ailand.plus.com	01631 710264
Garrett, William	3 Braeface, Tayvallich, Lochgilphead PA31 8JN	we.garrett@btinternet.com	
Logue, David	Courtyard Cottage, Barmor View, Kilmartin PA31 8UN	david@loguenet.co.uk	01546 870647
Malcolm, James	Tigh Na Criche, Cairndow, Argyll PA27 8BY	jgmalcolm@btinternet.com	01546 510540
McHugh, Douglas	West Drimvore, Lochgilphead PA31 8SU	dmchugh6@gmail.com	01369 860147
McLellan, James A.	Northton, Ganavan, Oban PA34 5TU	james.mclellan8@btinternet.com	01546 606403
Mills, Peter A.	Tigh na Barnashaig, Tayvallich, Lochgilphead PA31 8PN	peter@peteramills.com	
Morrison, John L.	Tigh na Barnashaig, Tayvallich, Lochgilphead PA31 8PN	jolomo@thejolomostudio.com	01546 870637
Ramsay, Matthew M.	Portnastorm, Carradale, Campbeltown PA28 6SB	kintyre@fishermensmission.org.uk	01583 431381
Scouller, Alastair	15 Allanwater Apartments, Bridge of Allan, Stirling FK9 4DZ	scouller@globalnet.co.uk	01786 832496
Sinclair, Margaret (Ms)	2 Quarry Place, Furnace, Inveraray PA32 8XW	margaret_sinclair@btinternet.com	01499 500633
Stather, Angela (Ms)	1 Dunlossit Cottages, Port Askaig, Isle of Islay PA46 7RB	angstat@btinternet.com	01496 840726
Thornhill, Christopher R.	4 Ardfern Cottages, Ardfern, Lochgilphead PA31 8QN	c.thornhill@btinternet.com	01852 300011
Waddell, Martin	Fasgadh, Clachan Seil, Oban PA34 4TJ	waddell1715@btinternet.com	01852 300395
Zielinski, Jeneffer C. (Mrs)	7 Wallace Court, Ferguslie Street, Sandbank, Dunoon P A23 8QA	jenefferzielinski@gmail.com	01369 706136

22. FALKIRK

Name	Address	Email	Phone
Duncan, Lorna M. (Mrs) BA	28 Solway Drive, Head of Muir, Denny FK6 5NS	ell.dee@blueyonder.co.uk	01324 813020
Jalland, Darren	62 Rosebank Avenue, Falkirk FK1 5JP	larbertred@googlemail.com	01324 558436
McMillan, Isabelle (Mrs)	17 Castle Avenue, Airth, Falkirk FK2 8GA		07896 433314
Scoular, Iain W.	15 Bonnyside Road, Bonnybridge FK4 2AD	scoulariain@gmail.com	01324 812395 / 07717 131596
Stewart, Arthur MA	51 Bonnymuir Crescent, Bonnybridge FK4 1GD	arthur.stewart1@btinternet.com	01324 812667
Struthers, Ivar B.	7 McVean Place, Bonnybridge FK4 1QZ	ivar.struthers@btinternet.com	01324 841145 / 07921 778208

23. STIRLING

Name	Address	Email	Phone
Grier, Hunter	17 Station Road, Bannockburn, Stirling FK7 8LG	anneandhunter@gmail.com	01786 815192
McPherson, Alistair M.	Springpark, Doune Road, Dunblane FK15 9AR		01786 826850

24. DUNFERMLINE

Name	Address	Email	Phone
Brown, Gordon	Nowell, Fossoway, Kinross KY13 0UW	brown.nowell@hotmail.com.uk	01577 840248
Grant, Allan	6 Normandy Place, Rosyth KY11 2HJ	allan75@talktalk.net	01383 428760 / 07449 278378
McCaffery, Joyce (Mrs)	53 Foulford Street, Cowdenbeath KY4 9AS	mccafferyjo@tiscali.co.uk	01383 515775
Mitchell, Ian G. QC	17 Carlingnose Point, North Queensferry, Inverkeithing KY11 1ER	igmitchell@easynet.co.uk	01383 416240
Monk, Alan	36 North Road, Saline KY12 9UQ	alanmonk@talktalk.net	01383 851283
Muirhead, Sandy		sandy_muirhead@hotmail.com	

25. KIRKCALDY

Name	Address	Email	Phone
Biernat, Ian	2 Formonthills Road, Glenrothes KY6 3EF	ian.biernat@btinternet.com	01592 741487

26. ST ANDREWS

Name	Address	Email	Phone
Elder, Morag Anne (Ms)	5 Provost Road, Tayport DD6 9JE	benuardin@tiscali.co.uk	01382 552218
Peacock, Graham	6 Balgove Avenue, Gauldry, Newport-on-Tay DD6 8SQ	grahampeacock6@btinternet.com	01382 330124
Smith, Elspeth (Mrs)	Glentarkie Cottage, Glentarkie, Strathmiglo, Cupar KY14 7RU	elspeth.smith@btinternet.com	01337 860824

27. DUNKELD AND MEIGLE

Name	Address	Email	Phone
Howat, David P.	Lilybank Cottage, Newton Street, Blairgowrie PH10 6HZ	david@thehowats.net	01250 874715
Patterson, Rosemary (Mrs)	Rowantree, Golf Course Road, Blairgowrie PH10 6LJ	pattersonrose.c@gmail.com	01250 876607

28. PERTH

Name	Address	Email	Phone
Archibald, Michael	Wychwood, Culdeessland Road, Methven, Perth, PH1 3QE	michael.archibald@gmail.com	01783 840995
Begg, James	8 Park Village, Turretbank Road, Crieff PH7 4JN	bjimmy37@aol.com	01764 655907
Benneworth, Michael	7 Hamilton Place, Perth PH1 1BB	mbenneworth@hotmail.com	01738 628093
Davidson, Andrew	95 Needless Road, Perth PH2 0LD	a.r.davidson.91@cantab.net	01738 620839
Laing, John	10 Graybank Road, Perth PH2 0GZ	johnandmarylaing@hotmail.co.uk	01738 623888
McChlery, Stuart	22 Kirkfield Place, Auchterarder PH3 1FP	s.mcchlery@gcu.ac.uk	01764 662399
Ogilvie, Brian	67 Whitecraigs, Kinnesswood, Kinross KY13 9JN	brianj.ogilvie1@btopenworld.com	01592 840823 07815 759864
Stewart, Anne	Ballcraine, Murthly Road, Stanley, Perth PH1 4PN	anne.stewart13@btinternet.com	01738 828637
Yellowlees, Deirdre (Mrs)	Ringmill House, Gannochy Farm, Perth PH2 7JH	d.yellowlees@btinternet.com	01738 633773 07920 805399

29. DUNDEE

Name	Address	Email	Phone
Sharp, Gordon	6 Kelso Street, Dundee DD2 1SJ	gordonsharp264@gmail.com	01382 643002
Xenphontos-Hellen, Tim	23 Ancrum Drive, Dundee DD2 2JG	tim.xsf@btinternet.com	01382 630355 01382 567756 (Work)

30. ANGUS

Name	Address	Email	Phone
Beedie, Alexander W. (William)	6B Carnegie Street, Arbroath DD11 1TX	a.wbeedie38@gmail.com	01241 875001
Gray, Linda (Mrs)	8 Inchgarth Street, Forfar DD8 3LY	lindamgray@sky.com	01307 464039
Walker, Eric	12 Orchard Brae, Kirriemuir DD8 4JY	eric.line15@btinternet.com	01575 572082
Walker, Pat (Mrs)	12 Orchard Brae, Kirriemuir DD8 4JY	pat.line15@btinternet.com	01575 572082

31. ABERDEEN AND SHETLAND

Name	Address	Email	Phone
Cooper, Gordon	1 Kirkbrae View, Cults, Aberdeen AB15 9RU	ga_cooper@hotmail.co.uk	01224 964165
Gray, Peter (Prof.)	165 Countesswells Road, Aberdeen AB15 7RA	pmdgray@bcs.org.uk	01224 318172
Greig, Martin	85 Macaulay Drive, Aberdeen AB15 8FL	mgreig@aberdeencity.gov.uk	07920 806332

32. KINCARDINE AND DEESIDE

Name	Address	Email	Phone
Bell, Robert	27 Mearns Drive, Stonehaven AB39 2DZ	r.bell282@btinternet.com	01569 767173 07733 014826
Broere, Teresa (Mrs)	3 Balnastraid Cottages, Dinnet, Aboyne AB34 5NE	broere@btinternet.com	01339 880058
Coles, Stephen	43 Mearns Walk, Laurencekirk AB30 1FA	steve@sbcco.com	01561 378400
McCafferty, W. John	Lynwood, Cammachmore, Stonehaven AB39 3NR	wjmccafferty@yahoo.co.uk	01569 730281 07768 925122
Middleton, Robin B. (Capt.)	7 St Ternan's Road, Newtonhill, Stonehaven AB39 3PF	robbiemiddleton7@hotmail.com	01569 730852
Platt, David	2 St Michael's Road, Newtonhill, Stonehaven AB39 3RW	daveplatt01@btinternet.com	01569 730465
Simpson, Elizabeth (Mrs)	Connemara, 33 Golf Road, Ballater AB35 5RS	connemara33@yahoo.com	01339 755597

33. GORDON

Name	Address	Email	Telephone
Bichard, Susanna (Mrs)	Beechlee, Haddo Lane, Tarves, Ellon AB41 7JZ	smbichard@aol.com	01651 851345
Doak, Alan B.	17 Chievres Place, Ellon AB41 9WH	alanbdoak@aol.com	01358 721819
Findlay, Patricia (Mrs)	Douglas View, Tullynessle, Alford AB33 8QR	p.a.findlay@btopenworld.com	01975 562379
Lord, Noel (Dr)	15 Milton Way, Kemnay AB51 5EW	drnolly@gmail.com	01467 643937
Mitchell, Jean (Mrs)	6 Cowgate, Oldmeldrum, Inverurie AB51 0EN	j.g.mitchell@btinternet.com	01651 872745
Robb, Margaret (Mrs)	Chrislouan, Keithhall, Inverurie AB51 0LN	mdmrobb@btinternet.com	01651 822310

34. BUCHAN

Name	Address	Email	Telephone
Barker, Tim	South Silverford Croft, Longmanhill, Banff AB45 3SB	tbarker05@aol.com	01261 851839
Brown, Lillian (Mrs)	45 Main Street, Aberchirder, Huntly AB54 7ST	mabroon64@gmail.com	01466 780330
Forsyth, Alicia (Mrs)	Rothie Inn Farm, Forgue Road, Rothienorman, Inverurie AB51 8YH	aliciaforsyth56@gmail.com	01651 821359
Givan, James	Zimra, Longmanhill, Banff AB45 3RP	jim.givan@btinternet.com	01261 833318
Grant, Margaret (Mrs)	22 Elphin Street, New Aberlour, Fraserburgh AB43 6LH	mgrant3120@gmail.com	07753 458664 / 01346 561341
Hine, Kath (Ms)	2 Burnside Cottage, Rothiemay, Huntly AB54 7JX	kath.hine@gmail.com	01542 870680
Lumsden, Vera (Mrs)	8 Queen's Crescent, Portsoy, Banff AB45 2PX	veralumsden53@gmail.com	01261 842712
McColl, John	East Cairnchina, Lonmay, Fraserburgh AB43 8RH	solfolly11@gmail.com	07757 303195
McDonald, Rhoda (Miss)	16 St Andrew's Drive, Fraserburgh AB43 2PX	techmc@callnetuk.com	01346 514052
McFie, David	The Manse, Fordyce Terrace, New Deer, Turriff AB53 6TD	waverley710@gmx.co.uk	01771 644631
MacLeod, Ali (Ms)	11 Pitfour Crescent, Fetterangus, Peterhead AB42 4EL	aliowl@hotmail.com	01771 622992 / 07821 670705
Macnee, Anthea (Mrs)	Wardend Cottage, Alvah, Banff AB45 3TR	macneeiain4@googlemail.com	01261 815647
Mair, Dorothy L.T. (Miss)	Flat F, 15 The Quay, Newburgh, Ellon AB41 6DA	dorothymair2@aol.com	01358 788832 / 07505 051305
Simpson, Andrew C.	10 Wood Street, Banff AB45 1JX	andy.louise1@btinternet.com	01261 812538
Sneddon, Richard	100 West Road, Peterhead AB42 2AQ	richard.sneddon@btinternet.com	

35. MORAY

Forbes, Jean (Mrs)	Greenmoss, Drybridge, Buckie AB56 5JB	dancingfeet@tinyworld.co.uk	01542 831646 / 07974 760337
Harrison, Christine BA	29 Seaview Park, Findhorn Road, Kinloss IV36 3TF	chrstnhrsn42@googlemail.com	07930 048565

36. ABERNETHY

Name	Address	Email	Telephone
Bardgett, Alison (Mrs)	Tigh an Iasgair, Street of Kincardine, Boat of Garten PH24 3BY	iasgair10@icloud.com	01479 831751
Black, Barbara J. (Mrs)	Carn Eilrig, Nethy Bridge PH25 3EE	bjcarneilrig54@gmail.com	01479 821641

37. INVERNESS

Name	Address	Email	Phone
Appleby, Jonathan	91 Cradlehall Park, Inverness IV2 5DB	jon.wyvis@gmail.com	01463 791470
Cazaly, Leonard	9 Moray Park Gardens, Culloden, Inverness IV2 7FY	len_cazaly@btinternet.com	01463 794469
Cook, Arnett D.	66 Millerton Avenue, Inverness IV3 8RY	arnett.cook@btinternet.com	01463 224795
Dennis, Barry	5 Loch Ness View, Dores, Inverness IV2 6TW	barrydennis@live.co.uk	01463 751393
MacInnes, Ailsa (Mrs)	Kilmartin, 17 Southside Road, Inverness IV2 3BG	ailsa.macinnes@btopenworld.com	01463 230321 / 07704 485055
Robertson, Hendry	Park House, 51 Glenurquhart Road, Inverness IV3 5PB	hendryrobertson046@btinternet.com	01463 231858 / 07929 766102
Roberston, Stewart J.H.	6 Raasay Road, Inverness IV2 3LR	sjhro@tiscali.co.uk	01463 417937
Roden, Vivian (Mrs)	15 Old Mill Road, Tomatin, Inverness IV13 7YW	vroden@btinternet.com	01808 511355 / 07887 704915

38. LOCHABER

Gill, Ella (Mrs)	5 Camus Inas, Acharacle PH36 4JQ	ellagill768@gmail.com	01967 431834
Skene, William	Tiree, Gairlochy, Spean Bridge PH34 4EQ	bill.skene@lochaber.presbytery.org.uk	01397 712594

39. ROSS

Finlayson, Michael R.	Amberlea, Glenskiach, Evanton, Dingwall IV16 9UU	finlayson935@btinternet.com	01349 830598
Greer, Kathleen (Mrs) MEd	17 Duthac Wynd, Tain IV19 1LP	greer2@talktalk.net	01862 892065
Jackson, Simon	Broomton Farm, Balintore IV20 1XN	simonjackson@procam.co.uk	01862 832831
Jamieson, Patricia A. (Mrs)	9 Craig Avenue, Tain IV19 1JP	happjam179@yahoo.co.uk	01862 893154
McAlpine, James	5 Cromlet Park, Invergordon IV18 0RN	jmca2@tiscali.co.uk	01349 852801

40. SUTHERLAND

Baxter, A. Rosie (Dr)	Daylesford, Invershin, Lairg IV27 4ET	drrosiereid@yahoo.co.uk	01549 421326 / 07748 761694
Roberts, Irene (Miss)	Flat 4, Harbour Buildings, Main Street, Portmahomack, Tain IV20 1YG	ireneroberts43@hotmail.com	01862 871166 / 07854 436854
Weidner, Karl	6 St Vincent Road, Tain IV19 1JR	kweidner@btinternet.com	01862 894202

41. CAITHNESS

MacDonald, Morag (Dr)	Orkney View, Portskerra, Melvich KW14 7YL	liliasmacdonald@btinternet.com	01641 531281
O'Neill, Leslie	Holytree Cottage, Parkside, Lybster KW3 6AS	leslie_oneill@hotmail.co.uk	01593 721738
O'Neill, Maureen (Mrs)	Holytree Cottage, Parkside, Lybster KW3 6AS	oneill.maureen@yahoo.com	01593 721738

42. LOCHCARRON-SKYE

Lamont, John H. BD	6 Tigh na Filine, Aultbea, Achnasheen IV22 2JE	jhlamont@btinternet.com	07714 720753
MacRae, Donald E.	Nethania, 52 Strath, Gairloch IV21 2DB	dmgair@aol.com	01445 712235

43. UIST			
MacNab, Ann (Mrs)	Druim Skilivat, Scolpaig, Lochmaddy, Isle of North Uist HS6 5DH	annabhan@hotmail.com	01876 510701
44. LEWIS			
Macleod, Donald	14 Balmerino Drive, Stornoway, Isle of Lewis HS1 2TD	donaldmacleod25@btinternet.com	01851 704516
Macmillan, Iain	34 Scotland Street, Stornoway, Isle of Lewis HS1 2JR	macmillan@brocair.fsnet.co.uk	01851 704826 / 07775 027987
45. ORKNEY			
Dicken, Marion (Mrs)	12 MacDonald Park, St Margaret's Hope, Orkney KW17 2AL	mj44@hotmail.co.uk	01856 831687
Gillespie, Jean (Mrs)	16 St Colm's Quadrant, Eday, Orkney KW16 3PH Moorside, Firth, Orkney KW17 2JZ	jrw2810@btinterent.com / yetminstermusic@googlemail.com	01856 701406 / 01856 761899
Jones, Josephine (Mrs) BA CertEd LRAM			
Pomfret, Valerie (Mrs)	3 Clumly Avenue, Kirkwall, Orkney KW15 1YU Essonquoy, Eday, Orkney KW17 2AB	vpomfret@btinternet.com / essonquoy@btinternet.com	01857 622251
Robertson, Johan (Mrs)			
47. ENGLAND			
Menzies, Rena (Mrs)	40 Elizabeth Avenue, St Brelade's, Jersey JE3 8GR	menzfamily@jerseymail.co.uk	01534 741095
Milligan, Elaine (Mrs)	16 Surrey Close, Corby, Northants NN17 2TG	elainemilligan@ntlworld.com	01536 205259
48. INTERNATIONAL CHARGES			
Campbell, Cindy (Mrs)	9 Cavello Heights, Sandys MA 05, Bermuda	cindyfcampbell@gmail.com	001 441 234 3797
Goodman, Alice (Mrs)	Route de Sallaz 23, Rivaz 1071, Switzerland	alice-goodman@epfl.ch	0041 21 946 1727
49. JERUSALEM			
Oakley-Levstein, Joanna (Mrs) BA	Mevo Hamma, 12934, Israel	j.oak.lev@gmail.com	00972 50584 2517

LIST I – MINISTRIES DEVELOPMENT STAFF

Ministries Development Staff support local congregations, parish groupings and presbyteries in a wide variety of ways, bringing expertise or experience to pastoral work, development, and outreach in congregation and community. Some may be ministers and deacons undertaking specialist roles: they are listed also in Section 5 (Presbyteries), with deacons further in List C of the present section.

1. EDINBURGH

Crocker, Liz DipComEd DCS	Edinburgh: Tron Kirk (Gilmerton and Moredun) – Parish Assistant	ECrocker@churchofscotland.org.uk
Fejszes, Violetta (Dr)	Edinburgh: Old Kirk and Muirhouse – Parish Development Worker	VFejszes@churchofscotland.org.uk
de Jager, Lourens (Rev) PgDip MDiv BTh	Edinburgh: Portobello and Joppa – Associate Minister	LDeJager@churchofscotland.org.uk
Hirani, Hina	Edinburgh: Old Kirk and Muirhouse – Project Development Worker	HHirani@churchofscotland.org.uk
Laoshe, Fadeke	Edinburgh: St Margaret's – Children, Youth and Family Worker	FLaoshe@churchofscotland.org.uk
Lewis, Christein	Edinburgh: Old Kirk and Muirhouse – Young Person Development Worker	CLewis@churchofscotland.org.uk
Luscombe, Kenneth L. (Rev)	Edinburgh: Greyfriars Kirk – Associate Minister	KLuscombe@churchofscotland.org.uk
McMullin, Michael BA	Edinburgh: Craigmillar Park; Priestfield; Reid Memorial – Ministries Development Worker	MMcMullin@churchofscotland.org.uk
MacPherson, Gigha K.	Edinburgh: St David's Broomhouse – Children and Family Worker	GMacPherson@churchofscotland.org.uk
Marshall, Zoe	Edinburgh: Willowbrae – Community Development Worker	ZMarshall@churchofscotland.org.uk
Midwinter, Alan	Edinburgh: St David's Broomhouse – Pastoral Assistant	AMidwinter@churchofscotland.org.uk
Moodie, David	Edinburgh: Granton – Parish Assistant	DMoodie@churchofscotland.org.uk
Richardson, Ian (Dr)	Edinburgh: Holy Trinity – Discipleship Team Leader	IRichardson@churchofscotland.org.uk
Robertson, Douglas S. BEng BA MTh	Edinburgh: Gracemount – Church Leader	Douglas.Robertson@churchofscotland.org.uk
Stark, Jennifer MA MATheol	Edinburgh: Richmond Craigmillar – Community Development Worker	JStark@churchofscotland.org.uk
Wilson-Tagoe, Jacqueline	Edinburgh: Meadowbank - Programme and Outreach Worker	JWilson-Tagoe@churchofscotland.org.uk

2. WEST LOTHIAN

Brown, Kenneth (Rev)	Livingston United – Church and Community Development Worker	Kenneth.Brown@churchofscotland.org.uk
Corrie, Margaret (Miss) DCS	Armadale – Mission Development Worker	MCorrie@churchofscotland.org.uk
Philip, Darrren BSc	Livingston United – Youth and Children's Worker	DPhilip@churchofscotland.org.uk

3. LOTHIAN

Glen, Ewen A.	Tranent Cluster and Presbytery – Family and Youth Development Worker	EGlen@churchofscotland.org.uk
McKenzie, Susan	Newton – Mission and Discipleship Outreach Worker	SMcKenzie@churchofscotland.org.uk
Morley, Anthea	Newbattle – Project Development Worker	AMorley@churchofscotland.org.uk
Muir, Malcolm T. (Rev)	Newbattle – Associate Minister	MMuir@churchofscotland.org.uk
Pryde, Erika	Newton – Mission and Discipleship Outreach Co-ordinator	EPryde@churchofscotland.org.uk

4. MELROSE AND PEEBLES

5. DUNS

6. JEDBURGH

7. ANNANDALE AND ESKDALE

Name	Description	Email
Brydson, Angela (Mrs) DCS	Lochmaben, Moffat and Lockerbie grouping – Deacon	ABrydson@churchofscotland.org.uk
Hislop, Donna	Canonbie, Langholm & Border grouping - Youth Worker	DHislop@churchofscotland.org.uk

8. DUMFRIES AND KIRKCUDBRIGHTSHIRE

9. WIGTOWN AND STRANRAER

10. AYR

Algeo, Paul	North Ayr Parish Grouping – Family/Development Worker	PAlgeo@churchofscotland.org.uk

11. IRVINE AND KILMARNOCK

Name	Description	Email
Wardrop, Elaine	Kilmarnock: St Andrew's and St Marnock's: Mission Development Worker	EWardrop@churchofscotland.org.uk

12. ARDROSSAN

Beck, Isobel BD DCS	Kilwinning Old – Deacon	IBeck@churchofscotland.org.uk
Blair, Fiona DCS	Beith – Parish Assistant	FBlair@churchofscotland.org.uk
Boyd, Carol	Kilwinning Mansefield Trinity – Young Adults Community Development W.	CBoyd@churchofscotland.org.uk
Devlin, Brian	Stevenston: Ardeer linked with Livingstone – Community Mission Worker	BDevlin@churchofscotland.org.uk
Hunter, Jean C.Q. BD	Brodick linked with Corrie linked with Lochranza and Pirnmill linked with Shiskine – Parish Assistant	JHunter@churchofscotland.org.uk
Isbister, Gordon (Dr)	Ardrossan: Park – Family and Outreach Worker	GIsbister@churchofscotland.org.uk
McKay, Angus	Cumbrae linked with Largs St John's – Parish Assistant	AMcKay@churchofscotland.org.uk

13. LANARK

14. CLYDE

Burke, Maureen	Dumbarton churches – Pastoral Assistant	MBurke@churchofscotland.org.uk
Dungavell, Marie Claire	Dumbarton: Riverside linked with West, Development Worker	MCDungavell@churchofscotland.org.uk
Graham, Gillian	Clydebank: Waterfront linked with Dalmuir: Barclay – Children, Young People and Family Worker	GGraham@churchofscotland.org.uk
Kemp, Tina (Rev) MA	Helensburgh linked with Rhu and Shandon – Associate Minister	TKemp@churchofscotland.org.uk
McCallum, Graham	Paisley North End – Outreach Worker	GMcCallum@churchofscotland.org.uk
Wilson, Lorraine	Clydebank: Waterfront linked with Dalmuir: Barclay – Pastoral Assistant	LWilson@churchofscotland.org.uk

16. GLASGOW

Baird, Janette Y.	Glasgow: Castlemilk – Community Development Worker	JBaird@churchofscotland.org.uk
Cameron, Lisa	Glasgow: St James' (Pollok) – Youth and Children's Ministry Leader	LCameron@churchofscotland.org.uk
Cathcart, John Paul DCS	Glasgow: Castlemilk – Deacon	Paul.Cathcart@churchofscotland.org.uk
Christie, Jacqueline F. (Dr)	Glasgow: Ruchazie – Project Support Worker	Jacqueline.Christie@churchofscotland.org.uk
Evans, Andrew	Glasgow: Gorbals – Community Development Worker	AEvans@churchofscotland.org.uk
Gargrave, Mary S. (Mrs) DCS	Glasgow: Carnwadric – Deacon	Mary.Gargrave@churchofscotland.org.uk
Goodwin, Jamie	Glasgow: Govan and Linthouse – Arts and Worship Development Worker	JGoodwin@churchofscotland.org.uk
Hamilton, James DCS	Glasgow: Maryhill – Parish Assistant	James.Hamilton@churchofscotland.org.uk
Hamilton, Karen (Mrs) DCS	Cambuslang – Deacon	KHamilton@churchofscotland.org.uk
Herbert, Claire BD DCS	Lodging House Mission, Glasgow - Chaplain	CHerbert@churchofscotland.org.uk
Hyndman, Graham	Church House, Bridgeton – Youth Worker	GHyndman@churchofscotland.org.uk
Lyall, Ann DCS	Glasgow: Baillieston Mure Memorial linked with Baillieston St Andrew's – Parish Assistant; Glasgow: Govan and Linthouse – Pastoral Support Development Worker	ALyall@churchofscotland.org.uk
Macdonald-Haak, Aileen D.	Glasgow: Carntyne – Development Worker, Older People	AMacdonald-Haak@churchofscotland.org.uk
McDougall, Hilary N. (Rev) MA PGCE BD	Presbytery – Depute Clerk and Congregational Facilitator	HMcDougall@churchofscotland.org.uk
McElhinney, Amy	Glasgow: Garthamlock and Craigend – Research and Development Facilitator	AMcElhinny@churchofscotland.org.uk
McIlreavy, Gillian M.	Glasgow: Govan and Linthouse – Community Development Worker	GMcIlreavy@churchofscotland.org.uk
McMahon, Deborah	Glasgow: Easterhouse – Children's Development Worker	DKeenan@churchofscotland.org.uk
Marshall, Kirsteen	Glasgow: St Christopher's Priesthill and Nitshill – Parish Assistant	KMarshall@churchofscotland.org.uk
Morrin, Jonathan	Glasgow: Barlanark Greyfriars – Youth and Children's Worker	JMorrin@churchofscotland.org.uk
Morrison, Iain J.	Glasgow: Colston Milton – Community Arts Worker	IMorrison@churchofscotland.org.uk
Mubengo, Eddison	Rutherglen: West and Wardlawhill – Mission and Discipleship Worker	EMubengo@churchofscotland.org.uk
Peat, Derek A. (Rev) BA BD MTh	Presbytery – Local Church Review Co-ordinator	DPeat@churchofscotland.org.uk
Pettigrove, Kaila	Glasgow: Drumchapel St Mark's – Children, Youth and Family Development Worker	KPettigrove@churchofscotland.org.uk
Quinteros Virreira, Marcos	Glasgow: Ruchazie – Congregational Leader	MQuinterosVirreira@churchofscotland.org.uk
Robertson, Douglas J.	Glasgow: Shettleston New – Discipleship Facilitator	DJRobertson@churchofscotland.org.uk
Smith, Stephen	Glasgow: Toryglen – Research and Development Facilitator	Stephen.Smith@churchofscotland.org.uk
Sutton, Naomi	Glasgow: St Christopher's Priesthill and Nitshill – Children and Family Worker	NSutton@churchofscotland.org.uk
Usher, Eileen	Glasgow: Cranhill, Ruchazie, Garthamlock and Craigend Parish Grouping – Family Worker	EUsher@churchofscotland.org.uk
Willis, Mags	Glasgow: Easterhouse – Youth Development Worker	MWillis@churchofscotland.org.uk
Wilson, Marie	Netherlee and Stamperland – Pastoral Assistant	Marie.Wilson@churchofscotland.org.uk
Young, Neil J.	Glasgow: St Paul's – Youth Worker	NYoung@churchofscotland.org.uk

17. HAMILTON

Douglas, Ian	Motherwell: Crosshill linked with St Margaret's – Parish Assistant	IDouglas@churchofscotland.org.uk
Pope, Helen	Motherwell: North linked with Wishaw: Craigneuk and Belhaven – Church and Community Development Worker	HPope@churchofscotland.org.uk

Quammie, Shannon E.M.	Strathaven: Trinity – Children's and Young People Development Worker	SQuammie@churchofscotland.org.uk
Wood, Elaine	Airdrie: Cairnlea linked with Calderbank – Family/Youth Ministry Co-ordinator	EWood@churchofscotland.org.uk
19. ARGYLL		
Fulcher, Christine P. (Rev) BEd	Team Minister – South Argyll	CFulcher@churchofscotland.org.uk
D'Silva, Emily	Kilmore and Oban – Parish Assistant	EDSilva@churchofscotland.org.uk
Hay, Alison	Presbytery Ministries Co-ordinator – North and East Argyll	AHay@churchofscotland.org.uk
Whyte, Susan	Presbytery – Youth Worker – Team Leader	SWhyte@churchofscotland.org.uk
Wilson, John K. (Kenny)	Presbytery - Youth and Children's Worker	KWilson@churchofscotland.org.uk
22. FALKIRK		
Bogle, Albert O. (Very Rev) BD MTh	Sanctuary First (Presbytery Mission Initiative) – Pioneer Minister	AlbertBogle@churchofscotland.org.uk
Boland, Susan (Mrs) DipHE(Theol)	Cumbernauld: Abronhill and Cumbernauld: Kildrum – Family Development Worker	SBoland@churchofscotland.org.uk
Cuthbertson, Valerie S. (Miss) DCS	Cumbernauld: Old – Deacon	VCuthbertson@churchofscotland.org.uk
du Toit, George (Erick) (Rev)	Falkirk: Camelon – Associate Minister	EduToit@churchofscotland.org.uk
Nicholson, David DCS	Cumbernauld: Kildrum – Deacon	DNicholson@churchofscotland.org.uk
23. STIRLING		
Allen, Valerie L (Rev) BMus MDiv DMin	Presbytery – Chaplain	VL2allen@btinternet.com
Anderson, Dorothy U. (Rev) LLB DipPL BD	Dunblane: Cathedral – Associate Minister	DAnderson@churchofscotland.org.uk
Porter, Jean T. (Mrs) BD DCS	Stirling: St Mark's – Deacon	JPorter@churchofscotland.org.uk
24. DUNFERMLINE		
Christie, Aileen	Lochgelly and Benarty: St Serf's – Outreach Worker	Aileen.Christie@churchofscotland.org.uk
Crawford, Morag (Miss) MSc DCS	Rosyth – Deacon	MCrawford@churchofscotland.org.uk
Scott, Pamela (Mrs) DCS	Lochgelly and Benarty: St Serf's – Parish Assistant	PScott@churchofscotland.org.uk
25. KIRKCALDY		
Hutchison, John BA	Rothes Trinity Parish Grouping – Families Worker and Parish Assistant	JHutchison@churchofscotland.org.uk
Kerr, Fiona	Methil: Wellesley – Parish Assistant	FKerr@churchofscotland.org.uk
Livingstone, Ruth M.	Glenrothes: St Margaret's – Congregational Support Worker	RLivingstone@churchofscotland.org.uk
Pringle, Iona M. BD	Kennoway, Windygates and Balgonie: St Kenneth's – Parish Assistant	IPringle@churchofscotland.org.uk
Thomson, Jacqueline (Mrs) MTh DCS	Buckhaven and Wemyss – Deacon	Jaqueline.Thomson@churchofscotland.org.uk
26. ST ANDREWS		
Thorburn, Susan (Rev) MTh	Eden Tay Cluster – Mission Development Worker	SThorburn@churchofscotland.org.uk

27. DUNKELD AND MEIGLE

Pringle, James	Dull and Weem – Parish Assistant	Jamie.Pringle@churchofscotland.org.uk
Wittman, Sam	Aberfeldy – Youth Work Co-ordinator	SWittman@churchofscotland.org.uk

28. PERTH

Smith, Jane	Perth: Riverside – Community Development Worker	JSmith@churchofscotland.org.uk
Stewart, Alexander T. (Rev) MA BD FSAScot	Perth: St John's Kirk of Perth linked with Perth: St Leonard's-in-the-Fields – Associate Minister	alex.t.stewart@blueyonder.co.uk
Stott, Anne M. (Rev)	Presbytery Pioneer Worker – Bertha Park	AStott@churchofscotland.org.uk

29. DUNDEE

Berry, Gavin R.	Dundee: Camperdown/Lochee - Parish Assistant	GBerry@churchofscotland.org.uk
Campbell, Neil MA	Dundee: Craigiebank linked with Douglas and Mid Craigie – Youth and Young Adult Development Worker	Neil.Campbell@churchofscotland.org.uk
Clark, Ross	Dundee: Fintry – Discipleship, Mission and Development Worker	Ross.Clark@churchofscotland.org.uk
McKenzie, Matthew	Dundee: Lochee / Dundee: Camperdown – Youth and Families Worker	MMcKenzie@churchofscotland.org.uk
Stirling, Diane BSc DipCPC BTh	Dundee: Craigiebank linked with Douglas and Mid Craigie – Parish Assistant	DStirling@churchofscotland.org.uk

30. ANGUS

Read, Rebecca	Montrose area churches - Youth and Children's Worker	RRead@churchofscotland.org.uk
Stevens, Linda (Rev) BSc BD PgDip	The Glens and Kirriemuir: United – West Angus Area Team Minister	LStevens@churchofscotland.org.uk

31. ABERDEEN AND SHETLAND

Amalanand, John C.	Aberdeen: South Holburn – Parish Assistant	JAmalanand@churchofscotland.org.uk
Angus, Natalie	Dyce – Youth and Family Worker	NAngus@churchofscotland.org.uk
Brankin, Cheryl (Mrs) BA	Presbytery – Depute Clerk	aberdeenshetland@churchofscotland.org.uk
Broere, Teresa	Aberdeen: Mastrick – Parish Assistant	PBroere@churchofscotland.org.uk
Griesse, Dorte	Aberdeen: Mannofield – Children's and Family Worker	DGriesse@churchofscotland.org.uk
Lightbody, Philip (Rev)	Presbytery - Mission Development Leader and Presbytery Planning Officer	PLightbody@churchofscotland.org.uk
Mitchell, William	Aberdeen: High Hilton – Community Development Worker	WMitchell@churchofscotland.org.uk
Richardson, Frances	Shetland	FRichardson@churchofscotland.org.uk
Sangbarini, Curtis	Aberdeen: St Nicholas Kincorth, South of / Torry St Fittick's – Parish Assistant, Mission Development	CSangbarini@churchofscotland.org.uk
Taylor, Valerie AssocCIPD PGDip	Aberdeen: Torry St Fittick's – Ministry Assistant	VTaylor@churchofscotland.org.uk
Thomas, Jay MA BA	Aberdeen: 'West End' churches – Youth Ministry Leader	JThomas@churchofscotland.org.uk
Weir, K. Ellen	Presbytery – Youth and Children's Worker	EWeir@churchofscotland.org.uk

32. KINCARDINE AND DEESIDE

33. GORDON

Name	Role	Email
Adam, Pamela BD	Ellon – Parish Assistant	PAdam@churchofscotland.org.uk
Bruce, Nicola P.S. BA MTh	Ellon – Parish Assistant, Mission Development	NBruce@churchofscotland.org.uk
Cross, Peter	Ellon – Parish Assistant	PCross@churchofscotland.org.uk
Mikelson, Heather (Rev)	Presbytery - Mission Development Worker	HMikelson@churchofscotland.org.uk
Stigant, Victoria J.	Presbytery - Youth Work Facilitator	VStigant@churchofscotland.org.uk

34. BUCHAN

Dick, Janet	Presbytery – Mission and Discipleship Development Worker	Janet.Dick@churchofscotland.org.uk

35. MORAY

Name	Role	Email
Baker, Paula (Mrs)	Birnie and Pluscarden linked with Elgin: High – Parish Assistant	PBaker@churchofscotland.org.uk

36. ABERNETHY

Black, Barbara	Tomintoul, Glenlivet and Inveraven – Parish Assistant	BBlack@churchofscotland.org.uk
Orr, Gillian BA	Presbytery - Youth Worker	GOrr@churchofscotland.org.uk

37. INVERNESS

Name	Role	Email
Getliffe, Dot L.J. (Mrs) BA BD DipEd DCS	Inverness: Old High St Stephen's – Mission Development Worker	DGetliffe@churchofscotland.org.uk

38. LOCHABER

39. ROSS

40. SUTHERLAND

41. CAITHNESS

Petersen, Robert	Wick: Pulteneytown and Thrumster – Mission Development Worker	RPetersen@churchofscotland.org.uk

42. LOCHCARRON-SKYE

43. UIST

44. LEWIS

45. ORKNEY

47. ENGLAND

48. INTERNATIONAL CHARGES

LIST J – OVERSEAS LOCATIONS

AFRICA
MALAWI

Church of Central Africa Presbyterian Synod of Livingstonia		
Dr Linus Malu (2018)	Legal Officer, Church and Society Department, Church and Society Department, PO Box 112, Mzuzu, Malawi nnabuikemalu@yahoo.com	office +265 265 1 311 133 mobile +265 994 652 345 www.ccapsolinia.org
Mr Gary Brough (2019)	Resource, Mobilisation & Communications Manager, Church and Society Department, PO Box 112, Mzuzu, Malawi churchsociety@sdnp.org.mw	office +265 265 1 311 133 mobile +265 883 626 500 www.ccapsolinia.org

MALAWI: CCAP Livingstonia, Nkhoma and Blantyre; MOZAMBIQUE: **Evangelical Church of Christ**; SOUTH SUDAN: **Presbyterian Church of South Sudan and Sudan**

Rev Dr Kenneth R Ross (2019)	Theological Educator: Africa, based at Zomba Theological College, PO Box 130, Zomba KRoss@churchofscotland.org.uk	+265 1 524 419

ZAMBIA

United Church of Zambia		
Mr Keith and Mrs Ida Waddell (2016)	UCZ Synod, Nationalist Road at Burma Road, PO Box 50122, 15101 Ridgeway, Lusaka, Zambia keithida2014@gmail.com	office 00260 964 761 039 mobile +260 977 143 692 http://uczsynod.org

ASIA

NEPAL — Mr Joel Hafvenstein (2015) — c/o United Mission to Nepal, PO Box 126, Kathmandu, Nepal ed@umn.org.np — 00 977 1 4228 118 www.umn.org.np

LAOS — Mr Tony and Mrs Catherine Paton (2009) (Mission Associates, staff of CMS) — Church Mission Society, Church of the Holy Spirit, Vientiane Lao People's Democratic Republic — www.the-chs.org.

EUROPE

PRAGUE — Rev Dr David I. Sinclair (2017) — Evangelical Church of the Czech Brethren, Jungmannova 9, CZ111 21, Prague 1 DSinclair@churchofscotland.org.uk — 00 420 224 999 230

ROME — Ms Fiona Kendall (2018) (Ecumenical appointment: Methodist Church UK; Global Ministries USA) — Mediterranean Hope, Federation of Protestant Churches in Italy, Via Firenze 38, 00138 Roma, Italy FKendall@churchofscotland.org.uk — 00 39 (0)6 4825 120 www.mediterraneanhope.com

MIDDLE EAST

ISRAEL & PALESTINE

JERUSALEM — Rev Dr John McCulloch (2018) — St Andrew's Jerusalem, PO Box 8619, Jerusalem 91086, Israel JMcCulloch@churchofscotland.org.uk — +972 2 673 2401 www.standrewsjerusalem.org/

TIBERIAS — Rev Kate McDonald (2015) — St Andrew's Galilee, PO Box 104, Tiberias 14100, Israel KMcDonald@churchofscotland.org.uk — +972 54 244 6736 https://standrewsgalilee.com/

See also the Presbyteries of International Charges and Jerusalem (Section 5: 48 and 49)

LIST K – PRISON CHAPLAINS

SCOTTISH PRISON SERVICE CHAPLAINCY ADVISER (Church of Scotland)
Rev. Sheena Orr — SPS HQ, Calton House, 5 Redheughs Rigg, Edinburgh EH12 9HW sheena.orr@sps.pnn.gov.uk — 0131 330 3575

ADDIEWELL — Rev. Jim Murphy — HM Prison Addiewell, Station Road, Addiewell, West Calder EH55 8QA jim.murphy@sodexogov.co.uk — 01506 874500

CASTLE HUNTLY — Rev. Anne E. Stewart — HM Prison Castle Huntly, Longforgan, Dundee DD2 5HL anne.stewart2@sps.pnn.gov.uk — 01382 319388

CORNTON VALE — Rev. Sheena Orr / Mrs Deirdre Yellowlees — HM Prison and Young Offender Institution, Cornton Vale, Cornton Road, Stirling FK9 5NU sheena.orr@sps.pnn.gov.uk deirdre.yellowlees@sps.pnn.gov.uk — 01786 835365

DUMFRIES
Rev. Neil Campbell

HM Prison Dumfries, Terregles Street, Dumfries DG2 9AX
neil.campbell2@sps.pnn.gov.uk

01387 294214

EDINBURGH
Mr Gordon Pennykid DCS
Rev. Keith Graham
Rev. David Swan
Rev. Dr Bob Akroyd (Free Church)

HM Prison Edinburgh, 33 Stenhouse Road, Edinburgh EH11 3LN
gordon.pennykid@sps.pnn.gov.uk
keith.graham@sps.pnn.gov.uk
david.swan@sps.pnn.gov.uk
robert.akroyd@sps.pnn.gov.uk

0131 444 3115

GLASGOW: BARLINNIE
Rev. Jill Clancy
Rev. Jonathan Keefe
Rev. Ian McInnes
Rev. John Murfin (Elim)

HM Prison Barlinnie, 81 Lee Avenue, Riddrie, Glasgow G33 2QX
jill.clancy@sps.pnn.gov.uk; JClancy@churchofscotland.org.uk
jonathan.keefe@sps.pnn.gov.uk
ian.mcinnes@sps.pnn.gov.uk
john.murfin@sps.pnn.gov.uk

0141 770 2059

GLENOCHIL
Rev. Graham Bell (Baptist)
Rev. Elizabeth Kenny

HMPrison Glenochil, King o' Muir Road, Tullibody FK10 3AD
graham.bell@sps.pnn.gov.uk
elizabeth.kenny@sps.pnn.gov.uk

01259 767211

GRAMPIAN
Rev. Alison Harvey (Episcopal)

HM Prison and Young Offender Institution, South Road, Peterhead AB42 2YY
alison.harvey@sps.pnn.gov.uk

01779 485744

GREENOCK
Rev. Neil Campbell

HM Prison Greenock, Old Inverkip Road, Greenock PA16 9AH
neil.campbell2@sps.pnn.gov.uk

01475 787801
ext. 393287

INVERNESS
Rev. Dr Hugh Watt
Rev. John Beadle (Methodist)

HM Prison Inverness, Duffy Drive, Inverness IV2 3HN
hugh.watt@sps.pnn.gov.uk
john.beadle@methodist.org.uk

01463 229020

KILMARNOCK
Vacant

HM Prison Kilmarnock, Mauchline Road, Kilmarnock KA1 5AA

01563 548928

LOW MOSS
Rev. Martin Forrest
Rev. Paul Innes (Assemblies of God)
Rev. John Craib (Baptist)

HM Prison Low Moss, 190 Crosshill Road, Bishopbriggs, Glasgow G64 2QB
martin.forrest@sps.pnn.gov.uk
paul.innes@sps.pnn.gov.uk
john.craib@sps.pnn.gov.uk

0141 762 9727

PERTH
Rev. Margaret Shuttleworth
Mrs Deirdre Yellowlees

Chaplaincy Centre, HM Prison Perth, 3 Edinburgh Road, Perth PH2 7JH
margaret.shuttleworth@sps.pnn.gov.uk
deirdre.yellowlees@sps.pnn.gov.uk

01738 458216

POLMONT
Rev. David Swan

Chaplaincy Centre, HM Young Offender Institution Polmont, Brightons, Falkirk FK2 0AB
david.swan@sps.pnn.gov.uk

01324 722241

SHOTTS
Ms Dorothy Russell
Rev. Murdo MacLean
HM Prison Shotts, Canthill Road, Shotts ML7 4LE
dorothy.russell@sps.pnn.gov.uk
murdo.maclean@sps.pnn.gov.uk
01501 824071

LIST L – UNIVERSITY CHAPLAINS

ABERDEEN
Rev. Marylee Anderson MA BD — m.anderson@abdn.ac.uk — 01224 272137
Rev. David S. Hutchison BSC BD ThM — d.hutchison@abdn.ac.uk — 01224 272137

ABERTAY, DUNDEE
Rev. Robert A. Calvert BSc BD DMin PhD — RCalvert@churchofscotland.org.uk — 07532 029343

CAMBRIDGE
Rev. Nigel Uden (U.R.C. and C. of S.) — minister@stcolumbaschurch.org — 01223 314586

DUNDEE
Rev. Fiona C. Douglas MBE MA BD PhD — f.c.douglas@dundee.ac.uk — 01382 384157

EDINBURGH
Rev. Harriet A. Harris MBE BA DPhil — chaplain@ed.ac.uk — 0131 650 2595
Rev. Alison M. Newell BD (Associate Chaplain) — ali.newell@ed.ac.uk — 0131 650 2597
Rev. Geoffrey Baines (Associate Chaplain) — g.baines@ed.ac.uk — 0131 650 9502

EDINBURGH NAPIER
Rev. Michael J. Mair BD — chaplaincy@napier.ac.uk — 0131 334 1730 / 0131 447 7943
Rev. Steven Manders LLB BD STB MTh — chaplaincy@napier.ac.uk — 07808 476733

GLASGOW
Rev. Carolyn Kelly PhD — chaplain@glasgow.ac.uk — 0141 330 5419

GLASGOW CALEDONIAN
Rev. Alastair S. Duncan MA BD — ADuncan@churchofscotland.org.uk — 07968 852083

HERIOT-WATT, EDINBURGH
Rev. Alistair P. Donald MA PhD BD — chaplaincy@hw.ac.uk — 0131 451 4508

OXFORD
Rev. Helen Garton (U.R.C. and C. of S.) — minister@saintcolumbas.org — 01865 606910 / 07399 027532

ROBERT GORDON, ABERDEEN
Rev. Canon Isaac. M. Poobalan BD MTh DMin   chaplaincy@rgu.ac.uk   01224 640119

ST ANDREWS
Rev. Donald G. MacEwan MA BD PhD   dgm21@st-andrews.ac.uk   01334 462866 / 07713 322036 / 01334 461766 / 07546 526280

Rev. Samantha J. Ferguson MTheol (Assistant Chaplain)   sjf6@st-andrews.ac.uk

STIRLING
Rev. Janet P. Foggie MA BD PhD   janet.foggie1@stir.ac.uk   07899 349246

STRATHCLYDE, GLASGOW
Vacant (Honorary Chaplain)   chaplaincy@strath.ac.uk   0141 548 4144

LIST M – WORK PLACE CHAPLAINS

INTERIM CHIEF EXECUTIVE OFFICER, WORK PLACE CHAPLAINCY SCOTLAND
Chic Lidstone   info@wpcscotland.co.uk   0131 441 2271

For a full list of Regional Organisers, Team Leaders and Chaplaincy Locations see: www.wpcscotland.co.uk > Contact Us

Outwith WPCS:
Chaplain to the UK Oil and Gas Industry   Rev. Gordon T. Craig   gordon.craig@ukoilandgaschaplaincy.com   01224 882600

LIST N – REPRESENTATIVES ON COUNCIL EDUCATION COMMITTEES

Aberdeen City	Rev. Shuna M. Dicks	SDicks@churchofscotland.org.uk	01224 861692
Aberdeenshire	Vacant		
Angus	Mr Eric A.D. Summers	eadsummers@gmail.com	01575 572133
Argyll and Bute	Mr W. Stewart Shaw	shawwilliam@sky.com	01700 504102; 07470 520240
City of Edinburgh	Mrs Fiona E. Beveridge	fbeveridge1@gmail.com	0131 661 8831
Clackmannanshire	Rev. Sang Y. Cha	SCha@churchofscotland.org.uk	01259 213872
Comhairle nan Eilean Siar	Rev. Hugh M. Stewart	berneralwuig@btinternet.com	01851 672388
Dumfries and Galloway	Mr Robert McQuistan	mcquistan@mcquistan.plus.com	01671 820327
Dundee City	Miss Kathleen Mands	kathmands@blueyonder.co.uk	01382 451140
East Ayrshire	Mr Ian Rennie	i.rennie@btinternet.com	01563 538932

East Dunbartonshire	Mrs Barbara Jarvie	bj@bjarvie.fsnet.co.uk	01360 319729
East Lothian	Ms Elizabeth Malcolm	malcolm771@btinternet.com	01875 813659
East Renfrewshire	Ms Mary McIntyre	mmmcintyre@ntlworld.com	0141 639 2513
Falkirk	Mrs Evelyn Crosbie	evelyncrosbie@yahoo.co.uk	
Fife	Mr William Imlay	imlay@btinternet.com	
Glasgow City	Mr James Hamilton DCS	James.Hamilton@churchofscotland.org.uk	0141 558 3195; 07584 137314
Highland	Mr William Skene	bill.skene@lochaber.presbytery.org.uk	01397 712594
Inverclyde	Rev. David W.G. Burt	DBurt@churchofscotland.org.uk	01475 633914
Midlothian	Mrs Elizabeth Morton	elizabethmorton180@gmail.com	
Moray	Rev. John A. Morrison	JMorrison@churchofscotland.org.uk	01343 550199
North Ayrshire	Mr Andrew J. Bruce	andrew_bruce2@sky.com	01294 605113
North Lanarkshire	Mr Derrick Hannan	derrickhannan@blueyonder.co.uk	01236 609517
Orkney Islands	Mr Hugh Halcro-Johnston	hugh@halcro-johnston.fsworld.co.uk	01856 811200
Perth and Kinross	Mrs Pat Giles	patgiles190@yahoo.co.uk	01738 625805
Renfrewshire	Miss Mary Jane Bird	mjbird55@gmail.com	
Scottish Borders	Mr Ian Topping	ian@itfotos.co.uk	01573 223720
Shetland Islands	Rev. Thomas Macintyre	the2macs.macintyre@btinternet.com	01950 477549
South Ayrshire	Rev. David R. Gemmell	DGemmell@churchofscotland.org.uk	01292 864140
South Lanarkshire	Ms Gillian Coulter	gillcoulter55@yahoo.com	01899 810339
Stirling	Mr Colin O'Brien	cobrien20@btinternet.com	01360 660616
West Dunbartonshire	Miss Sheila Rennie	sheilarennie@tiscali.co.uk	01389 763346
West Lothian	Mrs Lynne McEwen	lynnemcewen@hotmail.co.uk	01506 855513

LIST O – MINISTERS ORDAINED FOR SIXTY YEARS AND UPWARDS

For a full list see: www.churchofscotland.org.uk > Resources > Yearbook > Section 6-O

LIST P – DECEASED MINISTERS AND DEACONS

The Editor has been made aware of the following ministers and deacons who have died since the compilation of the previous volume of the Year Book.

Alexander, William McLeish   (Berriedale and Dunbeath with Latheron)
Barr, John   (Kilmacolm: Old)
Blyth, James George Stewart   (Glenmuick (Ballater))
Brown, Joseph   (Linton with Morebattle and Hownam with Yetholm)

Cashman, Patrick Hamilton	(Dirleton with North Berwick: Abbey)
Collier, Francis Charles	(Forgue-Inverkeithny with Ythanwells Auchaber)
Currie, Gordon Christopher Macleod	(Assistant, Linlithow: St Michael's)
Donaldson, Robert Bell	(Kilchoman with Portnahaven)
Fowler, Richard Cecil Allan	(Gask with Methven)
Frizzell, Robert Stewart	(Wick: Old)
Gordon, Alasdair Bothwell	(Aberdeen: Summerhill)
Gordon, David Cowser	(Gigha and Cara)
Hannah, William	(Muirkirk)
Higham, Robert David	(Tiree)
Hodge, William Neilson Thomson	(Longside)
Hunter, James Edward	(Blantyre: Livingstone Memorial)
Jeffrey, Stewart Duncan	(Banff with King Edward)
Jones, Robert Alexander	(Marnoch)
Kirkpatrick, Alice Harkins	(Northmavine)
Lamb, Alan Henry Worbey	(Associate, Fort Augustus with Glengarry)
Logan, David Dudley John	(Caerlaverock with Dumfries: St Mary's-Greyfriars)
McCabe, George	(Airdrie: High)
McCallum, John	(Falkirk: Camelon Irving)
McCance, Andrew Maltman	(Coatbridge: Middle)
Macdonald, Peter James	(Edinburgh: Broughton St Mary's)
McGregor, Alistair Gerald Crichton	(Edinburgh: Leith North)
Maciver, Norman	(Newhills)
Mackenzie, Angus Cameron	(Biggar)
MacLennan, Donald Angus	(Kinloch)
MacLeod, Ada Vanbeck	Hurlford
McPhee, Duncan Cameron	(Department of National Mission)
Macpherson, Colin Campbell Reith	(Dunfermline: St Margaret's)
Martin, Jane Millar DCS	(Deacon, Dundee: Chalmers Ardler)
Neill, William George	(Ayr: St Andrew's)
Pryce, Stuart Franklin Astey	(Dumfries: St George's)
Rae, Andrew Whittingham	(Annan: St Andrew's Greenknowe Erskine)
Ramage, Alastair Edward	(Auxiliary Minister, Bearsden: Westerton Fairlie Memorial)
Seath, Thomas James Grant	(Motherwell: Manse Road)
Sefton, Henry Reay	(Christ's College, University of Aberdeen)
Shaw, Douglas William David	(Professor of Divinity, University of St Andrews)
Sinclair, James Harvey	(Auchencairn and Rerrick with Buittle and Kelton)
Smart, David Dominic	(Aberdeen: Gilcomston South)
Strong, Clifford	(Creich, Flisk and Kilmany with Monimail)
Tamas, Bertalan	(Budapest: St Columba's)
Taverner, Glyn Rees	(Maxton and Mertoun with St Boswells)
Thomas, Shirley Ann	(Auxiliary Minister, Dunnichen, Letham and Kirkden)
Walton, Ainslie	(Lecturer, University of Aberdeen)
Watt, John Hubert Innes	(Mochrum)

White, Brock Ainslie	(Kirkcaldy: Templehall)
Wigglesworth, John Christopher	(General Secretary, Board of World Mission and Unity)
Wilkie, Ian	Falkirk: Grahamston United
Wilkie, William Edwards	(Aberdeen: South of St Nicholas Kincorth)
Wilson, Mary Dallas	(Auxiliary Minister, Presbytery of Sutherland)
Youngson, Peter	(Kirriemuir: St Andrew's)

SECTION 7

Legal Names and Scottish Charity Numbers for Congregations

All congregations in Scotland, and congregations furth of Scotland which are registered with OSCR, the Office of the Scottish Charity Regulator

For a complete list of legal names see:
  www.churchofscotland.org.uk > Resources > Yearbook > Section 7

Further information

All documents, as defined in the Charities References in Documents (Scotland) Regulations 2007, must specify the Charity Number, Legal Name of the congregation, any other name by which the congregation is commonly known and the fact that it is a Charity. For more information, please refer to the Law Department circular on the Regulations on the Church of Scotland website.

  www.churchofscotland.org.uk > Resources > Law Department Circulars > Charity Law

SECTION 8

Church Buildings: Ordnance Survey National Grid References

Please go to: www.churchofscotland.org.uk > Resources > Yearbook > Section 8

SECTION 9

Parish and Congregational Changes

The parish structure of the Church of Scotland is constantly being reshaped as the result of unions, linkages and the occasional dissolution.

Section 9A, 'Parishes and Congregations: names no longer in use', records one of the inevitable consequences of these changes, the disappearance of the names of many former parishes and congregations. There are, however, occasions when for legal and other reasons it is important to be able to identify the present-day successors of those parishes and congregations whose names are no longer in use and which can therefore no longer be easily traced. A list of all such parishes and congregations, with full explanatory notes, may be found at:

www.churchofscotland.org.uk/Resources/Yearbook > Section 9A

Section 9B, 'Recent Readjustment and other Congregational Changes', printed below, incorporates all instances of union, linkage and dissolution, together with certain other congregational changes, which have taken place since the publication of the 2019–20 Year Book.

9: Wigtown and Stranraer	**Inch** linked with **Portpatrick** linked with **Stranraer: Trinity**: both linkages severed
	Inch linked with **Luce Valley**
	Stranraer: High Kirk and **Stranraer: Trinity** united as **Stranraer**
	Portpatrick linked with **Stranraer**
11: Irvine and Kilmarnock	**Irvine: Mure** linked with **Irvine: Relief Bourtreehill**
12: Ardrossan	**Kilwinning: Old** renamed **Kilwinning: Abbey**
13: Lanark	**Coalburn and Lesmahagow: Old** and **Lesmahagow: Abbeygreen** united as **Coalburn and Lesmahagow**

14: Greenock and Paisley	**Howwood** linked with **Johnstone: St Paul's**
	Langbank linked with **Port Glasgow: St Andrew's**: linkage severed
	Lochwinnoch dissolved
	Paisley: Lylesland and **Paisley: St Luke's** united as **Paisley: South**
	Paisley: St Ninian's Ferguslie dissolved
	Port Glasgow: Hamilton Bardrainney linked with **Port Glasgow: St Martin's**: linkage severed
	Port Glasgow: St Andrew's and **Port Glasgow: St Martin's** united as **Port Glasgow: New**
16: Glasgow	**Moodiesburn** erected as new parish
	Netherlee and **Stamperland** united as **Netherlee and Stamperland**
	Glasgow: Garthamlock and Craigend East renamed **Glasgow: Garthamlock and Craigend**
18: Dumbarton	**Alexandria** and **Jamestown** united as **Lomond**
	Kilmaronock Gartocharn linked with **Lomond**
19: Argyll	**Campbeltown: Highland** linked with **Saddell and Carradale** linked with **Southend**
	Craignish: severed from linkage with **Kilbrandon and Kilchattan** and **Kilninver and Kilmelford**
	Cumlodden, Lochfyneside and Lochgair and **Glenaray and Inveraray** united as **West Lochfyneside: Cumlodden, Inveraray and Lochgair**
	Kilarrow and **Kildalton and Oa** united as **South Islay**
	Jura linked with **North and West Islay** additionally linked with **South Islay**
	Kilninian and Kilmore, Salen and Ulva, Tobermory and **Torosay and Kinlochspelvie** united as **North Mull**
23: Stirling	**Stirling: Allan Park South** and **Stirling: St Columba's** united as **Stirling: Park**
31: Aberdeen	**Aberdeen: Garthdee** dissolved
	Aberdeen: High Hilton and **Aberdeen: Middlefield** united as **Aberdeen: High Hilton**
	Aberdeen: Kirk of St Nicholas Uniting renamed **Aberdeen: Kirk of St Nicholas**

46: Shetland

Burra Isle, Delting, Dunrossness and St Ninian's inc. Fair Isle, Lerwick and Bressay, Nesting and Lunnasting, Northmavine, Sandsting and Aithsting, Sandwick, Cunningsburgh and Quarff, Tingwall, Unst and Fetlar, Walls and Sandness, Whalsay and Skerries and **Yell** united as the single parish of **Shetland** in the united Presbytery of Aberdeen and Shetland

Presbytery of Greenock and Paisley and **Presbytery of Dumbarton** united as **Presbytery of Clyde**

Presbytery of Aberdeen and **Presbytery of Shetland** united as **Presbytery of Aberdeen and Shetland**

Historical Note
The presbyteries created in 1581 (or shortly thereafter) included the Presbytery of Paisley and Dumbarton. In 1590 that was separated into presbyteries of Paisley and of Dumbarton. In 1834 Greenock was disjoined from Paisley. In 2003 Paisley and Greenock were united as Greenock and Paisley. So the new Presbytery of Clyde reflects its historical roots.

The 1581 presbyteries included the Presbyteries of Aberdeen and of Lerwick. In 1830 Burravoe was disjoined from Lerwick and in 1848 Olnafirth was disjoined from Lerwick. Following the 1929 union, Lerwick, Burravoe and Olnafirth presbyteries were united as the Presbytery of Shetland.

SECTION 10

Congregational
Statistics
2019

Comparative Statistics: 1979–2019

	2019	2009	1999	1989	1979
Communicants	308,797	464,355	626,665	804,468	970,741
Elders	27,247	36,215	44,131	46,106	48,056

NOTES ON CONGREGATIONAL STATISTICS

Com   Number of communicants at 31 December 2019.

Eld   Number of elders at 31 December 2019.

G   Membership of the Guild including Young Woman's Groups and others as recorded on the 2019 annual return submitted to the Guild Office.

In 19   Ordinary General Income for 2019. Ordinary General Income consists of members' offerings, contributions from congregational organisations, regular fund-raising events, income from investments, deposits and so on. This figure does not include extraordinary or special income, or income from special collections and fund-raising for other charities.

M&M   Final amount allocated to congregations to contribute for Ministries and Mission after allowing for Presbytery-approved amendments up to 31 December 2019, but before deducting stipend endowments and normal allowances given for locum purposes in a vacancy or guardianship.

–18   This figure shows 'the number of children and young people aged 17 years and under who are involved in the life of the congregation'.

The statistics for the congregations now in the united Presbyteries of Clyde and of Aberdeen and Shetland are shown under those new presbyteries.

Some congregations were united or dissolved after 31 December 2019. Their statistics are shown as the entities they were at that date, but their names are shown in italics – details of the readjustment are given in Section 9B. The charge of Moodiesburn (Presbytery of Glasgow) is not listed as it was created on 1 January 2020.

Figures may also not be available for congregations which failed to submit the appropriate schedule. Where the figure for the number of elders is missing, then in nearly every case the number of communicants relates to the previous year.

Congregation	Com	Eld	G	In19	M&M	–18
1. Edinburgh						
Balerno	511	63	25	127,925	81,357	10
Barclay Viewforth	267	23	-	147,471	127,416	67
Blackhall St Columba's	626	64	-	192,221	116,213	4
Bristo Memorial Craigmillar	39	4	-	-	31,247	80
Broughton St Mary's	166	23	-	57,188	55,460	20
Canongate	333	35	-	159,797	80,650	-
Carrick Knowe	323	42	59	63,357	42,389	250
Colinton	788	49	-	199,852	120,042	46
Corstorphine: Craigsbank	381	27	-	91,133	69,328	121
Corstorphine: Old	371	29	40	127,584	70,908	20
Corstorphine: St Anne's	360	54	55	111,392	71,634	42
Corstorphine: St Ninian's	581	74	56	168,720	102,876	28
Craiglockhart	354	43	21	134,799	86,743	50
Craigmillar Park	168	11	25	56,523	47,420	2
Reid Memorial	268	14	-	128,007	59,247	-
Cramond	932	86	-	239,047	188,396	46
Currie	440	30	49	138,917	92,268	57
Dalmeny	106	9	-	37,568	23,856	15
Queensferry	543	53	46	114,032	70,931	96
Davidson's Mains	418	61	-	-	119,609	55
Drylaw	65	11	-	23,263	10,627	10
Duddingston	398	41	-	114,692	76,870	157
Fairmilehead	499	56	35	113,905	86,227	59
Gorgie Dalry Stenhouse	194	22	-	-	76,292	96
Gracemount	22	5	-	17,432	7,492	24
Liberton	688	56	40	226,701	125,683	47
Granton	164	22	-	48,794	31,351	8
Greenbank	665	77	34	341,365	143,187	205
Greenside	102	21	-	-	34,431	7
Greyfriars Kirk	298	31	-	-	101,056	19
High (St Giles')	453	26	-	334,784	185,792	17
Holy Trinity	218	27	-	151,936	92,668	144
Inverleith St Serf's	305	32	21	102,178	72,114	100
Juniper Green	281	26	-	105,455	64,485	20
Kirkliston	231	32	43	108,319	62,322	38
Leith: North	143	22	-	73,524	51,461	4
Leith: St Andrew's	166	21	-	70,874	55,554	20
Leith: South	270	46	-	119,321	77,126	86
Liberton Northfield	164	13	-	57,865	30,627	327
Marchmont St Giles'	212	25	13	132,284	75,618	70
Mayfield Salisbury	483	58	-	257,190	149,933	-
Meadowbank	58	5	-	35,340	23,799	2
Morningside	393	62	-	185,363	128,071	252
Morningside United	98	10	-	63,630	1,150	19
Murrayfield	460	23	-	-	94,346	97
Newhaven	147	15	-	87,732	49,858	139
Old Kirk and Muirhouse	93	17	-	25,874	25,129	103
Palmerston Place	357	39	-	162,111	111,951	89

Congregation	Com	Eld	G	In19	M&M	–18
Pilrig St Paul's	200	13	19	47,809	35,106	3
Polwarth	147	23	17	71,846	60,602	4
Portobello and Joppa	779	72	69	218,277	146,482	223
Priestfield	105	16	-	85,880	56,392	54
Ratho	181	12	-	43,233	39,754	11
Richmond Craigmillar	83	8	-	-	10,506	3
St Andrew's and St George's West	314	45	-	255,241	171,706	14
St Andrew's Clermiston	164	9	-	-	31,816	9
St Catherine's Argyle	105	6	-	59,676	37,259	38
St Cuthbert's	259	32	-	-	91,765	6
St David's Broomhouse	118	15	-	27,378	16,657	28
St John's Colinton Mains	196	19	-	59,935	39,723	54
St Margaret's	193	28	24	54,353	43,123	-
St Martin's	84	11	-	21,467	2,859	4
St Michael's	306	26	32	66,348	49,973	13
St Nicholas' Sighthill	316	17	-	-	28,782	39
St Stephen's Comely Bank	122	7	-	-	59,035	18
Slateford Longstone	178	10	26	37,752	23,051	40
Stockbridge	181	17	-	122,892	61,933	21
Tron Kirk (Gilmerton and Moredun)	81	8	-	33,769	13,785	90
Wardie	486	45	48	-	87,889	159
Willowbrae	105	16	-	47,835	42,573	27

2. West Lothian

Congregation	Com	Eld	G	In19	M&M	–18
Abercorn	63	8	-	16,182	10,396	-
Pardovan, Kingscavil and Winchburgh	238	28	-	82,735	42,585	96
Armadale	460	38	24	80,920	50,614	101
Avonbridge	40	6	-	13,337	7,210	2
Torphichen	118	16	-	34,307	22,347	8
Bathgate: Boghall	212	24	24	94,485	58,350	197
Bathgate: High	437	38	31	89,679	56,680	88
Bathgate: St John's	321	15	25	-	40,015	-
Blackburn and Seafield	237	41	-	50,274	47,153	56
Blackridge	56	8	-	21,827	11,130	2
Harthill: St Andrew's	175	10	21	58,810	36,501	36
Breich Valley	101	11	17	30,827	25,068	8
Broxburn	322	24	21	83,822	49,207	9
Fauldhouse: St Andrew's	175	10	-	43,217	33,932	5
Kirknewton and East Calder	288	34	31	98,605	67,223	71
Kirk of Calder	473	37	23	88,724	54,755	7
Linlithgow: St Michael's	1,265	91	46	330,353	165,000	315
Linlithgow: St Ninian's Craigmailen	364	35	40	75,093	45,960	159
Livingston: Old	288	33	16	90,963	59,791	61
Livingston: United	252	32	-	83,076	45,050	177
Polbeth Harwood	156	17	-	28,531	15,544	10
West Kirk of Calder	223	16	12	59,654	46,216	70
Strathbrock	263	21	17	80,668	68,353	60
Uphall South	172	23	-	55,573	41,453	24
Whitburn: Brucefield	175	17	23	92,554	57,221	8
Whitburn: South	325	31	-	72,241	54,167	69

Congregation	Com	Eld	G	In19	M&M	–18
3. Lothian						
Aberlady	182	18	-	49,207	24,854	6
Gullane	337	19	25	67,727	41,274	25
Athelstaneford	183	12	-	21,751	17,645	12
Whitekirk and Tyninghame	128	12	-	-	21,714	10
Belhaven	509	35	65	91,923	55,975	43
Spott	96	5	-	16,858	11,034	3
Bilston	78	4	15	13,931	6,140	-
Glencorse	284	12	19	25,532	16,684	-
Roslin	198	8	-	27,140	17,483	-
Bonnyrigg	538	50	48	96,260	71,345	9
Cockenzie and Port Seton: Chalmers Memorial	157	26	25	89,756	53,294	81
Cockenzie and Port Seton: Old	202	17	27	-	36,155	15
Cockpen and Carrington	143	25	42	32,730	25,367	6
Lasswade and Rosewell	236	19	-	31,618	25,723	25
Dalkeith: St John's and King's Park	468	35	28	189,750	64,317	70
Dalkeith: St Nicholas' Buccleuch	309	16	-	61,863	33,609	-
Dirleton	173	14	-	-	39,455	6
North Berwick: Abbey	239	31	32	98,658	56,454	59
Dunbar	316	16	27	90,062	76,385	38
Dunglass	266	10	-	22,863	21,171	25
Garvald and Morham	34	9	-	-	7,332	5
Haddington: West	194	15	24	48,934	35,833	3
Gladsmuir	144	15	-	-	16,538	4
Longniddry	289	43	25	78,282	48,187	7
Gorebridge	140	12	-	132,081	67,928	120
Haddington: St Mary's	473	47	-	110,945	71,819	29
Humbie	66	9	-	27,886	17,046	19
Yester, Bolton and Saltoun	264	32	-	56,440	36,277	36
Loanhead	277	27	27	73,292	37,861	35
Musselburgh: Northesk	274	25	22	64,017	38,608	96
Musselburgh: St Andrew's High	257	25	18	68,843	42,657	-
Musselburgh: St Clement's and St Ninian's	63	10	-	13,268	14,800	-
Musselburgh: St Michael's Inveresk	356	36	-	90,612	53,698	5
Newbattle	300	22	12	74,946	39,022	147
Newton	81	1	-	13,788	13,592	9
North Berwick: St Andrew Blackadder	557	32	34	176,057	101,288	70
Ormiston	134	9	27	40,022	26,286	11
Pencaitland	132	3	-	-	28,372	6
Penicuik: North	371	30	-	76,995	45,484	34
Penicuik: St Mungo's	183	18	18	146,092	45,359	-
Penicuik: South and Howgate	79	11	-	52,414	52,641	2
Prestonpans: Prestongrange	237	19	14	53,349	39,780	3
Tranent	210	16	29	60,737	35,737	21
Traprain	395	29	33	82,460	55,720	30
Tyne Valley	277	27	-	77,311	58,486	79
4. Melrose and Peebles						
Ashkirk	34	4	-	10,760	6,226	1
Selkirk	333	20	-	73,272	39,003	37

Congregation	Com	Eld	G	In19	M&M	–18
Bowden and Melrose	650	53	22	119,722	79,185	72
Broughton, Glenholm and Kilbucho	137	9	18	18,200	12,019	1
Skirling	58	5	-	-	5,129	-
Stobo and Drumelzier	80	6	-	20,309	16,268	2
Tweedsmuir	36	5	-	-	4,162	3
Caddonfoot	152	13	-	17,428	10,856	3
Galashiels: Trinity	340	28	25	59,467	37,348	1
Carlops	50	12	-	25,208	13,309	15
Kirkurd and Newlands	80	12	8	13,868	16,244	5
West Linton: St Andrew's	163	15	-	41,396	24,778	50
Channelkirk and Lauder	379	20	16	-	33,969	3
Earlston	338	21	8	46,137	34,209	33
Eddleston	98	7	-	-	10,212	-
Peebles: Old	378	26	-	97,304	66,262	-
Ettrick and Yarrow	162	15	-	31,108	32,143	-
Galashiels: Old and St Paul's	217	15	26	55,728	41,514	2
Galashiels: St John's	171	9	-	39,441	25,056	60
Innerleithen, Traquair and Walkerburn	291	26	29	-	38,019	2
Lyne and Manor	84	7	-	33,333	21,676	2
Peebles: St Andrew's Leckie	464	31	-	120,350	65,674	-
Maxton and Mertoun	77	9	-	-	11,403	-
Newtown	106	9	-	19,709	10,800	-
St Boswells	163	20	16	33,309	16,721	-
Stow: St Mary of Wedale and Heriot	165	10	-	27,471	23,551	9

5. Duns

Congregation	Com	Eld	G	In19	M&M	–18
Ayton and District Churches	282	17	11	31,811	30,399	4
Berwick-upon-Tweed: St Andrew's						
Wallace Green and Lowick	290	17	-	64,802	38,852	5
Chirnside	88	5	12	16,451	10,499	-
Hutton and Fishwick and Paxton	59	-	10	16,423	10,593	-
Coldingham and St Abb's	63	13	-	39,361	28,156	5
Eyemouth	102	15	16	45,002	25,316	17
Coldstream and District Parishes	402	32	-	48,465	41,587	-
Eccles and Leitholm	131	7	12	27,247	15,474	-
Duns and District Parishes	599	32	33	92,055	71,733	110
Fogo	47	9	-	10,590	5,031	37
Gordon: St Michael's	59	6	-	-	7,659	10
Greenlaw	82	6	11	16,385	12,173	-
Legerwood	58	6	-	7,412	5,842	5
Westruther	37	1	-	4,246	4,497	-

6. Jedburgh

Congregation	Com	Eld	G	In19	M&M	–18
Ale and Teviot United	375	19	17	32,165	39,395	-
Cavers and Kirkton	96	6	-	12,403	10,350	-
Hawick: Trinity	479	34	38	45,158	29,316	45
Cheviot Churches	284	25	35	-	46,589	-
Hawick: Burnfoot	65	9	-	19,781	15,502	59
Hawick: St Mary's and Old	336	18	19	50,497	23,100	91
Hawick: Teviot and Roberton	188	13	9	61,382	31,127	10

Congregation	Com	Eld	G	In19	M&M	–18
Hawick: Wilton	251	19	-	-	30,753	64
Teviothead	52	3	-	4,828	3,343	-
Hobkirk and Southdean	123	18	12	11,010	16,261	5
Ruberslaw	229	17	10	32,577	24,330	7
Jedburgh: Old and Trinity	542	12	31	58,982	46,028	-
Kelso Country Churches	175	16	12	20,571	30,806	-
Kelso: North and Ednam	906	72	26	-	75,376	1
Kelso: Old and Sprouston	432	20	-	52,927	31,337	5
Oxnam	123	9	-	9,884	8,074	12

7. Annandale and Eskdale

Congregation	Com	Eld	G	In19	M&M	–18
Annan: Old	321	36	41	64,385	41,336	11
Dornock	101	10	-	-	6,407	-
Annan: St Andrew's	444	38	42	65,552	38,212	70
Brydekirk	43	3	-	-	6,710	10
Applegarth, Sibbaldbie and Johnstone	110	7	12	8,564	9,703	-
Lochmaben	220	8	30	68,990	41,102	3
Canonbie United	84	14	-	34,680	8,690	7
Liddesdale	94	6	-	30,187	22,585	-
Dalton and Hightae	169	6	-	21,437	15,063	4
St Mungo	73	11	-	11,651	9,868	-
Gretna: Old, Gretna: St Andrew's, Half Morton and Kirkpatrick Fleming	291	20	15	46,545	37,824	22
Hoddom, Kirtle-Eaglesfield and Middlebie	183	19	12	24,418	19,881	21
Kirkpatrick Juxta	97	6	-	11,783	6,637	-
Moffat: St Andrew's	317	26	20	75,240	45,962	41
Wamphray	53	5	-	8,475	5,188	3
Langholm Eskdalemuir Ewes and Westerkirk	423	-	9	54,910	52,358	-
Lockerbie: Dryfesdale, Hutton and Corrie	423	37	31	64,996	45,657	10
The Border Kirk	271	44	-	62,834	39,668	25
Tundergarth	26	4	-	10,253	5,639	-

8. Dumfries and Kirkcudbright

Congregation	Com	Eld	G	In19	M&M	–18
Balmaclellan, Kells and Dalry	118	14	12	35,643	27,419	-
Carsphairn	76	6	-	8,750	6,896	3
Caerlaverock	100	7	-	12,037	7,502	3
Dumfries: St Mary's-Greyfriars	322	28	26	-	45,185	7
Castle Douglas	329	19	17	72,079	38,977	8
The Bengairn Parishes	153	22	-	24,944	27,833	2
Closeburn	171	14	-	30,887	20,078	20
Kirkmahoe	197	12	-	32,620	19,319	-
Colvend, Southwick and Kirkbean	173	11	17	69,533	60,949	-
Corsock and Kirkpatrick Durham	46	10	-	-	15,217	9
Crossmichael, Parton and Balmaghie	198	10	15	26,002	20,759	2
Cummertrees, Mouswald and Ruthwell	172	15	-	-	23,686	-
Dalbeattie and Kirkgunzeon	482	22	-	-	34,477	-
Urr	153	9	-	-	17,490	-
Dumfries: Maxwelltown West	319	35	27	88,077	57,000	56
Dumfries: Northwest	249	8	-	-	26,970	2
Dumfries: St George's	458	46	21	114,094	70,870	54

Congregation	Com	Eld	G	In19	M&M	–18
Dumfries: St Michael's and South	618	40	19	88,751	63,665	29
Dumfries: Troqueer	225	16	23	-	58,313	17
Dunscore	172	17	-	32,509	20,107	23
Glencairn and Moniaive	142	7	-	31,171	25,831	-
Durisdeer	126	6	-	21,840	15,015	10
Penpont, Keir and Tynron	150	10	-	23,878	19,973	11
Thornhill	124	7	-	17,633	24,909	1
Gatehouse and Borgue	253	18	-	56,574	35,895	12
Tarff and Twynholm	130	12	22	23,798	18,355	15
Irongray, Lochrutton and Terregles	157	22	-	33,295	24,135	-
Kirkconnel	206	11	-	21,951	22,029	-
Sanquhar: St Bride's	351	17	11	35,194	28,150	-
Kirkcudbright	434	25	-	78,948	55,928	43
Kirkmichael, Tinwald and Torthorwald	360	-	15	-	38,584	-
Lochend and New Abbey	189	17	11	40,569	23,357	-

9. Wigtown and Stranraer

Congregation	Com	Eld	G	In19	M&M	–18
Ervie Kirkcolm	163	13	-	21,395	13,342	11
Leswalt	256	16	-	-	18,688	12
Glasserton and Isle of Whithorn	84	6	-	-	12,873	-
Whithorn: St Ninian's Priory	293	6	16	36,203	27,286	32
Inch	215	13	6	17,048	14,481	46
Luce Valley	209	15	24	52,338	34,337	19
Portpatrick	204	9	18	-	18,004	-
Stranraer: Trinity	465	-	25	85,242	64,818	-
Kirkcowan	100	10	-	32,310	21,214	5
Wigtown	139	14	12	32,511	22,347	40
Kirkinner	127	6	6	21,318	11,486	-
Mochrum	216	8	19	17,759	15,913	18
Sorbie	93	8	-	18,381	14,246	-
Kirkmabreck	113	10	20	19,782	13,200	5
Monigaff	232	6	-	17,273	16,938	7
Kirkmaiden	157	12	-	-	21,005	9
Stoneykirk	250	15	17	29,463	27,551	1
Penninghame	383	21	19	97,558	62,527	45
Stranraer: High Kirk	477	31	-	62,827	54,447	221

10. Ayr

Congregation	Com	Eld	G	In19	M&M	–18
Alloway	928	89	-	253,518	118,349	440
Annbank	235	20	15	24,357	21,878	-
Tarbolton	276	24	27	50,749	38,272	24
Auchinleck	303	15	24	-	22,867	6
Catrine	95	8	-	19,939	16,013	-
Ayr: Auld Kirk of Ayr	469	48	-	69,310	53,068	-
Ayr: Castlehill	510	34	50	76,368	59,952	151
Ayr: Newton Wallacetown	333	37	38	105,400	73,240	64
Ayr: St Andrew's	266	21	17	-	39,856	86
Ayr: St Columba	1,121	109	75	278,993	158,927	40
Ayr: St James'	317	27	-	64,806	49,259	136
Ayr: St Leonard's	345	43	20	104,592	54,658	-

Congregation	Com	Eld	G	In19	M&M	–18
Dalrymple	119	13	-	-	16,242	-
Ayr: St Quivox	131	19	-	36,487	34,900	3
Ballantrae	224	15	9	38,650	30,737	4
St Colmon (Arnsheen Barrhill and Colmonell)	201	8	-	-	18,940	12
Barr	36	2	-	8,803	2,937	-
Dailly	102	8	-	-	9,490	-
Girvan: South	237	22	27	32,652	21,853	10
Coylton	303	18	-	36,334	24,854	8
Drongan: The Schaw Kirk	153	15	12	-	25,055	40
Craigie and Symington	268	21	18	44,934	35,759	12
Prestwick: South	235	29	32	86,189	60,915	95
Crosshill	165	9	28	16,496	8,825	-
Maybole	290	25	17	69,055	42,900	2
Dalmellington	127	12	-	20,906	18,172	10
Patna: Waterside	129	10	-	-	17,622	-
Dundonald	455	36	41	-	50,847	32
Fisherton	115	13	-	14,995	9,016	4
Kirkoswald	186	18	20	35,438	22,352	11
Girvan: North	536	39	-	73,967	31,838	26
Kirkmichael	187	15	21	33,237	13,695	4
Straiton: St Cuthbert's	153	11	22	-	13,093	6
Lugar	149	12	15	21,794	14,668	6
Old Cumnock: Old	314	17	26	62,584	42,488	12
Mauchline	353	19	30	86,532	47,890	3
Sorn	128	11	15	18,057	12,290	-
Monkton and Prestwick: North	247	25	19	87,685	60,049	15
Muirkirk	149	13	-	19,603	12,631	7
Old Cumnock: Trinity	283	21	24	43,430	32,370	11
New Cumnock	438	27	17	69,032	42,274	-
Ochiltree	212	23	12	28,588	21,739	12
Stair	205	17	21	46,137	27,312	21
Prestwick: Kingcase	557	74	45	95,772	77,095	168
Prestwick: St Nicholas'	495	63	40	131,905	80,031	32
Troon: Old	875	58	-	131,566	82,624	120
Troon: Portland	451	47	-	-	81,939	-
Troon: St Meddan's	588	69	31	-	75,038	121

11. Irvine and Kilmarnock

Congregation	Com	Eld	G	In19	M&M	–18
Caldwell	196	19	-	63,905	40,875	-
Dunlop	365	-	19	79,760	54,895	-
Crosshouse	228	30	23	58,500	39,115	40
Darvel	289	-	29	49,876	35,493	-
Dreghorn and Springside	365	-	23	82,041	57,580	-
Fenwick	283	-	27	-	35,837	-
Kilmarnock: Riccarton	221	-	17	65,180	42,899	-
Galston	507	-	56	85,431	69,515	-
Hurlford	283	-	20	58,255	41,049	-
Irvine: Fullarton	364	33	44	118,864	64,289	260
Irvine: Girdle Toll	153	-	18	32,617	22,599	-
Irvine: St Andrew's	223	-	23	61,742	30,421	-

Congregation	Com	Eld	G	In19	M&M	–18
Irvine: Mure	260	21	22	55,634	40,732	44
Irvine: Relief Bourtreehill	186	19	20	37,204	26,161	4
Irvine: Old	314	-	-	66,116	47,685	-
Kilmarnock: Kay Park	432	62	23	139,070	84,580	206
Kilmarnock: New Laigh Kirk	762	68	46	223,753	133,841	140
Kilmarnock: St Andrew's and St Marnock's	715	89	35	177,407	105,384	385
Kilmarnock: St John's Onthank	176	-	17	-	32,045	-
Kilmarnock: St Kentigern's	269	-	-	51,245	32,307	-
Kilmarnock: South	201	15	14	39,178	23,302	15
Kilmaurs: St Maur's Glencairn	280	-	20	64,088	34,715	-
Newmilns: Loudoun	173	-	-	-	24,409	-
Stewarton: John Knox	242	-	29	108,438	61,335	-
Stewarton: St Columba's	400	-	38	80,359	59,518	-

12. Ardrossan

Ardrossan: Park	368	30	29	74,058	47,087	120
Ardrossan and Saltcoats: Kirkgate	194	28	24	73,287	53,791	2
Beith	640	56	21	96,343	69,102	44
Brodick	118	16	-	48,087	34,864	8
Corrie	26	5	-	23,718	11,490	-
Lochranza and Pirnmill	54	9	-	35,073	14,823	-
Shiskine	60	10	17	27,029	24,071	6
Cumbrae	207	24	33	57,378	38,207	48
Largs: St John's	619	41	41	125,694	79,627	22
Dalry: St Margaret's	477	55	24	-	90,201	50
Dalry: Trinity	156	16	-	96,618	53,597	97
Fairlie	187	16	23	71,579	49,034	62
Largs: St Columba's	293	22	46	74,389	56,612	36
Kilbirnie: Auld Kirk	264	24	-	49,564	37,930	5
Kilbirnie: St Columba's	475	32	-	64,806	39,761	35
Kilmory	28	4	-	-	8,702	-
Lamlash	78	10	24	-	26,038	12
Kilwinning: Abbey	485	54	24	102,833	70,655	24
Kilwinning: Mansefield Trinity	175	13	20	54,957	36,436	11
Largs: Clark Memorial	605	77	47	138,323	84,978	132
Saltcoats: North	231	17	19	-	30,960	12
Saltcoats: St Cuthbert's	223	32	12	84,853	54,333	78
Stevenston: Ardeer	182	22	28	35,546	27,619	67
Stevenston: Livingstone	211	26	19	55,362	34,458	3
Stevenston: High	206	19	17	75,468	59,829	36
West Kilbride	387	42	7	115,327	74,331	122
Whiting Bay and Kildonan	67	9	-	40,280	26,869	6

13. Lanark

Biggar	284	20	25	97,241	61,025	30
Black Mount	67	4	14	13,372	12,829	8
Cairngryffe	134	12	14	22,324	21,509	2
Libberton and Quothquan	76	11	-	16,850	11,161	15
Symington	129	13	19	31,610	22,930	2
Carluke: Kirkton	613	42	27	138,061	84,504	420

Congregation	Com	Eld	G	In19	M&M	–18
Carluke: St Andrew's	176	11	16	50,289	33,600	45
Carluke: St John's	518	47	27	95,299	57,844	45
Carnwath	116	10	18	-	12,911	-
Carstairs	162	12	19	40,642	32,195	115
Coalburn and Lesmahagow: Old	433	29	27	84,675	52,171	5
Crossford	132	5	-	32,799	22,545	35
Kirkfieldbank	72	6	-	-	11,579	-
Douglas Valley	268	21	31	63,578	34,791	-
Forth: St Paul's	307	26	27	65,545	40,331	118
Kirkmuirhill	148	9	46	81,931	50,343	25
Lanark: Greyfriars	474	46	27	111,412	56,554	130
Lanark: St Nicholas'	459	39	18	101,216	69,075	61
Law	169	10	29	51,918	29,759	81
Lesmahagow: Abbeygreen	100	12	-	-	38,157	135
Upper Clyde	175	8	14	21,155	23,178	9

14. Clyde

Congregation	Com	Eld	G	In19	M&M	–18
Arrochar	58	17	-	-	11,427	-
Luss	93	16	8	-	38,371	1
Baldernock	167	13	-	32,828	22,838	1
Milngavie: St Paul's	809	-	85	210,741	117,936	-
Barrhead: Bourock	410	37	32	93,029	60,513	200
Barrhead: St Andrew's	335	34	22	145,592	88,290	267
Bearsden: Baljaffray	358	7	36	92,024	54,407	100
Bearsden: Cross	646	68	26	170,354	100,019	47
Bearsden: Killermont	547	53	48	157,842	92,235	75
Bearsden: New Kilpatrick	1,223	113	75	-	181,947	40
Bearsden: Westerton Fairlie Memorial	317	33	46	110,427	62,234	40
Bishopton	608	51	-	108,986	67,517	137
Bonhill	425	48	-	-	44,520	85
Renton: Trinity	244	12	-	34,008	20,850	6
Bridge of Weir: Freeland	368	47	-	131,888	79,207	33
Bridge of Weir: St Machar's Ranfurly	294	26	26	100,928	59,328	21
Cardross	357	39	24	85,163	54,901	50
Clydebank: Faifley	171	15	32	42,702	27,533	8
Clydebank: Kilbowie St Andrew's	226	21	23	-	29,137	107
Clydebank: Radnor Park	104	16	12	31,674	28,587	-
Clydebank: Waterfront	147	23	-	47,974	34,639	22
Dalmuir: Barclay	155	19	-	47,275	23,797	61
Craigrownie	134	16	-	31,343	29,672	-
Garelochhead	133	11	-	-	34,828	35
Rosneath: St Modan's	92	13	25	30,196	15,056	-
Dumbarton: Riverside	439	60	36	107,809	69,574	234
Dumbarton: St Andrew's	98	17	-	31,577	19,580	-
Dumbarton: West Kirk	139	22	-	-	36,630	136
Duntocher: Trinity	183	18	46	37,523	24,861	-
Elderslie Kirk	409	35	34	-	64,302	123
Erskine	305	30	55	94,249	63,038	150
Gourock: Old Gourock and Ashton	565	56	19	125,711	75,132	356
Gourock: St John's	386	46	-	114,657	79,164	256

Congregation	Com	Eld	G	In19	M&M	–18
Greenock: East End	50	6	-	10,317	5,601	12
Greenock: Mount Kirk	298	30	-	57,575	42,635	100
Greenock: Lyle Kirk	696	47	18	-	88,395	85
Greenock: St Margaret's	150	25	-	36,351	24,735	12
Greenock: St Ninian's	207	16	-	-	18,053	28
Greenock: Wellpark Mid Kirk	434	47	13	-	60,162	66
Greenock: Westburn	514	64	23	116,930	78,808	36
Helensburgh	798	63	32	234,492	123,443	28
Rhu and Shandon	230	16	28	62,931	40,264	7
Houston and Killellan	653	56	60	154,627	90,122	224
Howwood	129	14	20	44,961	28,179	8
Johnstone: St Paul's	327	59	-	81,397	50,208	135
Inchinnan	237	33	29	-	39,269	17
Inverkip	291	28	17	75,414	50,889	10
Skelmorlie and Wemyss Bay	212	29	-	87,208	52,655	6
Johnstone: High	178	31	21	97,102	60,546	88
Johnstone: St Andrew's Trinity	181	23	-	37,614	24,767	49
Kilbarchan	402	49	41	111,564	77,059	120
Kilmacolm: Old	351	42	-	-	80,128	25
Kilmacolm: St Columba	131	17	-	88,663	62,868	4
Kilmaronock Gartocharn	198	10	-	22,127	20,222	10
Lomond	362	39	26	96,012	68,250	22
Langbank	116	14	-	-	27,141	1
Linwood	160	19	27	50,425	35,538	6
Lochwinnoch	87	9	-	-	26,547	-
Milngavie: Cairns	324	34	-	147,000	94,181	20
Milngavie: St Luke's	334	13	-	82,616	28,447	-
Neilston	407	27	19	105,687	70,826	140
Old Kilpatrick Bowling	215	14	-	-	39,510	40
Paisley: Abbey	682	43	-	111,375	106,808	76
Paisley: Glenburn	134	12	-	45,033	29,164	35
Paisley: Lylesland	242	36	26	87,831	60,571	49
Paisley: Martyrs' Sandyford	325	-	21	86,905	72,550	100
Paisley: Oakshaw Trinity	411	63	-	149,227	65,678	18
Paisley: St Columba Foxbar	149	20	-	23,875	20,061	4
Paisley: St Luke's	169	20	-	-	32,060	10
Paisley: St Mark's Oldhall	405	54	41	-	70,074	84
Paisley: St Ninian's Ferguslie	27	7	-	-	5,000	1
Paisley: Sherwood Greenlaw	502	58	20	128,941	78,876	130
Paisley: Stow Brae Kirk	283	63	41	92,029	67,422	9
Paisley: Wallneuk North	305	29	-	-	40,166	8
Port Glasgow: Hamilton Bardrainney	212	18	13	41,474	30,445	47
Port Glasgow: New	436	64	16	76,741	72,118	270
Renfrew: North	577	64	28	101,077	79,121	153
Renfrew: Trinity	283	21	31	90,989	65,048	50

16. Glasgow

Banton	56	8	-	7,577	4,729	3
Twechar	66	10	-	20,228	9,482	1
Bishopbriggs: Kenmure	229	18	32	92,116	70,767	90

Congregation	Com	Eld	G	In19	M&M	-18
Bishopbriggs: Springfield Cambridge	554	36	81	132,088	81,312	137
Broom	412	48	16	116,413	79,116	28
Burnside Blairbeth	431	35	76	241,251	142,927	157
Busby	204	27	20	-	46,815	20
Cadder	566	72	46	-	91,977	121
Cambuslang	539	41	34	108,910	90,057	174
Cambuslang: Flemington Hallside	293	27	35	60,669	39,834	50
Campsie	134	18	20	56,791	38,453	11
Chryston	400	24	12	-	112,660	72
Eaglesham	475	50	38	133,168	87,339	198
Fernhill and Cathkin	218	22	10	43,688	32,916	72
Gartcosh	74	13	-	21,766	13,787	85
Glenboig	104	5	-	18,469	8,833	-
Giffnock: Orchardhill	294	35	10	161,539	95,151	206
Giffnock: South	560	63	31	174,869	99,045	22
Giffnock: The Park	232	24	-	66,888	43,504	18
Greenbank	726	68	63	240,637	134,563	330
Kilsyth: Anderson	236	22	46	-	39,143	94
Kilsyth: Burns and Old	352	28	30	78,249	59,005	31
Kirkintilloch: Hillhead	65	8	9	-	11,220	-
Kirkintilloch: St Columba's	198	27	34	106,373	56,713	10
Kirkintilloch: St David's Memorial Park	488	49	28	94,527	55,330	95
Kirkintilloch: St Mary's	612	40	-	-	69,946	18
Lenzie: Old	404	43	-	126,120	69,520	82
Lenzie: Union	538	53	59	185,558	110,910	200
Maxwell Mearns Castle	245	25	-	162,339	96,752	180
Mearns	564	41	-	-	122,553	33
Milton of Campsie	291	30	40	80,851	50,504	115
Netherlee	558	62	33	203,443	118,034	-
Stamperland	270	24	15	70,573	55,069	11
Newton Mearns	347	37	30	108,955	72,698	91
Rutherglen: Old	205	24	-	69,161	38,768	4
Rutherglen: Stonelaw	282	29	-	141,419	85,799	25
Rutherglen: West and Wardlawhill	424	42	34	-	49,779	92
Stepps	198	16	-	-	36,924	61
Thornliebank	131	12	24	-	31,066	11
Torrance	188	18	-	100,300	63,159	96
Williamwood	379	58	26	101,816	69,858	561
Glasgow: Baillieston Mure Memorial	316	31	54	-	54,135	17
Glasgow: Baillieston St Andrew's	243	19	26	69,940	44,938	130
Glasgow: Balshagray Victoria Park	115	26	12	84,525	63,453	3
Glasgow: Barlanark Greyfriars	70	16	8	33,738	15,770	103
Glasgow: Blawarthill	155	18	20	27,272	11,693	53
Glasgow: Bridgeton St Francis in the East	74	11	11	36,103	23,264	23
Glasgow: Broomhill Hyndland	448	68	30	171,799	108,464	148
Glasgow: Calton Parkhead	78	10	-	14,101	5,446	2
Glasgow: Cardonald	281	43	-	104,418	68,725	92
Glasgow: Carmunnock	272	22	14	47,627	32,423	30
Glasgow: Carmyle	73	3	-	20,660	12,871	47
Glasgow: Kenmuir Mount Vernon	109	11	22	59,882	40,259	55

Congregation	Com	Eld	G	In19	M&M	–18
Glasgow: Carntyne	240	17	33	59,203	46,037	105
Glasgow: Carnwadric	76	10	-	24,413	21,725	20
Glasgow: Castlemilk	121	-	21	-	17,491	-
Glasgow: Cathcart Old	233	42	26	-	53,881	200
Glasgow: Cathcart Trinity	305	46	28	182,900	109,889	26
Glasgow: Cathedral (High or St Mungo's)	388	32	-	93,028	80,499	-
Glasgow: Causeway (Tollcross)	152	27	20	-	32,117	87
Glasgow: Clincarthill	193	28	34	86,916	57,658	6
Glasgow: Colston Milton	54	7	-	19,101	6,852	7
Glasgow: Colston Wellpark	86	11	-	25,636	20,638	32
Glasgow: Cranhill	33	3	-	-	4,791	164
Glasgow: Croftfoot	238	36	31	-	50,691	75
Glasgow: Dennistoun New	159	27	-	83,383	59,485	74
Glasgow: Drumchapel St Andrew's	144	36	-	37,678	28,036	35
Glasgow: Drumchapel St Mark's	75	8	-	13,351	1,370	45
Glasgow: Easterhouse	54	7	-	-	14,591	152
Glasgow: Eastwood	160	40	18	74,427	63,508	107
Glasgow: Gairbraid	119	-	-	23,719	18,680	-
Glasgow: Gallowgate	32	6	-	25,880	18,871	-
Glasgow: Garthamlock and Craigend	53	12	-	-	2,799	85
Glasgow: Gorbals	92	-	-	29,501	18,298	-
Glasgow: Govan and Linthouse	155	43	37	-	61,393	648
Glasgow: Hillington Park	265	32	26	58,449	40,115	110
Glasgow: Ibrox	115	27	-	47,500	27,801	52
Glasgow: John Ross Memorial (for Deaf People)	51	3	-	-	-	-
Glasgow: Jordanhill	336	58	23	164,721	99,412	21
Glasgow: Kelvinbridge	46	14	-	31,893	34,922	29
Glasgow: Kelvinside Hillhead	145	21	-	-	46,692	93
Glasgow: King's Park	489	58	-	120,350	85,626	18
Glasgow: Kinning Park	120	12	-	38,282	24,236	-
Glasgow: Knightswood St Margaret's	144	18	-	-	27,885	8
Glasgow: Langside	200	42	-	92,271	63,062	32
Glasgow: Maryhill	145	10	8	35,481	20,402	84
Glasgow: Merrylea	234	43	-	67,652	48,041	16
Glasgow: Newlands South	387	45	-	136,908	83,728	15
Glasgow: Partick South	106	12	-	67,196	45,630	15
Glasgow: Partick Trinity	119	20	-	-	55,165	40
Glasgow: Pollokshaws	89	16	-	41,959	27,480	10
Glasgow: Pollokshields	133	21	14	-	47,738	60
Glasgow: Possilpark	85	20	-	31,159	17,710	22
Glasgow: Queen's Park Govanhill	117	32	26	89,793	70,955	8
Glasgow: Robroyston	54	4	-	33,386	4,390	24
Glasgow: Ruchazie	26	5	-	-	1,958	20
Glasgow: Ruchill Kelvinside	64	10	-	-	33,333	25
Glasgow: St Andrew and St Nicholas	296	28	11	66,802	54,665	292
Glasgow: St Andrew's East	52	12	19	28,434	18,196	1
Glasgow: St Andrew's West	142	14	16	-	64,442	7
Glasgow: St Christopher's Priesthill and Nitshill	184	13	-	28,382	23,476	54
Glasgow: St Columba	123	14	-	-	12,704	-
Glasgow: St David's Knightswood	175	17	26	-	49,950	25

Congregation	Com	Eld	G	In19	M&M	–18
Glasgow: St Enoch's Hogganfield	102	11	16	-	21,393	2
Glasgow: St George's Tron	65	9	-	-	1,342	4
Glasgow: St James' (Pollok)	113	21	33	46,121	27,732	60
Glasgow: St John's Renfield	273	43	-	150,298	85,819	136
Glasgow: St Paul's	33	5	-	11,432	3,267	250
Glasgow: St Rollox	72	6	-	41,904	24,668	32
Glasgow: Sandyford Henderson Memorial	156	16	-	132,178	108,019	10
Glasgow: Sandyhills	217	24	43	61,406	49,148	19
Glasgow: Scotstoun	76	5	-	53,502	38,214	-
Glasgow: Shawlands Trinity	270	29	-	85,877	72,247	100
Glasgow: Sherbrooke Mosspark	319	48	18	-	109,594	25
Glasgow: Shettleston New	199	25	23	-	50,136	200
Glasgow: Springburn	185	25	18	-	43,077	64
Glasgow: Temple Anniesland	228	24	-	96,653	62,228	116
Glasgow: Toryglen	54	8	-	10,149	10,793	8
Glasgow: Trinity Possil and Henry Drummond	45	5	-	68,524	34,816	6
Glasgow: Tron St Mary's	84	12	-	-	25,837	18
Glasgow: Wallacewell	126	-	-	7,774	1,513	-
Glasgow: Wellington	151	30	-	86,233	71,282	9
Glasgow: Whiteinch	76	5	-	-	35,855	16
Glasgow: Yoker	91	7	-	19,863	14,097	7

17. Hamilton

Airdrie: Cairnlea	477	46	24	-	83,354	93
Calderbank	113	10	14	29,013	14,165	-
Airdrie: Clarkston	316	36	16	77,791	55,504	133
Airdrie: High	270	32	-	69,735	40,781	154
Caldercruix and Longriggend	145	6	-	54,084	34,306	77
Airdrie: Jackson	319	49	18	98,115	56,842	185
Airdrie: New Monkland	274	30	26	72,033	44,667	73
Greengairs	111	9	-	21,633	15,098	3
Airdrie: St Columba's	201	14	-	-	11,434	-
Airdrie: The New Wellwynd	691	86	-	174,299	99,063	157
Bargeddie	81	6	-	-	44,271	8
Bellshill: Central	150	30	19	60,182	35,506	14
Bellshill: West	430	32	-	69,505	40,148	16
Blantyre: Livingstone Memorial	183	25	-	56,238	29,920	233
Blantyre: St Andrew's	168	20	-	51,874	31,493	13
Blantyre: Old	242	15	21	57,263	50,902	25
Bothwell	472	51	37	184,940	74,457	83
Chapelhall	189	25	30	46,039	27,456	36
Kirk o' Shotts	157	9	-	29,324	16,937	13
Cleland	137	8	-	27,726	16,738	-
Wishaw: St Mark's	256	25	40	70,177	46,175	120
Coatbridge: Blairhill Dundyvan	221	22	24	55,300	38,161	77
Coatbridge: Middle	241	30	30	46,360	29,756	19
Coatbridge: Calder	250	13	-	39,787	37,144	-
Coatbridge: Old Monkland	93	18	-	57,825	32,921	25
Coatbridge: New St Andrew's	539	65	31	-	75,263	188
Coatbridge: Townhead	121	17	-	33,878	22,687	30

Congregation	Com	Eld	G	In19	M&M	–18
Dalserf	176	21	23	51,300	50,219	2
East Kilbride: Claremont	387	37	-	128,197	83,276	10
East Kilbride: Greenhills	140	11	15	32,057	21,207	4
East Kilbride: Moncrieff	547	53	43	133,885	74,497	190
East Kilbride: Mossneuk	250	12	-	21,492	17,739	113
East Kilbride: Old	636	62	33	-	78,588	17
East Kilbride: South	201	22	-	82,522	50,523	115
East Kilbride: Stewartfield	25	5	-	14,327	7,000	5
East Kilbride: West	262	21	-	-	37,564	15
East Kilbride: Westwood	306	23	-	-	51,517	40
Hamilton: Cadzow	357	49	36	-	80,798	70
Hamilton: Gilmour and Whitehill	116	18	-	38,375	28,533	5
Hamilton: West	173	30	-	62,879	42,914	45
Hamilton: Hillhouse	356	38	-	74,454	60,997	153
Hamilton: Old	441	67	17	-	100,223	46
Hamilton: St John's	476	49	55	166,000	78,911	246
Hamilton: South	142	17	19	50,166	38,738	6
Quarter	91	11	-	26,249	14,622	-
Hamilton: Trinity	254	18	-	55,665	34,310	-
Holytown	138	22	17	44,164	31,382	70
New Stevenston: Wrangholm Kirk	81	11	15	30,107	24,705	12
Larkhall: Chalmers	78	5	-	22,088	18,655	5
Larkhall: St Machan's	307	56	34	-	67,112	120
Larkhall: Trinity	145	16	24	38,968	29,231	90
Motherwell: Crosshill	242	37	47	74,922	58,792	55
Motherwell: St Margaret's	349	16	-	41,968	24,680	10
Motherwell: Dalziel St Andrew's	442	62	42	142,179	81,039	180
Motherwell: North	124	22	25	49,213	39,237	90
Wishaw: Craigneuk and Belhaven	114	22	-	56,731	26,774	10
Motherwell: St Mary's	636	92	55	147,913	90,050	452
Motherwell: South	388	72	48	93,040	62,741	25
Newarthill and Carfin	200	27	14	63,219	52,778	63
Newmains: Bonkle	105	17	-	37,072	21,630	13
Newmains: Coltness Memorial	172	20	12	-	34,187	4
Overtown	249	32	49	69,573	32,271	150
Shotts: Calderhead Erskine	383	34	30	88,319	58,569	14
Stonehouse: St Ninian's	362	55	34	-	8,956	160
Strathaven: Avendale Old and Drumclog	492	44	35	125,372	84,795	25
Strathaven: Trinity	875	118	62	188,668	114,791	143
Uddingston: Burnhead	257	23	9	53,060	34,797	47
Uddingston: Old	394	42	29	139,580	86,248	-
Uddingston: Viewpark	376	65	17	117,195	69,156	150
Wishaw: Cambusnethan North	396	31	-	78,006	48,690	32
Wishaw: Cambusnethan Old and Morningside	360	31	16	58,477	61,095	130
Wishaw: Old	178	21	-	33,619	22,186	32
Wishaw: South Wishaw	268	25	25	68,875	60,542	40

19. Argyll

Congregation	Com	Eld	G	In19	M&M	–18
Appin	84	12	16	24,720	16,744	1
Lismore	36	6	-	-	8,815	-

Congregation	Com	Eld	G	In19	M&M	–18
Ardchattan	80	10	-	21,875	18,014	3
Coll	18	3	-	5,657	2,751	-
Connel	104	17	10	-	28,149	9
Ardrishaig	117	17	24	32,515	22,810	-
South Knapdale	31	4	-	-	7,622	-
Barra	32	3	-	-	10,064	-
South Uist	51	7	-	17,178	12,325	6
Bute, United Church of	444	34	29	69,644	50,973	50
Campbeltown: Highland	347	30	-	37,882	27,670	10
Saddell and Carradale	178	16	21	30,042	23,850	20
Southend	209	16	14	29,521	20,038	12
Campbeltown: Lorne and Lowland	689	40	29	153,579	55,245	62
Colonsay and Oronsay	11	3	-	15,185	5,919	-
Craignish	40	3	-	-	4,520	-
Dunoon: St John's	110	23	30	-	30,191	-
Kirn and Sandbank	260	31	-	46,966	33,625	10
Dunoon: The High Kirk	273	31	25	-	41,301	2
Innellan	53	-	-	6,164	10,422	-
Toward	51	5	-	20,040	12,609	-
Gigha and Cara	28	6	-	8,324	6,953	4
Kilcalmonell	36	12	-	8,780	7,250	1
Killean and Kilchenzie	116	13	16	24,087	14,561	30
Glassary, Kilmartin and Ford	91	10	-	-	15,147	7
North Knapdale	47	6	-	20,811	21,571	4
Glenorchy and Innishael	39	6	-	-	6,878	-
Strathfillan	40	6	-	6,415	6,307	-
Iona	12	5	-	-	9,338	-
Kilfinichen and Kilvickeon and the Ross of Mull	25	4	-	10,393	5,320	4
Jura	21	5	-	8,133	2,522	-
North and West Islay	102	25	7	30,790	30,687	10
South Islay	115	22	-	-	45,792	16
Kilbrandon and Kilchattan	88	19	-	21,711	20,129	6
Kilninver and Kilmelford	53	5	-	9,104	7,754	-
Kilchrenan and Dalavich	33	9	-	14,925	12,217	24
Muckairn	106	20	-	-	16,836	-
Kilfinan	29	5	-	8,041	4,797	-
Kilmodan and Colintraive	73	8	-	16,595	14,432	-
Kyles	84	14	-	-	21,651	-
Kilmore and Oban	418	45	21	74,360	58,687	30
Kilmun, Strone and Ardentnny: The Shore Kirk	159	15	13	-	33,627	-
Kilninian and Kilmore	20	5	-	11,471	5,932	-
Salen and Ulva	32	-	-	22,672	7,733	-
Tobermory	61	11	-	34,956	21,860	13
Torosay and Kinlochspelvie	23	3	-	-	4,369	1
Lochgilphead	121	-	19	37,281	24,466	-
Lochgoilhead and Kilmorich	63	10	-	30,391	23,205	3
Strachur and Strachlachlan	104	11	11	20,435	19,951	-
Rothesay: Trinity	289	33	12	55,731	38,690	45
Skipness	17	3	-	12,103	5,185	1
Tarbert, Loch Fyne and Kilberry	93	11	17	29,916	23,374	5

Congregation	Com	Eld	G	In19	M&M	–18
Tiree	72	-	-	-	13,851	-
West Lochfyneside: Cumlodden, Inveraray and Lochgair	116	20	12	-	36,644	1

22. Falkirk

Airth	135	8	18	40,814	27,578	38
Blackbraes and Shieldhill	142	21	18	30,892	20,219	-
Muiravonside	162	18	-	-	29,454	2
Bo'ness: Old	305	24	9	59,390	35,624	40
Bo'ness: St Andrew's	341	11	-	39,557	45,116	70
Bonnybridge: St Helen's	196	13	-	-	35,722	8
Bothkennar and Carronshore	182	16	-	33,301	24,297	8
Brightons	562	28	41	168,377	81,525	190
Carriden	354	40	21	51,296	40,916	-
Cumbernauld: Abronhill	181	12	23	53,967	46,755	12
Cumbernauld: Condorrat	280	24	33	72,567	50,697	84
Cumbernauld: Kildrum	241	21	-	-	41,540	4
Cumbernauld: St Mungo's	146	32	-	38,029	28,016	16
Cumbernauld: Old	294	43	-	73,606	53,188	38
Denny: Old	285	36	20	58,748	41,182	40
Haggs	217	29	-	35,049	22,570	36
Denny: Westpark	393	29	23	94,467	66,204	85
Dunipace	314	20	-	63,055	37,997	91
Falkirk: Bainsford	112	13	-	38,948	22,993	100
Falkirk: Camelon	172	13	-	-	44,590	80
Falkirk: Grahamston United	400	56	21	-	43,837	46
Falkirk: Laurieston	164	15	17	34,217	23,680	-
Redding and Westquarter	110	12	-	25,802	16,223	-
Falkirk: St Andrew's West	382	27	-	79,529	54,379	20
Falkirk: Trinity	462	50	17	-	106,978	64
Grangemouth: Abbotsgrange	303	45	-	64,358	47,119	106
Grangemouth: Kirk of the Holy Rood	290	20	-	58,215	34,698	2
Grangemouth: Zetland	502	59	51	112,398	70,283	164
Larbert: East	584	53	34	131,132	83,769	227
Larbert: Old	269	19	-	84,609	46,957	58
Larbert: West	327	31	33	76,152	48,045	56
Polmont: Old	323	25	29	101,415	65,166	72
Slamannan	94	7	-	-	18,766	24
Stenhouse and Carron	305	27	-	-	46,073	5

23. Stirling

Aberfoyle	64	5	12	14,027	15,966	2
Port of Menteith	55	9	-	13,150	5,876	-
Alloa: Ludgate	278	20	14	88,758	44,586	5
Alloa: St Mungo's	313	40	27	-	46,913	16
Alva	418	54	31	78,730	52,255	64
Balfron	119	12	-	-	27,784	8
Fintry	98	11	13	18,550	20,019	2
Balquhidder	53	4	-	23,945	11,927	2
Killin and Ardeonaig	78	8	8	26,601	14,835	7

Congregation	Com	Eld	G	In19	M&M	–18
Bannockburn: Allan	252	33	-	57,663	29,569	-
Cowie and Plean	147	8	-	12,057	7,488	-
Bannockburn: Ladywell	352	17	-	31,188	19,756	14
Bridge of Allan	643	39	58	110,124	76,931	72
Buchanan	93	7	-	37,656	14,681	3
Drymen	242	25	-	78,225	47,782	19
Buchlyvie	152	14	15	25,156	20,892	16
Gartmore	56	8	-	18,496	16,946	5
Callander	488	24	31	95,579	69,522	79
Cambusbarron: The Bruce Memorial	270	24	-	83,493	42,589	40
Clackmannan	330	23	29	86,099	53,064	49
Dollar	222	25	54	89,546	59,425	7
Glendevon	27	3	-	2,963	3,020	-
Muckhart	77	7	-	20,364	16,490	12
Dunblane: Cathedral	761	72	29	223,663	126,610	194
Dunblane: St Blane's	291	25	34	104,293	67,715	20
Lecropt	133	16	-	46,080	27,189	6
Fallin	244	7	-	-	21,125	70
Gargunnock	110	9	-	19,445	21,094	15
Kilmadock	78	11	-	17,292	16,924	1
Kincardine-in-Menteith	71	5	-	15,254	12,536	-
Killearn	319	19	43	89,726	60,361	22
Kippen	175	14	17	28,954	25,791	6
Norrieston	84	9	9	23,662	18,768	-
Logie	465	30	25	79,306	62,779	20
Menstrie	309	19	25	58,660	43,947	-
Sauchie and Coalsnaughton	388	22	12	55,623	39,343	7
Stirling: Allan Park South	138	22	-	40,524	32,517	14
Stirling: Church of The Holy Rude	132	16	-	-	29,093	1
Stirling: Viewfield Erskine	219	20	19	29,504	20,793	7
Stirling: North	325	25	21	72,245	37,583	17
Stirling: St Columba's	416	45	-	113,199	59,992	40
Stirling: St Mark's	161	9	-	24,892	22,473	35
Stirling: St Ninian's Old	589	58	-	110,259	61,011	67
Strathblane	159	18	40	81,148	43,483	20
Tillicoultry	521	58	27	-	56,583	80
Tullibody: St Serf's	309	20	25	59,254	35,992	7

24. Dunfermline

Aberdour: St Fillan's	335	17	-	72,682	52,384	10
Beath and Cowdenbeath: North	204	23	21	58,993	38,475	11
Cairneyhill	87	17	-	28,729	16,387	-
Limekilns	222	30	-	80,352	50,366	8
Carnock and Oakley	148	18	23	57,637	35,991	4
Cowdenbeath: Trinity	257	23	11	64,764	50,037	15
Culross and Torryburn	59	10	-	-	34,179	20
Dalgety	473	39	25	120,544	81,995	85
Dunfermline: Abbey	582	58	-	145,596	87,086	25
Dunfermline: East	86	6	-	72,982	14,060	50
Dunfermline: Gillespie Memorial	120	18	13	-	26,576	16

Congregation	Com	Eld	G	In19	M&M	–18
Dunfermline: North	134	15	-	29,423	19,256	1
Dunfermline: St Andrew's Erskine	166	20	14	49,249	32,613	20
Dunfermline: St Leonard's	283	21	26	84,596	51,081	63
Dunfermline: St Margaret's	200	29	-	93,149	46,466	34
Dunfermline: St Ninian's	140	16	19	41,685	32,063	22
Dunfermline: Townhill and Kingseat	190	22	24	72,163	43,238	42
Inverkeithing	185	15	-	59,030	43,682	23
North Queensferry	49	7	-	18,857	10,230	6
Kelty	225	19	27	68,173	49,652	10
Lochgelly and Benarty: St Serf's	348	33	-	61,597	43,507	13
Rosyth	201	18	-	-	22,848	157
Saline and Blairingone	133	18	15	37,954	32,019	9
Tulliallan and Kincardine	244	29	38	-	43,038	73
25. Kirkcaldy						
Auchterderran Kinglassie	277	-	15	52,484	38,980	-
Auchtertool	62	6	-	16,309	6,471	3
Kirkcaldy: Linktown	207	30	28	59,826	41,137	5
Buckhaven and Wemyss	212	22	16	42,615	36,988	1
Burntisland	253	32	20	-	46,501	25
Dysart: St Clair	392	30	13	-	37,128	25
Glenrothes: Christ's Kirk	173	14	20	45,607	27,789	2
Glenrothes: St Columba's	368	43	-	76,990	41,002	91
Glenrothes: St Margaret's	248	26	26	61,617	32,930	50
Glenrothes: St Ninian's	200	29	18	81,000	47,135	6
Kennoway, Windygates and Balgonie: St Kenneth's	398	46	50	104,446	63,001	3
Kinghorn	213	20	-	87,178	46,216	-
Kirkcaldy: Abbotshall	426	31	-	81,751	47,799	10
Kirkcaldy: Bennochy	387	37	17	-	54,210	9
Kirkcaldy: Pathhead	303	29	39	79,072	49,253	130
Kirkcaldy: St Bryce Kirk	311	30	21	82,941	59,820	31
Kirkcaldy: Templehall	122	13	15	31,678	25,472	-
Kirkcaldy: Torbain	185	28	-	50,073	29,666	70
Leslie: Trinity	129	12	-	21,817	18,000	-
Leven	407	33	32	92,440	67,587	5
Markinch and Thornton	416	37	-	88,229	61,729	12
Methil: Wellesley	266	28	15	51,634	34,767	115
Methilhill and Denbeath	171	17	33	27,782	23,149	7
26. St Andrews						
Anstruther and Cellardyke: St Ayle	363	33	34	85,510	52,476	12
Crail	297	22	44	42,279	30,065	3
Balmerino	105	11	-	-	15,750	-
Wormit	165	14	32	38,678	23,950	19
Boarhills and Dunino	126	8	-	23,181	18,343	-
St Andrews: Holy Trinity	296	27	31	-	66,361	45
Cameron	89	10	9	21,484	13,721	6
St Andrews: St Leonard's	407	44	19	120,193	81,956	10
Carnbee	84	12	13	13,863	10,623	-
Pittenweem	206	12	16	19,334	14,452	3

Congregation	Com	Eld	G	In19	M&M	–18
Ceres, Kemback and Springfield	329	20	15	-	69,744	42
Creich, Flisk and Kilmany	74	8	-	19,882	18,604	-
Cupar: Old and St Michael of Tarvit	474	31	23	128,970	83,928	40
Monimail	72	11	-	20,226	15,309	3
Cupar: St John's and Dairsie United	601	43	33	-	72,654	9
East Neuk Trinity	287	24	50	78,906	54,725	6
St Monans	234	12	22	62,291	48,885	15
Edenshead	293	22	12	-	37,527	-
Falkland	109	11	-	33,044	26,252	-
Freuchie	123	20	20	26,485	16,744	14
Howe of Fife	275	19	-	57,404	41,857	19
Kilrenny	93	12	-	35,292	21,495	-
Kingsbarns	62	8	-	-	12,490	-
Largo	280	33	16	91,090	48,911	3
Largoward	44	8	-	15,533	5,158	4
Leuchars: St Athernase	283	24	19	-	34,868	13
Lindores	330	27	-	40,125	31,917	6
Newport-on-Tay	323	38	-	73,747	50,267	28
St Andrews: Hope Park and Martyrs'	481	44	22	-	97,913	-
Strathkinness	78	7	-	21,115	11,695	-
Tayport	214	10	-	-	34,433	6

27. Dunkeld and Meigle

Aberfeldy	155	9	-	-	29,675	208
Dull and Weem	129	14	12	34,069	23,320	1
Grantully, Logierait and Strathtay	126	9	7	32,741	28,227	5
Alyth	616	34	23	81,839	55,347	10
Ardler, Kettins and Meigle	369	20	34	49,514	33,811	10
Bendochy	73	12	-	24,030	17,121	-
Coupar Angus: Abbey	252	20	-	-	26,781	40
Blair Atholl and Struan	102	14	-	17,535	23,900	-
Braes of Rannoch	18	5	-	-	6,808	-
Foss and Rannoch	77	8	-	6,919	9,295	3
Blairgowrie	780	44	39	112,778	77,523	91
Caputh and Clunie	132	14	-	21,371	21,462	-
Kinclaven	127	13	15	24,711	14,268	5
Dunkeld	312	26	-	111,637	73,316	40
Fortingall, Glenlyon, Kenmore and Lawers	98	14	19	45,758	31,294	-
Kirkmichael, Straloch and Glenshee	75	5	-	11,375	13,561	-
Rattray	259	15	-	36,698	24,354	5
Pitlochry	309	30	18	96,577	58,964	32
Tenandry	36	8	-	22,260	18,716	-

28. Perth

Aberdalgie and Forteviot	167	14	-	29,323	12,834	13
Aberuthven and Dunning	180	14	-	51,652	35,647	15
Abernethy and Dron and Arngask	267	26	27	37,214	35,969	10
Almondbank Tibbermore	180	14	18	-	31,363	4
Methven and Logiealmond	143	15	-	-	16,066	-
Ardoch	163	15	28	47,297	23,948	22

Congregation	Com	Eld	G	In19	M&M	–18
Blackford	87	11	-	22,080	17,619	11
Auchterarder	529	35	43	149,672	94,760	35
Auchtergaven and Moneydie	455	27	20	-	37,654	5
Redgorton and Stanley	298	17	30	35,822	30,067	57
Cargill Burrelton	91	15	17	-	23,949	19
Collace	104	7	12	16,494	9,182	8
Cleish	126	10	11	36,261	28,557	10
Fossoway: St Serf's and Devonside	191	16	-	55,442	36,259	10
Comrie	342	27	23	91,596	69,987	60
Dundurn	53	7	-	17,769	11,191	-
Crieff	556	31	20	98,750	61,057	7
Dunbarney and Forgandenny	499	31	24	90,375	58,812	15
Errol	253	22	28	49,758	30,467	28
Kilspindie and Rait	63	-	-	14,220	8,804	-
Kinross	618	36	34	134,843	78,188	118
Mid Strathearn	305	26	14	50,944	49,549	29
Muthill	236	20	13	50,436	33,950	16
Trinity Gask and Kinkell	37	4	-	-	5,953	-
Orwell and Portmoak	375	33	28	83,475	57,140	28
Perth: Craigie and Moncrieffe	510	25	28	-	63,339	95
Perth: Kinnoull	353	38	25	-	50,406	91
Perth: Letham St Mark's	437	9	-	121,252	71,209	63
Perth: North	808	43	35	224,129	130,504	53
Perth: Riverside	64	-	-	44,996	27,471	-
Perth: St John's Kirk of Perth	372	29	-	105,405	66,471	-
Perth: St Leonard's-in-the-Fields	400	34	-	79,470	54,809	3
Perth: St Matthew's	588	27	18	125,522	60,184	120
St Madoes and Kinfauns	273	30	-	49,218	46,969	42
Scone and St Martins	782	43	41	107,932	71,594	49

29. Dundee

Congregation	Com	Eld	G	In19	M&M	–18
Abernyte	83	11	-	17,858	13,903	10
Inchture and Kinnaird	150	26	-	41,621	28,387	9
Longforgan	162	15	22	-	29,322	2
Auchterhouse	125	11	14	26,432	19,656	6
Monikie and Newbigging and Murroes and Tealing	430	19	14	54,431	37,294	5
Dundee: Balgay	294	29	-	57,926	39,508	12
Dundee: Barnhill St Margaret's	664	44	55	160,644	94,987	29
Dundee: Broughty Ferry New Kirk	578	44	36	104,825	66,468	70
Dundee: Broughty Ferry St James'	128	10	15	-	18,859	6
Dundee: Broughty Ferry St Luke's and Queen Street	282	34	18	-	45,406	6
Dundee: Broughty Ferry St Stephen's and West	275	29	-	59,987	31,763	-
Dundee: Dundee (St Mary's)	487	35	-	-	57,649	-
Dundee: Camperdown	83	10	-	23,351	19,751	10
Dundee: Chalmers Ardler	157	16	-	79,529	54,099	136
Dundee: Coldside	178	18	-	43,562	36,316	66
Dundee: Craigiebank	133	9	-	27,713	18,864	30
Dundee: Douglas and Mid Craigie	102	9	-	25,454	15,032	-

Congregation	Com	Eld	G	In19	M&M	–18
Dundee: Downfield Mains	238	20	21	93,621	58,090	131
Dundee: Fintry	87	5	-	50,096	32,136	56
Dundee: Lochee	441	19	30	71,048	47,361	193
Dundee: Logie and St John's Cross	190	13	21	69,638	47,862	18
Dundee: Meadowside St Paul's	273	24	15	64,443	32,767	7
Dundee: St Andrew's	386	41	23	120,390	66,808	40
Dundee: Menzieshill	220	12	-	-	25,727	-
Dundee: St David's High Kirk	180	33	19	48,300	31,941	40
Dundee: Steeple	195	18	-	131,167	84,149	26
Dundee: Stobswell	352	32	-	-	44,553	2
Dundee: Strathmartine	229	21	22	-	30,230	3
Dundee: Trinity	366	28	-	51,924	37,844	59
Dundee: West	247	18	18	61,550	52,390	-
Dundee: Whitfield	33	4	-	-	8,516	60
Fowlis and Liff	133	12	-	-	29,044	22
Lundie and Muirhead	257	24	-	46,739	30,543	45
Invergowrie	237	44	34	57,973	40,121	10
Monifieth	910	51	42	132,586	87,517	108

30. Angus

Congregation	Com	Eld	G	In19	M&M	–18
Aberlemno	185	8	-	27,664	17,819	14
Guthrie and Rescobie	209	10	11	-	15,370	15
Arbirlot	131	8	-	38,866	16,130	1
Carmyllie	92	12	-	-	16,636	-
Arbroath: Old and Abbey	381	26	-	71,268	61,350	35
Arbroath: St Andrew's	503	44	39	146,432	80,225	75
Arbroath: St Vigeans	440	39	14	-	46,066	100
Arbroath: West Kirk	836	85	56	99,619	92,037	30
Barry	178	8	16	27,443	15,940	3
Carnoustie	276	20	17	73,293	47,986	6
Brechin: Cathedral	407	26	25	-	50,882	-
Brechin: Gardner Memorial	414	18	-	51,240	38,688	14
Farnell	115	12	-	9,457	9,966	10
Carnoustie: Panbride	599	31	-	75,659	50,037	25
Colliston	161	5	6	18,621	13,031	4
Friockheim Kinnell	124	9	18	21,692	14,326	1
Inverkeilor and Lunan	109	7	15	19,628	16,217	1
Dun and Hillside	358	45	31	-	36,935	-
Dunnichen, Letham and Kirkden	221	15	18	33,618	26,860	3
Eassie, Nevay and Newtyle	189	15	16	23,427	20,490	30
Edzell Lethnot Glenesk	326	24	20	34,624	33,557	10
Fern Careston Menmuir	92	9	-	13,440	14,903	14
Forfar: East and Old	483	48	42	-	68,984	135
Forfar: Lowson Memorial	564	43	28	106,274	74,599	221
Forfar: St Margaret's	427	27	18	78,509	47,903	80
Glamis, Inverarity and Kinettles	325	27	-	46,056	48,181	12
Montrose: Old and St Andrew's	549	39	17	84,560	52,492	38
Montrose: South and Ferryden	275	18	-	55,830	36,291	1
Oathlaw Tannadice	113	7	-	17,563	18,529	3

Congregation	Com	Eld	G	In19	M&M	–18
The Glens and Kirriemuir United	1,093	82	50	-	99,398	150
The Isla Parishes	137	17	11	29,532	30,583	9

31. Aberdeen and Shetland

Congregation	Com	Eld	G	In19	M&M	–18
Aberdeen: Bridge of Don Oldmachar	175	11	-	50,020	33,288	76
Aberdeen: Craigiebuckler	707	64	24	-	70,807	85
Aberdeen: Ferryhill	291	39	-	82,021	55,053	100
Aberdeen: Garthdee	182	15	-	-	18,658	50
Aberdeen: High Hilton	281	27	17	51,778	33,633	55
Aberdeen: Holburn West	305	36	30	91,389	72,978	13
Aberdeen: Mannofield	821	94	38	-	92,156	15
Aberdeen: Mastrick	182	19	-	52,878	33,131	-
Aberdeen: Middlefield	89	4	-	-	3,891	-
Aberdeen: Midstocket	411	38	43	-	63,802	50
Aberdeen: Northfield	135	8	16	24,051	19,587	5
Aberdeen: Queen's Cross	365	47	-	-	83,105	-
Aberdeen: Rubislaw	379	57	36	141,566	85,649	24
Aberdeen: Ruthrieston West	296	27	15	86,764	49,702	6
Aberdeen: St Columba's Bridge of Don	216	13	-	92,232	57,643	100
Aberdeen: St George's Tillydrone	82	7	-	-	6,086	-
Aberdeen: St John's Church for Deaf People	85	4	-	-	-	-
Aberdeen: St Machar's Cathedral	460	37	-	170,318	90,844	12
Aberdeen: St Mark's	385	40	40	114,136	74,363	15
Aberdeen: St Mary's	282	34	-	67,039	47,091	90
Aberdeen: St Nicholas Kincorth, South of	304	25	-	66,768	46,670	80
Aberdeen: St Nicholas, Kirk of	278	28	12	86,195	15,194	4
Aberdeen: St Stephen's	147	20	13	-	42,065	28
Aberdeen: South Holburn	385	34	51	86,756	71,279	3
Aberdeen: Stockethill	86	6	-	35,444	9,869	19
Aberdeen: Summerhill	99	19	-	27,646	21,242	6
Aberdeen: Torry St Fittick's	273	15	18	-	44,402	1
Aberdeen: Woodside	235	-	18	43,290	34,446	-
Bucksburn Stoneywood	377	12	-	32,211	21,431	-
Cults	664	59	40	169,594	108,661	45
Dyce	841	52	41	-	70,977	135
Kingswells	294	23	16	45,542	33,675	-
Newhills	340	21	36	-	74,652	93
Peterculter	509	43	-	105,263	67,458	74

Shetland

Congregation	Com	Eld	G	In19	M&M	–18
Burra Isle	29	5	11	-	9,783	14
Tingwall	45	6	24	23,814	23,578	-
Delting	55	4	11	12,418	10,027	6
Northmavine	45	3	-	5,483	5,808	-
Dunrossness and St Ninian's	35	-	-	10,771	10,335	-
Sandwick, Cunningsburgh and Quarff	50	4	9	-	18,994	6
Lerwick and Bressay	291	22	4	72,091	42,787	8
Nesting and Lunnasting	24	4	-	5,131	5,278	-
Whalsay and Skerries	155	11	18	-	10,740	12
Sandsting and Aithsting	22	7	-	6,617	7,187	15
Walls and Sandness	31	10	-	-	7,807	-

Congregation	Com	Eld	G	In19	M&M	–18
Unst and Fetlar	69	6	17	16,506	11,451	1
Yell	32	8	12	-	7,721	-

32. Kincardine and Deeside

Congregation	Com	Eld	G	In19	M&M	–18
Aberluthnott	99	7	6	14,232	11,007	-
Laurencekirk	337	8	-	20,579	13,509	-
Aboyne-Dinnet	259	10	11	44,829	30,183	45
Cromar	177	13	-	25,482	25,617	2
Arbuthnott, Bervie and Kinneff	324	24	26	81,300	50,716	45
Banchory-Ternan: East	484	26	22	79,326	64,004	136
Banchory-Ternan: West	565	28	22	-	77,465	60
Birse and Feughside	197	15	-	-	31,079	24
Braemar and Crathie	172	25	-	-	41,076	28
Drumoak-Durris	368	11	-	62,055	37,998	25
Glenmuick (Ballater)	235	14	-	38,925	28,842	14
Maryculter Trinity	129	12	8	41,549	33,276	40
Mearns Coastal	204	8	-	21,932	21,360	-
Mid Deeside	485	33	22	-	43,255	12
Newtonhill	215	11	14	33,513	20,898	85
Portlethen	261	14	-	52,017	46,732	65
Stonehaven: Carronside	742	28	-	-	58,656	4
Stonehaven: Fetteresso	519	38	39	-	99,349	142
West Mearns	410	18	25	-	38,164	-

33. Gordon

Congregation	Com	Eld	G	In19	M&M	–18
Barthol Chapel	68	7	8	-	6,677	15
Tarves	246	14	29	46,132	24,882	51
Belhelvie	315	31	15	89,732	50,612	64
Blairdaff and Chapel of Garioch	295	25	12	-	24,217	8
Cluny	172	11	-	25,240	19,144	9
Monymusk	96	5	-	19,471	14,460	52
Culsalmond and Rayne	153	6	-	12,726	10,810	6
Daviot	138	8	-	-	10,022	7
Cushnie and Tough	228	9	-	22,983	18,055	1
Echt and Midmar	254	11	-	25,197	29,020	24
Ellon	1,301	67	-	208,750	101,281	137
Fintray Kinellar Keithhall	140	10	-	21,977	25,436	-
Foveran	207	10	-	55,574	36,882	5
Howe Trinity	460	18	24	70,872	52,043	-
Huntly Cairnie Glass	568	6	9	-	39,225	-
Insch-Leslie-Premnay-Oyne	319	29	14	-	27,348	93
Inverurie: St Andrew's	713	32	-	-	63,401	10
Inverurie: West	554	45	26	91,727	55,733	11
Kemnay	428	36	-	72,905	55,241	211
Kintore	635	33	-	-	58,723	40
Meldrum and Bourtie	371	22	33	-	50,728	2
Methlick	318	25	20	69,917	45,879	50
New Machar	350	18	-	52,009	54,036	18
Noth	190	6	-	30,029	20,050	1
Skene	1,067	62	41	143,646	85,315	131

Congregation	Com	Eld	G	In19	M&M	–18
Strathbogie Drumblade	382	35	21	54,756	43,299	15
Udny and Pitmedden	230	21	10	77,652	46,998	75
Upper Donside	318	18	-	33,873	32,368	25

34. Buchan

Congregation	Com	Eld	G	In19	M&M	–18
Aberdour	100	8	10	13,192	8,367	12
Pitsligo	75	8	-	23,220	8,319	-
Auchaber United	100	9	-	12,410	14,149	2
Auchterless	167	18	-	21,882	18,299	5
Banff	359	35	-	-	57,630	257
King Edward	136	12	8	23,250	13,603	2
Crimond	152	-	-	27,114	18,242	-
Lonmay	94	8	13	14,650	13,800	-
Cruden	323	18	16	47,000	31,003	20
Deer	528	18	20	48,635	44,620	46
Fraserburgh: Old	434	46	39	-	78,705	60
Fraserburgh: South	238	16	-	-	30,821	-
Inverallochy and Rathen: East	69	7	-	17,556	12,353	12
Fraserburgh: West	415	44	-	55,632	49,870	109
Rathen: West	69	8	-	11,832	8,066	-
Fyvie	166	13	17	42,404	30,177	-
Rothienorman	104	7	-	17,915	9,455	14
Longside	379	25	-	64,988	49,491	57
Macduff	553	28	32	97,855	62,208	150
Marnoch	339	16	12	40,122	28,591	36
Maud and Savoch	172	13	-	27,633	19,518	11
New Deer: St Kane's	250	13	22	52,956	32,130	6
Monquhitter and New Byth	250	18	8	18,453	19,800	2
Turriff: St Andrew's	431	26	12	-	30,635	70
New Pitsligo	237	5	-	-	16,501	30
Strichen and Tyrie	343	9	21	45,662	37,072	-
Ordiquhill and Cornhill	132	11	13	10,975	8,444	20
Whitehills	260	11	18	37,874	29,515	8
Peterhead: New	483	25	25	45,862	64,935	20
Peterhead: St Andrew's	378	20	19	48,856	32,684	28
Portsoy	267	11	22	62,289	29,433	20
St Fergus	150	8	9	15,299	9,540	-
Sandhaven	65	5	-	6,985	3,392	30
Turriff: St Ninian's and Forglen	517	20	15	81,058	47,990	43

35. Moray

Congregation	Com	Eld	G	In19	M&M	–18
Aberlour	196	13	30	41,193	31,283	8
Alves and Burghead	128	-	27	40,180	28,739	8
Kinloss and Findhorn	70	19	-	24,742	21,991	-
Bellie and Speymouth	316	21	19	63,615	42,052	90
Birnie and Pluscarden	190	20	17	54,634	31,395	-
Elgin: High	386	37	-	68,928	42,493	30
Buckie: North	314	29	28	50,390	38,217	8
Rathven	60	12	14	-	12,285	7
Buckie: South and West	210	17	23	46,159	27,129	-

Congregation	Com	Eld	G	In19	M&M	–18
Enzie	63	4	-	4,848	8,692	-
Cullen and Deskford	251	16	17	49,724	40,912	2
Dallas	43	6	10	14,548	10,879	1
Forres: St Leonard's	136	9	22	14,217	34,002	6
Rafford	41	-	-	16,237	10,102	-
Duffus, Spynie and Hopeman	210	31	13	71,489	40,722	36
Dyke and Edinkillie	165	18	10	44,682	32,851	20
Elgin: St Giles' and St Columba's South	458	43	39	106,436	70,727	42
Findochty	36	8	10	-	10,606	18
Portknockie	55	9	14	22,627	13,239	47
Forres: St Laurence	315	15	21	68,950	55,231	-
Keith: North, Newmill, Boharm and Rothiemay	433	43	16	-	63,230	6
Keith: St Rufus, Botriphnie and Grange	813	58	31	63,835	54,224	15
Knockando, Elchies and Archiestown	222	-	5	41,777	29,987	-
Rothes	264	16	17	42,132	28,471	18
Lossiemouth: St Gerardine's High	167	9	23	55,820	35,472	-
Lossiemouth: St James'	182	12	25	50,777	34,822	10
Mortlach and Cabrach	276	12	12	30,143	25,673	4
St Andrew's-Lhanbryd and Urquhart	303	38	21	65,543	46,025	12

36. Abernethy

Abernethy	131	11	-	55,331	33,960	39
Boat of Garten, Carrbridge and Kincardine	142	17	28	41,628	27,603	17
Alvie and Insh	67	5	-	26,944	24,065	20
Rothiemurchus and Aviemore	61	7	-	16,226	13,277	5
Cromdale and Advie	53	2	-	-	16,225	-
Dulnain Bridge	32	6	-	9,696	9,398	-
Grantown-on-Spey	174	17	-	52,080	29,588	25
Kingussie	70	15	-	-	20,790	10
Laggan and Newtonmore	103	18	-	55,823	30,607	20
Tomintoul, Glenlivet and Inveraven	122	9	-	23,276	19,046	25

37. Inverness

Ardersier	47	7	-	23,408	11,180	12
Petty	34	6	11	22,807	10,790	5
Auldearn and Dalmore	43	-	-	12,024	6,746	-
Nairn: St Ninian's	159	11	21	50,586	37,304	6
Cawdor	143	10	-	29,444	18,443	7
Croy and Dalcross	55	-	15	20,236	12,107	-
Culloden: The Barn	221	14	-	84,558	61,123	66
Daviot and Dunlichity	45	5	7	10,038	12,323	6
Moy, Dalarossie and Tomatin	30	5	12	-	7,441	12
Dores and Boleskine	51	6	-	16,742	12,758	-
Inverness: Crown	475	67	27	-	77,117	88
Inverness: Dalneigh and Bona	135	9	14	51,078	35,509	10
Inverness: East	206	24	-	108,369	75,968	21
Inverness: Hilton	215	10	-	72,123	48,755	30
Inverness: Inshes	233	16	-	161,111	96,694	64
Inverness: Kinmylies	68	8	-	46,472	38,063	60
Inverness: Ness Bank	513	48	29	159,284	88,455	15

Congregation	Com	Eld	G	In19	M&M	–18
Inverness: Old High St Stephen's	369	32	-	95,170	74,190	3
Inverness: St Columba	61	4	-	60,383	16,800	33
Inverness: Trinity	191	-	11	57,193	45,707	-
Kilmorack and Erchless	86	10	16	-	36,300	30
Kiltarlity	55	6	-	-	15,817	23
Kirkhill	70	8	11	-	15,953	30
Nairn: Old	346	43	17	120,795	71,482	22
Urquhart and Glenmoriston	98	8	-	65,583	35,422	15

38. Lochaber

Congregation	Com	Eld	G	In19	M&M	–18
Acharacle	30	4	-	21,321	11,890	17
Ardnamurchan	14	4	-	11,945	8,721	-
Ardgour and Kingairloch	44	6	12	13,335	6,489	3
Morvern	33	5	8	8,708	6,687	10
Strontian	24	3	-	5,758	3,590	3
Duror	32	6	14	11,766	9,712	2
Glencoe: St Munda's	41	8	-	19,084	9,598	-
Fort Augustus	60	9	-	18,817	13,456	4
Glengarry	26	5	13	-	7,427	5
Fort William: Duncansburgh MacIntosh	304	29	14	66,052	52,769	52
Kilmonivaig	52	13	10	-	20,236	9
Kilmallie	92	11	20	25,262	24,646	2
Kinlochleven	41	6	13	23,814	13,240	-
Nether Lochaber	39	8	-	16,474	12,829	-
North West Lochaber	72	11	11	32,782	20,157	17

39. Ross

Congregation	Com	Eld	G	In19	M&M	–18
Alness	62	8	-	30,764	18,347	14
Avoch	17	3	-	17,152	9,064	3
Fortrose and Rosemarkie	68	5	-	33,103	21,326	9
Contin	36	12	-	-	14,314	-
Fodderty and Strathpeffer	87	17	-	29,092	19,932	12
Cromarty	38	6	-	10,043	6,475	-
Resolis and Urquhart	82	9	-	-	27,149	4
Dingwall: Castle Street	126	16	-	55,252	30,855	22
Dingwall: St Clement's	160	29	18	73,950	43,152	18
Fearn Abbey and Nigg	38	5	-	-	16,505	-
Tarbat	33	4	-	52,035	9,143	2
Ferintosh	139	19	16	55,974	30,643	12
Invergordon	92	8	-	49,029	40,232	10
Killearnan	110	-	-	36,682	30,120	-
Knockbain	28	7	-	16,106	13,740	-
Kilmuir and Logie Easter	56	8	14	36,978	25,381	-
Kiltearn	51	8	-	34,094	22,333	8
Lochbroom and Ullapool	35	5	-	31,506	19,856	1
Rosskeen	101	12	9	43,938	36,325	35
Tain	85	7	13	-	31,480	8
Urray and Kilchrist	80	15	-	58,039	33,088	14

Congregation	Com	Eld	G	In19	M&M	–18
40. Sutherland						
Altnaharra and Farr	22	-	-	-	6,084	-
Melness and Tongue	28	-	-	-	15,546	-
Assynt and Stoer	7	2	-	12,175	7,860	2
Clyne	40	12	-	-	19,858	1
Kildonan and Loth Helmsdale	29	2	-	-	8,652	-
Creich	17	6	-	12,759	11,501	-
Kincardine Croick and Edderton	21	4	-	18,181	14,530	-
Rosehall	19	2	-	10,591	6,830	-
Dornoch Cathedral	296	-	50	-	69,932	-
Durness and Kinlochbervie	27	3	-	17,056	12,148	30
Eddrachillis	6	2	-	17,891	8,291	1
Golspie	29	9	4	19,283	30,707	1
Lairg	19	8	11	24,836	15,002	1
Rogart	12	-	-	-	10,529	-
41. Caithness						
Halkirk Westerdale	79	6	9	12,544	7,753	-
Watten	14	1	-	5,497	6,771	-
Latheron	53	12	7	21,458	16,096	18
North Coast	37	10	15	23,137	14,007	8
Pentland	96	10	22	-	25,229	19
Thurso: St Peter's and St Andrew's	120	19	-	-	37,822	20
Thurso: West	164	23	21	52,292	33,114	9
Wick: Pulteneytown and Thrumster	180	12	23	49,360	38,727	110
Wick: St Fergus	178	25	20	43,239	31,877	1
42. Lochcarron-Skye						
Applecross, Lochcarron and Torridon	51	5	6	34,016	22,707	15
Bracadale and Duirinish	39	-	6	-	20,608	-
Gairloch and Dundonnell	73	5	-	71,061	44,429	18
Glenelg Kintail and Lochalsh	60	9	7	28,272	36,066	-
Kilmuir and Stenscholl	44	-	-	-	23,294	-
Portree	85	16	-	69,501	43,893	12
Snizort	29	-	-	-	22,917	-
Strath and Sleat	110	6	-	94,830	65,942	-
43. Uist						
Benbecula	63	10	15	42,914	25,667	22
Carinish	72	11	14	51,907	26,799	11
Berneray and Lochmaddy	28	2	7	14,099	12,306	-
Kilmuir and Paible	26	4	-	30,472	20,776	1
Manish-Scarista	22	4	-	26,537	25,120	3
Tarbert	67	7	-	83,769	42,192	18
44. Lewis						
Barvas	71	8	-	69,920	43,578	28
Carloway	45	4	-	27,247	15,500	5

Congregation	Com	Eld	G	In19	M&M	–18
Cross Ness	63	4	-	25,230	29,513	50
Kinloch	32	4	-	40,139	26,326	16
Knock	24	1	-	31,659	19,609	6
Lochs-Crossbost	8	3	-	16,674	12,252	7
Lochs-in-Bernera	28	3	-	25,147	10,537	8
Uig	15	3	-	22,581	14,044	15
Stornoway: High	83	3	-	71,246	39,589	25
Stornoway: Martin's Memorial	329	11	-	156,016	88,188	60
Stornoway: St Columba	137	8	40	95,793	56,991	148

45. Orkney

Birsay, Harray and Sandwick	288	22	32	36,963	27,039	10
East Mainland	224	-	11	25,660	17,990	-
Eday	8	3	-	-	1,727	-
Evie	22	-	-	4,915	8,755	8
Firth	67	3	-	-	16,595	17
Rendall	44	-	-	14,191	8,957	-
Rousay	11	2	-	104	3,805	-
Flotta	21	4	-	3,794	3,246	-
Hoy and Walls	40	6	-	8,985	4,868	2
Orphir and Stenness	137	12	-	21,238	18,708	5
Kirkwall: East	300	21	20	75,786	45,684	15
Shapinsay	38	7	-	-	4,950	5
Kirkwall: St Magnus Cathedral	469	-	28	92,325	52,067	-
North Ronaldsay	5	2	-	-	1,049	-
Papa Westray	6	4	-	9,558	2,749	4
Westray	79	20	21	20,998	21,444	40
Sanday	47	7	7	-	7,011	4
South Ronaldsay and Burray	129	3	14	18,900	11,678	16
Stromness	280	30	13	-	28,238	1
Stronsay: Moncur Memorial	47	6	-	12,289	8,030	8

47. England

Corby: St Andrew's	196	16	-	44,904	23,953	9
Corby: St Ninian's	272	13	-	36,064	24,553	3
Guernsey: St Andrew's in the Grange	174	21	-	72,374	45,783	13
Jersey: St Columba's	112	10	-	55,959	36,595	7
London: Crown Court	203	29	3	-	62,247	18
London: St Columba's	802	58	-	-	235,438	-
Newcastle: St Andrew's	106	15	-	-	6,175	20

48. International Charges

Amsterdam: English Reformed Church	364	15	-	-	-	20
Bermuda: Christ Church Warwick	489	41	-	-	-	60
Brussels: St Andrew's	337	22	-	-	-	34
Budapest: St Columba's	27	-	-	-	-	-
Colombo, Sri Lanka: St Andrew's Scots Kirk	103	8	-	-	-	14
Costa del Sol	13	3	-	-	-	-
Geneva	216	15	-	-	-	-
Gibraltar: St Andrew's	25	-	-	-	-	-

Congregation	Com	Eld	G	In19	M&M	–18
Lausanne: The Scots Kirk	116	-	-	-	-	-
Lisbon: St Andrew's	50	-	-	-	-	-
Malta: St Andrew's Scots Church	67	-	-	-	-	-
Paris: The Scots Kirk	86	10	-	-	-	-
Rome: St Andrew's	81	-	-	-	-	-
Rotterdam: Scots International Church	192	16	-	-	-	46
Trinidad: Greyfriars St Ann's, Port of Spain with Arouca and Sangre Grande	244	-	-	-	-	-

INDEX OF MINISTERS

Ministers who are members of a Presbytery are designated 'A' if holding a parochial appointment in that Presbytery, 'B' if in other appointments or 'C' if demitted. 'A-1, A-2' etc. indicate the numerical order of congregations in the Presbyteries of Edinburgh, Clyde, Glasgow, and Hamilton.

Also included are ministers listed in Section 6:

(1) Ministers who have resigned their seat in Presbytery but registered as Retaining or Employed (List 6-D);

(2) Ministers who have resigned their seat in Presbytery but registered as Inactive (List 6-E);

(3) Ministers serving overseas (List 6-J) – see also Presbyteries 48 and 49;

(4) Ordained Local Ministers and Auxiliary Ministers, who are listed both in Presbyteries and in List 6-A and List 6-B respectively; and

(5) Ministers who have died since the compilation of the last *Year Book* (List 6-P)

For a list of the Diaconate, see List 6-C.

INDEX OF PARISHES AND PLACES

Numbers on the right of the column refer to the Presbytery in which the district lies. Names in brackets are given for ease of identification. They may refer to the name of the parish, which may be different from that of the district, or they distinguish places with the same name, or they indicate the first named place within a union.

INDEX OF SUBJECTS

Lightning Source UK Ltd.
Milton Keynes UK
UKHW020640080621
385138UK00011B/816

9 780715 209950